Geoffrey Hill and the ends of poetry

Manchester University Press

Geoffrey Hill and the ends of poetry

Tom Docherty

MANCHESTER UNIVERSITY PRESS

Copyright © Tom Docherty 2024

The right of Tom Docherty to be identified as the author
of this work has been asserted in accordance with the
Copyright, Designs and Patents Act 1988.

Published by Manchester University Press
Oxford Road, Manchester, M13 9PL

www.manchesteruniversitypress.co.uk

British Library Cataloguing-in-Publication Data
A catalogue record for this book is available from the British
Library

ISBN 978 1 5261 8189 3 hardback

First published 2024

The publisher has no responsibility for the persistence or
accuracy of URLs for any external or third-party internet
websites referred to in this book, and does not guarantee that
any content on such websites is, or will remain, accurate or
appropriate.

Typeset
by Cheshire Typesetting Ltd, Cuddington, Cheshire

In piam memoriam

ALICE MCMULLIN
(1925–2016)

THOMAS DOCHERTY
(1954–2020)

ALIZA NICOLE SPARTI
(2002–2023)

I haue seene an end of all perfection

PSALM 119.96

At once a Sonne is promis'd her, and gone,
Gabriell gives Christ to her, He her to John;
Not fully a mother, Shee's in Orbitie,
At once receiver and the legacie.
All this, and all betweene, this day hath showne,
Th'Abridgement of Christs story, which makes one
(As in plaine Maps, the furthest West is East)
Of the'Angels *Ave,* 'and *Consummatum est.*

DONNE

Contents

Acknowledgements	*page* viii
Abbreviations	ix
Introduction	1
1 Puns	18
2 Dead ends	46
3 Rhymes	78
4 Syntaxes	110
5 Forms	146
End notes	198
Notes	201
Bibliography	252
Index	271

Acknowledgements

The fourth section of the third chapter, 'Impossible rhymes', was published in an earlier version, titled 'Impossible Rhyme in Geoffrey Hill', in *Essays in Criticism*, 72.1 (January 2022), pp. 77–93. The second section of the fifth chapter, 'Unrhymed sonnets: Lowell and "Funeral Music"', was also published in an earlier version, titled 'Crying Out for a Companion: Hill's and Lowell's Unrhymed Sonnets', in *Literary Imagination*, 23.1 (March 2021), pp. 1–18.

I thank:

> Michael Hurley and Kathryn Murphy, for their continued helps, indispensable guidance, and generous friendship;
>
> Ruth Abbott, Archie Burnett, Rebecca Lamb, Robert Macfarlane, Seamus Perry, Christopher Ricks, John Talbot, and Rosanna Warren, for edits, suggestions, kindnesses;
>
> my mother and late father, Edwina and Thomas Docherty;
>
> my mother- and father-in-law, Diana and Robert Vogel;
>
> my children, Clementine, Pia, Sylvia, and Felix, for their easy perfections;
>
> my wife, Molly, with whom I am well bound and without whom am to no end;
>
> and St Joseph, for happy conclusions.

Abbreviations

Geoffrey Hill's works

BBGJ	*The Book of Baruch by the Gnostic Justin*, ed. by Kenneth Haynes (Oxford: Oxford University Press, 2019)
BH	*Broken Hierarchies: Poems 1952–2012*, ed. by Kenneth Haynes (Oxford: Oxford University Press, 2013)
C	*Canaan* (1996), in *BH*
CCW	*Collected Critical Writings*, ed. by Kenneth Haynes (Oxford: Oxford University Press, 2008)
Cl.	*Clavics* (2007–2012), in *BH*
CP (1985)	*Collected Poems* (Harmondsworth: Penguin, 1985)
EV	*Expostulations on the Volcano* (2007–2012), in *BH*
HOLC	*Hymns to Our Lady of Chartres* (1982–2012), in *BH*
KL	*King Log* (1968), in *BH*
L	*Ludo* (2011), in *BH*
LIV	*Liber Illustrium Virorum* (2007–2012), in *BH*
MCCP	*The Mystery of the Charity of Charles Péguy* (1983), in *BH*
MH	*Mercian Hymns* (1971), in *BH*
O	*Oraclau*	*Oracles* (2007–2012), in *BH*
OB	*Odi Barbare* (2007–2012), in *BH*
OS	*The Orchards of Syon* (2002), in *BH*
P	*Pindarics* (2005–2012), in *BH*
SC	*Scenes from Comus* (2005), in *BH*
SS	*Speech! Speech!* (2000), in *BH*
T	*Tenebrae* (1978), in *BH*
TCP	*A Treatise of Civil Power* (2007), in *BH*
TCP (2005)	*A Treatise of Civil Power* (Thame: Clutag Press, 2005)
TL	*The Triumph of Love* (1998), in *BH*
TT	*Al Tempo de' Tremuoti* (2007–2012), in *BH*
U	*For the Unfallen* (1959), in *BH*
WT	*Without Title* (2006), in *BH*

x   *Abbreviations*

Other works

ELW   *Geoffrey Hill: Essays on his Later Work*, ed. by John Lyon and
        Peter McDonald (Oxford: Oxford University Press, 2012)
EW   *Geoffrey Hill: Essays on his Work*, ed. by Peter Robinson (Milton
        Keynes: Open University Press, 1985)
GHC   *Geoffrey Hill and his Contexts*, ed. by Piers Pennington and
        Matthew Sperling (Bern: Peter Lang, 2011)
OED   *The Oxford English Dictionary*, ed. by J. A. Simpson and E.
        S. C. Weiner, 3rd edn, rev. by J. A. Simpson and others, *OED
        Online*, www.oed.com/. All quotations from the *Oxford English
        Dictionary* are cited by lemma, part of speech (where necessary),
        and sense number (e.g., 'instinct, *adj.*', sense 3).

All quotations from the Bible, following Hill's own practice, are from *The
Authorised Version of the English Bible 1611*, ed. by William Aldis Wright,
5 vols (Cambridge: Cambridge University Press, 2010), and are cited by
book, chapter, and verse (e.g., Revelation 22.21).

Introduction

Mots, mythes, myrthes, morts

Mots, êtes-vous des mythes, et pareils aux myrthes des morts?

'Words, are you myths, and similar to the myrtle-leaves of the dead?'[1] The question belongs to the French poet Robert Desnos, who died in the concentration camp at Terezín in 1945. Geoffrey Hill, as well as citing these words in an early notebook, translates them in the second poem of *Expostulations on the Volcano*: '*Words, are you myths and like | Unto the myrtles of the shades?*' (p. 630).[2] The quotation in the notebook comes from a larger quoted passage, handwritten by Hill, from Wallace Fowlie's *Age of Surrealism* (1950). Here is Fowlie's commentary on Desnos's words, with some succeeding thoughts:

> The line is curiously composed of four key-words, each beginning with *m*: *mots, mythes, myrthes, morts*, the last three of which – *myths, myrtle-leaves, dead* – serve as elliptical and provocative explanations for the first term, *words*. Perhaps the best starting-point in this problem of language would be to remember the sacred importance of words in all the major religions of the world. Words, and very often related words, are the masters and disciplinarians of religious systems. According to *Genesis*, the universe itself came into existence by an utterance or a word of God: 'And God said, Let there be light.' [...] Words are myths, because they are not understandable in any ordinary sense. They are similar to the myrtle-leaves of the dead, because they do not describe or reveal or resurrect the dead, but because they symbolize the glory and achievement of the dead.[3]

Desnos's 'curiously composed' sentence brings to mind the early journals of Hopkins: meditations on the slight variations of colour, of connotation, in verbal series such as '*Flick, fillip, flip, fleck, flake*'.[4] Passages of Hill's poetry also suggest themselves: 'the lost are blest, the scarred most sacred [...] Patience hardens to a pittance, courage | unflinchingly declines into sour rage' (*MCCP* 5, pp. 147–48). The attention to the crucial subtleties of language that Desnos demonstrates is a hallmark also of Hill's writing.

2   *Geoffrey Hill and the ends of poetry*

The achievement, the being finished, of the dead is both honoured and sought after in Hill's poetry.

The last poem in Hill's *Broken Hierarchies: Poems 1952–2012* is a *soi-disant* 'picnic party' of the dead (*TT* 95, pp. 935–36). It is populated by Brunelleschi, Donatello, the Virgin Mary, the Christ-child, God the Father, Abraham, John the Baptist, Judith, Holofernes, the Apostles, Pontius Pilate, and, by another name, God the Father again: 'Yahweh himself not wholly disabused ‖ Of procreation' (p. 936). Apart from God the Father, and, depending on one's theological opinion, the Virgin Mary, all of these have experienced death. This picnic party, though not explicitly the heavenly banquet, is a vision of the end. Having written, in 1952, a poem called 'Genesis', which would be the first in Hill's first collection, it is fitting that Hill's compilation of sixty years' poetry should finish with an apocalypse.

The end of this last poem, though, is hardly like an end. If it is, it is a cliffhanger:

> Time is the demiurge
> For which our impotence cannot atone.
> Nothing so fatal as creation's clone.
> The stars asunder, gibbering, on the verge
>
> (p. 936)

The line teeters on the verge of a verb, which would be its completion. The rhyme is fulfilled but not the sentence. Hill is aware of the word that marks the end of his own speaking, the verge at the end of his life. The word recalls Regan speaking to her father, King Lear:

> O Sir, you are old,
> Nature in you stands on the very Verge
> Of his confine[5]

Nature cannot exist without the confinements of ends. Lear's soul appears to be on the point of flying his body; but its exact 'confine', at least in terms of duration, is unknown until death occurs. The 'Verge' hangs in expectation at the end of the previous line; Hill takes this effect and maximises it by omitting the remainder of his clause. Hill's line, it is implied, cannot be completed; perhaps such a consummation is impossible until his death, or even the end of the world – in what may be the poem's first hint of this, Hill (never averse to testing out uncommon theological positions) calls the sculpted Biblical figures described in the poem 'enraptured gazers'.

For Francophones such as Charles Péguy, a poet revered by Hill, Christ is *le Verbe*: 'Avant le commencement sera le Verbe'.[6] In both linguistic and

Introduction   3

theological senses, the last utterance in *Broken Hierarchies* appears to lack the verb. In the latter sense, this verb is the second coming of the Word, and the 'restitution of all things' (Acts 3.21). But Christ is linguistically present in this last line. Alluding to the prophecy of Isaiah, Christ tells his Apostles that at the end of the world 'the Starres of heauen shall fall' (Mark 13.25).[7] If Hill's stars are 'asunder' (which may constitute another allusion to Christ's words), such a time cannot be far off.[8]

The consummation foreseen in the seventh of Hill's 'Psalms of Assize' in the collection *Canaan*, which reckons 'how it ends | how it goes at the last day' (p. 229), is different. It hears the 'O' of the O Antiphons, liturgical texts sung at Advent, as a kind of verbal revelation, one that is both reconciled and reconciling. It is the 'great O of advent', the 'O that nothing may touch', bringing about the end with a consummate flourish of words: 'its ultimate | cadence | its fall impeccable'.

The central contention of this book is that Hill's poetry is characteristically 'end-directed'. I argue that, for Hill, the chief ends of poetry are twofold: the reconciliation of antagonists in word and thought; and the poem's own perfect articulation. What 'reconciliation' and 'perfect articulation' denote in this context will become clearer over the course of this book's discussions with reference to Hill's poetry and literary criticism. (But allow me to stress from the beginning that 'reconciliation' need not always be entirely happy, amicable, or harmonious; one may be reconciled to an unpleasant state of affairs.) The acknowledgement of failure to achieve such ends provides its own impetus to Hill's work. The book examines in detail Hill's puns, repeating figures, rhymes, syntaxes, and forms – their local reconciliations and entrenched contrarieties – and establishes their essential place, until now barely explored, in the study of Hill's poetry, particularly with regard to its sustained concern with ends and endings.

The way in which the book's argument connects technical and formal with thematic and intentional ends has further-reaching implications for the study of twentieth-century poetry and of literature more broadly. By its use of Hill's poetry as an example, the book indicates the potential for an approach to others' work that begins with its ends. What do puns, repeating figures, rhymes, syntaxes, and forms entail, not only for a work's aesthetic realisation or finishedness but also for its final worth (moral, theological, or other) and its own idea of this worth? I hope that the discussions here, which focus on Hill's work almost exclusively, will nevertheless address in a small way the large questions of poetry's ultimate value: what are its ends; where does it wish to end up?

Critics and contexts

Scholarship on the poetry of Geoffrey Hill is extensive and steadily growing, but it is also necessarily limited by the complexity, recentness, and volume of the work, especially the later work. Very little has yet been written that takes a comprehensive view of his poetry. This is not least because the definitive *Broken Hierarchies*, which introduces five new books, greatly expands another, and makes numerous revisions, was published only in 2013; while *The Book of Baruch by the Gnostic Justin*, published posthumously and including 271 new poems, appeared only in 2019.[9]

There is to my knowledge no work that takes the ends, or endings, of Hill's poetry as its subject. Neither is there any work that concentrates specifically on any of the elements of technique and form with which the individual chapters of this book are concerned: puns; repeating figures and tautologies; rhymes; syntaxes; forms. Questions of syntax and form have been instructively raised in some of the scholarly work on Hill; but there has been little at length, and very little connected with ideas of the end.[10]

For a poet as interested in form and elements of form as Hill, it is surprising that so few critics have taken the technical and formal features of Hill's poetry as their primary focus. The three chapters that discuss Hill in Christopher Ricks's *The Force of Poetry* (1984) perhaps come closest; though naturally these deal with what is now a relatively small portion of Hill's poetic oeuvre.[11]

Ricks is in many ways Hill's first critic. In November 1964, only five years after the publication of Hill's first collection, Ricks's article 'Cliché as "Responsible Speech"', later adapted to make up one of the three chapters on Hill in *The Force of Poetry*, brought Hill's attempts to resurrect dead language to the attention of readers.[12] More recently, 'Hill's Unrelenting, Unreconciling Mind', Ricks's contribution to a book of essays, published in 2012, on Hill's later work, reiterates his argument in 1984 that 'there can be no atonement of atonement and at-one-ment', that Hill's attempt to unify the word with its etymological root is impossible.[13] Where in the earlier essay the primary hinge of Ricks's thoughts about the possibilities and impossibilities of reconciliation is the hyphen, the later essay studies what might hang on such a hinge: a suffix.[14] The particular suffix is *-ble*, as in 'possible'. Matthew Sperling calls this Ricks out-Ricksing himself.[15] But the insistence on a link between the intricacies of Hill's language and its attempt to enact seemingly impossible reconciliations is just and useful.

The book-length surveys of Hill's poetry, most of which appeared before the 1996 collection *Canaan*, have mainly intended to locate and measure its significance and to address its thematic concerns.[16] E. M. Knottenbelt's *Passionate Intelligence* (1990) in particular includes many detailed readings

Introduction 5

and helpful investigations of the poems' literary contexts. It is perhaps the closest thing to an annotated edition of Hill's early work (while Ann Hassan's *Annotations to Geoffrey Hill's 'Speech! Speech!'* (2012) is the sole monograph devoted to annotation of any of Hill's work).

The first book of criticism to deal with most of the published poetry, as well as with archival materials, is Matthew Sperling's *Visionary Philology: Geoffrey Hill and the Study of Words* (2014). The book studies Hill's engagement with etymology and claims for it a preeminent importance in the understanding of his writing. For Sperling, Hill has from the early days pursued a 'vision of language' in which history, politics, and theology are 'embedded, or encoded', a mythological vision of language's 'historical drama'.[17] Alex Pestell's *Geoffrey Hill: The Drama of Reason* (2016) focuses on delineating the various philosophical influences on the style and content of argument in Hill's poetry and critical prose. Two more recent books – the thematic survey of *Geoffrey Hill's Later Work: Radiance of Apprehension* by Alex Wylie (2019) and *Strangeness and Power: Essays on the Poetry of Geoffrey Hill*, a collection of essays edited by Andrew Michael Roberts (2020) – show that there is a growing interest in Hill's work since his death in 2016.

Several critics, especially in recent years, have included Hill in monographs on various but related subjects, such as the meanings of seriousness and value; the question of authority; the position of the poetic voice and to whom it is addressed; poetic difficulty; and the ethics, Christian and other, which complicate and are complicated by poetics.[18] In addition to these, there have been numerous articles and reviews of Hill's work since the 1960s, increasing in volume since 2007 amid the flurry of *Daybooks* and the release of Hill's collected critical writings and poems (see Bibliography). The magazine *Agenda* has devoted four issues to discussion of Hill (17.1 (1979), 30.1–2 (1992), 34.2 (1996), 50.1–2 (2016)). Five collections of essays have also been compiled, with many rich contributions to Hillian criticism.[19]

Kathryn Murphy, whose work features in two of these collections of essays, has been among the most acute readers of Hill. Her review of the *Collected Critical Writings* refers, like Sperling, and as in the title of Pestell's book, to a 'drama' in Hill's work: 'the *drama* of Reason' (quoting Hill quoting Coleridge).[20] This drama is more internal than historical. Murphy's two essays consider Hill's attempts at reconciliation in sacramental language: 'Geoffrey Hill and Confession' and 'Hill's Conversions'. Murphy parses Hill's words and indeed Hill's parsings, discriminating between kinds of confession, conversion, and expression in ways that display their likeness as well as their 'major unlikeness'.[21] Noting, in her review of the critical work, what Hill calls the 'requirement to make

6   *Geoffrey Hill and the ends of poetry*

incoherencies cohere' (*CCW*, p. 579), she writes: 'In Hill, however, even the urge towards coherence is cross-biased by the urge to dissent.'[22] This observation demands questions to which this book is addressed: what is the meaning of Hill's 'cross-biased' urge towards coherence; how does it manifest itself in his poetry; and how do language's own coherencies and incoherencies, as seen by Hill, inflect and shape his poetry?

This book is the first to benefit from a full view of Hill's poetic work, published and unpublished. It takes up both Sperling's verbal–historical drama and Murphy's rational–religious drama and situates them in an encompassing and multifarious play of ends: not only features of language, or terminations in time, but also consummating purposes.

Ends of definition

It will be noted that the word *end* is already working multiple shifts here. A few remarks about the word and my uses of it in this study are required. Firstly, my question is not one of philosophy but of poetic criticism and analysis; not one of teleology per se but of the ends of poetry. Even this, admittedly, is too large a field of enquiry for this book. Accordingly, its main focus and concern is the poetry of only one man, albeit one of the most significant English-language poets of the last hundred years; but my intention is that this book provide a wide-ranging introduction to the polyvalent idea of the ends of poetry, and that it indicate this idea's applicability to technical and formal studies of literature. I recognise that applying the same word across numerous levels of poetic thought and composition, from sonic minutiae to questions of theology, is a fraught business. But it is among the aims of this book to demonstrate the essential connectedness of all these ends, in the first place as they pertain to Hill's poetry.

The broadest distinction between senses of the noun *end*, as suggested by the *OED* (of which Hill was an ardent user and significant critic, and to which I shall often have recourse), is that it can pertain to both space and time.[23] The *OED*'s entry for 'end, *n.*' lists three categories of definitions: 'I. With reference to space'; 'II. With reference to time or serial order'; 'III. Idiomatic phrases'. In the first two categories, forty-four separate senses (under fifteen main entries) are listed; in the third, twenty-five idiomatic phrases (under nine main entries). The entry also includes fifty-seven compound phrases and six draft additions (five of which are compound phrases). The verb 'end, *v.1*' has sixteen different senses (under nine main entries).[24] On the whole, my use of *end* here is limited to the senses regarding 'time or serial order'.

Introduction

There are three primary definitions I have in mind, which I imagine as constant lodestars over the other, thematic and prosodic, definitions: these are the end as *terminus*, the point at which a process stops (see *OED*, sense 7a); as *attained perfection or good* (senses 12, 13a); and as *aimed-at or intended thing* (sense 14).[25] These ends, then, are terminative; perfective; and intentional. The three senses are easily interwoven: for instance, one's end (intention) may be that, at one's end (termination), one will have reached one's end (perfection). At the same time, there can be (as in Hill's work) a tension between these senses: one may seek finally something unfinished, imperfect, open-ended, or unending.[26] These three senses also relate to the thematic and prosodic 'ends' that emerge in this study due to their specific relevance to Hill's work.

As to the thematic ends, many of these also correspond directly to *OED* entries: 'termination of existence; destruction, abolition' (e.g., the 'end of the world'; sense 8a); 'death (of a person)' (sense 8b); '[u]ltimate state or condition' (sense 9); 'a resolution' ('*Obsolete*', sense 11). Other thematic ends align more clearly with the definitions of 'consummation', such as: '[t]he action or an act of consummating a marriage or relationship. Also more generally: the action or an act of having sexual intercourse' (*OED*, sense 2b).[27]

The prosodic ends, which provide the structure of this book, concern specific end-directed figures and features of the finished ('[c]onsummate, perfect, accomplished') poem, with frequent emphasis throughout on the closing sections, lines, and words of poems.[28] These prosodic ends progress through the five chapters from the smallest end-directed unit, the single word, to the largest, the poem. (The broader units of collection (or book) and entire corpus are also considered throughout and particularly towards the end of this book.)

My discussion of the thematic ends is necessarily looser, more ad hoc, than that of the prosodic ends. It would be unwise to attempt to associate specific thematic ends with prosodic ones: no such association exists in the work. The interaction between both kinds of ends in Hill's poetry is naturally various, and this is variously shown in the course of these chapters. When the word *end* is used here, the polyvalency of the word should be obliquely discernible; but I rely on context to indicate which of the above senses of the word is, or are, being emphasised in a given instance.

Both the thematic and prosodic ends at issue could be described as ends in poetry; but a remaining, and interpenetrative, question hovering over this study – because it hovers over much of Hill's own work – concerns more properly the ends of poetry: that is, the question of poetry's purposes (*OED*, 'end, *n.*', sense 15: 'A final cause; the object for which a thing exists; the purpose for which it is designed or instituted'). There are several

8 *Geoffrey Hill and the ends of poetry*

writers whose thoughts on poetry's purposes, of which I shall now give brief sketches, are relevant both to Hill's writing and to this book's approach.

The notion of a purpose or final cause, at least as understood here, derives in the first place from Aristotle.[29] The four αἰτίαι or causes – the four answers to the *why* of a thing; the four explanations for a thing's existence – that Aristotle outlines in the *Physics* are foundational to much subsequent thought about ends; my own limited understanding of them forms part of this book's considerations of poetry's ends. The causes are: (1) the 'that out of which' or material cause; (2) the 'what it is to be' or formal cause; (3) the 'that from which the origin of motion or rest comes' or efficient cause; and (4) the 'that for the sake of which' or final cause. For example, a table's material cause is wood; its formal cause is its design; its efficient cause is carpentry; and its final cause is its use. As for the poem, its material cause could be called words; its formal cause its form; and its efficient cause writing; suffice it for now to say that its final cause, and even whether it can be said to have one, is a matter of dispute. All four of these causes are germane to this book. The prosodic ends I discuss relate to the first three causes: my analyses of puns, repeating figures, and rhymes are concerned with poems' material cause; the analyses of rhymes are also concerned, along with those of syntaxes and forms, with poems' formal causes. Their efficient cause, writing, may be related to the discussions of Hill's creative process throughout the book, particularly revisions, which are examined in the third and fourth chapters. The notion of the final cause of poetry, even when not under discussion, is continually under the discussion in this book; but that may be appropriate for what is fundamental.

Although art is not their primary subject, the first three chapters of the second book of the *Physics* suggest the importance of the causes, especially the formal and final causes, to art and, by extension, life.[30] The inquiry into the nature of a thing, Aristotle argues,

> must embrace both the purpose or end and the means to that end. And the 'nature' is the goal for the sake of which the rest exist; for if any systematic and continuous movement is directed to a goal, this goal is an end in the sense of the purpose to which the movement is a means. (A confusion on this point betrayed the poet into the unintentionally comic phrase in reference to a man's death: 'He has reached his end, for the sake of which he was born.' For the 'goal' does not mean any kind of termination, but only the best.) [...] In the crafts, then, it is we that prepare the material for the sake of the function it is to fulfil, but in natural products Nature herself has provided the material. In both cases, however, the preparation of the material is commanded by the end to which it is directed.[31]

In Aristotle's quotation from the 'poet', I cannot help but see and hear a knowing pun in the apparent misuse of the word *end*: 'He has reached

Introduction   9

his end, for the sake of which he was born.' Is this a befuddlement of the terminative and the perfective ('only the best' as Aristotle writes); or is it an insight that they can be made one? Aristotle contends that, in both nature and art (which for him imitates nature), the design of anything 'is commanded by the end to which it is directed'. This might be said to presuppose a designer on both counts; and though the question of the metaphysics behind or involved in Aristotle's teleology is significantly beyond the scope of this book, the two poems in Hill's *Canaan* that take their titles from Aristotle's works ('Of Coming into Being and Passing Away' and 'De Anima', *C*, pp. 174–75), which I examine in the fourth chapter, forge clear connections between the endings and ends of the artist ('ending as praise itself') and the evident ends of God ('terms of grace | where grace has surprised us'; 'typology || incarnate').[32]

Aristotle's teleology (of both nature and art), as well as his artistic criticism, are of great importance to two poets who have written about poetry's ends in ways that I suggest have bearings on Hill's work: Philip Sidney and David Jones. Sidney's *Defence of Poesie* provides a beginning and a recurring touchstone for what is perhaps Hill's most celebrated essay, 'Our Word is Our Bond'.[33] The essay's (and Hill's) sense of language is strongly influenced by the *Defence*'s discussion of poetry's relation to nature, specifically man's fallen nature, which can be summarised in a quotation that Hill contemplates with a measure of awe in his inaugural lecture as Oxford Professor of Poetry: 'our erected wit, maketh vs know what perfection is, and yet our infected will, keepeth vs from reaching vnto it'.[34] Sidney evokes Aristotle (for the first of numerous times) in the *Defence*'s first definition of the end of poetry: 'Poesie therefore is an arte of imitation, for so *Aristotle* termeth it in his word *Mimesis*, that is to say, a representing, counterfetting, or figuring foorth; to speake metaphorically, a speaking picture: with this end, to teach and delight'.[35] Sidney goes on to bring the idea of the 'infected will' to bear on a definition of the final purpose of the 'purif[y]ing wit, this enritching of memory, enabling of iudgment, and enlarging of conceyt, which commonly we call learning': 'the final end is, to lead & draw vs to as high a perfection, as our degenerate soules made worse by theyr clayey lodgings, can be capable of'.[36] Poetry, for Sidney, is the fittest vehicle for such an end; by contrast, he finds that astronomy, philosophy, and mathematics are

> but seruing Sciences, which as they haue each a priuate end in themselues, so yet are they all directed to the highest end of the mistres Knowledge, by the Greeks called *Arkitecktonike*, which stands (as I thinke) in the knowledge of a mans selfe, in the Ethicke and politick consideration, with the end of well dooing and not of well knowing onely; euen as the Sadlers next end is to make a good saddle: but his farther end, to serue a nobler facultie, which is

10 *Geoffrey Hill and the ends of poetry*

> horsemanship, so the horsemans to souldiery, and the Souldier not onely to haue the skill, but to performe the practise of a Souldier: so that the ending end of all earthly learning, being vertuous action, those skilles that most serue to bring forth that, haue a most iust title to bee Princes ouer all the rest.[37]

For Sidney, poetic 'skilles' merit the status of 'Princes ouer all the rest' because they best serve the 'ending end', the final purpose, of all learning, which is 'vertuous action'.[38] It may seem almost ridiculous to ask whether the end, or an end, of Hill's poetry also is to lead its recipients to a more virtuous life; but if the scope were narrowed a little and the word 'life' replaced by *language* or *speech*, the question might begin to sound more reasonable. (Additionally, the 'knowledge of a mans selfe, in the Ethicke and politick consideration' is also a clear thematic end in Hill's poetry and critical prose.)

Later in the *Defence*, Sidney considers the local ends of speech, which is significant to this book's central examination of prosodic ends:

> For if *Oratio*, next to *Ratio*, Speech next to Reason, bee the greatest gyft bestowed vpon mortalitie: that can not be praiselesse, which dooth most pollish that blessing of speech, which considers each word, not only (as a man may say) by his forcible qualitie, but by his best measured quantitie, carrying euen in themselues, a Harmonie: (without (perchaunce) Number, Measure, Order, Proportion, be in our time growne odious.)[39]

The word 'pollish' should not be overlooked or misconstrued. The prosodic ends that constitute this book's chapter titles – puns; dead ends (repeating figures); rhymes; syntaxes; and forms – are understood to be constituents of completedness in Hill's poetry. They are not finishing touches or merely ornamental flourishes but ingredient signs of consummate and consummative artistry; further to this one can adduce these poetic figures' and structural features' reconciling attributes, in that they bring disparate verbal senses and connotations, and accidents of language, into motivated alignment or atonement. While Sidney's 'pollish' may at first suggest the improvement of only the surface appearance of the 'blessing of speech', as polish is added as the finish to a table, the rest of the sentence confirms that the finish Sidney has in mind is something integral to every moment of composition: 'which considers each word'. The elements of this 'pollish' are 'forcible qualitie' (for which Sidney elsewhere uses the terms 'forciblenes, or *Energia* (as the Greekes cal it) of the writer') and 'best measured quantitie'.[40] The first element, rhetorical power or persuasiveness, is 'pollish' without being a final sheen added to speech; even more so, the second element, corresponding to the harmony of rhythm and form ('Number, Measure, Order, Proportion'), is not superimposed on speech but is among that through which speech exists.

Introduction   11

To return to the question of poetry's purposes, there is an important counter to Sidney's 'ending end' of art as stimulant to 'vertuous action'; it can be found in the arguments of many writers, but an account that seems particularly significant for the purposes of this study of Hill is Rowan Williams's *Grace and Necessity: Reflections on Art and Love*, the published version of his Clark Lectures in 2005.[41] In *Grace and Necessity*, Williams discusses the thoughts on art of a theologian (Jacques Maritain), a painter-poet (David Jones), and a novelist (Flannery O'Connor). Both Jones and O'Connor are treated as following Maritain's lead in crucial respects. For Maritain, and contra Sidney, Williams writes, 'art is not *of itself* either grounded in or aimed at moral probity. [...] Virtuous making aims not at the good of humanity but at the good of what is made.'[42] Williams's exploration of art through the writers he examines is notable for its intense engagement with ends, both as art's (and especially poetry's) purposes and as its sense of finishedness, which tends to represent an unfulfilled, even unfulfillable, desire: 'The mature Maritain, in the Mellon lectures, speaks of finite beauty or finishedness in the work being always incomplete at some level'; 'art aims always at the formally finished work [...], not at the stimulating of particular felt response'.[43] But when Williams goes on to ask, 'if things "give more than they have" in the artist's world, what exactly can be said about that redundancy and excess of gift that does not sooner or later have to connect with a picture of divine *poiesis*?', the distance travelled from Sidney's 'speaking picture' may begin to have seemed wider than it is.[44] Sidney too likens the poetic maker ('Poet' coming from 'this word *Poiein*, which is, to make') to the 'heauenly Maker'; and both agree with Aristotle on the essentially mimetic nature of the artwork.[45]

Williams, via Maritain, writes of art's purpose in a way distinct from both Sidney's 'end' and the nineteenth-century notion of art for art's sake. The perfecting of the artwork itself has a central place; but whether this is the final end of art is not entirely decided between Williams and the subjects of his book. One of these is David Jones, for whom the 'natural end of man (i.e. the end conformable to man's nature) is eternal felicity'; in this he follows Aristotle by way of Thomas Aquinas.[46] Jones writes (in a passage not cited by Williams) of the etymology of *art*, which leads into an evaluation of art's end:

> the word 'art' from *artem* has, probably, at root, the meaning of something fitted together, because here the Latin element *ar-* means 'to fit'. [...] Art concerns a means or process, a means by which is achieved a 'perfect fit'.
>
> One could say that the 'end' of Ars *is* that 'perfect fit'. Or we might, for convenience' sake, say that Ars has no end save the perfecting of a process by which all sorts of ends are made possible. It *is* that process. It is concerned

12   *Geoffrey Hill and the ends of poetry*

with perfecting a means. In so far as art has an end that end is a 'fitting together' and the word art means a fitting together.[47]

Hill, in *The Book of Baruch*, may be seen to agree with Jones: 'Art's aim is to scheme for a tight fit even so' (*BBGJ* 191, p. 105).[48] The two chief ends that I ascribed, in the first section of this introduction, to Hill's poetry, 'the reconciliation of antagonists in word and thought' ('a fitting together') and 'the perfect articulation of the poem' ('perfecting of a process'; 'perfecting a means'), are traceable in Jones's words. Together, these two ends are Jones's 'perfect fit'.

But, of course, it is not a perfect fit for Hill. It will be evident throughout this study that unfinishedness is a continual, countering urge and characteristic of Hill's poetry. Unfinishedness is not antithetical but complementary to the argument that Hill's poetry is end-directed. At every level of Hill's work there is awareness, at times regretful, at others resigned, at yet others pugnacious, of the universally unavoidable imperfection and incompletion of artistic endeavour. It is also true that Hill, especially in the poetry from *Canaan* (1996) onwards, frequently seeks a felt sense of unfinishedness; whether, finally, this is a matter of relinquishing desires for mastery and unattainable order or of furthering such desires by another means, pursuing the perfectly imperfect, must depend on the poem. The tempting sorrow of the unfinished is deeply involved in the end-directedness of Hill's poetry. In addition, the sense of the failure of language itself, and the careful speaker's unending struggle with that failure, is manifested in Hill's use of the poetic figures considered here: it is in the pitiful puns of 'September Song' (discussed in the first chapter); in all of the second chapter's linguistic and other 'Dead ends'; in the pained autorhymes of 'The Pentecost Castle' (discussed in the third chapter). The fourth chapter in particular addresses the lure of broken language.

A natural concomitant is the moral failure not of language but of its user. Praising the critical work of another Williams, that is, Charles Williams, near the end of his penultimate collected essay, Hill evokes Rowan Williams's 'divine *poiesis*' while remaining equally aware of converse poetic impulses:

As a Christian [C. Williams] would have understood the fundamental dilemma of the poetic craft: that it is simultaneously an imitation of the divine fiat and an act of enormous human self-will. [...] Poetry can be in, or out of, grace; and the mind of the maker can imitate either God's commandment or Lucifer's 'instressing of his own inscape' as Hopkins splendidly and humbly described it: 'it was a sounding, as they say, of his own trumpet and a hymn in his own praise.' (*CCW*, p. 563)

Introduction

13

That poetry can imitate the 'divine fiat' and 'God's commandment', and even be in a state of 'grace', does not preclude it from the pitfall of hubris; it suggests that both poetry's means and its end should be discerned with caution, but does not say exactly what that end may be. The next paragraph comes closer, quoting Alice Mary Hadfield's paraphrase of Williams: 'The call of poetry in word and thought is to be final' (*CCW*, p. 563). This is a call that echoes through Hill's poetry from beginning to end. Whatever else Hill's poetry's end is, it is to be an end: 'something | incomparably finished, something beyond change | as by design, yes, the great memory-surge | of raw beginning' (*SC* 2. 38, p. 449).

The doubling of the 'poetic craft' that Hill outlines above is in every sense typical of his thought and his expression. What does not turn on itself seems unworthy of Hill's notice. Directly after observing the oxymoronic doubleness of the word 'sacrifice' (*CCW*, p. 99) in his essay 'Redeeming the Time', Hill quotes a letter written by Hopkins to Robert Bridges in 1887. It functions not only as his own *Defence* against charges of obscurity and difficulty but also as a bounding suspicion of his own deep desire for poetic consummation:

> Plainly if it is possible to express a sub[t]le and recondite thought on a subtle and recondite subject in a subtle and recondite way and with great felicity and perfection, in the end, something must be sacrificed, with so trying a task, in the process, and this may be the being at once, nay perhaps even the being without explanation at all, intelligible.

Figures and features

This book's five chapters can be split down the middle in two categories, because the third chapter belongs to both: poetic figures and structural features. The first three chapters examine the local consummations (whether reconciliations or head-buttings) that Hill tries and tests: puns; repeating figures and tautologies; and rhymes. Crucially, each of these features is a verbal coupling (or consummation), a coming together of two or more distinct words or senses of words. The single-word pun is a joining of meanings and connotations, sometimes harmonious, sometimes dissonant. The repeating figure combines a word with its derivatives or aural relatives; the tautology has a word address itself; and the rhyme, depending on the kind, draws words into more or less oblique communications and closures. Rhyme introduces the element of organisational function in the poem; and the fourth and fifth chapters, on syntaxes and forms respectively, look more broadly at the structures of Hill's poems. They ask to what extent these structures are end-directed (that is, indicative of the poems' intent; driven to thematic ends; and accruing force and attention to the endings of poems).

The first chapter is on Hill's puns. The pun is in one sense a very minimal linguistic end, bringing together disparate meanings or connotations in a single word or phrase. The first section of the chapter cites a wide range of puns from Hill's poetry in order to establish the characteristics of the figure for Hill and how these change over the course of his career. The second section begins by considering the implications of the pun's 'ambiguity', its capacity to represent doubled or coupled 'reality'. Referring to Empson, Weil, and T. S. Eliot, it asks why an 'accurate' ambiguity may be poetically and ethically desirable, and discusses the '[r]e-cognition' that may follow. The final section of the chapter analyses Hill's puns in light of two persistent themes, which themselves have affinities with puns: sexual love and alchemy. Looking predominantly at poems from *Scenes from Comus* (2005) and *Oraclau | Oracles* (2007–2012), and noting the debts owed to both Donne and Jung, this section regards the pun as both witness and minister to Hill's 'alchemic-carnal' marriages of meanings.

The title of the second chapter is 'Dead ends'. Reiterations and quasi-repetitions of words play dangerously close to dull redundancy; they are potential 'dead ends'. This chapter's four sections, the first on repeating figures and the latter three on tautologies, look at the expressions of language's limitations in Hill's poetry, focusing particularly on *The Triumph of Love* (1998), *The Orchards of Syon* (2002), and *The Book of Baruch by the Gnostic Justin* (2019). With the help of a Chestertonian allusion to Aristotle's sense of *meson*, or balance, the first section argues that repeating figures can present discrete rebalances of language, which aim to transcend the corrupt histories of words. The next three sections are devoted to tautologies, in which a superficial balance of words is already evident. After a preliminary investigation of the link between tautology, infancy, and speechlessness, with reference to Tennyson, the second section claims that tautologies, for Hill especially, are the closest thing in language to expressions of 'mute desire'. The third section examines the 'evenness' of tautologies, understood as necessary for the potential transcendence of their expression; and the fourth section, following this logic of tautologies to its intended end, considers Hill's tautology as a childlike plea to God for reconciliation.

The third chapter deals with Hill's rhymes. The rhyme is a significant end-point of poetry, coupling words that are often otherwise unfamiliar to each other. This chapter starts by reflecting on rhyme's importance in the context of Hill's 'antiphonal' poetics, and reviews some of the suspicions of rhyme's 'easy mellifluousness', citing Stevens and Pope. The second section

Introduction 15

asks how Hill's rhyme might be influenced by, and how it differs from, the suggestions of T. S. Eliot and the example of Allen Tate. A survey of rhyme in Hill's poetry is offered in the third section, with a distinction drawn between the work before and after the 1985 *Collected Poems*. The culminating fourth and fifth sections of the chapter posit two paradoxical kinds of rhyme in Hill's work: the impossible and the inevitable. Admitting that it is a question of emphasis rather than strict definition, the chapter studies at length two poems from Hill's early work, 'The Pentecost Castle' (1978) and 'Ovid in the Third Reich' (1968), as examples of impossible rhyming; and several poems from *Al Tempo de' Tremuoti* (2007–2012) as examples of inevitable rhyming. The chapter ends with a short suggestion of the relation between rhyme and Hill's idea of equity.

Beginning the book's perspectival ascent to the larger structural features of poetry, the fourth chapter, on syntaxes, examines the ends Hill seeks at the level of the sentence. It takes *A Treatise of Civil Power* (2007) as its point of reference for an analysis of the tension between order and disorder in Hill's syntax. It notes the '[u]rge to unmake | all wrought finalities' in the collection's last poem, 'Nachwort', and regards this urge as essential to the troubled and diverse energies of Hill's syntaxes. The metatextual rhetoric of language undressing or undoing itself in the later poems sheds light on the struggle for 'plain speaking' in Hill. The remaining two sections of the chapter evaluate one of the key orchestrators of Hill's syntax: his punctuation. The second section looks at poems of 'limited punctuation' in *Canaan* (1996), arguing that these, somewhat surprisingly, provide some of the clearest examples of 'satisfactory', conclusive endings in Hill's work. The third section assesses the punctuational changes made between revisions of *Odi Barbare* (2007–2012), reading the helpful additions of punctuation marks in the latter version as revealing a deepened 'trust' in syntax in Hill's late poetry.

The fifth and final chapter is on the forms of Hill's poems: do they arrive at ends; and if so what are they? The chapter's introductory section attends to the notion of the 'ideal' in Hill's thought. Quoting at length from remarks Hill made in 2008 and in 2016 at his last public reading, it relates the ideal shaping of the poem to what Hill calls its 'necessary closure'. The chapter goes on to examine four of Hill's forms: unrhymed sonnets; versets; clavics; and sapphics. The first two of these appear in Hill's early work (1968–1971), the latter two in his late work (2007–2012). Hill's use of each is distinctive; together, they illustrate Hill's resourceful and attentive handling of various forms to reach, or deflect from, a sense of closure. There is a closing discussion of the thought of 'yearning', which is taken as fundamental to Hill's end-directed language and forms. What F. H. Bradley calls 'the idea of perfection' is deemed an essential stimulus not only of

16 *Geoffrey Hill and the ends of poetry*

the sapphic's short final line but of Hill's poetry as a whole. The chapter ends with a summary of the nature of forms in Hill's early and late work, including the pointedly unbounded end of his posthumous collection, *The Book of Baruch by the Gnostic Justin*.

Lastly, there are two short 'End notes', which constitute a last reflection on this book's intentions; and on the ends of Hill's poetry taken as a whole.

Titles and *tetelestai*

In the first of his series of lectures (between 1999 and 2004) as Professor of Poetry at the University of Oxford, titled *The End of the Poem*, Paul Muldoon begins by saying 'a word or two' about his 'choice of this somewhat booming, perhaps even slightly bumptious phrase, "the end of the poem"'.[49] Nothing approaching an explanation of the choice or the phrase arrives at this point; but, in the course of the fifteen lectures, Muldoon takes up numerous senses and connotations of a poem's end, some of which this book sets aside. These include the sense that a poem is an 'epilogue' to another poet's work; the 'notion of there being "no barriers" between the poem and the biography of its author'; the 'influence of one poem on another within the body of work of a single poet, whereby the "gaps" or "blanks" in one poem are completed or perfected by another'; the 'extent to which', in 'the relationship between any writer and any reader', 'one determines the role of the other, one completing the other'; and the poet's attempted '*limiting* of readings of the poem'.[50] Muldoon's approach to senses of *end* is broader and somewhat more freewheeling than my own but indicates many of the potential paths an end-directed poetics could take.

Muldoon also points out the existence of a 1999 book by Giorgio Agamben, 'unfortunately titled' *The End of the Poem: Studies in Poetics*.[51] As for this book's title, though accusations of booming bumptiousness may equally pertain, I hope I have justified already my titular pluralising of *End*. A still nicer distinction exists between *the Poem* and *Poetry*. There are forfeited benefits of the former term, firstly that *the Poem* trains the mind on the abstracted finished form of the poem in a way that would suggest some of this book's key concerns. Secondly, this book, as I have mentioned, is structured as though it were a lens zooming out from the smallest verbal details to the largest designs of a poem; the individual poem, viewed thus, is the image of the book's broadening analysis. But while *the Poem* emphasises the creation sans creator, *Poetry* is the 'art or work of a poet', as the *OED* has it (sense 2).[52] As well as including this important sense of labour, the latter term seems to me slightly wider, more reconciling of forms and

Introduction   17

of definitions. It occurs to me, too, that a poem can be finished, but, at least this side of the eschaton, poetry cannot. There is, then, a quietly oxymoronic friction between *Ends* and *Poetry* that may suggest the troubles of discerning what comes to an end and what does not in Hill's work and elsewhere.

The original title of this book was *Consummatum est* (to which the current one was a subtitle). The phrase remains crucial to the book (though as if it were its ghost, given up). It is Jerome's translation into Latin of the single Greek word in John 19.28 and 19.30, the only two places in the Bible where it occurs, and the second of which is attributed to Christ, dying on the Cross. The word is τετέλεσται (*tetelestai*). In the Vulgate it becomes the two words *consummatum est*. This title had been arguably impertinent for at least two reasons, neither of which accounts for its absence here. One is that it is found nowhere in Hill's work (though 'consummation' and its relatives are found throughout).[53] The other is its unavoidable audacity. The use of the words of Christ was no claim to virtue or holiness, either on Hill's behalf or mine. Rather, it struck me that these words, which the King James Version (1611) translates as 'It is finished' (John 19.30), mark the moment of a consummate accomplishment; to be able to say them truly, at least with regard to poetry, seems to me to have been a major part of Geoffrey Hill's aspiration. As Henry Hart writes of Hill: 'Many writers have written about becoming artists and writing poems, but few have put so much emphasis on the actual moment of finishing a poem.'[54]

As two of his best essays, and a significant part of his poetry, demonstrate, Hill greatly honours and believes in sacrifice.[55] (Hopkins: 'in the end, something must be sacrificed'.) Christ's sacrifice, which was to undo the effects of original sin – the doctrine of which is the beginning (if not the end) of Hill's personal theological credo – is present in shadow (as in Jean-Léon Gérôme's 1867 painting *Consummatum est*) throughout Hill's reflections on human conduct, sacrifice, and death. 'You are the castaway of drowned remorse, | you are the world's atonement on the hill'.[56]

1

Puns

Transfigurations

And *glowery* is a mighty word with two meanings
if you crave ambiguity in plain speaking
as I do.

And *glowery* is a mighty word because it has two meanings.[1] Hill quotes the word from Kate Fletcher's *The Old Testament in the Dialect of the Black Country* (1975); there it describes the face of Moses glowing (and yet, if one is to incorporate the double-meaning of *glower* (*OED*), also scowling) after having encountered the Lord on Mount Sinai. Moses appears also in the New Testament, when Jesus is 'transfigured' before the three Apostles, 'and his face did shine as the Sunne' (Matthew 17. 2).

Does using a 'word with two meanings' constitute a transfiguration? To complicate the question further, Hill gives two shades of meaning to the word *transfiguration* itself: 'The term connotes both "metamorphosis" and "elevation"' (*CCW*, p. 33). Using a word with two meanings, deliberately lifting up both meanings in the use, can be described as an elevating 'metamorphosis' (*OED*, sense 1: 'The action or process of changing in form, shape, or substance'). In the case of using a word with two meanings, the change – in contrast with what I call repeating figures, which I examine in the second chapter – is in substance: combining meanings in the use of a word alters its substance by inviting inferences, generating new meaning from the combination.

The definition of *pun* in this chapter may be at once too narrow and too broad. Too narrow because I impose a tighter limit to the pun than is normally applied even to the classical term *paronomasia*; too broad because, after all the limitations, one appears to be left with a phenomenon that might simply be called (following Hill above) 'ambiguity'. Eleanor Cook's entry for 'paronomasia' in *The Princeton Encyclopedia of Poetry and Poetics* begins with a broad stroke: 'Wordplay based on like-sounding

Puns 19

words, e.g., a pun.'[2] This is not how I wish to define *pun* here. More useful to my purpose is Cook's later summation of the distinction between two kinds of puns: 'homophonic puns (like-sounding, as in "done" and "Donne") and homonymic or semantic puns (different meanings in one word, as in railroad "ties" and "ties" of the heart in Bishop's "Chemin de Fer").'[3] The pun, as I define it here, is homonymic; but my range is narrower still: the meanings should inhere in a single use of a word (rather than in the same word being repeated in different senses). (One qualification here is that 'word' may apply also to a short phrase, usually a set phrase.) The reason for this narrow definition is that I want to concentrate discretely on the smallest complete lexical unit, the single word, as a locus of ends and end-directedness before moving (in the second and third chapters) to the play of word with or against word. There is a marked difference to me between, on one hand, the interaction of meanings in a single use of a word; and, on the other, the interaction of separate words (even when they are the same word repeated). The single-word homonymic pun can be less self-advertising than repeating figures; the juxtaposition it presents can be quieter (though often more startling for its quietness); its bringing together of sense and connotation is a more intimate affair and seems more easily than the repeating figure to afford tragedy as well as comedy. Hill's use of the pun, as I hope to show, bears this out.

But what of Hill's use of *pun*? Does it align with the one outlined above? It seems so. Certainly, in his criticism, Hill identifies what I am calling puns as such – Bunyan's '*damnable*' (CCW, p. 387), for instance, which I shall look at later – and nowhere does he use the word in a way that contradicts my definition.[4] His use of 'paronomasia', following Henry Peacham's *The Garden of Eloquence* (1593), tends instead to refer to repeated figures.[5] In Hill's poetry, references to puns and punning, while predictably offering less in the way of definition, give nonetheless a strong impression of the importance of puns for Hill – particularly the proclivity for puns in a given language, which undoubtedly he views as a positive attribute.

The main language in question here is Hebrew. 'Not | music,' Hill writes in the twentieth poem of *Speech! Speech!*, adapting Pater's famous dictum, 'Hebrew. Poetry aspires | to the condition of Hebrew' (SS 20, p. 298).[6] Later, in *Pindarics*, he writes: 'Hebrew mates word and thing, the acting word, | the basic punning language though not all | punsters are poets nor would wish to be', adding tellingly at the end of the stanza, 'How strange you have to be to stay faithful' (P 13, p. 535). The Welsh language is lent favour by association in *Oraclau | Oracles*: 'Welsh like Hebrew is a punning language' (O 127: *Marwnad William Phylip, Hendre Fechan* (1), p. 783). What Hill intends to suggest by all this is not made wholly clear; though it is certainly clear that Hebrew, as in that of the Old Testament

20 *Geoffrey Hill and the ends of poetry*

or Hebrew Bible, is replete with puns.[7] Biblical puns often occur in the naming of people, places, or things. In this sense they are somewhat one-sided, as it were hewn by force out of the language – the thing named is made to connect with that which names it. Perhaps the most famous example in Scripture comes not from Hebrew but from Greek, when Jesus gives Simon the new name 'Peter', meaning *rock*, and goes on to explain: 'and vpon this rocke I will build my Church' (Matthew 16.18). This is not a pun of chance or spontaneity; it is not that Simon already happened to be called Peter, and that Jesus was merely using the word to point to the aptness of the coincidence. But other puns, with which Hill and this book are more concerned, are the result of contingency, the chance double-nature of a word or phrase, which can be turned to motive, to purposed use, by the deliberate speaker.

The word 'pun' does not occur in the poetry until *Speech! Speech!* (2000); seven other instances follow.[8] It is, I suggest, at this point in Hill's poetic career that his poetry's attitude towards the contingencies of language, and at the same time the character of its puns, change. The collections that in my view gravitate most towards punning may serve to show this change: in the early work, *King Log* (1968); in the later work, *Speech! Speech!* and *The Daybooks* (2007–2012).

The first poem in *King Log*, 'Ovid in the Third Reich' (*KL*, p. 39), offers some quiet puns: the speaker has learned 'not to look down | So much upon the damned', in which there is the added suggestion of a literal glance to the underworld; and the damned are said to '[h]armonize strangely with the divine | Love', 'strangely' taking advantage of at least two distinct senses (*in a foreign or unusual way* – since the damned are estranged from, foreign to, divine love – and *exceptionally*; see *OED*, senses 1, 4, and 5). The next poem, 'Annunciations', includes in its second section perhaps the most commented-on, since among the loudest, of all Hill's early puns: 'Our God scatters corruption' (*KL*, p. 40). The extreme opposition of meanings jarring together in 'scatters' is paradoxical but not necessarily self-negating: it would be in fact rather orthodox for a Christian to claim that God allows corruption to be dispersed among humanity while ultimately dispersing with it altogether in His judgement. The boldness of this pun has drawn attention away from one only three lines down in the last words of the poem: 'strive | To recognize the damned among your friends'. The word 'recognize' is doing at least a double shift: the imperative is both *discern which of your friends are going to be damned* and *acknowledge that the damned are among your friends* (possibly also *show appreciation to the damned when you are among your friends*). Further along in *King Log*, there are the grim puns of 'September Song', on which I focus in the next section of this chapter;

and there are three occurrences of the word 'end' that play on the familiar juxtaposition of *terminus* and *purpose*.[9]

The first of 'Three Baroque Meditations' begins with a very direct pun: 'Do words make up the majesty | Of man [...]?' (*KL*, p. 66). Again, Hill's pun is poised between grandeur and (often self-redounding) suspicion of it: do words, such as his own, constitute or counterfeit the high stature of mankind? A subtler pun comes in the third meditation, 'The Dead Bride': 'His sacramental mouth || That justified my flesh' (*KL*, p. 68). Prepared by 'sacramental', 'justified' twins a religious absolution with psychological validation. The poem ends: 'He weeps, | Solemnizing his loss', where '[s]olemnizing' shades together ritual and performance.

King Log concludes with 'The Songbook of Sebastian Arrurruz', a sequence of pained love-lyrics. The second part, 'Coplas', ends its first stanza with a familiar but well-employed pun made clearer by repetition: 'I can lose what I want. I want you' (*KL*, p. 70). Here, 'want' is both *lack* and *desire* in both instances; in the first, the pun effects the poignant meaning that even what one does not have can be taken from one (cf. Matthew 13.12: 'whosoeuer hath not, from him shall be taken away, euen that hee hath').[10] The two 'want's also play off of one another: the resigned and petulant air of the first instance of 'want' – *I can lose whatever I wish to lose* – is undone by the honesty of 'I want you' (that is, *I did not wish to lose you*). A similar explanation accompanies the pun in the fifth part: 'The metaphor holds; is a snug house' (*KL*, p. 73). The latter clause alerts the reader to the double sense of *remains valid* and *embraces* in 'holds'. There are hints of puns elsewhere in the poem: sexual contentment and hauteur merge in 'satisfied women' ('From the Latin', *KL*, p. 75); and in the last part, '11' (itself a visual symbol of the lovers' separation), the speaker wakes to 'caress propriety with odd words' (*KL*, p. 79): that is to say, with whatever words come piecemeal to mind, which happen also to be peculiar.

A few general characteristics of Hill's early puns can be assumed from this sample. The first is their lack of cheer. The dark poems of *King Log* seem at first unfit for puns, which, in their most familiar linguistic surroundings, are usually in the service of comedy. Hill writes in a late notebook: 'I'm a comedian'; but his early puns, like his early use of clichés, are usually for 'tragic rather than comic purposes'.[11] Secondly, and relatedly, these puns mark a deep suspicion of the double-sidedness of words, and the puns' activation of their disparate meanings is very cleverly and very carefully managed. The first sentence of Hill's first collected essay offers a useful shorthand: these are puns with 'raised eyebrows'.[12] Thirdly, these are often softer and subtler puns than in the later work, rarely pointing to themselves; they are studious, though never bookish.

22   *Geoffrey Hill and the ends of poetry*

Compare the later puns of *Speech! Speech!*, which represents perhaps the largest gathering of puns in all Hill's work, and which is both studious and bookish (beginning as it does – after two epigraphs, one in Latin and one in German – with the single-word sentence 'Erudition' (*SS* 1, p. 289)). But neither bookish nor erudite means without humour. While it includes an obscure reference, the tenth poem is a bawdy riot of puns that demonstrates that talk of the 'end' need not be entirely gloomy:

> From the beginning the question how to end
> has been part of the act. One cannot have sex
> fantasies (any way) as the final
> answer to life. Shiftless,
> we are working at it, butt-headed
> Sothsegger for one, between bouts of sleep
> and community arm-wrestling, elbows
> in spilt beer. TALK ABOUT LAUGH, TALK ABOUT
> ANGRY. But don't count, don't bet,
> on who or what ends uppermost, the franchise
> of slavishness being free to all comers
> without distinction.

> (p. 293)

With Hill's poems one may have to get to the 'end' in order to go back to 'the beginning' and enumerate all the puns. Once one has read 'Sothsegger' (and perhaps, as I did, looked it up), a reference to a fifteenth-century alliterative poem called 'Mum and the Sothsegger' of which both the beginning and end are lost, this poem's first sentence begins to ring with the potential for new meaning. But new meaning is already retroactively injected by the second sentence: the dramatic 'act' becomes also the sexual act; 'how to end' becomes also how to reach climax. Continuing down the poem, the parenthetical 'any way', crucially two words, sounds less like either confirming the point or changing the subject and more like the content of the 'sex | fantasies'. 'Shiftless', meaning *lazy* (as well as *without work*), also gains meaning from this context, a 'shift' being (now chiefly in North American use) a 'straight, loose dress', or (in older use) a woman's undergarment (*OED*, 'shift', *n.*, senses 10a, b). This in turn gives 'working at it' an eye-opening new colour (leaving alone 'butt-headed', which may just confuse matters). After 'arm-wrestling', 'who or what ends uppermost' can refer to both elbows on tables and entangled whole bodies. The crude pun 'comers', then, hardly requires explanation; and the poem concludes with another, less salacious, example: 'without distinction' is both *without discrimination* and *with no outstanding qualities*.

Before getting to my reason for listing them, it is worth asking what Hill's reason is for writing all these saucy puns. Though *Speech! Speech!*, with its 120 poems, is not in the same world of degradation as its stated analogue, de Sade's *120 Days of Sodom* (1785), the tenth poem's informal sexual puns indicate one way in which Hill is depicting the decay of democratic society and culture, encapsulated in the phrase 'the franchise | of slavishness'. Hill is using a consciously slippery language; the difference in this later work is that he appears to be relishing it. The puns are looser, more off-hand.

Other puns in *Speech! Speech!* follow suit. There are far too many to cite here – usually more than one in each poem – but I will give a few representative examples. The sixty-fourth poem ends with a cliché unexpectedly becoming a philosophical definition: 'Liebniz's | monad is one thing. One thing or another— | we are altogether something else again' (p. 320). The initial cliché 'is one thing' is the first of a hat trick ('If I can cap this it will be a hat trick'), being expanded into two further double-edged clichés to complete the poem.[13] (Meanwhile the 'we' in question could be speaker and lover, addressed in the previous poem, or humanity as a whole.) Elsewhere, in one of the best uses of the collection's newspaper-headline voice, Hill imagines Donne's death: 'Face | the all but final degradation—FAMED | PILLAR OF THE CHURCH A STIFF' (p. 327). Two nouns are punningly literalised here: 'degradation' is a loss of bodily integrity as well as pride; 'PILLAR' a corpse's as well as a doctrinal solidness. In the ninety-first poem Hill goes deliberately too far, spelling out his puns and offering meta-commentary on them and himself:

> This lays it ón | a shade: in the arms
> of his claustral love. A pun, then, *arms*? He's that
> sort of a mind. Another one on *lays*:
> lays it | on a sháde—are you still with me
> yet wandering, blocked words hung round neck
> on a noose of twine: his own name included.
>
> (p. 334)

The comic image in the last two lines here is of a poet weighed down (as Coleridge's mariner) by his puns, his verbal ingenuity.[14] Even 'his own name' is a pun: the indignity! (It is employed in Bunyan-fashion thirty-one poems earlier (*SS* 60, p. 318): 'Up the Hill Difficulty'.) The vertical marks and stress marks, which, as with several other collections, Hill mostly removes between the initial publication of *Speech! Speech!* and its final version in *Broken Hierarchies*, are retained here to point out condescendingly the (hardly unfamiliar or inscrutable) puns 'lays', 'arms', and 'shade'. Hill then has the temerity to ask 'are you still with me', which gains its own punning shade in the possibility that it is addressed to the ghost or (newly accented) 'sháde'. Hill's apparent disdain for the reader becomes more

24   *Geoffrey Hill and the ends of poetry*

pardonable in the context of this poem and the entire sequence of 'blocked words', which sees Hill continually presenting bitterly satirical caricatures, including several of himself. He is interminably, almost (he claims) involuntarily, 'laying' his 'name', his poetic reputation, on a 'shade' of meaning over and over again in *Speech! Speech!* and elsewhere. He is betting that the power of this nuance will be great enough to bear the weight of the paired and pairing words with which he burdens himself, to save him in his 'noose of twine', his terminal twinning.

In these late puns and those in later work, all the way to *The Book of Baruch by the Gnostic Justin* (2019), it cannot be said that Hill has become less serious about language and its gravity. What has happened, though, is that the poetry has become more welcoming of, and less suspicious of, language's contingencies. Its puns have become more easy-going, more casually associative; the daft sexual puns of the tenth poem of *Speech! Speech!* would be unimaginable in any of the previous collections (with the possible exception of *The Triumph of Love* (1998) in its most waggish moments). The chance alignments of meaning in a word, which beforehand tended to give cause to agonised revelation, become, in the later work, almost universally ripe for prompt gathering and repurposing.

This is not to say that Hill's earlier motivations of contingency are to him doomed or wholly pessimistic ventures. Indeed, the notion of a redemptive or atoning kind of 'transfiguration', to pick up again the word that sparks this section's discussion, is brightly present throughout Hill's first two collected essays. In the second, 'The Absolute Reasonableness of Robert Southwell', Hill calls Southwell's style 'an art of "transfiguration"' (*CCW*, p. 33), and also (quoting Southwell himself) a 'wonderful alteratio[n]' (*CCW*, p. 35). What Southwell is said to transfigure is the mendaciousness and violence surrounding his life, and his own suffering, into a 'positive oblation' (*CCW*, p. 36). Fittingly, the Transfiguration of Christ is invoked and compared in Southwell's own words to His Crucifixion: 'Christ 'transfigured in *Mounte Thabor* ... was also at the same time, heard talkinge *de excessu* of his bitter passion' (*CCW*, p. 36).[15]

In the first essay, 'Poetry as "Menace" and "Atonement"', Hill, praising Coleridge's redrawings of sense in both poetry and prose, writes: 'It is a transfiguring of weakness into strength, a subsuming' (*CCW*, pp. 14–15); he goes on to quote Kathleen Coburn on her own adjective for Coleridge in *The Self Conscious Imagination*: 'The two senses of the word are thus antithetical, *self-conscious* (1) as being realistically accurate about one's identity, and *self-conscious* (2) as being anything but clear, in fact painfully in doubt' (*CCW*, p. 15). A little later, employing (not for the last time) some awkward sexual imagery, Hill writes: 'I attempt to set at one the piercing insight and the carnal blundering, in which I intentionally recollect

Puns   25

Coleridge's capacity to "transfigure his own dissipation by a metaphor that perfectly comprehends it"' (*CCW*, p. 17). The pun, a compacted metaphor, is something that Hill intends to do precisely this job for him. Hill wonders, with a measure of fear and loathing, whether such attribution of power to language approaches Wallace Stevens's declaration of religion decapitalised and given the boot by poetry (which Hill quotes in *CCW*, p. 18: 'After one has abandoned a belief in god, poetry is that essence which takes its place as life's redemption'). The essay's final paragraph, without concurring with Stevens, attempts not a theological vision of literature but the clearing of a ground for one, and in so doing comes near to a poetic manifesto with which Hill's entire corpus-in-waiting can be atoned. The poet's vocation is 'that of necessarily bearing his peculiar unnecessary shame in a world growing ever more shameless' (*CCW*, p. 19); one would not be surprised to read this on the back cover of *Speech! Speech!* or indeed *The Book of Baruch*. The poet, Hill goes on, 'may even transfigure and redeem that "word-helotry" to which George Steiner sees the merely literate man ultimately condemned' (*CCW*, p. 19). Not only to transfigure but to 'transfigure and redeem'. To reshape words' meanings in puns is not a zero-sum game: words can end both metamorphosed and elevated.

This quasi-theological reconciling and redemption is one of the central ends of Hill's puns. From the opening pages of this first essay, Hill has ends and endings in mind: 'The poet will occasionally, in the act of writing a poem, experience a sense of pure fulfilment which might [...] be misconstrued as the attainment of objective perfection. It seems less fanciful to maintain that, however much a poem is shaped and finished, it remains to some extent within the "imprisoning marble" of a quotidian shapelessness and imperfection' (*CCW*, pp. 3–4). A little further on: 'the technical perfecting of a poem is an act of atonement, in the radical etymological sense—an act of at-one-ment, a setting at one, a bringing into concord, a reconciling, a uniting in harmony; [...] this act of atonement is described with beautiful finality by two modern poets' (*CCW*, p. 4); Hill goes on to quote Yeats ('a poem comes right with a click like a closing box', a phrase which recurs with frequency in Hill's writing and speaking) and T. S. Eliot ('when the words are finally arranged in the right way [...] [the poet] may experience a moment of exhaustion, of appeasement, of absolution, and of something very near annihilation'). 'From the depths of the self', Hill writes in the same paragraph, 'we rise to a concurrence with that which is not-self' (*CCW*, p. 4). One can read this as both a summary of puns and a summa of life.

In the remaining two sections of this chapter, I examine the ethical burdens of ambiguity in Hill's punning language, chiefly a concern of the early work (pre-*Canaan*); and the double theme of alchemy and sexual love, expressed with a telling recourse to puns, which emerges solely in the late

26   *Geoffrey Hill and the ends of poetry*

work. I suggest that, as with the constructively negative labour of 'Poetry as "Menace" and "Atonement"', it is possible to conceive of the early work around ambiguity as clearing the ground for the freer punning expression, the easier reconcilings, exemplified in the 'alchemic-carnal' language that builds slowly from *Canaan* into the last collections.

Accurate ambiguities

> And *glowery* is a mighty word with two meanings
> if you crave ambiguity in plain speaking
> as I do.

I reuse this epigraph to point out that 'ambiguity in plain speaking' would be a contradiction in terms by William Empson's definition. In the preface to the second edition of *Seven Types of Ambiguity*, Empson responds to a review by James Smith that posits objections to his uses of his keyword:

> I have also to answer this sentence: 'We do not ordinarily accuse a pun, or the better type of conceit, of being ambiguous because it manages to say two things at once; its essence would seem to be conciseness rather than ambiguity.' We call it ambiguous, I think, when we recognise that there could be a puzzle as to what the author meant, in that alternative views might be taken without sheer misreading. If a pun is quite obvious it would not ordinarily be called ambiguous, because there is no room for puzzling. But if an irony is calculated to deceive a section of its readers I think it would ordinarily be called ambiguous, even by a critic who has never doubted its meaning.[16]

Hill's use of the word above does not align with either Smith's or Empson's definition of ambiguity. Whatever the intention of Hill's 'ambiguity in plain speaking' might be, it is not 'to deceive a section of its readers'.[17] For Empson, an 'ambiguity, in ordinary speech, means something very pronounced, and as a rule witty and deceitful'; if anything, Hill's ambiguity is as a rule opposed to deceit.[18] He remarked to John Haffenden:

> I resent the implication [...] of my using words in a double sense in order to mislead. [...] It may be that the subjects [of my poetry] present themselves to me as being full of ambiguous implications, but this is surely a different matter. The ambiguities and scruples seem to reside in the object that is meditated upon.[19]

To present ambiguities and scruples in the poetry, then, is simply an attempt to be faithful to the reality of the poetry's subject. ('How strange you have to be to stay faithful'.) James Smith's defence and description of the pun, quoted above by Empson, seems much closer to Hill's sense of his 'mighty word', except that Smith wishes to call its quality 'conciseness rather than ambiguity'.

The divergence of opinion demonstrates the ambiguity in the word itself: the *OED* (sense 3a) offers 'double or dubious signification', in which 'or' leaves a lot of room for the word in question. Hill asserts that his ambiguity is not frivolously or even wilfully dubious; it is double signification because of the dubiousness of both word and world. One may even wonder whether there is something in words' ambiguity that renders the writer deceived rather than deceiving: when Hill says that the 'ambiguities and scruples seem to reside in the object that is meditated upon', it is easy, following Hill's sense, to ignore that a seeming residence may be a completely illusory one.

Such discussion, for Hill, is semantic but not pedantic.[20] Hill's linguistic precision strives for moral rigour: it is precisely ambiguous because it wishes to avoid deceit. Hill is always on guard against 'tyrannical simplification', of a language grossly oversimplified, 'because propaganda requires that the minds of the collective respond primitively to slogans of incitement'.[21] Hill writes elsewhere: 'It is the precise detail, of word or rhythm, which carries the ethical burden.'[22] Even the appearance of his poetry, particularly from *Speech! Speech!* onwards, indicates this precision: round and square brackets; passages in italics and in small capitals; vertical marks to indicate caesurae, as in music; and stress marks, influenced by Hopkins (though not tied to his use of them: at times they seem to inflect sense more than rhythm). Hill's poetry challenges the eye's and ear's powers of discernment. It rewards meticulous attention. It fears to be interpreted on the basis of misreadings and mishearings, though such are frequently its subject.

It is apparently paradoxical, then, that what Hill's poems often take pains to convey are imprecisions, or, put another way, conscious ambiguities. The pun is an apparent imprecision that, in Hill, can become an unexpected furtherance of precision (even across languages). 'It is also | furtherance of slow exile, but enjoy— | best to enjoy—riding that *vague*' (*OS* V, p. 355): here the French word for a wave becomes vague simply because it resembles an English word.[23] By deliberately employing a word with numerous potential senses in its context, the distance between those senses is not only acknowledged but confronted, scrutinised, pressed for significance. A greater precision can be attained by tackling the vague. As Hill said in a radio interview, it is 'precision of a certain kind, because it's precision that can't rule out ambiguity. [...] The ambiguities can't come in accidentally, because that's a solecism. You've got to be accurate in your ambiguities.'[24] By way of contrast, in his final Professor of Poetry lecture at Oxford, Hill commented on the 'colloquial ambiguity' of Larkin's 'Church Going'.[25]

Hill's compulsion to make his ambiguities 'accurate', avoiding the sin of 'solecism', suggests questions that this section of the chapter endeavours to answer. Where may such a compulsion come from? Why, for Hill, is

28   *Geoffrey Hill and the ends of poetry*

accuracy to be so prized? And, most importantly, do Hill's puns reach this intended end of 'accurate' ambiguity?

An inspection of Hill's early critical work is useful in addressing the first question. Hill's scrupulosities are not far removed from those of G. K. Chesterton, quoted in Hill's first collected essay: 'a saint after repentance will forgive himself for a sin; a man about town will never forgive himself for a *faux pas*. There are ways of getting absolved for murder; there are no ways of getting absolved for upsetting the soup' (*CCW*, p. 9). The notion of forgiving oneself speaks resonantly to Hill's life of writing. Hill demands an idealistic accuracy from poetry, at least in part, because of fear and guilt, and the anxieties that accompany them: fear because he wishes not to add to the 'perpetration of "howlers", grammatical solecisms, mis-statements of fact, misquotations, improper attributions' (*CCW*, p. 9); guilt because, by writing, it is inevitable that he will.

'It is an anxiety', Hill continues, 'only transiently appeased by the thought that misquotation may be a form of re-creation' (*CCW*, p. 9). This 're-creation' is itself poised delicately between opposite meanings: the working of a hyphen into a word of play renders it a word of work, and a reworked word. Hill, in the knowledge that he cannot be completely accurate at all times, tentatively suggests that the inaccuracy 'may be' a kind of *felix culpa*, a happy fault. The pun is a paragon of re-creation, a play on words and a working with words.

In the strophe of the seventeenth ode in *Pindarics*, Hill offers, in italicised quotation, an oblique rationale for punning:

> *Eternity irradiates couple*
> jigs a fair recreation of sound bite.

(P 17, p. 539)

Is this recreation also a disguised re-creation? This quotation, the accuracy of which I cannot ascertain, from the Italian poet and writer Cesare Pavese (1908–1950, to whom *Pindarics* is dedicated, and who is its imagined inter-locutor), is nonetheless a 'sound bite', dragged out of context and onto its own line to become a kind of aphorism. (It cropped up earlier too, in *Clavics* (2011), before disappearing from that work as collected in *Broken Hierarchies*.[26]) In the antistrophe of the ode from which these two lines come, the italics reappear and seem to follow from the thought of eternal coupling or coupled eternity, this time ironically demanding context from spliced citations:

> What assigns *double, treble, reality*
> *to a single word*? Make that *in context,*
> I'm yours, free spirit, dead cobber. All in all
> Simone outwitted us: *L'enracinement*:
> working on multiple planes.

The second question I ask above – why, for Hill, is accuracy to be so prized? – begins to be answered in relation to this passage. The pun, particularly as a '*single word*', can have a special accuracy, by being uniquely faithful to the reality that is '*double, treble*'. It is interesting that the wording of Hill's question presupposes that the double or treble reality – which might mean the coexistence, the harmony or disharmony, the overlap, of thoughts and things – precedes the pun. It suggests that the pun is capable of accurate representation; that it is not wholly a result 'of being at the mercy of accidents, the prey of one's own presumptuous energy'; that it is arbitrary, but in the full, self-contradictory double sense of that word.[27] For Hill, then, the pun is not simply evidence of but an eloquent answer to the doubling, the coupling, the blurring of reality: 'Beauty stemming from the aboriginal fault' (*TT* 32, p. 901).

The passage from Weil alluded to in the seventeenth ode of *Pindarics* is cited by Hill on numerous occasions (and with special approval):

> Simultaneous composition on several planes at once is the law of artistic creation, and wherein, in fact, lies its difficulty.
>
> A poet, in the arrangement of words and the choice of each word, must simultaneously bear in mind matters on at least five or six different planes of composition.[28]

L'enracinement is the book from which this quotation comes. In a previous chapter, Weil claims that it is urgent to consider a 'plan for re-establishing the working-class by the roots', in which society's 'goal would be, not, according to the expression now inclined to become popular, the interest of the consumer – such an interest can only be a grossly material one – but Man's dignity in his work, which is a value of a spiritual order'.[29] Hill is convinced of the spiritual value of work, which, he repeatedly emphasises, includes the 'composition' of poetry.[30] The 'working on multiple planes' to which he refers itself works on multiple planes: the pun is the word 'working'. If a pun or a poem is 'working' on multiple planes it is succeeding in various respects. At the same time it is, perhaps visibly, travailing to cohere, trying hard to achieve all that it intends.

The complexity is that, for Hill, to work with language is to work with a mysterious and even dangerous entity; and to explore this complexity is to answer more fully the question of why 'accurate' ambiguities are so prized by Hill. In an essay, Hill quotes from Hobbes's treatise on *Humane Nature*: 'there is scarce any word that is not made *equivocal* by divers contextures of speech'.[31] The Word that can become flesh can elsewhere become a blasphemy. As words are made up 'of both acoustic images and concepts', as they turn 'a side to things and a side to the speaker', so they do 'not only have dual meanings; they are dual in their very essence'.[32] By these accounts, words, with their unsystematic assortments of association and connotation, have something like split personalities. The pun, being a word, is also essentially 'dual'; but it can make its duality coherent and meaningful. In this sense it is language's own divinely inspired *felix culpa*, which, to reappropriate Ernest B. Gilman's words, 'is partially able to repair the split suffered in the Fall – to approximate the unity of the divine mind'.[33]

Hill takes the ethics of aesthetics very seriously, and the pun is at the heart of his enquiry into that complicated matter. Since, according to St Paul, one must 'worke out' one's own salvation in fear and trembling (Philippians 2.12), it is no wonder that one's language, and in particular the pun, can be a matter of eternal life or death, as Hill detects in his reading of *The Pilgrim's Progress*:

> Bunyan's ability is to make a passage of emblematic discourse suddenly become the mind's activity: 'but that Lock went *damnable* hard'. The word is caught at the precise moment of translation from imprecation to recognition.
>
> It so happens that this particular, and in context exemplary, instance of recognition takes the form of a pun; and it is a fact that, as numerous commentators have noted, 'many meanings can have *one word*' and that 'Donne is really the kind of being to whom the word *done* can be applied'. But that which unites the pun with other types of semantic recognition is the common factor of attention (which, in its time, has been the 'diligence' which the first Lutheran and Calvinist translators of the Bible attributed— rightfully for the most part—to themselves and, in its time, has been the phrase *sedem animae in extremis digitis haberit* which commended itself to Robert Burton, 'their Soule, or *intellectus agens*, was placed in their fingers ends'). (*CCW*, p. 387)

Few people would connect puns with a notion of sixteenth-century Protestant diligence. But this is Hill's way of attempting to raise the pun from its reputation, its association with glib jokes and low-wattage advertising. Hill observes that Bunyan's pun signifies the 'precise moment' in which Christian's exacting labour is rewarded. It is a transfiguring of earthly work into divine play.

Hill has spoken about inspiration with similar emphasis on toil recompensed: 'you struggle for hours, days, even weeks, in agony of mind trying a hundred variants, and suddenly the word or phrase is there with that marvellous click like a closing box that Yeats talks about'.[34] The poet works for that grace – a gift in different senses theological and prosodic – so that it might work for the poet.

> The labours of the months are now memory,
> indigent wordplay, stubborn, isolate
> language of inner exile.
>
> (*OS* VIII, p. 358)

Puns   31

Again, here, 'labours' have become 'wordplay'. 'The labours of the months' is a pun on a medieval decorative subject: Hill is likening his own labours to the agricultural activities proper to each month of the year.[35] The 'inner exile' is, in part, language's fallen state, frequently exiled from history in its use, and from reality by euphemism or misuse; and the pun itself is a word of inner exile, where significations can be far from their natural homes.[36] Seeming to run counter to this, there may also be a sense (the syntax in this passage allowing for various distinct readings) in which Hill is commenting, harshly but not dismissively, on the 'labours' of his early work, which 'are now memory'. This poem, from *The Orchards of Syon* (2002), instantiates the notion that, at least linguistically, Hill has been finally, demonstrably loosed from a former 'inner exile'; the puns exemplify such loosening. By this logic, it is the earlier puns (among other linguistic figures) that are 'indigent', 'stubborn, isolate', in Hill's judgement.

A pun may be 'indigent' in many ways; one way, which Hill has from the first taken great pains to avoid, is when it lacks a necessary precision, when it is only loosely or accidentally (to return to Hobbes's word) *'equivocal'*. By being able to elide contradictory meanings of words, a pun can allow the writer room for what Hill calls an 'illicit persuasiveness' (*CCW*, p. 111). But, when used with accuracy, it is also capable of reconciling lost meanings and connotations, capable of eliciting the 'attention' (Hill's word on Bunyan) of both writer and reader.

In Hill's comments on Bunyan above, he defines the pun in passing as a type of 'semantic recognition'. But Hill's puns themselves have to work to attain the recognition he has in mind; and, in these puns' pursuit of accuracy, the attainment of this recognition is crucial. Two meanings sometimes seem not to belong in one word; the shock of that recognition produces an enlivened conversation between the senses of a word, a rethinking of meaning. The word 'recognition' has triggered its own polysemic recognitions in Hill's writing.[37] Sperling, discussing Coleridge and Hill in *Visionary Philology*, points to an index card in Hill's archives that explores some of the word's associations:

> Re-cognition
> + know the place for the first time (metaphor, statement, redemption)
>   THE CRUX IS RE-COGNITION
>   to recognise & be recognised.
>   (etym. of the word)[38]

The presence of 'Little Gidding' here ('+ know the place for the first time') is notable. In the second part of that poem, there is a chance meeting of the speaker and 'one walking, loitering and hurried', in whose

32   *Geoffrey Hill and the ends of poetry*

eyes the speaker discerns a 'familiar compound ghost | Both intimate and unidentifiable'.[39] (With the help of Eliot's drafts, there has been a recognition in this ghost of the 'brown baked features' of Dante's loved and damned mentor, Brunetto Latini, whom, in a scene of startling pathos, the Pilgrim meets in the seventh circle of hell.[40]) The unfathomable process and potency of language, operating at a level beyond the very speaker, reveals itself:

> the words sufficed
> To compel the recognition they preceded.
> And so, compliant to the common wind,
> Too strange to each other for misunderstanding,
> In concord at this intersection time
> Of meeting nowhere, no before and after,
> We trod the pavement in a dead patrol.[41]

The thinking-again of recognition produces a strange concord. As with the metaphor, the pun's 'intersection' of things in a single word or phrase can seem to work best when these things are disparate, when their meanings are obviously distinct, '[t]oo strange to each other for misunderstanding'. Magnetically, this strangeness attracts – and attracts 'attention'.

This recognition, this strange meeting, requires an acknowledgement on the poet's part of similarity and of difference, of what can be easily reconciled and what cannot:

> though the grading and measuring of words presupposes the ability to recognise ambiguities, there are some ambiguities so deeply impacted with habit, custom, procedure, that the 'recognition' is in effect the acknowledgement of irreducible bafflement. Dryden and Pound are alike in their feeling for a language that is as expressive of the labour and bafflement as it is of the perfected judgement. (*CCW*, p. 228)

The particular ambiguity of the pun can be, for Hill, a linguistic admission of the 'irreducible bafflement' that results from linguistic labour and from working with the deeply rooted ambiguities of the wordly, the worldly, and the otherworldly. It is in a spirit of shared recognition and friendship with Dryden and Pound, as well as Wordsworth, whose 'blind understanding' is, according to Hill, 'both bafflement and groping intuition', that Hill declares, in a 2008 lecture on Milton, 'I think I have always felt myself to be a kind of blind-mouthed, blind-understanding poet'.[42]

Hill's 'recognition', in the passage on Bunyan, also at least bears a family resemblance to Aristotle's *anagnorisis*, the moment of tragic discovery examined in the *Poetics*.[43] The recognition Hill sees in Bunyan's pun – 'but that Lock went *damnable* hard' – is a discovery of a tragic possibility (the

Puns   33

potential imminence of damnation), though not in fact a tragic discovery (because it is not the actual imminence of damnation; the gate, after all, opens). Kathy Eden, in her book *Poetic and Legal Fiction in the Aristotelian Tradition*, notes the strong similarities between Aristotle's types of *anagnorisis*, listed in order of artistic merit, and his assessment and ranking of legal proofs in the *Rhetoric*.[44] To 'dramatize the change' from ignorance to knowledge, the tragic playwright 'relies on the very same instruments of proof available to the forensic orator'.[45] What Hill spots in Bunyan is such a dramatisation of change. Hill's 'attention' to the text's language proves the text's attention to language. In Bunyan too, the pun of recognition is a type of proof, an ostensibly superstitious type of proof, that words are never mere words; that their collisions might reveal unexpectedly the realities sustaining them; that one works '*damnable*' hard because one is damnable. This word, to some degree truly by accident, does 'change': it begins as a curse and becomes, is italicised into, a kind of blessed realisation. '[O]ur language', Hill has written, 'is a blessing and a curse; but in the right hands it can mediate within itself, thereby transforming blessing into curse, curse into blessing'.[46]

Hill's puns are evidence of both curses and blessings. ('The word for *bless*, in some tongues, is the same as the word for *curse*.'[47]) But before they can mediate within themselves and transform, they have to come together. This, as I have suggested, and as Hill believes, is an ethically risky meeting. The final question I pose at the beginning of this section is whether Hill's puns reach their intended ends of 'accurate' ambiguity. His most remarked-upon poem, 'September Song', provides an illuminating perspective.

'September Song' is addressed to a Jewish child deported to a concentration camp in 1942. This is Hill's only poem to include subtitled dates: 'born 19.6.32—deported 24.9.42' (*KL*, p. 44). An entry in one of the notebooks for *King Log* demonstrates that it is written for a young girl named Edita Pollaková.[48] She was born and deported (to Terezín) on the dates in Hill's subtitle; and she was killed at Auschwitz.[49] The odd meeting of congruence and incongruence that a pun represents is, in keeping with other puns in *King Log*, a source of pain in 'September Song'. There is an added pain in the subtle sense that, by dint of their association with comedy, the puns may trivialise the matter of the poem. Hill, born the day before the child to whom the poem is addressed, makes an implicit connection with her and is simultaneously repulsed by his own presumption to present it. The poem is a lament that jars with itself by questioning its own capacity to offer such lament.[50] Yet it perseveres, doing so in the face of Adorno's famous eschatological dictum for poetry.[51] It does so, too, against Arnold, who claims that there are human situations 'in which the suffering finds no vent in action', from which 'no poetical enjoyment can be derived'; 'the

34 Geoffrey Hill and the ends of poetry

representation of them in poetry', Arnold writes, 'is painful'.[52] 'September Song' acknowledges the pain, and the ethical peril, of that representation. Part of its triumph is in the admission of its failure.

> Undesirable you may have been, untouchable
> you were not. Not forgotten
> or passed over at the proper time.
>
> As estimated, you died. Things marched,
> sufficient, to that end.
> Just so much Zyklon and leather, patented
> terror, so many routine cries.
>
> (I have made
> an elegy for myself it
> is true)
>
> September fattens on vines. Roses
> flake from the wall. The smoke
> of harmless fires drifts to my eyes.
>
> This is plenty. This is more than enough.
>
> (*KL*, p. 44)

This is, appropriately, far from the most musical of Hill's poems. Its power resides instead in its puns, beginning with the first word: 'Undesirable'. It is an uncomfortable word, especially as apparently legitimised by the first line's 'may'. (The line, therefore, can be read as both *maybe you were deemed undesirable* and *maybe you were undesirable*.) This word, the plural of which is the usual translation of *Untermenschen*, borrows from the terminology of the Third Reich. The pun that ends the first line, 'untouchable', extends this association. By virtue of her innocence, the child ought to have been untouchable, that is, not seized for deportation. Yet she was seized, and proved to be touchable: a real person, not an abstraction; and not too undesirable to be abducted (see *OED*, 'untouchable, *adj*.', senses 1a and 3).

The abundance of negations here follows the first two lines of the poem: the bookending *un-* words in the first line and the repetition '[...] not. Not [...]' in the second. The latter is stopped from being a double negative only by the full stop: 'you were not. Not forgotten'. The difference between remembering and forgetting can be subtle; it may even hang on a voice's inflection. By her captors, the child was not forgotten 'or passed over at the proper time'. The Lord passed over and did not put to death the children of Israel in Egypt (Exodus 12); but this child's fate is not to be passed over (either by her captors or by the poem).

Puns 35

In the second stanza, the punning language begins to insinuate the efficiency, and officiousness, of the Nazis' system of killing. 'As estimated' derives ambiguity from its missing pronoun: who has done the estimating? On one hand, the estimation is an educated guess from Hill's, and our, side of history; one might expect such a child to have died. On the other hand, the estimation is that of an imagined Nazi administrator, a sinister calculation. Puns and their shadows run through the rest of the stanza: the echo of the guards' boots in 'Things marched', their image returning in 'leather, patented'; the conflated senses of purpose and death in 'that end'; and then the word 'routine', attributed to the victims' cries instead of the procedure by which the cries were induced. The qualifiers 'just so much' and 'so many' have the same double-sided perspective: they denote either superabundance or precise sufficiency ('sufficient'), depending on who is saying them.

In particular, 'patented' sounds like a needless pun. Is a pun on patent leather appropriate to a poem about a young victim of genocide? It may be that this is part of the point: the child's victimhood is needless; the poem's inadequate tribute is needless; Hill is laying bare the blunt instruments of his own language. In this case, to write puns after Auschwitz is barbaric. But is it barbaric to point out, using only one word, that it is barbaric to patent, or license, 'terror'; and to patent a poison gas, 'Zyklon', to which Hill's careful adjective also refers? The third, parenthetical stanza follows, breaking off for good the first seven lines' meditation, almost as an apology for them (if not explicitly for their puns). Its line breaks fall unexpectedly, unsure of themselves, seeking to avoid the appearance of pride by shaping the assertion 'it is true' into 'it | is true'.[53]

The idea of superabundance is transposed to the present in the fourth and fifth stanzas, which have moved on from the direct relation of the child's fate and into the speaker's time and place. 'September fattens on vines': the language (personifying the month), and the earth itself, suddenly seem repellently indulgent. It is as though the earth is living on death. The images of roses that 'flake from the wall' and 'smoke' are also abhorrent reminders, aftershocks. And yet there is the quiet implication of peace in these stanzas: these are, after all, roses falling; the fires are 'harmless'; and grapes are fattening, late in the season.[54] The final stanza offers both renunciation and hope: 'This is plenty. This is more than enough.' In Hill's present September, the earth's fullness is an unfair, unwanted gift; moreover, his own words have tried to do too much, tried to offer more than they can, and so must be withdrawn here. But what appears to be the present may also be a foresight of the child's fate beyond death, a vision of transcendence; this may be a heavenly harvest. The intensification of 'plenty' to 'more than enough' works in several ways: the earth is found to be abundant, and then

36   *Geoffrey Hill and the ends of poetry*

distastefully so; the poem is found to have come to an end, and then to have gone too far; yet, in another sense, the peaceful scene is found to represent true 'plenty', and then even 'more than' this. It is found to be a spiritual vision, grander than a barbaric and narrow understanding of satisfactoriness, more than 'sufficient' (cf. John 10.10: 'I am come that they might haue life, and that they might haue it more abundantly').[55]

'September Song' is a clear illustration, and even a justification, of the 'accurate' ambiguities of Hill's puns. The vision of 'plenty' at its end requires a fundamental 're-cognition': a capacity to see good, and to see the possibility of a different end, amid needless evil and suffering.[56] The poem admits that its ideas, which in its puns become coupled 'realities', sit uncomfortably together; but the success of its effort is in acknowledging such uneasy elisions.

A final word, in Hill's final collection: 'Our words drive us into dishonesty by their own recalcitrance. That is but a split root of the matter; and in such a strait as this few care whether we are or are not practitioners of deceit' (*BBGJ* 231, p. 124). What Sidney approaches in calling poetry a 'counterfetting', Empson full-throatedly declares in calling ambiguity 'as a rule witty and deceitful'.[57] Hill, in his poetry, and particularly in his puns, objects to both of these poet-critics by striving against the tendency of words towards 'dishonesty'. His puns' 'vocation' (*CCW*, p. 19) is to engage in semantic transfiguration, neither to deceive nor for a 'play of wit' (*CCW*, p. 152), but as a self-conscious effort towards words' redemption.

Alchemic-carnal marriages

The last collection of poems in Hill's *Broken Hierarchies*, titled *Al Tempo de' Tremuoti*, or *At the Time of Earthquakes*, has a word running through it like a fault. ('Geophysicists ‖ make much of *fault*' (*SC* 3. 18, p. 479).) It is an overused, even degraded and debauched, word. 'No matter', Hill tells the insufficiently shod Tony Blair reading the first epistle to the Corinthians at the funeral of Diana, Princess of Wales, 'You ‖ shall not degrade or debauch the word LOVE ‖ beyond redemption' (*SS* 114, p. 345).[58]

The difficulty of puns is not only the difficulty of ethics: it is also the difficulty of love. What can be reconciled everywhere coexists with what cannot be reconciled; purity everywhere coexists with impurity; desire for the Creator everywhere coexists with desire for the creature. Human love, in particular sexual love, is a persistent theme of Hill's poetry. The seventh and eighth poems in Hill's first collection ('The Turtle Dove' and 'The Troublesome Reign', *U*, pp. 10–11) are fable-like, yet terribly realistic, accounts of the breaking of an intimate relationship. Throughout the poetry, the notion of one person abiding in another, derived from Jesus's words in John 15.4–10 and 17.21–23, is found complicated in both human and human–divine relationships.[59] In the first 'Lachrimae' sonnet, the speaker addresses Jesus directly: 'You do not dwell in me nor I in you' (*T*, p. 121). The later work seems to view the same idea with different eyes. In *Speech! Speech!* there is a consistent thread of optimism about human love: 'Responsible | or not, I will hold you as if once | I would be held ín you' (*SS* 108, p. 342). In convoluted syntax, among the last poems in *Broken Hierarchies*, there is a similar possibility of successful reconciliation: 'Of density of being; of otherness; | That Eros alone, and rightly understood, | As some so marvellously have, his blood | Realigns with ours' (*TT* 87: *on the Marriage of a Virgin*, p. 930).

In a late essay, Hill sheds light on the connection between erotic and verbal consummations: 'The arbitrariness of the sexual signalling of compatibility, the arbitrariness of choosing the right word out of a thousand possibilities, constitute the heart of the erotic commonplace. What Charles Williams depicts, in his vision of eros, is that "profound contrariety" which is as much a part of love's truth as are adamic nuptials' (*CCW*, p. 572). In *Speech! Speech!*, this abstraction becomes personal in a touching celebration of married love: 'Togetherness after sixteen years? You're on. | There ís a final tableau of discovery | and rehabilitation' (*SS* 63, p. 320). The most chance meetings can be, despite the odds, abiding. '"It is chance if it includes life", said puckish Allison' (*BBGJ* 131, p. 70).

The paradox, struck repeatedly in Hill's late poetry (sometimes punningly), is between the arbitrariness of the meeting and at the same time its evident predestination: 'Unsurely | words appear to meet me on what I mean; || fumble eternity' (*HOLC* 13, p. 163); 'a kind | of sublime compromise with accident' ('On Reading *Blake: Prophet Against Empire*', §II, *TCP*, p. 569); 'The hapless connotations that denote | Elisions of choice and inadvertence' (*EV* 10, p. 638); 'Do I rhyme *friends: fiends* | Anywhere in my posthumous *oeuvre*? | Such accidents are like getting the bends | From reckless ascent' (*EV* 31, p. 659); 'I am, as ever, free to make captive | The genius of language' (*EV* 52, p. 680); 'With her unrivalled language at command, | Freed from subservience yet freely bound' (*O* 137: *Welsh apotheosis* (ii), p. 786); 'Must I conjure augur to rest with anger? [...] Word tag world' (*OB* XIX, p. 853); 'Surely much moved even by chance conjunction' (*OB* XX, p. 854); 'Into scrap language unpredicted landscape' (*OB* XXXV, p. 869); 'Let the inconsistencies pull together, | Breakup being nerve of induction' (*OB* XXXVII, p. 871); 'Hazardings unscathed by the harsh alignments | Made for survival' (*OB* XL, p. 874); 'Necessity by miracle made choice' (*TT* 23, p. 897); '*Uncanny gifts at once so free, so fated*' (*TT* 26, p. 898); '*The lots we drew | Teach us our inexorable freedom*' (*TT* 29, p. 899); 'Blessed apotheosis of mishap, | Less empathy than grace' (*TT* 74, p. 924); 'Its paradox, determinate free will, | cracked' (*TT* 77, p. 925); 'The serendipitous many times deceives with its priorities' (*BBGJ* 40, p. 19); 'Predestination and luck co-exist in hard-to-ride tandem; and the divinely choreographed many times performs as if it were random or stuck' (*BBGJ* 96, p. 45). Charles Tomlinson provides (some decades earlier) a simpler agreement with the above mass of quotations: 'The chances of rhyme are like the chances of meeting— | In the finding fortuitous, but once found, binding'.[60] If it is true of rhyme, it is (perhaps even more) true of puns.

In Hill, language is a thing of love: corrupted yet intrinsically valuable and capable of transcendence. Human love, and the love poem, are subject to what Hill, following Newman, calls the 'terrible aboriginal calamity' of fallen nature, but through their incomplete and imperfect reconciliations, a deeper and encompassing consummation can be glimpsed.[61]

> Sexual love—instinctively alchemical:
> early sexual love. Or is the dying
> recreation of it the real mystery?
>
> I say that each is true: words troth-plight
> to both of us, equal with her, truer
> now, than I was or ever could be,
>
> but knowing myself in her. I said
> *ask me to explain*—they won't remember,
> forty-six lines back and already buried
>
> with the short day.
>
> (*SC* 1. 11, p. 426)

Until *The Book of Baruch*, Hill's image of himself as a 'blind-mouthed, blind-understanding poet' is nowhere more evident than in *Scenes from Comus*. Poems such as this feel improvisatory, which, given the allusion to Milton's masque in the title and the dedication to the composer Hugh Wood, is fitting. The third sentence's peculiar syntax with its succession of commas (in lines four to seven) disturbs the reader's comprehension and sounds extemporised. But the doubling puns in 'dying | recreation' – sex as sport, itself a recreation of one of the most familiar puns in the language; and as an attempt to remake 'early' love in late life – are not the chance discoveries of improvisation. Nor are the sexual connotations of 'knowing myself in her' accidental. In Hill's awkward, 'blind-understanding' way, these puns bring together the bodies of lovers in their semantic meetings.[62] They indicate Hill's continuing faith in words, despite their corruption.[63] Words 'troth-plight | to both of us', Hill writes; and he accepts their promise

Puns 39

of marriage. (Hill also writes of Spenser's double-use of 'deare' in *Amoretti* LXVIII (*CCW*, p. 152): 'What happens here is more solemn than a play of wit; it is a form of troth-plight between denotation and connotation.') For two people to marry, and be spiritually and bodily joined, words of 'troth-plight' are required; the words approach corporeality because, like the bodies themselves, they enact the pledge.[64]

The first poem of *Scenes from Comus*, with its fragmentary, noun-heavy announcements of the work's subject, similarly sets love's and language's bonds side by side:

> Of *bare preservation,*
> of *obligation to mutual love;*
> and of our covenants with language
>
> contra tyrannos.
>
> (*SC* 1. 1, p. 421)

The italicised phrases are quotations from the second of Locke's *Two Treatises of Government*.[65] Uses of language, for Hill, are entrances into quasi-bodily 'covenants', which, immediately following the phrase '*obligation to mutual love*', implies the marital contract. The covenant of marriage, with its attendant restrictions (as 'contract' insinuates), is seen in Hill's poetry as a near-miraculous restitution of order: social and sexual.

The twenty-fourth poem of the second section of *Scenes from Comus* makes this 'vision' of marriage clear:

> Alongside these travesties stands my own
> vision of right order. Some forms, orders,
> travesty themselves. That is today's
> communiqué. Tomorrow's order book
> will read the same.
> World-webbed collusions, clouded diplomacies,
> are lightning when they strike and strike us down.
> Of marriages I speak, as of right order
> among the travesties.
>
> (*SC* 2. 24, p. 442)

The puns in this poem may appear haphazard: 'world-webbed' makes an indirect link between widespread conspiracy and the internet; 'lightning' emerges from 'clouded' with only a superficial impact. One may even call these 'travesties' of puns.[66] But another pun here is more telling. An 'order book', in the first sense, is a list of customers' orders kept by a company (see *OED*, sense 1); in the context, then, of a discussion of linguistic dodgy dealing, 'order book' suggests a book of words designed to combat such verbal 'collusions', to reinstate 'right order | among the travesties' (this phrase

40 *Geoffrey Hill and the ends of poetry*

itself a reinstatement of the poem's first sentence). 'Alongside these travesties stands my own | vision of right order': the line break, with a comic touch, threatens to spoil the vision before it has been relayed. Yet Hill contends that his stated vision 'stands', and that it is marital: 'Of marriages I speak'. Hill's words wish to invoke, and reproduce, the 'order' he sees in marriage; and words' own semantic marriages, in puns, are essential to the task. There is certainly something predestined about this order for Hill, something intractably contingent. Within parentheses, at the end of a later poem, which begins 'It is not long, not long to eternity', Hill writes: 'Good marriages are made by guardian | Spirits, whatever loves ourselves ordain' (*O* 134, p. 785).

In the second stanza of *Scenes from Comus* 1. 11, quoted earlier, Hill reaches the conclusion that both 'early sexual love' and its 'dying | recreation' are 'alchemical', but 'real', mysteries. This is the first time Hill professes a relation between alchemy and sexual love (which I, following Hill's practice, loosely align with marriage). The doubled adjective 'alchemic-carnal', which Hill uses twice, reinforces the mysterious bond.[67] Alchemy, for Hill, is an essential metaphor for the irreducibly mysterious symbioses of language and human experience, of which the pun, as an acknowledgement of strange semantic alignments in words, is both example and microcosm.[68] If, for example, the unremembering reader takes Hill's hint and goes back forty-six lines, three references to alchemy are discovered, one each in 1. 8, 1. 9, and 1. 10: 'The man who said this died of alchemy'; 'another remnant of alchemical twaddle'; 'the alchemy the primal infiltration' (pp. 424–25).[69] Alchemy is primal, in the same way that 'sexual love' comes 'instinctively'. The frequent references to alchemy in Hill's later work are continually related to the body and to sexual union. They are also evidence of Hill's prolonged and productive fascination with the literature of the Renaissance, in which alchemy is a distinct, diverting, and sometimes dangerous presence, at the edges of cultural and religious orthopraxy.[70]

Alchemical words of the Renaissance, such as *conjunction*, themselves often resound with sexual overtones. The religious alchemist Gerhard Dorn's *coniunctio*, the process by which the alchemist forms himself and unites his soul with the divine, is in the literal sense a bringing together under one yoke; *conjunction* is also, according to the *OED*: 'Union in marriage'; 'Sexual union, copulation'; 'Mixture or union of "elements" or substances; one of the processes in alchemy' (senses 2a, 2b, 2d).[71] Hill's pun is this kind of productive conjunction, bypassing the need for grammatical conjunction – the need for an *and* – by bringing about a direct mixture or union of words' various elements.[72]

The eightieth poem of *Al Tempo de' Tremuoti* reveals the intermingling of such thoughts, the conjunction of the diverse meanings of *conjunction*:

Black puddle crudely flares its mutant eye.
The word is generation, *Anima*
Mundi itself being the dynamo.
The toad unreels her fabulous progeny.

Earth, best-rhymed original alchemist,
Proclaims *the very natural true sperm*
Of the great world. Charged thus to procreant Adam
My fecund winter glitters its verbed crest.

(*TT* 80, p. 926)

The quotation between the sixth and seventh lines is from Thomas Vaughan's *Lumen de lumine* (1651).[73] Vaughan attaches the idea of sexual union to the creation of the world itself; Hill perceives this idea, as well as alluding to the alchemists' 'Black Sun', in the first line's black puddle with its 'mutant eye'.[74] The abundance of procreation here extends to the multiplying meanings of words. 'The word is generation': the word, the poem, are older words' and poems' offspring. In his life's 'winter', Hill finds himself still 'fecund', still capable of giving birth to words. 'Charged', in the penultimate line, is a lively pun. Firstly, the syntax renders the charging unclear: does it apply to the '*sperm*' or to the 'fecund winter'? If the former, the sperm is charged, or ascribed, to Adam, the 'original' man; the world's condition is his responsibility (*OED*, 'charge, *v.*', sense 16b). If the latter, Hill's late productivity is charged, as though with alchemical electricity, to the fullness of Adam's virility, even to the point that it 'glitters'. While 'glitters' and 'crest' both unpleasantly recall the great world's '*sperm*', and the toad's unreeling 'progeny', they also pun on Hill's newly charged up sense of self. By glittering, he makes 'a brilliant appearance or display', is 'showy' (*OED*, 'glitter, *v.*', sense 2); and his crest is his 'plume', his 'symbol of pride, self-confidence, or high spirits' (*OED*, 'crest, *n.1*', senses 2, 1b). Equally, 'glitters', with 'winter', conjures an image of fallen snow (to which Vaughan compares the strange substance he encounters).[75] It is also a 'verbed' crest: earth overlaid with words; and at the same time a poetic summit (*OED*, 'crest, *n.1*', sense 5). Hill's puns, his words of 'generation', alchemically mixing and transfiguring the senses of words, are his crest: his distinguishing badge; and representations of a peak of artistic ambition.

In *Odi Barbare*, Hill again sees the punning variety within words and is reminded of alchemy:

Words of three, four, characters, five if reckless,
Serve to keep this stirring alchemic portent.
Union played for in the limbeck's furor,
    Spiritus mundi.

(*OB* L, p. 884)

42 *Geoffrey Hill and the ends of poetry*

Hill does not write 'alembic'; he uses the alternative 'limbeck', described by the *OED* as archaic even in 1903, because that is Donne's word (as well as Spenser's, Shakespeare's, Milton's, Dryden's, Pope's). The word itself must, for Hill, be a distillation of its history. Like lovers, words of numerous unified senses, or 'characters', strive for '[u]nion' also with each other in the divinely inspired 'furor' of the poet–alchemist (*OED*, 'furor', sense 2). The word 'characters', here, is a pun. As well as meaning, here, a word's significations (and its traits, and even its reputations), it amalgamates the Christian, particularly Augustinian, definition of 'character' as the 'indelible quality which baptism, confirmation, and holy orders imprint on the soul' with the sense used by Milton in *Paradise Regained*: 'by what the Starrs | Voluminous, or single characters, | In thir conjunction met, give me to spell'.[76] This kind of 'character', according to the *OED*, is a 'cabbalistic or magical sign or emblem; the astrological symbol of a planet, etc.' (*n.*, sense 2a). Milton, too, is punning on 'conjunction'.

In another intersection of Hill's poetry with that of the seventeenth century, the nine-line stanza form of Donne's 'A nocturnall upon S. Lucies day' is revived in Hill's *Oraclau | Oracles*.[77] Donne's poem, also replete with alchemical imagery, sees its speaker purified out of earthly existence: 'I, by loves limbecke, am the grave'.[78] The parenthesis in Donne's sentence is itself a limbeck, a distilling apparatus, that connects the isolated 'I' with 'the grave' at the end of the line. The deathly connotations of Donne's limbeck transfer powerfully to Hill's poetic discussions of alchemy, particularly in *Oraclau | Oracles*.[79]

The nocturnal's 'dead thing' that is Donne is also resurrected in one of *Oraclau*'s poems: 'Whose is the spirit moving that dead thing?' (O 72: *Afal du Brogŵyr* (I), p. 764).[80] The line occurs in the very middle of the collection, amid a group of four poems with 'Afal du Brogŵyr' in their titles. The phrase is borrowed from the title of a series of paintings by the Welsh artist Ceri Richards, which Richards translated as 'Black Apple of Gower'. The *Afal du Brogŵyr* paintings, Richards wrote, were intended to capture 'the great richness, the fruitfulness and the great cyclic movement and rhythms of the poems of Dylan Thomas. The circular image [...] is the metaphor expressing the sombre germinating force of nature'.[81] One such cycle, or circle, which travels over to Hill's 'Afal' poems, is the mandala (Sanskrit for *disc*), a geometric figure representing the universe, which tends to consist of a circle surrounded by a square with four T-shaped gates. 'The final mysteries at length retired | Into themselves, and the First Circle squared' (O 56: *Marwnad Saunders Lewis* (III), p. 759). Squaring with that, there are four 'Afal' poems; the alchemists, too, wrote of the four elements, sustained invisibly by a fifth, which William Bloomfield called the 'privy quintessence'.[82]

Hill's 'Afal' poems are built from readings (Jung's and his own) of Renaissance alchemical texts, from 'the ruin of well-fathomed dreams' (*O* 71: *Bollingen, May 1958 (Afal du Brogŵyr)*, p. 764). Puns, in these poems, are thematically appropriate: they are the semantic meldings of words, '[p]atent as compost' (*O* 73: *Afal du Brogŵyr* (ɪɪ), p. 765). Hill's poetry has to root around for its punning experiments: it is '[p]oetry of such corruption and fire | Baking the lily in its dung' (*O* 73: *Afal du Brogŵyr* (ɪɪ), p. 765). Images of compacted black matter, of various kinds, recur in the 'Afal' poems. 'Alchemy itself', Hill writes in the last of these poems, 'is the Black Sun, | Absorption of convulsion, the *nigredo*, | The pitchblende of immortal sign' (*O* 74: *Afal du Brogŵyr* (ɪɪɪ), p. 765). The pun, like a symbol 'capable of many interpretations', emerges from this mixed soil, the *nigredo* of debased language.[83] It emerges lightly, playfully, from that worked dirt. 'Not everything', Hill punningly concludes, 'is rotten in Carl Jung' (*O* 73, p. 765).

The first of the 'Afal' poems, 'Bollingen, May 1958 (Afal du Brogŵyr)', mentions a 'black mandala', and the following three poems consider this image variously. Hill's '[i]ntrofusion of vision' (*O* 73, p. 765) in these poems, among others, is complex and condensed, so that it is not easy to distinguish a metaphor of alchemy from an alchemy of metaphor, an apple from a mandala from a sun. Puns abound as the symbols of Christianity, alchemy, and Eastern mysticism coincide. This is the second of the quartet, '*Afal du Brogŵyr* (ɪ)':

> That mandala, stone-black apple
> Made so by the charring of permafrost
>   Or the sun's giving up the ghost
> Of its corona: so some people
>   Dismayed. Nonetheless who shall say
>   Which of us claims the wrong
> Side of the myth in this catastrophe;
> Who to their own imperviousness belong;
> Whose is the spirit moving that dead thing?

The 'stone-black apple', found on the Gower Peninsula, in Richards's painting, and in Hill's poem above, is at once the *afal gauaf*, the winter-apple frostbitten by the ground's icy subsurface, and the Black Sun: it is life in a cloak of death, or death with latent life buried in it, a 'central seed'.[84] Hill considers two explanations for the apple's blackness: 'the charring of permafrost | Or the sun's giving up the ghost | Of its corona'. Even for Hill, 'the sun's giving up the ghost' is an extraordinary punning cliché. In the literal sense, the weather has turned sour; the sun is dying away. In an alchemical sense, the Black Sun, in which all life is consumed and reflected, is a limbeck, distilling it to pure spirit, giving up its ghost. And, in a theological sense, with 'darkness over the whole land' (Mark 15.33), this sun is the Son who 'gave up the ghost' in a death of latent eternal life (Matthew 27.50; Mark 15.37; Luke 23.46; John 19.30). From this last perspective, the apple might come to symbolise the Edenic fruit of the *felix culpa*, rotten but recoverable, a seed for atonement. The 'ghost' of Christ hovers over Hill's final question: 'Whose is the spirit moving that dead thing?' In terms of language, the pun is such a spirit. With the pun's help, Hill finds language redeemable. The phrase 'giving up the ghost', then, is a fitting description of overused language itself, emptied of meaning before being punningly regenerated, suddenly made fertile again, its dead matter distilled and replaced with new semantic life.

The language of alchemy – its ethereal, religious vocabulary, the ritualistic processes and unexpected relationships it describes – provided a new and exciting nexus of understanding for writers and thinkers of the Renaissance; crucially, it provided a lively metaphor for language itself, one that Hill's punning language is keen to reanimate. The 'simple, sensuous, passionate' poet is a linguistic alchemist.[85] Sidney's remarks on the matter are distinctly redolent of Ficino: 'onely the Poet [...], lifted vp with the vigor of his owne inuention dooth growe, in effect, another nature, in making things either better then Nature bringeth forth, or quite a newe formes such as neuer were in Nature [...]. Her world is brasen, the Poets only deliuer a golden.'[86] Sidney's argument is also peculiarly continuous with R. P. Blackmur's single-sentence note entitled 'Art and Manufacture', loved and quoted by Hill: 'The art of poetry is amply distinguished from the manufacture of verse by the animating presence in the poetry of a fresh idiom: language so twisted and posed in a form that it not only expresses the matter in hand but adds to the stock of available reality.'[87] Language twisted and posed may not sound (or look) particularly elegant, but the precise awkwardness, and the 'accurate' ambiguity, of Hill's poetry lend the idea some credence. What Blackmur is not saying, as Hill has stressed, is that poems add to the stock of actuality, which they do, but that is nothing to brag about; any tired old poem can be 'new'. Reality is, in Blackmur's sense, not simply that which can be experienced but that which can be conceived. F. H. Bradley writes: 'Everything phenomenal is somehow real.'[88] To add to the stock of available reality is alchemical, and it is also sexually generative: the invention of the poem brings new conceptions out of existing materials. It does not create *ex nihilo*; it procreates. Sidney's comparison of nature's brass world with the poets' golden one puts extraordinary faith in poets; for Hill, though, the poet cannot 'deliuer' the golden sun, the true heavenly elixir. The intended end of Hill's punning poetry is, instead, to deliver (give birth to, hand over, redeem) the Black Sun, the 'pitchblende' of dead language (O 74, p. 765), but with such powers of linguistic alchemy as to render 'available' a consummate production of light.

Comparing Donne's with Henry Wotton's use of alchemical tropes in the essay 'Caveats Enough in their Own Walks', Hill gives this purifying process a further Biblical turn: 'The "furnace" of alchemical "activity" which is also the "furnace of aduersitie" in Ecclesiasticus (chapter 2, verse 5) where "acceptable menne" show their worth like gold, will further purify qualities in Wotton [...] that, in turn, will prove the metal of those with whom he comes in contact' (CCW, p. 217). (As though by instinct when writing of alchemy, Hill cannot help but produce a homophonic pun in 'metal'.) The pun, like these furnaces – alchemical, spiritual, marital – is a testing ground whereby transfiguration is possible: from lead to gold; sinner to saint; lust to love; colloquially ambiguous to accurately ambiguous. Alchemy, as a persistent feature of Hill's late work, speaks to its increasing openness to the possibility of transfiguration: that of words, the mind, and reality itself. In this respect the later work's translation of the contingent into the motivated more heavily emphasises – and values for its own sake – the contingency. When Hill writes in *Al Tempo de' Tremuoti* of 'linguistic alchemy' as '[v]icarious redemption by the word' (*TT* 37, p. 904), one is tempted to wonder whether a shift of identity has subtly taken place over the course of Hill's poetic corpus. Redemption's vicar, here, is the 'word' – a word that is itself, being resolutely lower-case, on the verge between pun and no pun – and not the wordsmith taking it on himself to 'ravage and redeem the world' (*U*, p. 4). 'I still believe in words' (n. 63): Hill's early belief is lived out fully in his late loosening of alchemic-carnal puns.

2

Dead ends

Repeating figures

Are dead ends irreconcilable with the life of the word? If 'giving up the ghost' in *Oraclau | Oracles* is to be taken as a punning revitalisation of dead language, then the answer must be no. But there are linguistic dead ends that Hill approaches differently. The poverties and redundancies natural to language can result in repetitions of words and their roots. Dead ends in a broader sense are also the inevitable incompletenesses of expression – the failure of language to comprehend fully its referents – and the uses of language that, due to shortcomings of articulation belonging to either the language or its user, unwittingly deceive, mislead, confuse, or under-inform their audiences. (As I have suggested, wilful misuses of language are sometimes the subject but, I believe, never the substance of Hill's poems.) This chapter examines the repeating figures in Hill's poetry that both reflect these dead ends and seek to transcend them: this section looking at repeating figures generally; and the three shorter sections that follow all looking at tautologies in particular.

By the term 'repeating figures' I mean to include much that my *pun* leaves out, such as uses of a word more than once (with the same meaning (i.e., tautologies) and with different meanings); figures that combine words with their relatives, cognates, and so on; figures that combine words with like-sounding words (in a way that does not have an organisational function, as opposed to rhyme, which does); figures by which a word's letters are locally and noticeably recycled (such as anagram and palindrome); and also, by extension, figures by which the speaker makes a rhetorical return on himself (such as metanoia).

Although in this chapter I focus on later work, namely *The Triumph of Love* (1998); *The Orchards of Syon* (2002); *Scenes from Comus* (2005); *Pindarics* (2005–2012); *Liber Illustrium Virorum* (2007–2012); *Ludo* (2011); and *The Book of Baruch by the Gnostic Justin* (2019), collections in which such repeating figures are particularly obvious and telling, it may be said that Hill's attraction to these figures is present, though often less prominent, in his earliest poems. In an undated early poem one finds the Hopkinsian concatenations of 'grave-grove', '[l]ast-left-leaf', '[f]all wind, fall wing-will', and '[w]here wood meets Wold'.[1] More subtly, in the first of the 'Three Baroque Meditations' in *King Log* (1968), Hill writes of the demons: 'When I exorcized they shrivel and thrive' (p. 66). The genius of this figure, for which I know no name, is in its perfectly insidious affirmation of what is said: five-sixths of 'thrive' thrive, in exact order but voiced completely differently, even in the middle of 'shrivel'. A notebook for *Mercian Hymns* (1971) sees Hill trying out palindromes and near equivalents, written in majuscules as though to distinguish them from the ordinary work of drafting poems: 'MIRROR ADMIRER', 'TROPE REPORT', 'SEX AXES', 'I MA/RY TRAM-MART/YR AM I?', 'EMIT NO TROPE • REPORT ON TIME'.[2] Attention to repeating figures intensifies in the *'errata'* poems of *The Triumph of Love*: 'For wordly, read worldly; for in equity, inequity; I for religious read religiose; for distinction I detestation' (*TL* XL, p. 250).[3] From this point in Hill's corpus his repeating figures, like his puns, gain a newly free range of applicability. Their weight seems lifted, even when they are employed for serious matters: 'Semiotics I rule semiautomatics' (*SS* 19, p. 298). In less serious matters, Hill, probably unknowingly, masquerades as Jeremy Reed on Elvis: 'Short-changed and on short time let us I walk óh-so óh-so with all new gods. I Showmen kill shaman [...]. I had a line all I set to go; a lien now. Even the shadow- I death cues further shadows' ('Improvisations for Jimi Hendrix', §3, *WT*, p. 503).[4] Throughout the late work, including *The Book of Baruch*, repeating figures continue to abound, with a wide span of dynamics from 'near subliminal' (*BBGJ* 197, p. 109) to 'ff' (*BBGJ* 103, p. 49). Are these successful revivifications, or merely successful evasions, of the dead places of language to which Hill regrets seeing so many of its users resort?

An answer must be prefaced by attempting to find out the starting points of such linguistic dead ends. 'Syntax I is a dead language' according to *Speech! Speech!* (99, p. 338); *The Triumph of Love* speaks of 'the dead language of Canaan' (LXXXIX, p. 265).[5] Both of the poems quoted evoke the classroom, with Hill in the role of exasperated teacher; the suggested irony is that Hill's language – imbued with its own history and theology – is dead to its society. The audience's ears are deader than Hill's deaf ear; and Hill bemoans this fact with varying rhetorical success in his later work.

For Hill, as Murphy and Sperling have separately demonstrated, the fallen nature of language, its deathly concupiscence, is inextricably tied to the Augustinian–Lutheran notion of the twisted, inbent predisposition of sinful mankind: *homo incurvatus in se*.[6] With the 'colossal weight' of the Fall, man's inclination is to hunch over, curve inside himself, and be crushed by sin. In Hill's understanding, language, a mirror of this human fault, has the same tendency to seek within itself: puns, repeating figures, and rhymes are among the symptoms. Hill exploits these incurvations of language in the belief that, used thoughtfully and judiciously, they will rectify themselves. 'The mortifications are the fortifications', Hill offers as a single-line poem in *Ludo* (*L* 61, p. 622). It is another linguistic *felix culpa*: the injury becomes the source of the cure. In that single line above from *Ludo*, the rhyme is humorously jingling; the five-syllable rhyme risks sounding frivolous, despite its serious point. It is as though Hill is consciously reducing himself to the pat rhyme, oversimplifying his poetry, as a self-mortification. There is also, again, an acceptance of what the language gives, a suspension of suspicion about its contingencies.

The increasingly explicit use of repeating figures in Hill's work from *The Triumph of Love* onwards, combined with the greater profusion of inter-textual allusions, reveals Hill's growing desire to deal directly with the dead ends of language – and the poetry's growing sense of self-security against the deadly accidents of 'solecisms' (*CCW*, p. 9). The repeating figures are not themselves endpoints; as Hill suggests, one need not 'describe | *Finnegans Wake* as a dead end' for language, or for literature (*TL* CXXXIX, p. 282). Repeating figures exemplify and magnify words' capacity for regeneration. Anadiplosis, anagram, antanaclasis, antimetabole, epanalepsis, metanoia, palindrome, and polyptoton, used as examples here because they all occur in *The Triumph of Love*, are ways of engaging with the dead ends of language: they are mirrorings, scramblings, and twistings of words already stated; they are reactive figures, designed to overcome repetition's fatal anaemia. But such engagement and such design are no magical salve for the inevitable 'diremption' (*CCW*, pp. 100, 539, 578; *BBGJ* 215, p. 117) between language and language-user: 'I don't engage well with language. It takes me over—no, not "as a lover". As a cuckoo plants its progeny on some feathered sucker. I hatch its meanings and naively imagine them mine' (*BBGJ*, 123, §7, p. 66).

Homo incurvatus in se, man twisted in on himself, is reduced to an acknowledgement of his warped condition. (The verb 'reduce' derives partly from Latin *reducere*, to 'bring back' (*OED*).[7]) The 139th section of *The Triumph of Love*, alert to this '[c]oncerning' condition and where it may lead the soul, repeats and reworks its own words, as well as returning to the language of the dead. The theological dead end this poem discusses was a special concern for Luther: it is the question of predestination, a question that pervades much of the later poetry.[8] Here are the poem's opening lines:

> Concerning the elective will, *arbitrium*.
> Concerning wilfulness and determination:
> in so far as the elective is elect
> it will not now be chosen. It may choose
> non-election, as things stand. The Florentine
> academies conjoined
> grammar and the Fall, made a case of *casus*.
> All things by that argument are bound
> to the nature of disordinance,
> Judgement's two minds, the broken
> span of consequence.
>
> (p. 282)

The 'wilfulness' Hill refers to relates to his strongly held notion of man's fallen nature, as expressed in the essay 'Of Diligence and Jeopardy': 'Original sin may be described not only in terms of concupiscence and wilfulness, our nature "gredie to do euell" [...], but also as that imperfection which stamps all activity of the graceless flesh' (*CCW*, p. 282).[9] Repetitiveness can be a symptom of such 'imperfection'. The first five of the lines above contain three examples of polyptoton (the variation of different endings on the same morphological root). The prolonged wondering about theological concepts, which Hill affords himself in the sometimes lengthy free-verse lyrics of *The Triumph of Love*, produces the mouth-mulling of 'will' and 'wilfulness'; 'elective' (twice), 'elect', and 'non-election'; and 'chosen' and 'choose' (*electus*, Latin, meaning chosen). Repeating figures like these are not always playful or clever evasions of language's 'imperfection'; here, they are almost stifling.

One way out of such verbal inwardness is by another kind of repeating figure: the neologism, as in Hopkins's '*inscape*' and '*instress*', which appear later in the poem. 'All things by that argument are bound | to the nature of disordinance'. Here, the new use of an obsolete word appears and acts as a neologism: a reconfiguring of old parts, which, here, constitutes an immediate revival of dead language. *Disordinance* is last recorded by the *OED* in a text of 1502, a translation of de Worde's *Ordynarye of crystyanyte or crysten men*: 'Yf he haue notother dysordynaunce'. More pertinent might be the first recorded use, from Chaucer's translation of Boethius's *De Consolatione Philosophiae* (*c*. 1374): 'What place myȝt[e] ben left [...] to folie and to disordinaunce syn þat god lediþ [...] alle þinges by ordre?' The phrase 'all things' carries from Chaucer to Hill. Chaucer, too, connects disordinance with the idea of order. Disordinance is the way all things are ordered: the semantic nearness of the word to *disorder* is implicit.[10] The added sense of religious rite or observance in *ordinance* (*OED*, '*n*.', sense 4a) infects the meaning of Hill's word so that 'disordinance' becomes something akin to liturgical abuse, the twisting of sacred things.

50   *Geoffrey Hill and the ends of poetry*

The poem worries itself further before arriving at its own 'twist':

How can our
witty sorrows try the frame of such
unsecured security—nothing between
election and reprobation, except vertigo
and a household word-game of tit-for-tat
with family values. Milton writes of those
who 'comming to Curse … have stumbled into
a kind of Blessing'; but if you suppose him
to invoke a stirrup-and-ground-type mercy, think
again. It's a Plutarchan twist: even our foes
further us, though against their will
and purpose.

(p. 282)

Where does the 'Blessing' reside in the condition that Hill, in another instance of polyptoton, calls 'unsecured security'? The paradox, its trajectory following that of Milton's, fits Hill's discussion of election: the elect of God might at any time lose their salvation; if this were not the case they would not have free will; yet God already knows that they will not lose their salvation. 'The book is closed for your time,' Hill writes in *Canaan*'s 'Parentalia' ('Go your ways'), '[b]ut go, as instrumental, of the Lord, | life-bound to his foreknowledge' (p. 209). The security of election is known to God, but to no one else. '[N]othing between | election and reprobation, except vertigo | and a household word-game of tit-for-tat | with family values.' Hill's word-games are linked to his poetry's spiritual vertigo. As ever, they are concerned with the last things. ('[M]y sense of what I am', Hill explains in an interview, 'is inextricably caught up with a lifetime's anxiety about things, prominent among which is an anxiety about the fate of my own soul.'[11]) These word-games put pressure on a similar mystery to that of the Christian's unsecured security: how can there be any security of expression in words, which, by their mutable nature, are not secure in either sound or sense?

The answer for Hill's poetry may lie in the action of linguistic coupling that occurs in puns, repeating figures, rhymes, and syntactic and formal parallelisms. The sounds and the meanings of words change over time; the poet has no control over this. The security of expression, the curse made blessing, cannot come from the mere words themselves. The poet's likeliest way to transcend the corruptions of language and 'reach the steady hills above' (*U*, p. 3) might instead be the stabilising twists of words and their meanings into momentary, but revelatory, reconciliations.

Hill gives the notion a personal adjective. 'It's a Plutarchan twist: even our foes | further us, though against their will | and purpose.'[12] Hill claims

Dead ends   51

that the fallenness of language can be advantageous for knowledgeable and diligent users of it. *Lingua incurvata in se* is the perfect instrument for *homo incurvatus in se*. By Hill's logic, 'our foes' are, in the first place, ourselves, inbent and twisted with the help of 'Lucifer' (mentioned two lines later). And yet this condition of 'wilfulness', since it had to be redeemed by Christ, whose Incarnation and Crucifixion exalt the 'graceless flesh', becomes the cause of salvation. ('Cross- | dressing in mid-twist, salvation in mid-fall' (*SS* 103, p. 340).) Another sense could be strictly biographical: Plutarch furthered *Lives*; he also furthered the name of one of his literary 'foes', Herodotus, by lambasting his work. More to Hill's point here, Plutarch also wrote the *Moralia*, the sixth chapter of which is entitled 'How to Profit by One's Enemies'.[13]

Plutarch's *Lives*, commonly called *Parallel Lives*, is a collection of biographies, mainly paired in order to reveal correspondences of morality between the Greek and Roman noblemen it describes. The text is alluded to more obviously later in the same poem with another repeating figure: anadiplosis, the repetition of a clause's final word as the next clause's first.[14] 'You | can draw up Plutarch against yourself; yourself | the enemy (*do it and be damned*)' (p. 282).[15] This, as well as strengthening the introvert reading of 'our foes | further us', makes of Plutarch's *Parallel Lives* an exact parallel: 'yourself | yourself'.[16] This is *homo incurvatus in se* displayed in a verbal mirror. Looking at oneself and seeing only oneself is, in this light, a symptom of the Fall.[17] Several lines earlier in the poem, Hill praises Hopkins for his neologisms, or 'self-coinings', regarding this kind of self-absorption:

> Hopkins gave his best
> self-coinings of the self—*inscape*,
> *instress*—to inventing Lucifer:
> *non serviam*: sweetness of absolute
> hatred, which shall embrace self-hatred,
> encompass self-extinction, annihilation's
> demonic angelism.
>
> (p. 282)

Lucifer is the epitome, here, of the self turned inward. Having fallen by his pride (*non serviam* meaning *I will not serve*), his status as an angel has become emptied, oxymoronic: 'annihilation's | demonic angelism'. The latter word is not found in the *OED* (though 'Angelist' is); it is another neologism, this time from Jacques Maritain, a pejorative noun to describe a philosophy that refuses to accept the human condition and lays claim to angelic rights and capacities.[18] Lucifer, too, is seen by Hill to have refused to accept his condition; and so he negates himself. In F. H. Bradley's words, much admired by Hill, Lucifer has 'failed to get within the judgement the

52   *Geoffrey Hill and the ends of poetry*

condition of the judgement'.[19] Any rhetorical figure is, for Hill, empty unless its speaker understands the personal and linguistic circumstances in which it is produced.

Hill has persistently asserted that expressiveness is by no means the same thing as self-expression.[20] Consequently, Hill's disapprobation of the use of the word 'you' in Eliot's *Little Gidding* is voiced partly in terms of the narcissist expressing to himself: 'Is Eliot instructing himself, self-confessor to self-penitent[?]' (*CCW*, p. 377). Confessing to, and being absolved by, oneself would constitute a parody of a sacrament, a thorough 'disordinance'. The inbent man, the narcissist ignorant of his own condition, easily becomes a parody of a man. 'Why nót twist Luther,' asks Hill elsewhere, 'practised self-parodist?' (*SS* 117, p. 347).[21] In the context of the poem, Hill's repeating figures seek greater reconciliations: between 'wilfulness' and grace; between Milton's 'Curse' and 'Blessing'.

Not satisfied with its own reconciliations, the poem aptly dead-ends at the thought of a work replete with repeating figures and word-games, Joyce's *Finnegans Wake*. The pun of that title famously indicates both an end (a vigil held over a dead body) and a restart (a waking and rising again):

> As for the rest of us, must we describe
> *Finnegans Wake* as a dead end? (*Over*
> *my dead body*, says Slow.)
>
> (p. 282)

The invented critic Slow's cliché is also a waking-up of dead language.

Where repeating figures are successful in this rousing of language, then, they get within their use the 'condition' of their use. They turn away from complacent use of language, from verbal narcissism. Meditating again on the nature of words in the forty-third poem of *Liber Illustrium Virorum*, Hill considers how this turn and ascension from inbent language might be achieved:

> It is the simplest narrative that flies
> Together in double chronology;
> For that words are analogues of crisis;
> Cross-stress and dissonance bind eulogy:
> Obedience held axiomatic,
> The circle is not squared by dividers.
>
> (p. 727)

Words are analogues of crisis: in utterance they hold together their disparate meanings and connotations: they can speak in multiples, and to both past and present in 'double chronology'. Even 'analogues' here is a play on words; in fact it is a play on the word for *word*, since the Greek λόγος (*logos*) is at its root.[22] Hill sees crisis as necessary for good poetry:

Dead ends

'When you have *techne* without crisis, the result is poetry similar to that written by Movement poets of the 1950s.'[23] The crisis, the '[c]ross-stress', of words is a balance between two struggling forces: one of their divine nature and one of their fallen human nature; between the vertical beam and the horizontal beam.[24] 'Patent figuration', writes Hill elsewhere, 'lifts plus from minus' (*O* 138: *Welsh apotheosis* (III), p. 786). And again: 'Poetics is a cross with all its stations; | My theme in these devotions | Intemperate devotion to my theme' (*TT* 82: *i.m. R. B. Kitaj*, pp. 927–28); here the cross-word, the word on which the verbal near-palindrome of the clause turns, is 'intemperate', which aptly doubles as adjective to both the word preceding (though somewhat archly in this respect) and the word succeeding it.

The cross-stress is Aristotelian and Chestertonian: discussing its way of finding Aristotle's μέσον (*meson*), or balance, G. K. Chesterton characterises Christianity as 'like a huge and ragged and romantic rock, which, though it sways on its pedestal at a touch, yet, because its exaggerated excrescences exactly balance each other, is enthroned there for a thousand years'. In Christendom, he writes, 'apparent accidents balanced'.[25] The idea relates to Hill's vision of language: 'Cross-stress and dissonance bind eulogy'. Hill's rhetorical figures – the expansion of 'crisis' into '[c]ross-stress'; the puns of 'flies' and 'held' – are also apparent accidents that aim to rebalance (though frequently in a decidedly hazardous fashion) the out-of-shape language through which they work.

Martin Dodsworth writes of Hill that 'balance does not appeal to him', citing Hill's dislike of Empson's 'Arachne' (Dodsworth: 'a poem about "balance"') and his rejection of a simplified appraisal of John Crowe Ransom as 'the supreme equilibrist' (Hill: 'despite the consensus we may better appreciate Ransom's final achievement by not shirking the occasions when he is thrown off balance' (*CCW*, pp. 128–29)).[26] But, as Dodsworth admits, what Hill dislikes about the Empson poem is its 'banal obviousness'; if balance is being questioned it is because it has been falsely found. Similarly, the call to appreciate Ransom's moments 'off balance' does not negate an appreciation of achieved balance. When it comes to Hill's thoughts of the end, it is clear that balance not only appeals to him but is essential to his vision of an ultimate redemption, an artistic redemption that yet retains a religious temperament approaching 'strange Christian hope' (*MCCP* 5, p. 147): 'The implication so far is that there is somewhere a final equation: | As Péguy must have believed and, in his own fashion, proved as a type of sublime fiction' (*BBGJ* 252, p. 136).[27]

The desired balance in Hill is one of equal but hostile forces: a 'balance between lust and admonition' (*HOLC* 19, p. 167); 'when disparities get spliced and make | sense to each other' (*OS* XXXVIII, p. 387). It is often something ephemeral but epiphanic: 'Eternal orders flash balancing | acts in the East Window, random and wholly I articulate light' (*OS* XXV, p. 375); 'a wayward covey I of cabbage-whites this instant balanced I and prinking' (*OS* LXIII, p. 413).[28] Of the arrangement of the title-page of Ivor Gurney's *Severn & Somme*, Hill writes that Gurney 'briefly holds in balance what Lionel Trilling would later call "the reality of self" and "the reality of circumstance"' (*CCW*, p. 430). It is a difficult, perhaps momentary, but necessary balance whereby 'reality' can be expressed faithfully. But do Hill's repeating figures achieve this *meson*; if so, how; and to what end?

One of the ways in which Hill tries to attain this precarious balance, the cross-stress, is by using the rhetorical turn of changing one's mind, known as metanoia.[29] In a paradoxical way, the rhetorical turn is akin to the physical malady of *homo incurvatus in se*: Hill calls it a 'return upon the self' (*CCW*, p. 164).[30] This phrase, adapted from Arnold, describes an incurvation of its own, but a rectifying one. The return upon the self is a kind of repentance; it reverses the initial turn inwards, represented for Hill by original sin.

Kathryn Murphy's essay 'Hill's Conversions' illuminates the multivalence of the figures of turning and return in Hill. She draws attention to two lines of 'Canticle for Good Friday', from Hill's first collection: 'Spat on the stones each drop I Of deliberate blood' (*U*, p. 20). This 'poises', she writes,

> between choice and inevitability, free will and ineluctable gravity: indicating at once Christ's chosen self-sacrifice, and its necessity in providential history. A further irony is introduced by the parallel root of 'deliver', from a popular Latin skewing of 'deliberare', meaning 'to free completely'. The blood is delivered (released) from the body; it will also deliver the souls it saves. The etymon only enriches the resonances: 'deliberare' is ultimately from 'libra', a Roman weight of twelve ounces, a balance, or set of scales. (*GHC*, p. 72)

Hill's deliberation, his deliberateness with words, is a kind of balancing act. The notion is bound up with the idea of deliverance from the bounds of expression. The pun that turns on itself, that corrects and converts itself, looks to achieve this end of deliverance, which, etymologically, at once sets right and sets free.

There are numerous examples of metanoia, in the rhetorical sense, in Hill's poetry. The last line of the first poem in *Expostulations on the Volcano* is 'Better drama than in the theatre'. The first line of the collection's thirty-eighth poem is 'Not better drama than the theatre' (pp. 629, 666). The single-line bookends of *The Triumph of Love*, which constitute the first and 150th sections, make a subtler and even more distant amendment from 'Sun-blazed, over Romsley, a livid rain-scarp' to 'Sun-blazed, over Romsley, the livid rain-scarp' (pp. 239, 286). Sometimes Hill uses the figure to have his cake and eat it regarding word choice (while sneaking in a pun on his own metanoia's punctuation): 'See in what ways the river | lies padded—no, dashed—with light' (*SC* 2. 22, p. 441). Other returns upon the self are more abruptly personal and penitent: 'Still I anticipate. | I did not anticipate the marriage || that I destroyed' (*SC* 1. 16, p. 428).[31] The fifty-fifth section of *The Orchards of Syon*, which is partly concerned with the relationship between 'confession' and 'rhetoric', dramatises the feeling of responsibility to its reader as well as to God: 'To you I stand | answerable. Correction: must once have stood' (p. 405). Standing is a symbol of righteousness. The person living in accord with God's will is the *vpright man* of the Wisdom literature.[32] The act of standing is also significant in Milton, particularly as exemplifying the exercise of free will that would have saved mankind from the Fall: 'Sufficient to have stood, though free to fall'.[33] Hill's correction is a balance of acknowledgements: being human, he has fallen and can no longer stand proudly before God or reader; but, for that fall, he must 'stand | answerable', which requires him to get back up.

Elsewhere in *The Orchards of Syon*, the metanoia is even more strikingly posed; the tenth poem ends, 'Strophe after strophe | ever more catastrophic. Did I say | strophe? I meant salvo, sorry' (p. 360). The turn of this correction is a pun on 'strophe', which in Greek means *turning* (catastrophe is *downturn*). The balance here is found by way of a rhetorical last resort: Hill has fun at his own expense. He does so twice over: firstly with the jocular suggestion that work by work, '[s]trophe after strophe', his poems are worsening; and secondly by pretending to confuse his words.

In *Ludo*, the collection of 'Epigraphs and Colophons to *The Daybooks*' (*BH*, p. 603), the balances of each differently shaped poem are particularly awkward. The poems' guiding spirit is John Skelton, whose poems stand like leaning towers, their variously constructed metres held up by successions of repeated rhymes. The tenth poem turns in petition to him with a suitably off-kilter rhyme: 'Turbulent John Skelton | pray for us in meltdown' (p. 607). Hill's virtuosity is both assured and unsure of itself. Even in achieving the desired outcome, there can be an unpleasant return: 'something within the balance that repels' (*L* 60, p. 622). In the twenty-seventh poem of *Ludo*, steady footings are found even in the poem's denial of its own capacity to achieve balance:

> I cannot comprehend the situation
> > as I describe it;
> > let verse enrobe it
> with lively fantasy of time and motion.

                    56   *Geoffrey Hill and the ends of poetry*

As to what finally might merit diction
    I shall not here say,
    to ensure privacy
for the sordid act of begetting fiction;

conceding as I do some self-contusion—
    ah, the weak endings,
    mute understandings,
forlorn pacts between compaction, diffusion.
                                    (*L* 27, p. 613)

Wrestling with their language, several of *Ludo*'s poems look dejectedly on their repeating figures, seeing their reconciliations as merely 'weak endings, | mute understandings, | forlorn pacts'. Nevertheless, verbal pacts are made in the poem: the clearest are the weighty end-rhymes, the pattern of which travels over the stanza breaks: all of the longer lines rhyme on words ending with -*tion* or -*sion*. There are also the pacts between *com-* and *con-* words (beginning with the first line's 'comprehend' and ending with the last line's 'compaction'), which by their etymology signify togetherness. An especially close understanding exists in the ninth line between the self-humiliations of 'conceding' and 'contusion'. The turn of 'verse' is deemed a 'lively fantasy of time and motion'; but the poem's turning on itself, and over its words, is an achieved balance that transcends mere 'lively fantasy'.

In *Ludo*'s fourteenth poem, another definition of verse is given, before a repetition of that poem's first line: 'Verse is change-ringing. *Economic laws | survive their violation*' (p. 608).[34] One might wonder why the changes are rung on this specific quotation; is Hill's poem an economy – in the etymological sense, a household to be managed – with the layout of its rooms (or stanzas) having to be balanced as the books are balanced? Or is verse simply what is left after a transaction with thought, the change ringing being the jangle of pocketed coins, poetic fragments clinking together? (Offa's verse-leftovers in the final lines of *Mercian Hymns* are 'coins, for his lodging, and traces of | red mud' (*MH* XXX, p. 112).) Later, in *Ludo* 21, the motto recurs: 'For want of text, recycle: *verse is change- | ringing*' (p. 611). The change is metanoia. It is a kind of writerly repentance for repetitiveness, as well as for 'weak endings' and 'mute understandings'. It is an attempt to discover, or recover, a just balance between things. It takes language's 'forlorn pacts' and elevates them as offerings: to the reader, and, hesitantly, to God (as in *Ludo* 15, p. 609: 'How shall I sing the Lord in this strange land?— | if that is my brief | which I doubt'). The balancing sacrifice of the fifty-first Psalm, foreshadowing that of Christ, is 'a broken and a contrite heart' (Psalms 51.17). The repeating figures of *Ludo*, and of

Dead ends 57

Hill's work as a whole, are contrite, ungainly presentations of balance to an unbalanced language and world.

The sixth poem of *Ludo* expresses its equilibria even more elaborately:

Medieval bones deep that city to disinter.
Splinter to enter. Veil of equity in poor state.
Mortal temple ample to commote fear.
Violence uncivil. The dead, the kept ones
who toll silence as to berate:

Reversed prayer made for non-payment they aver.
  Rumor a maimed palindrome.
Malign lingam of lignum vitae; Vera ill-served.
Emerod-ridden rear end well-riddled by rod. And?
Viva revived. Review those long aggrieved.

(p. 606)

This kind of linguistic exploration is a return to the cramped, abbreviating style of *Speech! Speech!*: that collection's last five poems include the peregrinations of 'reveille. Re evil— | relive, revile, revalue | self- | revelation' and 'AMOR. MAN IN A COMA, MA'AM. NEMO. AMEN' (*SS* 115, 120, pp. 346, 348). The flirting with obscenity in the poem above (albeit obscure; 'lingam' is a phallus worshipped as a symbol of the Hindu god Siva, while an '[e]merod', not in the *OED*, is a haemorrhoid) also recalls the punning 'filthy talk' of *Speech! Speech!* (89, p. 333: 'Don't overstretch it, asshole [...] Don't let them hear CUR | DEUS HOMO'). This is metanoia by punchline, the humorous (or blasphemous) rebalancing of the poetry's lofty aspirations.

The poem obliquely apologises for turning on itself: 'Rumor a maimed palindrome.' *Rumor*, though its American spelling is truer to its French and Latin progenitors, and though it has been in occasional British use, is nevertheless, for Hill as a British speaker, a maimed version of *rumour*. Without spelling it this way, Hill could not have had his pun. The pun is a reflection on the shapes of the word's letters; if *o* had not been maimed, decapitated even, to become *u*, the word would read *romor*, a palindrome, but nonsense. ('Nonsense verses set down versus conscience', as the maimed palindrome of *Ludo*'s fifty-fourth poem reads (p. 620).) The line, the only one indented in the poem, sits in the centre of the line above (a line that is another failed self-reversal), as though to balance it, to make a feeble attempt to recover that '[v]eil of equity in poor state'. The palindrome's move backwards recalls again the peculiar metanoia of *Speech! Speech!*: 'Self-correction without tears: see me reverse | tango this juggernaut onto the road' (*SS* 116, p. 346). Given that *Ludo* is a group of poems that play, one might expect its metanoias, too, to be 'without tears'; but they are

58   *Geoffrey Hill and the ends of poetry*

regularly penitent, self-contusing. The poem above is sorry for its 'sordid act of begetting fiction'. The silence of the 'dead, the kept ones' (who are also perhaps 'those long aggrieved'), is heard as their rebuking response.

But if the dead who occupy these poems would only 'berate' their attempts to find a *meson*, all that work might seem a waste. Would Nathaniel Hawthorne not be pleased to find his word 'commote' resurrected in the third line (see *OED*)? In turning, Hill is often going back, and, as a result, bringing back. His repeating figures as a whole work in the same way as his metanoias: they acknowledge and try to rebalance errors of the poet and corruptions of the language. This *meson* is a balance that, when found by 'mankind turned, or bent, inwards upon itself', provides a platform for words 'to go higher' (*OS* XIX, p. 369), to become prayer. As the 'prayer made for non-payment' looks to the unacknowledged dead, it also looks up to the Cross of Christ, itself a transcendent 'payment' and consummate balancing act. The following three sections, all of which treat of Hill's tautologies, examine them by way of three deeply interrelated qualities (that they display or with which they are associated): muteness; evenness; and tendency to prayer. In a passage that suggests such qualities in *The Orchards of Syon*, the balance of words is figured as a 'rough concurrence', from which is derived nevertheless a hope of ascent:

> You have a knack, a way
> with broken speech; a singular welcome
> for rough concurrence. After a time it's all
> resolved, in part, through a high formal keening.
> And need to work on that and to go higher.

Mute tautologies

Tautologies are the purest and yet most fraught repeating figures. They are appropriately double-sided: dead ends of language that may (or may not) be the means of new expressive life. I understand *tautology*, then, as a neutral word. There are good and bad tautologies: both are exact verbal repetitions, but good tautologies produce new sense, even though they often appear at first to be redundancies. Bad tautologies simply are unredeemed redundancies. In this sense '[t]hey lie; they lie' (*U*, p. 15) is a bad tautology, since the double-meaning in the first instance renders the repetition not only needless but also an unintended insult to the reader's intelligence (see n. 15). This is a dead end from which no way out has been found. (There is also the even more egregious tautology of sense between two different words, for example *fatal murder* (see *OED*, sense 2).) Good tautologies are often simply emphatic. Others are meditative, ritualistic,

Dead ends

59

lulling. One may imagine that Hill, concerned to reach the ends of language through reconciliations, would be uninterested in, if not determined to avoid, tautologies, which can reconcile the word only with itself. But their perfect and intrinsic *meson* proves meaningful and powerful to Hill.

It is true, as Ewan James Jones remarks, that 'a genealogy of tautology reveals that the very term that is supposed to connote self-identity is not even identical with itself: rather, it is constituted in an unsuspected variety of ways'.[35] As Sol Saporta notes, while the 'clearest tautology is typically of the form, X is X', such sentences occur 'with meanings which are not circular'.[36] Clichés such as *boys will be boys* are clichés because of the catchiness, the repeatability, of such figures; the phrase is rescued from meaninglessness when the implied adjectival sense of the second *boys* (i.e., mischievous, etc.) is realised.[37] I wish instead here to consider the tautology as an exact verbal repetition without a distinct change in sense. Such a definition absorbs into it several related rhetorical terms, for example: *conduplicatio* (wherein a word or phrase is repeated in adjacent clauses, usually for emphasis); *epanadiplosis* (wherein a sentence begins and ends with the same word); and *epanalepsis* (wherein a word is repeated after intervening matter).

The Triumph of Love offers its own, unsurprisingly doubled, definition: 'tautology, which is at once *vain* | *repetition* and *the logic of the world* | (Wittgenstein)' (*TL* CXXV, p. 276).[38] Tautology, then, is language's self-revelation of vanities, its mirror. If it is also '*the logic of the world*', this may be because language, through tautologies, seeks in vain to represent reality with a mirror's accuracy, to weigh things justly; or even to make a statement that by its nature cannot be refuted (this being a more Wittgensteinian sense, as I shall go on to discuss). As Jones observes in Kant, writing about tautology tends towards inhabiting it; and so it will be necessary to return to this section of *The Triumph of Love*.[39] ('My theme in these intemperate devotions | Intemperate devotion to my theme'.)

In Hill, the tautology (as I define it) is, at the same time, a self-reflection and a cry for the deeper reflection of self afforded by a relationship of love (both human and divine). The tautology of human love, in Hill's early work, often distinguishes itself by 'cadence':

> Oh my dear one, I shall grieve for you
> For the rest of my life with slightly
> Varying cadence, oh my dear one.
>
> (p. 70)

This, the second of the 'Coplas', which themselves make up the second part of 'The Songbook of Sebastian Arrurruz' in *King Log*, is consummated in the very lack of consummation. The repetition, as poignant as it is clever,

60   *Geoffrey Hill and the ends of poetry*

completes the poem by expressing perfectly the speaker's feeling of incompleteness, his recourse to the same, unanswered cry – with the unimportant, yet all-important, 'slightly | Varying cadence' – as an artificial answer to itself. Its proximity to redundancy is its emotional and intellectual power. Near the other extreme of Hill's career, here is the beginning of the first of 'Six Variants on Montale, "Il gallo cedrone"':

> *Snapshot—that—the snapped shot. You foundered,*
> *Who had been ponderous; echo a travesty*
> *Of a mating-call, that 'guttural retching cry'.*
> *Desperately sheltering, I too am plundered.*
>
> > (*TT* 43 (a), p. 908)

Echo is indeed a travesty of a mating-call, at its worst a '*guttural retching cry*'. The same poem ends with '*a god among his gods*' going '*down into the earth to be re-born*'. As when it imitates a mating-call, the tautological echo can be a kind of false rebirth, keeping the word alive despite the steady depletion of its meaning.

More commonly in the early work, the tautology signifies an intensification of expression, often emotionally wrought. The increase in anxiety in 'shadows warned him | not to go | not to go | along that road', from 'The Pentecost Castle' (§1, *T*, p. 115), is attributable to the song-like refrain. In the same poem's second section, the first stanza is repeated whole (the only change being to the initial capital letter) as the third and last stanza: 'Down in the orchard | I met my death | under the briar rose | I lie slain' (p. 115). Again, this is very consciously a balladic trope; here, a kind of memorial inscription for a dead and spoken-for 'I' is at the same time a first-person narration of spiritual and emotional death. Repeating this resigned stanza nonetheless asserts the permanence of the speaker's state. Similarly, in a more straightforward posthumous inscription ('I speak this in memory of my grandmother'), the twenty-fifth hymn in *Mercian Hymns* repeats its first stanza as its fourth and last (p. 107).

Between *Speech! Speech!* and *The Orchards of Syon*, Hill's tautology moves through numerous diverse voices and pitches. It begins with the heckling or hectoring of the first book's title, repeated in the sixth poem: '(*speech! speech!*)' (*SS* 6, p. 291). Elsewhere, the tautology is found in such roles as ironic placeholder: 'BLANK BLANK BLANK BLANK' (*SS* 47, p. 312); slapstick caller-and-responder: 'Say this was my idea. THIS | WAS MY IDEA' (*SS* 69, p. 323); parroter of British history: 'PRETTY | BLOODY PRETTY BLOODY' (*SS* 72, p. 324); parodic stutterer: 'WHADDYA WHADDYA | call this—script or prescription?' (*SS* 107, p. 342); avian transcriber: '*chích | chích, chích chích*' (*OS* IX, p. 359); feigned rager: 'Lyric cry lyric cry lyric cry, I'll | give them lyric cry!' (*OS* XXX, p. 380); mock-plaintive

Dead ends   61

addresser: 'Memory! memory!' (*OS* LV, p. 405); 'My polity— | polity!' (*OS* LXV, p. 415); 'Syon! Syon!' (*OS* LXVI, p. 416); and repetitive reporter: 'Our people, | where áre they?—cranky old Barnes—*But óh, | our peóple, whére are théy?*' (*OS* LIX, p. 409).[40]

But what is the meaning of tautology in Hill? What is its end, and how might it constitute an end? In *The Book of Baruch*, the motif of repetition, and Hill's association of it with muteness, provide a way towards answering these questions. In the early part of the book Hill finds himself revelling in a repeated, titular kind of tautology: 'Clare, house of Clare, how beautifully the name twice takes its place here' (*BBGJ* 35, p. 15).[41] The link between tautology and muteness follows a few poems later. 'Repetitiousness of the mute' (38, p. 18) serves to describe the consistently silent mysteries of existence ('Eternity is in particulars that exclude pity? No-one explains'). Somewhat relatedly, the Biblical Job's 'repetitious but instructive grief' is later invoked (86, p. 40). Elsewhere, and almost as an apologia for his work: 'Obsession is repetitious when it is not mute' (131, p. 70). Hill is clearly agitated by the thought of repeating himself, drawn at once towards attack and defence: 'Repetitiousness stems from ignorance and distress; probably not both at once. | Scansion is repetition in pattern; and an enduring mansion' (181, p. 96).[42] An important distinction is drawn here between '[r]epetitiousness' and 'repetition': the first a solecism, the second neutral and even possibly redeeming. Later, in defence of both specific and general repeatings: 'This endless name-dropping [...] is not—I repeat—my form of coping with the nameless thing, our final and fatal lot. | Mere repetitiousness is not endurance; more a transference of oxymorons' (199, p. 110). With wry punning humour, having already dropped his name in full earlier in the poem, Hill writes of 'the repetitious scorn of Percy Wyndham Lewis' (169, p. 90). With his ageing self in mind, Hill comments on an unnamed woman: 'She writes well of people who are near-mutes [...]. *In extremis* will take speech from us, even the famous' (191, p. 105). On occasion those without speech are celebrated: 'Each is indebted to the mute and the mad for the roof over his worldly head' (123, §5, p. 65). There is found something admirable about choosing silence – particularly in Hopkins, one of Hill's firm heroes to the end: 'Gerard, tipped fervent by the Birmingham Oratory, had made a burnt offering of his vatic temerity, and become creatively dumb' (220, p. 119).[43] Hill approaches the end of this poem with a familial parallel: 'My grandmother, I recall, read well, moving her lips silently the while'.

In Hill's poetry, the tautology is language's nearest expression of a 'mute desire' for consummation (*P* 28, p. 550). This desired consummation, for Hill, is both perfectly weighed articulation and the final justice of the divine

62   *Geoffrey Hill and the ends of poetry*

Word. But, as the epode of the twenty-eighth ode in *Pindarics* indicates, prolonged repetition can be a circle of hell:

> Manipulate necessity to end
> even as salutation. Set us down
> into our loop; and we repeat ourselves
> only as mute desire. We do not open
> the fatal book nor match up sighs that steal.
>
> (p. 550)

Muteness, here, is not silence but inarticulacy. The infant (from Latin *infans*, meaning *speechless*) can cry but cannot eloquently express desires, having only 'broken speech' (*OS* XIX, p. 369). The silence of one's childhood, as poignantly depicted in *Scenes from Comus*, can instead be that of adults: 'Silence is dealt defending a loved child ‖ against incorrigible fact. Mute | suffering's a factor of countless decibels' (*SC* 1. 7, p. 424).

As infants 'we repeat ourselves'; this is the sign of our 'mute desire'. This characteristic of infancy is, as Hill notices, raised to a high articulation in Tennyson's poetry. Hill cites two lines of *In Memoriam* as a 'sublime instance' of the 'dramatised yearning' of the word *somehow*: 'Oh yet we trust that somehow good | Will be the final goal of ill' (*CCW*, p. 532).[44] The final stanza of the same poem conveys the yearning speechlessness of infancy and has a tautological structure:

> So runs my dream: but what am I?
>   An infant crying in the night;
>   An infant crying for the light:
> And with no language but a cry.[45]

The form itself gestures towards infancy, since it draws from the rhythmic and rhyming conventions of the ballad.[46] The childlike poet cries for divine 'light' to overturn his human sombreness. Like Tennyson's infant, Blake's child who climbs a ladder to the moon (in an engraving of 1793) expresses a larger human longing to go beyond the earthly: 'I want! I want!'[47] Hill, ever a devotee of Blake, quotes this in a darker hue (with reference to the composer Malcolm Arnold) in *The Book of Baruch*: 'Perfidious the irritant solace of alcohol. I want! I want!' (*BBGJ* 197, p. 109). In both the Blake and the Tennyson passages, the repetition of the cries expresses the desire's intensity, but the nature of the desire is unclear, due to the lack of a stated object. Seamus Perry mentions the 'pervasive "i" rhyme' in this stanza from *In Memoriam*; the stanza's cycle of these [aɪ] sounds exemplifies having 'no language but a cry'.[48] It also centralises the first-person subject.

Dead ends

In the 155th poem of *The Book of Baruch* Hill, with a coiling associativeness, travels from a yearning to define words, through tautology, then silence, and finally to infancy (and an enforced silence):

> As one or other has effectively said, resurrected is not exactly revived.
> *Define and yet again define* wears definition to ruin.
> Touch my lips and tongue with a live coal, I will not sing but recoil, as anyone
> would, not pre-selected by God, anathema riproaring among cosmic
> blips: a plethora of themes.
> In fact *speechless infant* does not appear anywhere in the New Testament. Why
> did I ever suppose that it is there between Christmas and the
> New Year?
>
> (p. 84)

The distinction drawn between 'resurrected' and 'revived' (cited from the amusingly undefined 'one or other') sees Hill again brooding on the soul's final fate.[49] What follows in the passage demonstrates the profound connection for Hill between several ends: death; the function of the poet; tautology; and speechlessness. The tautological enjoinment to '[d]efine and yet again define' is reminiscent of Housman's description of Bentley, 'his great predecessor in the emendation of Latin texts', pointing to the scribe's work and saying, '*thou ailest here, and here*' (cited in *CCW*, pp. 387, 414). Hill is also playing on the wearing away of meaning that occurs when repeating a word: to continually say 'define' would wear *define*'s 'definition to ruin'. Most importantly, though, '*Define and yet again define*' is a repetition of a quotation, from Ezra Pound, which Hill uses in the essay 'Our Word is Our Bond', and which is concerned with the ends of poetry: 'The poet's job is to *define* and yet again define till the detail of surface is in accord with the root in justice.'[50] Hill's reference to this in the poem plays with what he does not quote: the finish of a poem, its 'detail of surface' and its 'definition', is in danger of being worn 'to ruin' by the very process of constantly defining (Hill stepping aside from Pound's hopeful 'till', the foreseen end-point of the craft).

Shifting abruptly to the sixth chapter of Isaiah, but retaining his focus on the poet's job, Hill appears to react against the commentators' designation of him as a prophet: were the 'live coal' pressed to his mouth, Hill suggests, he would 'not sing but recoil', be mute: he is 'not pre-selected by God', which explains the things in his work that would be unsayable by a messenger of God, the 'anathema riproaring' through his 'plethora of themes' ('anathema' and 'themes' being a repeating figure, both from the etymon θέμα (*thema*), a 'proposition' or thing 'set up'; see *OED*, 'theme').

The thought of recoiling from utterance ostensibly leads Hill to look up '*speechless infant*' in the New Testament; the subsequent reference to his

64   *Geoffrey Hill and the ends of poetry*

having supposed that the words occur 'between Christmas and the New Year' confirms that Hill has in mind the Massacre of the Holy Innocents perpetrated by King Herod shortly after Christ's birth (Matthew 2. 16), traditionally commemorated on 28 December. Hill recalls the Holy Innocents in a poem from *The Triumph of Love* (CXXV, pp. 276–77) to which I attend further on in this chapter; and in one of the later-written *Hymns to Our Lady of Chartres* (1982–2012) he again invokes the events around Christ's birth: 'Herod was dire but he was not the Shoah. | What do you say, Vierge, to this Jewish child | fixed at your breast, in the great glass annealed, | Himself the threefold shattering of Chaos?' (*HOLC* 9, p. 161). The phrase '*speechless infant*' is a tautology of sense that gains poignancy from the apparent redundancy of the Holy Innocents' deaths. The Christ-child, for whom the Innocents are unwitting proxies and martyrs, has been called the speechless Word or *verbum infans*, more paradox than tautology. Eliot borrows the paradox from Lancelot Andrewes, who in turn borrows it from the Church Fathers; the next poem in *The Book of Baruch* gives room to all three: '"Christ is no wild-cat" says a preacher [...]. *Confer* for such matter "the Word of God became a babe that cried"—Justin Martyr. [...] [T]hough "Christ is no wild-cat" got to inspire Eliot I am not his sort of spoiled priest' (*BBGJ* 156, p. 84).[51] What connects the three names in this passage (and Hill too) is the Word made wordless in the Christ-child, to which all make reference. That Hill quotes the less memorable formulation attributed to Justin Martyr, 'the Word of God became a babe that cried', seems significant. It is not mere wordlessness that Hill notices but the cry born of wordlessness. The cry of the Christ-child, mirrored at Christ's death, can be interpreted in the light of His earthly intention: rendering Himself a helpless God to reconcile God with helpless man.[52] For Hill, thoughts of reconciliation, even an apocalyptic resurrection, accompany his tautologies as they do this crying 'Babe': 'Crawl home; rise reconciled | To the Christ-child' (*LIV* XVII, p. 701).

Even tautologies

The cry of Hill's tautologies is closely related to a child's speechlessness and a feeling of having 'no language'. As with Tennyson's 'infant', the 'mute desire' Hill's tautologies express is for transcendence, both linguistic and spiritual. In *The Orchards of Syon*, transcendence is called for as early as the epigraphs, all three of which (from Thomas Bradwardine, D. H. Lawrence, and Thomas Traherne respectively) describe preternatural, grace-imbued conditions or situations (*BH*, p. 349).[53] Even in the dedication, '*To my children and grandchildren*', some sight of what may lie beyond life's end is forming. This is all

Dead ends 65

perhaps preempted by the title, which conjures a vision of paradise ('*Orchard* and *Paradise* (from the Persian) | I would claim for my paradigm the two | most beautiful words we have' (*HOLC* 21, p. 168)). And, as with Hill's repeating figures, the transcendence desired in his tautologies requires the establishment of a poetic *meson*, a balanced platform from which words may 'go higher'. Hill writes that *The Orchards of Syon* 'is concerned with forms and patterns of reconciliation – not the easiest of states to move into, so there are numerous lapses and relapses throughout the sequence'.[54]

The word *even*, in *The Orchards of Syon*, is of particular importance in this regard. Though on the face of it a common word, *even* occurs peculiarly often in the collection; and many of its occurrences appear to be puns, playing off either its adverbial emphatic sense or its idiomatic use in verb phrases against the idea of a numinous (and noumenal) equilibrium: 'let what is | speak for itself, not to redeem the time | but to get even with it' (XVIII, p. 368); 'though why in the world this light is not | revealed, even so, the paths plum-coloured' (XXIV, p. 374); 'just to break even with you in despair' (XXVI, p. 376); 'Even | thinking at all earns points' (XXX, p. 380); 'Is this even | to be thought?' (LII, p. 402); 'Even | this much praise is hard going [...] I claim elective | affinities as of the root, even. | Even if unenduring' (LXV, p. 415); 'let us | presume to assume the hierarchies, | Goldengrove, even as these senses fall | and die in your yellow grass' (LXVI, p. 416).[55] Such a polyvalent word, and one that suggests justice, balance, reconciliation, could hardly fail to appeal to Hill; in its eighteen senses recorded by the *OED*, numerous definitions seem appropriate to these envisaged orchards and their descriptions: 'without inequality'; ''equal', equable, unruffled'; 'Equally balanced; in a state of equilibrium; "not inclining to either side" (Johnson)'; 'just, impartial'; while the phrase *even Stephen* captures the idea of balance in its equally weighted and rhymed pair of words (see *OED* (second edition), 'even', *adj.*, senses 2, 8, 9, 12, and 14d).[56] The tautology, characteristic of *The Orchards of Syon*, is as close to evenness as language can manage.

The Orchards of Syon is a collection infused both with tautologies and with yearning. Hill's Syon is, as Jeffrey Wainwright remarks, 'not a time or place but a mental vision'.[57] The title-phrase recurs frequently in the collection, a highly unusual motif for Hill.[58] The first instance is at the end of the first poem:

Has it ever been staged
seriously outside Spain, I mean
La vida es sueño? Tell me, is this the way
to the Orchards of Syon
where I left you thinking I would return?

(p. 351)

66   *Geoffrey Hill and the ends of poetry*

Hill returns throughout the collection not only to 'the Orchards of Syon' but to '*La vida es sueño*'. The latter, following *Tenebrae*'s 'The Pentecost Castle', itself brings Hill back to his interest in Spanish Golden Age literature. *La vida es sueño* ('Life Is a Dream') is a 1635 play by Pedro Calderón de la Barca, which is concerned, as is most of Hill's later work, with the paradox of coexistent free will and predestination (that though God knows what one will do, one is nonetheless free to do it), 'this | Augustinian-Pascalian thing about seeking | that which is already found' (*TL* CXXV, p. 276). As its title suggests, the play also considers the relationship between imagination and reality ('Call me fantasist | lately assigned to reality' (*SC* 2. 70, p. 465)). Calderón de la Barca's play contends that life is a dream in that it is a distorted prelude to the everlasting life after death, an infancy of one's existence. Accordingly, tautologies abound: the king (whose name, Basilio, is itself tautological, deriving from the Greek βασιλεύς (*basileús*), meaning *king*) dreams that he is a king ('[s]ueña el rey que es rey'); and dreams are, as one might expect, dreams ('y los sueños, sueños son').[59]

One reason for tautologies like these may be the desire to remember, to repeat in order not to lose something of value. In *The Orchards of Syon*, '*La vida es sueño*', a phrase that Rowan Williams calls the work's 'repeated burden', is always associated with the speaker seeking knowledge, forgetting, or remembering.[60] There is the doubled reference in the fifteenth poem:

> *La vida es sueño*? I ought
> to read it, before they say I haven't.
> Memory proves forgetting. [...]
> *Poiesis* a sufficient act; I almost
> forgot to say this. Otherwise
> the transient ever-repeated dream,
> the all-forgetful. *La vida es sueño*
> or something other. Other, that is, than death.
>   (p. 365)

Williams's critical meditation on this poem goes a long way in expounding what Hill is saying but omits the profound connection of tautology to remembering: '*Poiesis* is what makes the dream other than death, not just a repetition [...]; it does so by what I earlier called taking responsibility for what we know, owning our words as gestures towards the abiding Syon that continues to make speech both possible and doomed to the saving imperfection of always having more to say'.[61] Having more to say may imply a lack of time or a lapse of memory (which Hill at times makes much of: 'forgetting [...] almost forgot [...] all-forgetful'). But Hill's later work is full of remembering and repeating others' words. If the formulas that express truth, as Wittgenstein has it, are tautological, then it is surely fitting

Dead ends   67

that such formulas be remembered and repeated verbatim.[62] Hill even expresses the thought tautologically: 'Memory | finds substance in itself' (*OS* XIV, p. 364); 'let what is | speak for itself' (*OS* XVIII, p. 368). A related thought, which precedes a quotation (and the word 'infantile'), emerges in *Expostulations on the Volcano*: 'Thinking is repetitious so invent' (p. 680). Inventing (or, following that word's etymology, finding) the thoughts of others can be a remembrance that is not circular rhetoric.

This remembrance, when it happens, is cause for benediction:

> Perverse
> to persever: the Orchards of Syon
> not just any mirage. Bless poetics
> if this is what they are. *La*
> *vida es sueño*—see, I remembered!
>
> (*OS* XXV, p. 375)

The anagram in the first few words here, anagrams being a different kind of reiteration, indicates something about tautology. Since, according to Ecclesiastes 1.9, the 'thing that hath been, it is that which shall be; and that which is done is that which shall be done; and there is no new thing under the sun', it is perverse to persever: perverse simply to carry on making (which is the meaning of *poiesis*) without an end in mind.[63] Hill's restated end is the Orchards of Syon, 'not just any mirage' but a specific ideal, rooted in human history and understood by Hill to be a worthwhile end for poetry. This end is restated because it must be restated in order to preserve it (*preserve* being the third word ghosted in the letters of *perverse* and *persever*).[64]

The tautologies here are restatements of what is to be retained, of truths that remain, though time has passed, and though many have misunderstood them:

> Here are the Orchards of Syon, neither wisdom
> nor illusion of wisdom, not
> compensation, not recompense: the Orchards
> of Syon whatever harvests we bring them.
>
> (*OS* LXVIII, p. 418)

The repetitions, like the puns, like the turns of Hill's language, are attempts to find reconciliation in balance, in evenness. Extremities are ruled out: 'neither wisdom | nor illusion of wisdom' (this coming in the final lines of the work, perhaps a relation of 'Do not | mourn unduly' in its first lines).

When Hill gives the conditional benediction, 'Bless poetics | if this is what they are' (*OS* XXV, p. 375), he wishes to make an equation between his vision of poetics and poetics as 'they are'; he also wants to equate poetics with his own work.[65] He would like to say 'this is what they are' with the

68 Geoffrey Hill and the ends of poetry

proper force of the word *is*. For Wittgenstein, *is* is the central word of the tautology:

> In the language of everyday life it very often happens that the same word signifies in two different ways—and therefore belongs to two different symbols—or that two words, which signify in different ways, are apparently applied in the same way in the proposition.
>
> Thus the word 'is' appears as the copula, as the sign of equality, and as the expression of existence; 'to exist' as an intransitive verb like 'to go'; 'identical' as an adjective; we speak of *something* but also of the fact of *something* happening.
>
> (In the proposition 'Green is green'—where the first word is a proper name and the last an adjective—these words have not merely different meanings but they are *different symbols*.)[66]

The complexities, and also the simplicities, of Wittgenstein's philosophy are outside the purview and capacity of this book; but, because Hill quotes him on tautologies, passages such as the above merit attention. In the Preface to the *Tractatus*, having already admitted falling 'far short of the possible', Wittgenstein asserts nonetheless that 'the *truth* of the thoughts communicated here seems to me unassailable and definitive'.[67] The definitive word *is* is 'the sign of equality' and 'the expression of existence': the statement of something's existence, for Wittgenstein, depends on its being called equal to something else. The statement comes about through the combination of two '*symbols*', whether these are different words or the same word used differently. Wittgenstein's notion of statements of truth precludes singleness, requires a doubling.[68] The last sentence of the ninety-fourth poem of *The Book of Baruch* comes to mind: 'Words attract words as trouble attracts trouble and yet, to succeed, we must ditch all safeguards; and see and think and speak double' (*BBG* 94, p. 43). The sense of this verbal attraction, associated directly with 'trouble', is not positive and does not indicate a clarifying of meaning or faithful 'expression of existence'. This sentence's tautologies are indeed troubled: the doublings of 'words' and 'trouble' are not measured and measuring but merely accumulative, suggesting a process grown somewhat out of control.

The distinct troubles of the reconciling, tautology-making *is* are not lost on Hill. Indeed, they become associated directly with Wittgenstein in a late poem:

> I can tell you this, though; Poetry's not
> Imitation. Parallel worlds may better—
> Discontinuities—matter ignites matter—
> The mutual abruption: such our thought,

Workable grammar matching thrust to shove.
Syntax as coitus. Call Original Sin
Freedom being what it is (not Wittgenstein
Though something like him). Under and above,

Scattering bright (Donne). Angels and nematodes.
Even if in sex only, one can say
I will and yet my will does not obey.
Augustine's not all right stuck in his codes.

(*TT* 18, p. 895)

In this poem of 'matching', the Aristotelian notion of art as an attempted tautology of life is immediately dismissed: 'Poetry's not | Imitation' (though the capitalisation of 'Poetry' to match the line-beginning 'Imitation' confers a kind of equal weight on the two words). The second sentence here, with its own mirroring 'matter ignites matter' among its '[d]iscontinuities', gets unbalanced and lost in its own syntax. (The following sentence seems to pass comment on its impulsive obstreperousness: 'Syntax as coitus.') It seems a victim of what Hill then calls '*Freedom being what it is*'. It is significant and ironic that this tautological formulation fails even to be reconciled to Wittgenstein, of whom the phrase reminds Hill. It does not equal but only approximates; it is just 'something like him'. In addition, the phrase may reconcile the word *freedom* with itself; but it does not make the verb '*will*' in the penultimate line match up to its own replication as a noun.[69] The will for the non-tautological consummation of sex presents an 'abruption' of what one may '*will*' in a colder, more sober state – perhaps a state like Augustine's, once sex-driven but later striving for a higher equilibrium in 'his codes'.[70]

The unmanageable weight of *is* burdens the last poem in the first section ('The Argument') of *Scenes from Comus*:

That weight of the world, weight of the word, is.
Not wholly irreconcilable. Almost.
Almost we cannot pull free; almost we escape

the leadenness of things. Almost I have walked
the first step upon water. Nothing beyond.
The inconceivable is a basic service;

Not to be too Parnassian about it;
And not to put to strain their erudition
(I mean the learned readers of J. Milton);

And weight of the word, weight of the world, is.

(*SC* 1. 20, p. 430)

70   *Geoffrey Hill and the ends of poetry*

For all this balancing, one may notice another quirk concerning capitalisations: namely that this poem's are inconsistent. The last five lines all begin with majuscules, even though the precedent set by the preceding poems appears to dictate that three of them (the seventh, eighth, and tenth) should not. It may be argued, speciously, that the very letters begin to bespeak the weight of their words near the end of this poem, with 'Parnassian' and 'J. Milton' also taking on some bulk. Ultimately, though, it is an editorial oversight, of which there are remarkably few in *Broken Hierarchies*. What may explain it is that the poem has been revised since the original publication of *Scenes from Comus* in 2005. In the earlier version, the last five lines properly begin with majuscules: 'The inconceivable is a basic service. || Hyphens are not-necessary for things I say. | Nor do I put to strain their erudition— | I mean, the learned readers of J. Milton. || But weight of the world, weight of the word, is.'[71]

This difference – particularly the influence of that 'But' instead of the later version's 'And' in the last line – shifts the weight of 'is'. On the earlier version, Ricks comments:

> Weight of the world and weight of the word are distinguished without being posited as altogether distinct. Had the apothegm ended with *are*, they would have been more differentiated. Are they one and the same, as *is* might insist? Yes and no. Or might it be that they are two and the same?[72]

Tautologies render things two and the same. They are linguistic balances that seem to defy the weights and workings of language, 'the leadenness of things' from which one can 'almost [...] escape'. But the first line of this poem, even more so than the last line, puts a heavier weight on *is* than on the not altogether distinct weights of *world* and *word*: 'That weight of the world, weight of the word, is.'[73] It could be read as a fragment, which simply points to, even calls on, '[t]hat' word, *is*. One can imagine it in the vocative: '*Is*, weight of the world, weight of the word'. It is the balance of *is* that makes those weights, the weights of reality and its expression, '[n]ot wholly irreconcilable'.[74]

It is easy to read the first and last lines of this poem from *Scenes of Comus* as fragments, since many precede them in this first section, 'The Argument'. Eleven of the section's twenty poems begin with the word 'That': 'That we are inordinate creatures'; 'That *marriage is a hieroglyphic*'; 'That I mean what I say, saying it obscurely' (*SC* 1. 2, 1. 12, 1. 13, pp. 421, 426, 427). The phrasing appears to borrow from titling practices; *is*, or any verb, is missing but implied: *The Argument is: That....*[75] In this last of twenty poems attempting to make the argument, the clearest verb unqualified by 'almost' occurs in this poem's sixth line: 'The inconceivable is a basic service'. And the inconceivable is what *is* reaches for, what the tautology

Dead ends

71

reaches for: a perfect equation of words with themselves, which is indeed 'Parnassian' and would 'put to strain' anyone's erudition.

And yet, in the very next poem: 'How heartening it is when it goes right— | the moment of equipollence, a signal' (*SC* 2. 1, p. 431). The 'it' is both poetry and life, word and world; and it going 'right' is directly linked with 'equipollence'. The principal sense of this word in the *OED* is 'Equality of force, power, or signification'; the second, specific to '*Logic*', is 'equivalence between two or more propositions'.

In this first poem of *Scenes from Comus*'s second section, entitled 'Courtly Masquing Dances' (with the subtitle '*nello stile antico*', or, *in the old style*), there is a level of focus on conversion, opposition, and equipollence entirely appropriate to a dance. They make do with the awkward weights of words' dance, though it may be with 'one hip | acting up, strung on a wire' (*SC* 2. 1, p. 431). The balancing act continues in the subsequent poems. These are the second poem's first three lines:

> Indebtedness is resolved by paying debts,
> strangely enough; justice, not metaphysics;
> custom, restitution, setting to rights and rest.
>
> (*SC* 2. 2, p. 431)

This setting to rights does not quite sit right; metrically, it juts out of the blank verse it most resembles; and the characteristic fragments do not carry a great sense of sonic, semantic, or etymological equivalence. But Hill, as he suggests, pays debts 'strangely'. Here he bookends lines with related words, the latter words drawn out of the former: 'Indebtedness' and 'debts' in the first line; 'restitution' and 'rest' in the third.[76]

The latter pair is especially significant. For Hill, the connection between 'restitution' and 'rest' is profound. Only when things are set right, made just, can there be rest from the word or the world. In *The Book of Baruch* he writes: 'Restitution is the burden of what I am about' (*BBGJ* 25, p. 11). This is why the making-equal of tautology is so closely linked to the desire for consummation: if the end is not one of restitution, there can be no final rest.

Shakespeare's sixty-sixth sonnet, on which Hill comments at length in his first lecture as Oxford Professor of Poetry, balances imbalances along its lines, stringing together tautologies in prolonged desire for such rest:

> Tyr'd with all these for restfull death I cry,
> As to behold desert a begger borne,
> And needie Nothing trimd in iollitie,
> And purest faith vnhappily forsworne,
> And gilded honor shamefully misplast,
> And maiden vertue rudely strumpeted,

> And right perfection wrongfully disgrac'd,
> And strength by limping sway disabled,
> And arte made tung-tide by authoritie,
> And Folly (Doctor-like) controuling skill,
> And simple-Truth miscalde Simplicitie,
> And captiue-good attending Captaine ill.
>   Tyr'd with all these, from these would I be gone,
>   Saue that to dye, I leaue my loue alone.[77]

The column of bare conjunctions, the painful litany of 'And's, in enumerating the injustices of life, is by itself an act of mourning: it mourns that language's incessant attempts to make things equal only ever end with the same old inequalities. Nothing seems to be in proportion; a fourteen-line poem comes to sound, and feel, longer. The *is* of the equable tautology does not appear; the repeated imbalances are instead stuck with past participles, which end eight of the lines. The couplet breaks from the repetition only to repeat the sonnet's first four words: 'Tyr'd with all these'. In a flourish of rhetoric, the poem feigns tiredness even with itself as it comes to its end. The first and thirteenth lines arrive at subtly different responses to the tiredness: 'for restfull death I cry' is, if not an infant's cry, conceivably speechless; yet at the same time it is not only an active response but also a clever introduction to the verbal cries of the succeeding lines. On the other hand, 'from these would I be gone' is a wish truly tired out by these intervening lines; it is conditional and passive; where 'for' aspires to movement, 'from' aspires to withdrawal. But the poem is saved from pessimism, from redundancy, by the unexpected '[s]aue' of the last line. Why would it be undesirable, in this speaker's case, to die? Because death would be not merely imbalance but severance; reconciliation cannot take place without two. The 'I' of the last line, feeling unworthy of his 'loue', which is both a person and the whole unequal world, concludes that the greater injustice would be to 'leaue [...] alone', to break irremediably what he wishes to repair.

To this sonnet Hill applies the words of R. P. Blackmur, not about Shakespeare but about 'the poetry of Eros', in which 'the experience comes very near becoming thought': 'This is one of the great examples of tautology: where things become their own meaning: which is the condition of poetry—however great or narrow the selection of experience may be.'[78] The notion of things becoming their own meaning – and the added claim that this is the condition of poetry – appeals to Hill because his poetry is so involved not only with tautology but with the end. For a thing to become its own meaning is for it to reach its end, its consummate purpose. The tautology, at its most intentional, tries to make a word at rest with itself, to restore the relationship of its connotative distinctions and contradictions.

Dead ends 73

(At times it even blurs the distinctions: 'The river the forest, the river is the forest, | the forest the river' (*SC* 2. 3, p. 432).)

It is hard not to hear Blackmurian reverberations in a description found later in the Courtly Masquing Dances: 'Something towers and stoops to its own mind | exactly; it is good merely to sense this' (*SC* 2. 59, p. 460). The *meson* of Hill's repeating figures establishes a ground for prayer, for words that strive to transcend; Hill's intrinsically 'even' tautologies aspire to be these transcending words, to be prayers in themselves. The towering and stooping 'Something' of the poem above, which has a mysterious sway over the fox that traverses the same poem 'like a swift perfect image of itself', may point to the only being, God, who would be capable of such a return.

Tautologies, pleas

This precipitates at last a return to the 125th section of *The Triumph of Love*. As the above examples show, Hill's tautologies express the 'mute desire' for a consummate evenness. They do so through the evocation of recurring dreams and visions; the remembrance of quotation; and the emphasis on equation, typified by the use of *is* in *Scenes from Comus* 1. 20. Having now examined some of the tautologies and tautological tropes that appear in Hill's poetry, it remains to consider more fully how they may be called a kind of prayer.

The 'mute desire' of the infant, as heard in Tennyson, is expressed by crying. ('Tyr'd with all these [...] I cry'.) The infant is estranged from the world by speechlessness; and is joined to it by tautologically imitating the speech of his parents, of the world. The child learning to speak is not expected to soliloquise extemporaneously but to repeat a word or two. The tautology, in Hill's poetry, can be read as an infant's cry – tentatively, and not without complication, to God – for reconciliation. In this respect it is a cry to language's origin and its end, whose name, at least in English ('I AM THAT I AM'), is a tautology, and whose existence is manifested in an incarnated Word.[79]

> Estrangement itself
> is strange, though less so than the metaphysics
> of tautology, which is at once *vain*
> *repetition* and *the logic of the world*
> (Wittgenstein). Some of its moves—I mean
> tautology's—call to mind chess-moves: moves
> that are in being before you—even as
> you—make them.
>
> (*TL* CXXV, p. 276)

74   *Geoffrey Hill and the ends of poetry*

The ordering repetitiveness of the tautology, as here, is intrinsic to language, which means that no attempt to introduce something utterly disordered, or utterly new, in language can be successful; linguistic chaos is about as possible as a chess-move outside the board. The conundrum performs itself in *Oraclau | Oracles*: 'Disorder cannot be brought to the point | Which is the point of disorder. [...] This is a strange country, the words foreign' (*O* 51, p. 757). Wittgenstein is no stranger to the idea: 'We cannot think anything unlogical, for otherwise we should have to think unlogically. [...] The truth is, we could not *say* of an "unlogical" world how it would look.'[80] For Hill, the tautology's logicality is intrinsically connected with his sense of its 'metaphysics', that is, its transcendental logic. The wilful tendency towards redundancy in the passage quoted above – the three instances of 'moves' in two lines; the awkward parenthesis in 'before you—even as | you' – is strange, awkwardly coherent, and metaphysical.[81] If, in Wittgenstein's words, '[e]*ssence* is expressed by grammar', then it may be said that Hill, who in the poem above perceives tautologies as having or pointing towards a metaphysical grammar, or 'God's grammar', uses his tautologies to enquire into God's essence.[82]

Such an enquiry need not be haughty or presumptuous. The tautology used to seek knowledge of God may be instead like a child's repeated cry to hear a song again. The 'grammar' of the song can be described as metaphysical because it is beyond linguistic explanation but open to a primal and profound kind of understanding. The tautology's plea to God is like that of another Blakean child:

> Piping down the valleys wild
> Piping songs of pleasant glee
> On a cloud I saw a child.
> And he laughing said to me.
>
> Pipe a song about a Lamb;
> So I piped with merry chear,
> Piper pipe that song again—
> So I piped, he wept to hear.[83]

Beyond this 'Introduction' the *Songs of Innocence* are full of such pleading children, and full of beautifully propitiating tautologies. Their echo is resonant in Hill, who writes both early and late poems about Blake, and whose first published critical piece is a review of *Jerusalem*.[84]

The first of the *Mercian Hymns* ends in this Blakean vein: '"I liked that", said Offa, "sing it again."' (*MH*, p. 83). In *The Triumph of Love* CXXV, and repeatedly throughout Hill's later work, pleas are addressed, as though filially, to Mary, the Mother of God:

Dead ends 75

I have been working towards this for some time,
Vergine bella. I am not too far from the end
[...]
Vergine bella, forgive us the cunning
and the reactive, over-righteous
indignation, the self-approving
obtuse wisdom after the event,
our aesthetics and our crude arrangements.
I have been working up to this. The Scholastics
mean more to me than the New Science. All
things are eternally present in time and nature.

(pp. 276–77)

The first two lines here begin the poem; the next eight finish it.[85] Hill returns on himself by restating the name by which he addresses the Blessed Virgin and repeating that he has been working 'towards' (or 'up to') 'this'.[86] He also makes a rhetorical *conversio*, including his own work in the accusations of 'over-righteous | indignation', 'aesthetics', and 'crude arrangements'. The final sentence here, too, is a near-replication of a quotation earlier in the poem from Thomas Bradwardine's *De Causa Dei*, a text Hill follows by enquiring into the things of God.[87]

Earlier in the poem, Hill outlines 'Bradwardine's thesis' in a way that, by tracing a circular pattern ('springs from [...] returns to'), recalls the Scholastic schema of *exitus* and *reditus*, which imagines an orbit of procession from and return to God.[88]

> The intellectual
> beauty of Bradwardine's thesis rests
> in what it springs from: the Creator's grace
> *praecedentum tempore et natura* ['Strewth!
> 'already present in time as in nature'?—ED]
> and in what it returns to—our arrival
> at a necessary salvation.

(p. 277)

And directly before dealing with Bradwardine, Hill invokes Coleridge to make still grander claims for tautologies:

> Though certain
> neologisms—Coleridge's 'tautegorical'
> for example—clown out along the edge,
> τὸ αὐτό enjoys its essential being
> in theology as in logic.

(p. 277)

Neologisms, like tautologies, are here presented as linguistic performances, designed to attract attention, though it may be God's attention: they 'clown out'. The tautology, expressed here in Greek, enjoys its 'essential being' in theology because, by its attempt to arrive at metaphysical truth, it is elevated to a distinct affinity with God, the 'essential being' whose essence, for Scholastics such as Bradwardine, is existence (thus revealing 'essential being' itself as a tautology, at least etymologically or with regard to God).[89]

Coleridge's neologism presents the tautology as a kind of allegory: the 'Tautegory', he writes, 'is the consummate symbol'.[90] The tautegory may be defined as a kind of synecdoche, a symbol that symbolises something so perfectly as to be equated with it: the eye, by this logic, is a tautegory of vision.[91] Elsewhere, Coleridge acknowledges the tautology's heightened metaphysical status. He writes of

> that Law of Passion which inducing in the mind an unusual activity seeks for means to waste its superfluity – in the highest & most lyric kind, in passionate repetition of a sublime Tautology (as in the Song of Debora).[92]

For Coleridge, the expression of Scripture is not subject to the fallenness of language but 'consubstantial with its subject'; this is the aim of the tautology.[93] Wordsworth's accompanying note to his poem 'The Thorn' claims that 'repetition and apparent tautology are frequently beauties of the highest kind'.[94] This idea of the 'sublime Tautology' may occur to Coleridge, Wordsworth, and Hill because of the association, which goes back to Augustine, of the tautology with the very nature of God:

> You recall that one and the same Word of God extends throughout Scripture, that it is one and the same Utterance that resounds in the mouths of all the sacred writers, since he who was in the beginning God with God has no need of separate syllables; for he is not subject to time.[95]

What Augustine calls the 'Word of God', homologous throughout Scripture, can be likened to Bradwardine's 'image or form of Truth', which also exists outside time, and which is an 'Utterance' of God inseparable from God Himself ('God with God').[96] This tautology in God's nature, understood as a Trinity, a threefold expression of the same divine essence, is what sustains the strange distinction when Hill writes of 'the real being God or, more comprehensively, Christ' (*TL* XXXVIII, p. 250).

This is not to say that Hill's tautology is perfectly secure in the above understanding of God – or even at home with any understanding of Christian orthodoxy. After rewording Bradwardine's 'good news' in *The Triumph of Love* CXXV, Hill moves to 'its correlate', the 'bad' news: 'everlasting torments of the non-elect; guaranteed | damnation for dead children unbaptized' (p. 277). The notion that the child's cry, his own, might be ultimately ignored, is anathema to Hill; he condemns it as an expression of doctrinal 'Policy', with that word's looming majuscule and whiff of

Dead ends 77

tyranny. He names (for the first but, as we have seen, not the last time in his poetry) the blessed exceptions to this rule, whose beginnings were also their ends: 'The Church's first martyrs, the Holy Innocents, | unbaptized Jewish infants, surrogates | of the Jewish child we call our Child-King' (p. 277). After briefly disputing the notion of being '*baptized in blood*', Hill returns to the Innocents, crying in their muteness, unmoving symbols of purity and truth: 'Still, there they are: crying shame to the cant, | the unending *negotium*, | the expediencies, enforcements, and rigged evidence' (p. 277).

The child's cry is persistently 'there', if sometimes quiet, in Hill's tautologies. Its plea resounds against the 'cant' and the 'unending *negotium*', the world too loud, too full of itself and its lies for mute desire.[97] Hill's tautology is a prayer, a 'passionate repetition', to repeat Coleridge's words, that seeks divine truth through the divine trace in itself. Tautology is a connecting thread in Hill's poetry, bringing together several desired and attempted ends: to reconcile love with loss (as in the early 'Coplas'); to reconcile remembering (memorising, memorialising) with forgetting (as in *The Orchards of Syon*); to reconcile the muted 'child-soul' (*TL* II, p. 239) with the loquacious adult (as in *Mercian Hymns*, *The Triumph of Love*, and *The Book of Baruch*); and, finally, to make of language a true balance, a sufficiently even ground on which to stand before oneself and before what transcends one. 'So with a well-contrived | Thread of myth with which I have lived | Long enough, I embroider my prayer | Of forgetfulness layer by layer; | Petition petition, | Cross of station' (*LIV* XLI, p. 725).

Of the paradoxically sleepy end of Robert Frost's 'Stopping by Woods on a Snowy Evening', 'And miles to go before I sleep, | And miles to go before I sleep', Blackmur writes that the 'analogies multiply and deepen into surds of feeling', which is perfect not least because *surd* derives from the Latin *surdus*, meaning *mute*.[98] Very near the end of *The Triumph of Love* (CXLVIII, pp. 285–86), there is, in the repetition of a translated phrase from Leopardi, a similarly deepening lullaby. The repeated words, which end the poem, themselves serve to describe the transcendent shift that Hill's tautologies at their best successfully enact, a shift within language that makes its regrettable dead ends, its child's cries, into their own unexpected remedies:

>   What
> ought a poem to be? Answer, *a sad*
> *and angry consolation*. What is
> the poem? What figures? Say,
> *a sad and angry consolation*. That's
> beautiful. Once more? *A sad and angry*
> *consolation*.

3

Rhymes

Expectations

Gifts to those altars. Ye shall offer no
Strange incense-effect. Nor ponder rhyme late.

But Hill does ponder rhyme late; and the fact that he does indicates something about what rhyme is for him.[1] Hill, as he believes he should, offers the 'antiphonal voice of the heckler' (*CCW*, p. 94) within his own work, doing what he declaims against, and declaiming against what he is doing.[2] He ponders rhyme not only in this first poem of *The Daybooks*, the last published sequence of his life, but throughout, and often. It is striking that Hill describes the heckler's voice as 'antiphonal': a musical counterbalance, related to 'counterpoint', Hopkins's word.[3] Why, though, does the antiphonal voice have to be a heckler?

The last essay in Hill's *Collected Critical Writings* might help one to calculate an answer:

> What he [Yeats] is looking for in his late writings is a unit comprising antithetical, even mutually repellent, forces, in which the calculated is at one with the spontaneous: integration that is simultaneously diremption; a kind of monad of linguistic energy, a unit of speech itself becoming a Yeatsian form. (*CCW*, pp. 577–78)

Of Hopkins's commentary on Whitman, Hill writes: 'This may not be good Whitman criticism but it is good Hopkins criticism' (*CCW*, p. 106). The same may be said for Hill's commentary on Yeats here. The linguistic 'unit' in question is Hill's through and through. For Hill, the antiphony of words is never happy; there is insufficient 'energy' in happiness. Instead it ought to be a hostile meeting of perfect opposites.[4] His only criticism of the dual characteristics of 'aloof hauteur' and 'haughty rabble-rousing' in Yeats's last book are that these represent 'a difference that is complementary rather than antithetical' (*CCW*, p. 578). The heckler must be in the poem to avoid complacency, or monotony, in its voice. The heckler's presence provides the 'integration that is simultaneously diremption'; it is a 'repellent' force, introduced to deter presumption and elision and laziness. As Natalie Pollard writes, 'in *Speech! Speech!* the concluding stanzas concede to its audience's expected criticisms, as well as rudely heckling, speaking over and competing with, *your* hostile reception of the poem' (Pollard's emphasis; '*you*' signifies that imagined audience or reader).[5]

What Hill censures in language is a too easy joining of things. It is a meeting of what might be expected to go together; it is, or can become, reflexive. Rhyme, with its capacity for easy mellifluousness, has been heard suspiciously for centuries and by many. Wallace Stevens deprecated the facile rhymes in his own early work:

> In the 'June Book' I made 'breeze' rhyme with 'trees,' and have never forgiven myself. It is a correct rhyme, of course – but unpardonably 'expected.' Indeed, none of my rhymes are (most likely) true 'instruments of music.' The words to be rhymes should not only sound alike, but they should enrich and deepen and enlarge each other, like two harmonious notes.[6]

The 'expected' coupling is easy because it requires little thought; and unpardonable because even what thought is involved in bringing together the coupling's sounds is too easily ignored through overfamiliarity. Thomas Campion complained, in 1602, that rhyme simply made it too easy to be a poet: 'the facilitie & popularitie of Rime creates as many Poets, as a hot sommer flies'.[7] Stevens, with his quotation marks around 'expected', likely has Pope's famous censures of the 'tuneful Fools' in mind,

> Who haunt *Parnassus* but to please their Ear,
> Not mend their Minds [...],
> While they ring round the same *unvary'd Chimes*,
> With sure *Returns* of still *expected Rhymes*.
> Where-e'er you find *the cooling Western Breeze*,
> In the next Line, it *whispers thro' the Trees*[8]

Stevens has found himself guilty of the very rhyme Pope satirises here. The expected rhyme, though it may superficially please the ear, cannot, as Pope suggests, mend the mind; that is because it affects to bring together what is already a happy couple. The expected rhyme is a fraudulent invention: it purports to have found a living connection between words where it has found the remains of one. In its complacency, it comes to a false sense of conclusion.

Hill has a less than easy relationship with rhyme, though his prose barely indicates how profound or how troubled it is. He is, unsurprisingly, aware of Campion's, and Milton's, objections: 'That which Milton disdains as "the troublesom and modern bondage of Rimeing" is troublesomely binding as much because it is easy as because it is hard.' He goes on to notice what

80 *Geoffrey Hill and the ends of poetry*

Campion calls the 'childish titillation of riming' in that poet's own work: 'His own lyrics from the four books of ayres, in which "loue" rhymes with either "moue" or "proue", or their moods and cognates, in song after song, obligingly demonstrate his contention' (*CCW*, p. 322). Consequently, when Hill rhymes, it is always with a degree of scepticism, or mistrust. Even the 'no' and 'late' which end the lines from *Expostulations on the Volcano*, in the epigraph above, are rhymed with one eye (or ear) open, their respective partners in rhyme being 'nose' and 'Hamlet'.

Rhymes with Eliot and Tate

To avoid undue mistrust here, I shall briefly delimit my terms. The word *rhyme* will refer, here, to end-rhyme, unless otherwise stated.[9] This is both because it corresponds with the tradition of end-rhyming English poetry that Hill inherits and seeks to augment and because the rhyme that stands out visually and aurally at the end of a line is fundamentally important to a discussion of ends in poetry. In George Saintsbury's words, 'on the whole, rhyme should come at the end of something'.[10] To cover 'several varieties of rhyming practice that are related to yet do not fulfill the canonical definition' of end-rhyme, I use the term *half-rhyme*.[11] *Autorhyme* will denote end-rhymes of the same word.[12]

In his essay 'Why Rhyme Pleases', Simon Jarvis discusses what he deems 'the currently respectable definitions of rhyme'. For many of these definitions, in Jarvis's words, 'sheer sound replay is not enough'.[13] Instead, an organising principle must be at work. Jarvis quotes an unpublished fragment from Hugh Kenner, in which rhyme is described as 'the production of like sounds according to a schedule that makes them predictable'.[14] One need not read 'predictable' in the pejorative sense of Stevens's 'expected' to find this a rather strange and old-fashioned perspective on rhyme, especially in light of Eliot's century-old reflections:

> The rejection of rhyme is not a leap at facility; on the contrary it imposes a much severer strain upon the language. When the comforting echo of rhyme is removed, success or failure in the choice of words, in the sentence structure, in the order, is at once more apparent. Rhyme removed, the poet is at once held up to the standards of prose. Rhyme removed, much ethereal music leaps up from the word, music which has hitherto chirped unnoticed in the expanse of prose. Any rhyme forbidden, many Shagpats were unwigged.
>
> And this liberation from rhyme might be as well a liberation *of* rhyme. Freed from its exacting task of supporting lame verse, it could be applied with greater effect where it is most needed. There are often passages in an unrhymed poem where rhyme is wanted for some special effect, for a sudden

Rhymes

81

tightening-up, for a cumulative insistence, or for an abrupt change of mood. But formal rhymed verse will certainly not lose its place.[15]

In Eliot's formulation, rhyme need not be 'predictable'; indeed, its use in modern verse, as he saw it then, was best to be unpredictable, its effects 'sudden' and 'abrupt'. Eliot's notion of rhyme here brings to mind what Hill calls the 'change of time-signature' that Hopkins observes and praises in Wordsworth's 'Ode: Intimations of Immortality' (an observation Hill in turn praises as 'a major contribution to the study of rhythm' in *CCW*, p. 91). It is a musical change, a 'magical change' in Hopkins's words; and one that, for Eliot, occasional (as opposed to predictable) rhyme is capable of achieving.[16]

Eliot's conception of the rhyme being liberated is not quite as novel as it might sound; Milton, whose ambivalent relationship with rhyme is well known, wrote *Lycidas*, with its irregular, improvisatory rhyme scheme, which includes unrhymed lines, and has been considered 'a piece of blank verse carefully equipped with rhyme for the purpose technically speaking of providing it with a lyrical vehicle [...], completely devoid of regularity, and [...] intended to be so'.[17] I mention *Lycidas* here because Hill's first modernist master, not Eliot but Allen Tate, refers to Milton's poem as the 'model for the irregular rhyming' of 'Ode to the Confederate Dead', Tate's best-known poem.[18] Hill says that this poem 'struck' him

> like a bolt from heaven; overnight I became a modernist. The beauty of Tate's 'Ode' is that it succeeds in a double economy – the classical economy of the rhymed strophes, the minimal subsistence-economy of the broken unrhymed couplets. [...] I knew simply and immediately that this was the structural presence, the technical daimon, that would show me how to shape my own work so that its built-in strengths would prove self-sufficient, something quite distinct from an adolescent's yearning for self-expression. At that time I had not read Eliot's 'The Function of Criticism' and 'Tradition and the Individual Talent' but in being so abruptly and so profoundly affected by Tate's poetry, I was – as I now realize – receiving the Eliotian stresses at second hand.[19]

These Eliotic (or Eliotian) stresses may be presumed to have influenced rhyme in Hill's poetry, since so much else in Eliot has influenced Hill, and especially since they can be seen to have influenced Tate's ode. It is surprising, therefore, that not one of Hill's poems uses rhyme in the way Eliot describes. Of the very few instances of occasional rhyme in Hill's poems – if, going against Kenner's definition, we are to employ common sense and call such instances rhyme – none could be termed a 'sudden tightening-up', a 'cumulative insistence', or an 'abrupt change of mood'.

In one of the clearest examples, 'Annunciations', the occasional rhymes sound like internal half-rhymes. That the rhyming words end their respective

82 *Geoffrey Hill and the ends of poetry*

lines is not quite an accident; but it is the only thing that confirms them as rhymes. This, incidentally, shows the other problem with Kenner's definition of rhyme ('the production of like sounds according to a schedule that makes them predictable'): that it counts sound alone as rhyme's criterion and characteristic, ignoring its position on the line. Here is the end of the second, and final, part of 'Annunciations':

> Our God scatters corruption. Priests, martyrs,
> Parade to this imperious theme: 'O Love,
> You know what pains succeed; be vigilant; strive
> To recognize the damned among your friends.'
>
> (*KL*, p. 40)

The punning in both parts of 'Annunciations', what Hugh Haughton calls its 'unrelenting play on telling ambiguities', provides the real twist in the poem's meaning.[20] In his note to the poem in *The Penguin Book of Contemporary Verse: 1918–60*, Hill writes: '[Love] struggles to be heard in the last two lines but is twisted by a pun.'[21] The rhymes do not strengthen the effect. Two consecutive lines in the first part end with 'spawn', and the first three lines of the second part end 'grind/redeemed/assured'. The half-rhyme 'love/strive' is the fullest rhyme in the poem. But it is a let-down. On the page it draws the eye to the two surrounding lines to seek a pattern; but the pairing of 'martyrs' and 'friends' does not create a 'telling ambiguity'. The words do not 'play' on each other as 'scatters' plays on 'corruption' or as 'recognize' plays in the last line as to enable at least two wholly contradictory readings. The 'love/strive' half-rhyme, though it highlights the ironic distance of the speaker from both true loving and true striving, is, along with 'martyrs/friends', strangely superfluous. It does not swing or sharpen the double-edged linguistic sword that is at the heart of the poem. This is a surprise: not only does Hill's poetry rarely use occasional rhyme, one of the chief characteristics of the Tate poem that sparked Hill into poetic life; but, when he does use it, it lacks that life. Hill's precision, especially in matters of form, allows little and reluctant room for occasional rhyme. His best rhymes follow neither Eliot's suggestions nor Tate's example.

Odd symmetries

Hill's explicit pondering of rhyme is found in the late work, particularly *The Daybooks*, but, before examining that, it is worthwhile to consider the occurrence and nature of rhyme in his work from the beginning.

In his first collection, *For the Unfallen* (1959), with two exceptions, every poem has a rhyme scheme (the least 'expected' being that

Rhymes 83

of 'Canticle for Good Friday' (p. 20)).[22] *King Log* (1968) experiments more. 'Annunciations' (p. 40), as we have seen, rhymes only occasionally, while the 'Locust Songs' (pp. 41–42) move from autorhyme ('The Emblem') to rhyme ('Good Husbandry'), and finally to half-rhyme ('Amherst' and 'Shiloh Church, 1862: Twenty-three Thousand'), words' consonances gradually coming apart. As in *Tenebrae* (1978), there is a combination of rhymed and unrhymed poems in *King Log*; apart from the first collection, there are no others in Hill's oeuvre that present this mixture.

After *The Mystery of the Charity of Charles Péguy* (1983) and the first three *Hymns to Our Lady of Chartres* (which appeared in the *Collected Poems* of 1985), none of Hill's poems is rhymed for twenty-five years (*Oraclau | Oracles* being released in 2010). In *Broken Hierarchies*, *Hymns to Our Lady of Chartres* is dated '1982–2012'. *Ludo*, the next collection in *Broken Hierarchies* that is rhymed, is dated '2011', while *The Daybooks* is dated '2007–2012' (pp. xi, xiii). The difference between the rhymes of 1982 and those of 2012 is surprisingly obvious. The rhymes in the new *Hymns to Our Lady of Chartres* (of which eighteen out of twenty-one were written after 1985) are immediately more conspicuous, more readily approximate, often eccentric. Half-rhyme has become the clear norm. Some approach anagrams rather than rhymes: 'even? No/Byron' (3, p. 158); 'country/century'; 'Shoah/chaos' (9, p. 161).

Ludo, the reintroduction to rhyme in *Broken Hierarchies*, is an explosion of sonic effects; it reads like a release of pent-up rhyming energy, replete with internal rhyme and eye rhyme, displaying Hill's 'knack of half-rhyme' (which half-rhymes with 'Kenelm', 'psalm', and 'realm' in the twenty-sixth poem (p. 613)).

In *The Daybooks*, hosts of odd pairs appear. Since it is at the beginning of *Expostulations on the Volcano*, the first of the six *Daybooks*, that Hill playfully proscribes pondering rhyme, it will suffice to ponder (only a selection of) examples from that sequence: 'diffidence/dividends' (4, p. 632); 'place/neo-Nazi'; 'particle/inarticulate' (5, p. 633); 'I dis-/ideas' (6, p. 634); 'cover/*Ivre*' (15, p. 646); 'Merman/harmon- | y'; 'complexity/dyslexia' (18, p. 646); '*topoi*/top' (24, p. 652); 'perhaps it is/rhapsodies' (25, p. 653); 'to me/tome' (31, p. 659); 'decoded/ode-aid' (34, p. 662); 'heartfelt/kurtweillt' (35, p. 663); 'here I/hero' (36, p. 664); 'hand-en- | twined/abandonment' (38, p. 666); 'rue this/issue' (39, p. 667); 'once col-/dance school' (40, p. 668); '*Liturgy*/shit-purge, I' (44, p. 672). The second daybook, *Liber Illustrium Virorum*, presents fifty-four poems in an unusual form: each comprises twenty-one iambic lines, rhymed ABABCDDCDDEEFFGGHHICI.[23] The final C-rhyme in this sequence is so distant that it is seen (if seen at all) more than heard, particularly because it is often a half-rhyme (take, for

84   *Geoffrey Hill and the ends of poetry*

examples, 'joy/equity'; 'foreigners/ignorance'; 'rhyme/metrum'; 'portrays/ Patria's'; and 'stigma/phlegm').[24]

This 'knack of half-rhyme' is not merely a playful characteristic of Hill's late poetry but one that troubles it, and displays its troubles. It is strongly related to, but distinct from, the pun and the oxymoron; it is also inextricable from Hill's 'antiphonal voice of the heckler'. Half-rhymes, and the other approximate rhymes sounded off in Hill, are distorted or disturbed echoes; one mocks the other; one is heckled by the next; the latter is shackled by the former. Hill notes in Wilfred Owen, famed as a successful half-rhymer, his recognition 'that half-rhyme, which sustains order and expectation while maintaining its scepticism of them, also draws bidding power into the extremities of the lines' (*CCW*, p. 529). But one less obvious relation of Hill's late rhyme-heckling is a collection I have failed to mention, one of only two that eschews – at least ostensibly – the boundary of the line break that makes rhyme on the page possible: *Mercian Hymns* (1971). The other is *The Book of Baruch by the Gnostic Justin* (2019), which employs a similar (but not the same) form; and is similarly laced with autobiography.

Unease about the ease of rhyme seems built into the form of *Mercian Hymns*; the *Hymns* may not constitute 'grunts and shrieks' against the inadequacy and impropriety of rhyme, but appear to place it, distrust-fully, aside.[25] Nevertheless, in one of his notebooks for the collection, Hill experiments with rhyme for an 'Offa's Dynasty' poem (a title that does not appear in the final list of contents for *Mercian Hymns* in either the 1985 *Collected Poems* or *Broken Hierarchies*, which lists vary in one other respect).[26] The poem has not been completed but looks as though it is approaching a sonnet.[27] Elsewhere in the notebook, Hill indicates that he is considering a rhymed section of *Mercian Hymns*.[28] In the end, internal rhyme emerges – obliquely, but surely, at times even joyfully. If one were to construct a contradistinctive argument, for the prevalence of occasional rhyme in Hill's unrhymed poetry, *Mercian Hymns* would not be the place to begin but *The Book of Baruch*: its 'off-rhyme and internal rhyme', as described on the book jacket, are so widespread and often so obvious as to be unmissable.[29] Some rhymes in *The Book of Baruch* are endearingly, amusingly egregious: 'A great poet who fixates on landed estates is of course Yeats' (*BBGJ* 76, p. 35).[30] But *Mercian Hymns* has its own quieter rhymes. The poems appear as prose; Hill has called them 'versets of rhyth-mical prose', a designation somewhere between precise and precious.[31] The first two poems in particular are so complexly and conspicuously laden with echoes that they might sound as though they rhyme. The first (p. 83) could even be lineated to look like a rhyming poem – not only occasionally but in its entirety:

King of the perennial holly-groves,	A
the riven sandstone: overlord of the M5:	A
architect of the historic rampart and ditch,	B
the citadel at Tamworth, the summer hermitage	B
in Holy Cross: guardian of the Welsh Bridge	B
and the Iron Bridge:	B
contractor to the desirable new estates:	C
saltmaster:	D
money-changer:	D
commissioner	D
for oaths:	C
martyrologist: the friend of Charlemagne.	E
'I liked that,' said Offa, 'sing it again.'	E

The sweetest ring of rhyme in the poem comes at the end. It is a ring of antiphony – Offa providing an unexpected counterpoint as the 'antiphonal voice of the heckler' – and it is also a ring of repetition; Offa's simple and joyfully rhyming request to hear the hymn once more is a summary of the simple joy of rhyme, of hearing a sound at once changed and 'again'. Offa here is like the child in one of Chesterton's essays who, unlike the draughtsman who delights 'that his lines of charcoal, light and apparently loose, fall exactly right and in a perfect relation', delights merely 'in the fact that the charcoal makes marks of any kind on the paper'.[32] There is a tension in *Mercian Hymns*, as in Hill's poetry generally, between this 'simple pleasure' – the 'simple, sensuous, passionate' sort that Offa has here – with the 'sophisticated' pain of self-distrust and distrust of words, the going in fear of easy and 'expected' elision.[33]

In Hill's version of Henrik Ibsen's *Brand*, though each line has a rhyming counterpart, there are instances of extremity and heckling antiphony in the rhyme that point to this tension, at times stretching to paradox. Brand's castigation of Einar's happy-go-lucky piety at the end of the first Act finds such perfectly chiming opposites that Einar is moved to ironic tribute:

> [BRAND:] Sin if you dare, but have the grace,
>   at least, to be fulfilled in vice. [...]
>   A middling this, a middling that,
>   never humble, never great.
>   Above the worst, beneath the best,
>   each virtue vicious to the rest.
> EINAR: Bravo, Brand! Have your say,
>   just as you will. I'll play
>   'Amen' in the right place.[34]

The neat oxymoronic construction of Brand's speech – 'sin' and 'grace'; 'grace' and 'vice'; 'this' and 'that'; 'humble' and 'great'; 'above' and

86   *Geoffrey Hill and the ends of poetry*

'beneath'; 'worst' and 'best'; 'best' and 'rest'; 'virtue' and 'vicious' (all of which appropriately encircle the negating doublings of 'middling' and 'never') – finds its main performative charm in the rhymes, the last, full-rhyming couplet in particular being clearly and dramatically end-stopped as well as brightly sonorous. Einar responds in a markedly less elevated and more enjambed verse-style. Adrian Poole writes: 'Hill here seems to highlight what is only a hint in Ibsen by making Einar's consciously ironic applause retrospectively "place" the theatricality of Brand's speech.'[35] Brand does not expect a more powerful opposition than his own to be heckled into his soliloquy by Einar, as at the very end of the play he does not expect to be interrupted, his words both cancelled and consummated, by a heavenly Voice. That Voice, which may be God's, responds to Brand's desperate final questions about the role of human will in salvation by saying, 'He is the God of Love', which could signify either condemnation or consolation (or indeed both).[36]

In the final lines of Act Three, the lines with which Hill finished work on the play, at the terrible moment in which Brand and Agnes 'sacrifice' the life of their son Alf, the antiphonal rhyme reaches its starkest contrast.[37] It is a simple, even expected, meeting of opposites, which finds itself powerfully recharged by the severity of the dramatic situation:

> AGNES [*lifting the child high in her arms*]:
> That which you have dared
> to ask of me, O Lord,
> I dare to give to Heaven.
> Accept my sacrifice.
> Now lead me through your night.
> > *She goes into the house.* BRAND *stares blindly for a moment; bursts into tears; clasps his hands over his head and throws himself down on the steps.*
> BRAND [*crying out*]:
> Lord, grant me light![38]

Though the spouses are both addressing God, they are responding to each other in rhyme. The insistence on the possessive ('my sacrifice', 'your night') was more obvious in the first published edition of Hill's text, in which Brand's words fit the trimeter rather than disturbing it with an urgent dimeter: 'O Lord, grant me your light!'[39] In the later edition, the doubling of Agnes's 'my sacrifice/your night' is echoed not only by the paired requests for personal help (Agnes's 'lead me' and Brand's 'grant me') but by the concluding couplet, 'night/light'. Night is possessed, light desired.

Keeping the marital context of this rhyme in mind, the significance of it for Hill is difficult to overstate. Here is Hill on Henry Vaughan:

Rhymes 87

In Vaughan's poetry a rhyme which occurs with striking frequency is 'light: night', or 'night: light'. Here, too, basic mechanics assume ontological dimensions. S. L. Bethell has remarked on 'the light-darkness opposition in Vaughan', but such a rhyme embodies more than an opposition. It is a twinning: a separation which is simultaneously an atonement ('Wise *Nicodemus* saw such light | As made him know his God by night') and a conjunction which exacerbates the sense of divorce ('And by this worlds ill-guiding light, | Erre more then I can do by night'). In the pairing 'light': 'night' and 'night': 'light' itself, there is nothing remarkable except its bookish obviousness. [...]

It is reasonable to ponder what it is that draws or impels Vaughan towards this rhyme. Is it an instinctual gravitation, or a conscious application to the sensory material of his brother's and other hermetical writers' theories about magnetism and sympathetic attraction? Or is it that Vaughan has so concentrated his mind on the abstract eschatology of 'light-darkness opposition' that he is relatively or even totally indifferent to the monotonous uninventiveness of his word-finding?

[...] Vaughan's metaphysics, his bookish but spontaneous and sincere paradox of 'deep, but dazling darkness', or his persistent 'light-darkness opposition', working through the rhyme-pattern, poem after poem, transforms contingency itself into a density, an essential 'myre', though without the accidents of language thereby being denied or tamed. Each time the words 'light': 'night', 'night': 'light' chime they reassert 'merest coincidence' even while they are affirming a theological or hermetic theorem as clear and absolute in Vaughan's mind as 'the square of the hypotenuse'. (*CCW*, pp. 323–26)

Between the first and second passages quoted above, Hill cites without interruption no fewer than twenty-six occurrences of the rhyme in question in Vaughan's poetry. These words begin to indicate the general weight of rhyme in Hill's own work. As with the pun, Hill is interested in the 'twinning' of language, the way it 'seems to shuttle between two realms [...] without relinquishing touch with either'.[40] One might, after Hill's manner, quibble with 'theorem' as a description for the relationship evoked between 'light' and 'night' in Vaughan, a relationship which seems both less meticulously reasoned and more sensuous than one might expect a theorem to be.[41] Instead, the light–night opposition does what all rhyme does: it 'transforms contingency itself into a density'; it brings out the substance of accidents. Though less formulable than Fibonacci numbers, about which Hill develops a late fixation, such rhymes as Vaughan's represent truly mysterious and oxymoronic alignments, '[o]dd symmetries holding the mind at gaze' (*TT* 1, p. 889).[42]

Impossible rhymes

Rhyme, for Hill, is the archetypal example of such alignments. It is how words are 'mystically espoused' (*HOLC* 7, p. 160). The paradox in Hill's poetry is that rhyme's mystical espousal, a representation of consummation and itself a verbal consummation, is found to be both impossible and inevitable.

Both of these adjectives require some expansion. In *Gravity and Grace*, Simone Weil gives this fragment, as part of a larger one: 'Poetry: *impossible* pain and joy'.[43] Two such contradictory but simultaneous reactions to the same reality could be said to constitute Hill's rhyme. Similarly, and continuing the connection with Weil, Robert Macfarlane proposes that the 'two periods into which it is now conventional to divide Hill's poetry might usefully be characterised as the epoch of gravity and the epoch of grace'.[44] Hill's rhymes might be divided into those of impossibility and those of inevitability. But, as with gravity and grace, the two always coexist; what distinguishes the supposed types is the emphasis. The pairing I put forward shares at least two other characteristics with that of gravity and grace in Hill: the first is the significance of faith, which in Hill's poetry is the 'pain and joy' of seeking reconciliation before and with God; the second, as I implied in the previous section, is that the shift of emphasis can be traced to the same point in Hill's chronological line. The character of Hill's rhyme changes, after the three Chartres hymns of 1985, from one that accentuates consummation's impossibility to one that accentuates its inevitability. Accordingly, in looking at the impossible rhyme, I will consider two poems from Hill's early work, 'The Pentecost Castle' and 'Ovid in the Third Reich'; and in looking at the inevitable rhyme, I will consider a handful of poems from the last book collected in *Broken Hierarchies*, *Al Tempo de' Tremuoti*.

The epigraphs of 'The Pentecost Castle' give a strong foretaste of the poem's subjects, its tangled contradictions. The first is from Yeats: 'It is terrible to desire and not possess, and terrible to possess and not desire.' The second is another of Simone Weil's impossibilities: 'What we love in other human beings is the hoped-for satisfaction of our desire. We do not love their desire. If what we loved in them was their desire, then we should love them as ourself' (*T*, p. 115). Both recall Plato's definition of eros in the *Symposium*: the child of poverty and possession.[45] 'The Pentecost Castle' is more concerned with the first than the second part of the Yeats quotation: it is about desiring and not possessing, and consequently desiring not to desire. What the poem's narrator is seeking seems contradictory: he wishes both for an everlasting love with an ever-lost woman and for loss of desire in death. But these are two halves of the same desire: for consummation in love. And, just as the narrator cannot be 'mystically espoused' either to the human object of his desire or to Christ, the words, too, struggle to be reconciled in rhyme.

In 'The Pentecost Castle' rhyme is not predictable; it emerges only at times and, where it does, its pattern differs. It accrues gradually, and goes on to fade and reappear continually. The first rhymes of the poem are in the third section, and immediately their framing sounds fit into the short, song-like lines. There is nothing abrupt about their entrance; it is as though the poem has rhymed from the beginning, at which point one might look back to the first two sections and find the autorhymes of repeated lines ('not to go | not to go') in the first and the repeated stanza ('Down in the orchard') in the second (p. 115). The next rhymes, in the third section, also include autorhymes:

> You watchers on the wall
> grown old with care
> I too looked from the wall
> I shall look no more
>
> (p. 116)

Both rhymes are walls, affording the poem an audible structure, but both are audibly flawed. The autorhyme 'wall/wall' is mimetically restrictive; its echo is dull; it does not feel like a completion. The half-rhyme 'care/more' also sounds incomplete: it asks for 'more' even while the last line insists on the opposite. Even in the final stanza of this section, when the fourth 'wall', as it were, is broken, the clang of the rhyme does not fulfil the poem's or the reader's desire for consummation:

> you keepers of the wall
> what friend or enemy
> sets free the cry
> of the bell

The ultimate rhyme in the poem, replacing the expected autorhyme, is 'bell', which is indeed a cry set free; but this bell is as ambiguous as the wall preceding it. The reader has travelled from the 'road' of the first section to the 'orchard' of the second; and perhaps this is the orchard wall, and yet it sounds more like a prison wall. The desire that the bell announces, and that the wall obstructs, is to be beyond both bell and wall. It is to be set 'free', both from the spiritual and erotic pilgrimages the narrator describes and from the seeming incompatibility of these two pilgrimages. These physical realities cannot match up to the desire and therefore fail themselves to match. 'Bell' does not truly answer 'wall', just as the 'cry' of words does not truly answer the desire behind it. The rhymes enact the desire–fulfilment

90   *Geoffrey Hill and the ends of poetry*

paradigm in the epigraph from Yeats. When the rhymes are found they are left behind; and then they are sought again.

In the fourth section, there are only two rhymes, half-rhymes of religious frustration: 'stone/resurrection' and 'tears/altars' (p. 116). The 'stone' rolling away to reveal 'resurrection' chimes only imperfectly; such impossible reconciliations are all Hill's narrator has (as in the sixth section of 'Funeral Music': 'I believe in my | Abandonment, since it is what I have' (*KL*, p. 52)). Even the 'tears' of candle wax falling on 'altars' cannot distribute the words' emphasis correctly: they symbolise the pain of longing, but only through a distancing abstraction; and the stresses of these two half-rhyming words, one masculine and one feminine, are unbalanced. The separateness of what ought to have been put together is everywhere apparent.

The sections in which rhyme is strongest are the twelfth and thirteenth: they represent moments of desperation, in which the rhymes feel forced together, first in autorhyme and then in bold repetitive sequences. The last two stanzas of section twelve find difference even in the starkest reiterations:

> faithful to my desire
> lost in the dream's grasp where
> shall I find you everywhere
> unmatched in my desire
>
> each of us dispossessed
> so richly in my sleep
> I rise out of my sleep
> crying like one possessed

(p. 119)

Though the ends of the lines may match, one need only travel backwards to find them somewhere, somehow, 'unmatched', as in the parallels of the first and fourth lines. The second line's 'where', ending the line like a question, is answered unhelpfully by 'everywhere'; the 'us' who are 'dispossessed' contracts to 'one possessed'; and the reality 'in my sleep' is never encountered 'out of my sleep'.

In the thirteenth section, the linguistic likenesses ('likening us our unlikeness') are so close as to be confusing. The proximity of the words evokes frustration in their very sound: how can it be that consummation is tangibly near and yet unattainable? The effort prompts paradoxes:

> Splendidly-shining darkness
> proud citadel of meekness
> likening us our unlikeness
> majesty of our distress

> emptiness ever thronging
> untenable belonging
> how long until this longing
> end in unending song
>
> and soul for soul discover
> no strangeness to dissever
> and lover keep with lover
> a moment and for ever
>
> (p. 119)

Everything here speaks of impossibility. Seven of the first eight lines are self-contained oxymorons, which the last four are left to attempt to resolve. Seen another way, the first six lines describe a single oxymoron – the consummation so eminently imaginable that it can be experienced vicariously, but that is in reality impossible – and the next six lines explain what this vicarious experience looks like. In both the second and third stanzas, a kind of linguistic Occam's razor seems to be in action: the rhymes pare themselves away to their end or goal. In the first, 'thronging', 'belonging', and 'longing' are completed by 'song', which rhymes with the first syllables of each but cuts off the gerund. The gerunds move and are longing; but 'song' simply is, in nounal perpetuity. Similarly, in the second stanza 'discover' loses a phoneme and becomes 'dissever', which in turn drops a syllable to find 'lover', and this is at last reduced to 'ever'. Both 'song', in this context, and 'ever' are atemporal; and the eight lines above are all about the desire for atemporal consummation. The rhymes, not building to that end but dismantling to it, find themselves nevertheless having to start over again. The section seems to find conclusion with its 'end in unending song', but even this phrase is lengthened, as though in painful answer to the question 'how long', into another stanza. Here the 'strangeness to dissever' is constantly evident, as one rhyming word dissevers and estranges itself from another.

What is expressed about the impossibility of consummation in 'The Pentecost Castle' would not be possible without its fitful rhymes, its incomplete reconciliations of sound. Imperfection is consciously evoked in the poem, notably in the half-rhymes and absences of rhyme; but the poem's technical imperfection is another of its paradoxes. With its simple language and song-like cadences, 'The Pentecost Castle' is one of Hill's most effectively artless poems; the effort that has gone into this artlessness can be seen in one or two stiff spots. The pain of this particular fault might be why, for example, in *Broken Hierarchies*, the eleventh section of the poem has been significantly revised from the original. Though the revision itself says something about the anguish of the struggle for final reconciliation, there

92   *Geoffrey Hill and the ends of poetry*

is a loss of effect in the revised expression of it. Here is the original eleventh section:

> If the night is dark
> and the way short
> why do you hold back
> dearest heart
>
> though I may never
> see you again
> touch me I will shiver
> at the unseen
>
> the night is so dark
> the way so short
> why do you not break
> o my heart
>
>   (*CP*, p. 142)

And here the version in *Broken Hierarchies*:

> If the night is dark
> and the way short
> if the way you take
> is to my heart
>
> say that I never
> see you again
> touch me I shall shiver
> at the unseen
>
> the night is so dark
> the way so short
> yet you do not wake
> against my heart
>
>   (p. 118)

The desperateness, in the original poem, of 'why do you not break | o my heart', the way it asks life to imitate art, for the heart to break (that is, for the sorrow at last to break free and be allowed to overwhelm the speaker, removing the added torment of that sorrow's inexpressibility) as truthfully and clearly as a line breaks (or as day breaks), is lost in the revision. (The fourteenth section speaks similarly (p. 119): 'in grief desiring | still to grieve'.) The newer version's 'yet you do not wake | against my heart' also plays on the unbroken 'night' at the beginning of the stanza and is a subtle reminder that the lover being addressed has died. It is a death so close to the speaker's 'heart' that it is like his own death, as in the second section

(p. 115): 'Down in the orchard | I met my death'. Unlike the original, in which heartbreak is desired and not achieved, the revision, more straightforwardly and expectedly, achieves that heartbreak by its indication of the lover's death, which derives part of its meaning from the line break (in that it is a death that has come 'against' the desire of the speaker's 'heart').

Hill, when revising the poem, knew that the original had already been widely read and analysed; in removing the desire for, and impossibility of, heartbreak in the original eleventh section and replacing it with the arrived-at heartbreak itself, the later version detracts from the effective meaning of 'The Pentecost Castle' as it was, a poem of and about incompletions. More than this, for anyone who has read and remembered the original version (as I had when I read *Broken Hierarchies*), the new words seem shadowed by the old ones in a way not dissimilar to the effect of rhyme. For such a reader the meanings of the first words colour those of the next, as one sees 'break' in the dimness of the 'dark' that precedes it, or as 'wake' emerges from the night's 'dark' in the new version.[46]

In W. K. Wimsatt's influential essay 'One Relation of Rhyme to Reason', he argues that the 'characteristics of Pope's couplet, as opposed to Chaucer's, are, of course, its closure or completeness, its stronger tendency to parallel, and its epigrammatic, witty, intellectual point'.[47] In the course of the essay, Wimsatt is even less equivocal about his preference for Pope's kind of rhyme. Rhyme's capacity to draw together unexpectedly the senses of words, Wimsatt finds, is accentuated in Pope's rhyming of words that are different parts of speech, or that have different syntactical functions. In referring to the feeling of 'closure or completeness' in Pope's rhymes, Wimsatt, as his footnote shows, has in mind the relative frequency of end-stopping in Pope. Clearly, 'The Pentecost Castle' is not written in heroic couplets; but the considerations of 'closure' and 'completeness' are germane. 'The Pentecost Castle', with its total absence of punctuation (except perhaps, as Ricks has suggested, the half-punctuating hyphen), does not appear to be end-stopped; and yet, often, it is.[48] The lack of punctuation, rather than making every line seem to run on, has the opposite effect in this poem; the enjambments come as surprises. After the '[s]plendidly-shining darkness | proud citadel of meekness' and so on in the thirteenth section, it is startling to find the very word 'end' breaking the poem's end-stopping: 'how long until this longing | end in unending song'. Closure and completeness are ostensibly what this poem's rhymes aim to achieve; but their lack of punctuation, which results in a markedly different kind of end-stopping than Pope's, renders each section, and the poem as a whole, open-bordered and incomplete.

Despite that the poem has a lyric beauty to rival any in Hill's poetic corpus, and despite its strong 'tendency to parallel', it is irreparably imperfect, half-rhyming where it seems to want a full rhyme, unclear where

94 *Geoffrey Hill and the ends of poetry*

it desires most to be clear. This is a characteristic with which the poem engages, but which is ultimately unwanted. The final two stanzas, in section fifteen, express and exemplify this:

> beloved soul
> what shall you see
> nothing at all
> yet eye to eye
>
> depths of non-being
> perhaps too clear
> my desire dying
> as I desire

(p. 120)

Rhyming in this poem is generally hazy, floating in and out and approximating in a dreamlike way; but there is something also exhausted about these eight lines. Firstly, the poem's final two rhyming words have already been used as such: 'dying' in section fourteen (as well as 'death' twice in section two and once in section nine, 'dead' in section nine, and 'die' in sections nine and fourteen) and 'desire' once in section eight and twice in section twelve (as well as 'desiring' in section fourteen). Secondly, the last stanza here, comprising the rhymes 'being/clear/dying/desire', chimes too much with the fourteenth section's middle stanza, in which the lines break on 'dying/live/desiring/grieve'. The effect evokes the desperateness and persistence of the longing; and represents the many attempts to satisfy it. This recurrence of sounds and thoughts is a neighbour or a distant cousin of rhyme, but it is not, on the whole, gladly received: it renders the rhymes even weaker than they intend to be and, for the first time in the poem, they begin to sound boggy, struggling to support the weight of their concerns.

Hill's discussion of the word 'cry' in the poetry of John Crowe Ransom might begin to indicate what 'The Pentecost Castle' attempts, especially in its final sections:

> The word 'cry' and its derivatives form what is perhaps the most frequently recurring group of words in his poetry; and the 'cry' is peculiarly a 'monad' in which the physiological 'speaks out' for the ontological. It is the minimal utterance, which, paradoxically, is expressive of a multiplicity of psychic nuance: abandonment, affirmation, solitude, communion; as the medieval mystics perceived in their teaching on the efficacy of monosyllabic prayer. The particular characteristic of the reiterated cry is arguably its power to transform pure spontaneous reflex into an act of will. (*CCW*, p. 142)

'The Pentecost Castle' certainly has the character of 'monosyllabic prayer' – its ninth and eleventh sections, for instance, are almost entirely monosyllabic – but the attempted transformation of the 'reflex' of its repeated cry 'into an act of will' is finally unsuccessful. The speaker realises that no human will is strong enough to cry things into being. The 'minimal utterance, which, paradoxically, is expressive of a multiplicity of psychic nuance: abandonment, affirmation, solitude, communion' is powerfully realised in 'The Pentecost Castle'; but these nuances remain a 'multiplicity'. They are not reconciled, not rhymed together into an ontological 'monad'.

The recurring cry in the final section, attempting to distil the poem's thought, also risks nebulousness. What Hill calls 'perhaps too clear' in the final stanza is anything but. The metaphysical abstraction of 'depths of non-being' – somewhat like those he praises in Ransom's prose – arrives out of a different vocabulary from that of the rest of the poem. Perhaps it borrows from Eliot's 'Burnt Norton': 'Caught in the form of limitation | Between un-being and being.'[49] In Hill's case, it may help that 'non-being' is half-rhymed with 'dying'. The rhyme places the concepts together, as though to sort out their differences – and similarities. Non-being and dying would seem to be opposites. The notion of non-being, at least as it applies to human life, is only possible in a conception of life in which one's existence ends completely in death. Thus, the rhyme facilitates a reading of the stanza: that the frightening depths of the idea of non-being have come into 'too clear' a focus in the light of the speaker's 'dying' desire for divine (and erotic) consummation. But the abstruseness of the lines, and the frustrated awareness of the inability to speak with perfect lucidity, remain. The preceding stanza, also ambiguous, indicates as much: its second line might almost read 'what shall you say', since what is said in this poem about the impossibility of reconciling sacred and profane love is, particularly in this final section, both perfectly plain ('eye to eye') and perfectly opaque ('nothing at all'). The predicament described is reduced to a kind of philosophical formula in 'depths of non-being'. It is the poem's last and most strained attempt at a consummation, an attempt that may be 'too clear' in the speaker's mind but that is not clear enough in the listener's.[50]

Not only in 'The Pentecost Castle' but throughout Hill's poetry, the impossibilities of reconciling man with God, man with woman, and thought with poem, are bound together; a longing for one appears to imply or engender a longing for all. The advances and retreats of rhyme in the poem are so important to the expression of this longing that even two changes of rhyming words, as in the eleventh section, can alter the meaning, and the achievement, of the poem. Rhyme and revision in Hill, as I have implied, are both seeking to resolve the same impossibility.

Here, Hill's essay on Ransom is again relevant. Its title is 'What Devil Has Got into John Ransom?' It quickly transpires that the devil in question is that of 'ruinous rewriting', of 'compulsive revisions' (*CCW*, p. 127). And it is unlikely that Hill would pay such attention to this devilish trait

96   *Geoffrey Hill and the ends of poetry*

in Ransom if he had not noticed it in himself. The postscript of the first edition of *King Log* includes a revised version, subtitled 'An Attempted Reparation', of 'In Memory of Jane Fraser', a poem that appeared in *For the Unfallen*. In the notes, Hill writes: 'I dislike the poem very much and the publication of this amended version may be regarded as a necessary penitential exercise.'[51] The changes are surprisingly minimal; yet the poem's fourteen-year-old offences have clearly gnawed at Hill.[52] It is a 'penitential exercise' because it seeks an ethical reconciliation: even if it can never be perfect, Hill wishes to try to make up for what he considers the poem's most flagrant faults and deceptions.[53] The 'self-division and intestinal warfare of the ethical substance', a phrase from A. C. Bradley that Hill uses in the Ransom essay, is evident in all of Hill's poetic revisions – and in many of his rhymes.[54] The term 'ethical substance', itself borrowed from Hegel, is no less apposite to the discussion of the 'metaphysics of poetry' than to that of Bradley's 'metaphysics of tragedy' (*CCW*, p. 139). Because, for Hill, poetics are so implicated in ethics, he is pained by work that requires apology, that does not effect its own reconciliations. In such work, it is made clear that what rhyme cannot produce in the first place cannot be brought about by revision in the second place. In Knottenbelt's words, the poem offers 'the semblance of a quest or of a rite with a certain end'.[55] The pain and problem of the poem is that it ends in not mere uncertainty but inconclusiveness. Its two desires, for sacred love and for profane love, intertwine without meeting, without truly seeing 'eye to eye'. Its words, both rhyming and non-rhyming, are not 'mystically espoused' but irremediably separate.

Hill is well aware of the ethical failure of poems that enact a make-believe espousal of words, that use their rhymes to perform sham marriages. In this regard, throughout his early work, Hill distrusts the ease of poetry's elisions, in which rhyme is a significant instrument. The two stanzas that make up 'Ovid in the Third Reich', the first poem in *King Log*, convincingly illustrate the error of treating poetry's, and rhyme's, impossibilities as possibilities.

Before these two stanzas, though, there are two other stanzas in *King Log*, one prosaic and one poetic: the epigraphs, of the collection and of the poem. The first is part of a sentence from Francis Bacon's *The Advancement of Learning*: 'From morall vertue, let us passe on to matter of power and commandement ...' (*BH*, p. 37). The difference between this sentiment and that of the poem's epigraph, from Ovid's *Amores*, hints that the Ovid of the poem is not going to have a Baconian attitude to 'morall vertue'. It reads: 'non peccat, quaecumque potest peccasse negare, | solaque famosam culpa professa facit', which can be translated as: 'She does not sin who can deny her sin, and 'tis only the fault avowed that brings dishonour'.[56] In context, the speaker is entreating his lover not to confess her dalliances with others

Rhymes 97

but to allow him to 'enjoy a fool's belief' in her.[57] For this jocular Ovid to be dragged out of context and into the Third Reich might seem peculiar or even distasteful. But Hill appreciates that this advice to deceive is funny because it is true; and because it is true, it is also sinister. For Ovid's speaker, whose wit masks a void of 'ethical substance', words are fungible and serve merely practical (chiefly manipulative) purposes. He continues to his lover:

> What madness is this, to confess in the light of day the hidden things of night, and spread abroad your secret deeds? [...] Put on a better mind, and imitate, at least, the modest of your sex, and let me think you honest though you are not. What you are doing, continue to do; only deny that you have done, nor be ashamed to use modest speech in public.[58]

It is a stroke of invention, but in a sense no surprise, that Hill takes these recommendations and applies them to the poet himself.

Here is the dislocated Ovid's modest speech:

> I love my work and my children. God
> Is distant, difficult. Things happen.
> Too near the ancient troughs of blood
> Innocence is no earthly weapon.
>
> I have learned one thing: not to look down
> Too much upon the damned. They, in their sphere,
> Harmonize strangely with the divine
> Love. I, in mine, celebrate the love-choir.

(p. 39)

The technical and rhetorical poise of this poem, which steadies on its rhymes, allows it to sound perfectly unobjectionable. It is only the title that sheds light on the poem's 'hidden things'. With the title in mind, the reader can begin to perceive that the deceit of the speaker's effort to '[p]ut on a better mind' is revealed and subverted by the subtle conflations of its syntactical parallels, and most obviously of its rhymes. 'I love my work and my children. God': at first this appears to be a perfectly laudable list of priorities for a poet, or for anyone, in Nazi Germany. But it is no accident that the vague, tensile word 'work' comes first, before 'children', while 'God' is mentioned last and cut off on both sides by the full stop and the line break, grammatically isolated. He is made 'distant, difficult' by his position on the line. In the circumstances, the distance and difficulty of God for the speaker is ostensibly reasonable; but, followed by the suspiciously unemotional 'Things happen', the sentence's function as an equivocation and an excuse for complicity starts to become manifest. ('Things happen' anticipates 'September Song', which comes four poems later in *King Log*: 'Things marched, | sufficient, to that end' (p. 44).) Even the initial 'I love', looking back, assumes the character of an appeal to the reader's emotion, following the dishonest directions of *Amores*, and as insincere as its loves. The cut-off 'God' is rhymed with 'blood'. The rhyme, also 'distant, difficult', and distinctly unsettling in the context of the Third Reich, underwrites the poet: both words have ended up finishing their lines by default, having been pushed there, pushed as far out of the poet's conscious mind as possible (the words having been '[t]oo near', too close for comfortable thought); but, consequently, their off-key chime makes them stand out as extreme contradictions. The second rhyme is another dangerous parallel. 'Things happen' is, here, an eschewal of ethical responsibility; it is rhymed with 'earthly weapon'. Morality has been removed from the situation, and what is left is only the wielding of power over the weak, over those with '[i]nnocence'. The rhyme, another telling half-rhyme, is a demonstration of words' slipperiness and of their fragility under the pressure of authorial manipulation: the morally lax contingency of 'Things happen' is so easily reduced to the brutality of the 'earthly weapon'.

The question of what can be made to '[h]armonize strangely' is at the centre of this poem. The second stanza offers two more rhymes of contrast: 'down/divine' and 'their sphere/love-choir', in which 'their sphere' means the place of the 'damned'. These rhymes pair images of Heaven and Hell, claiming, in a Blakean fashion, a relationship of affinity and even mutual dependence between the two. But this is not the strange harmony that is in fact suggested by the lines. How can the damned be said to harmonise with God's love, and how can the poet be so sure that he belongs to a different 'sphere'? The answer is in the lack of a parallel word for 'damned' in the poem: no one is deemed saved; the sphere the poet calls 'mine' is unsubstantiated. The 'damned' here are not the spiritually damned but those damned, though innocent, by the regime. This is their strange harmony with God's 'Love', Christ, also damned though innocent. The speaker's 'sphere' is an insulated one, from which he composes harmonies for the 'love-choir' that are strange because falsely achieved. The fifth line on its own summarises his vantage point: 'I have learned one thing: not to look down'. He is like someone at a great height, with eyes closed, refusing to acknowledge the danger of falling.

Hill is painfully aware of this danger. The poet suffers an ethical fall by the very refusal to admit the possibility of falling (in this case, from the imagined 'sphere' of the poets' love-choir). The poet of 'Ovid in the Third Reich' chooses to remain stupefied by his own music. He dares not allow that some realities are, to the 'earthly' mind, incongruous; that some things cannot be forcibly harmonised. The rhymes in Hill that speak more clearly of inevitability than impossibility bear this lesson in mind. They attempt to avoid overlooking truth and resorting to 'beautification' and 'exaggerated

Rhymes 99

feeling'; but they accept graciously the mystical espousals, the données of language.[59]

Inevitable rhymes

In Hill's late work, and particularly in *Al Tempo de' Tremuoti*, the inevitable imperfection of rhyme is, as in his early work, admitted. The difference is that the inevitability of the rhymes themselves, the sheer fact that some words naturally rhyme with others, comes to be seen more vividly as a consummation in itself. (The word 'inevitable', including its relatives, appears just once in the poetry but twenty-six times in Hill's *Collected Critical Writings*.[60]) The coincidences of language, words' ever-surprising capacity to be reconciled and near-reconciled, 'held and set apart' (*TT* 17, p. 895), are considered at one with the contingencies of human life. In a late notebook, Hill quotes 'W. B. Yeats again: "our words must seem to be inevitable"'.[61] For Hill, life is uncompromisingly linguistic. At the end of life, in prayer, faith in the wedlock of language becomes paramount.

> Intractability of happenstance
> Reduced to final supplication: Mary
> Mediatrix, absolve my word-memory
> Uprisen in this late self-hallowing trance.
>
> (*TT* 19, p. 895)

Rhyme can be both a cause and an effect of 'word-memory'. Its connections can be as easily sought, and as difficult to leave behind, as memories. At the same time, it forges links in the hearer's mind that may seem, on the rhymer's part, automatic, even accidental. The danger of rhyme-as-reflex, of a too easy poetry, may be why Hill's speaker seeks absolution for such memory. Rhymes are caught up in the '[i]ntractability of happenstance', so much so that the rhyme of 'happenstance' is itself sleepwalking: 'trance'. But the etymology of the latter word, from the Latin *transire*, denotes a deeper sleep, meaning 'to go across'. If death is conceived as going across, then the dying are active rather than passive: going, not being pushed. That the trance is called 'self-hallowing' further suggests intentionality (since one usually has to mean to become holy). Hill's late rhymes demonstrate an acceptance of the going across from life's certainty to death's; but they also attempt to be, like the Blessed Virgin, a deliberate mediation between irreconcilable circumstance and consummating grace.

The thirtieth poem in *Al Tempo de' Tremuoti*, one of four that 'freely rewrite and adapt poems found in *Aleksandr Blok: The Journey to Italy*, trans. Lucy E. Vogel' (p. 939), appears, with its italicised confession of the

100   *Geoffrey Hill and the ends of poetry*

debt to Blok (and Vogel), to be going across its Sienese cemetery in a tran-
scending 'trance' of its own:

> *When—if—you brood: how our days are numbered*
> *And also fleeting, and are stalled in dread,*
> *Borne down by introspection, lift your head*
> *And count these graves, Siena's dead unnumbered.*
>
> *You may well ask, where are the eternal shades?*
> *I answer, here. The Sibylline mouthings*
> *For all their frenzy utter some true things,*
> *Christ's resurrection, the harrowing of the shades.*
>
> *Bear with what you are given. Given stone,*
> *The sculptor's chisel is our soothsayer.*
> *Live your life well, even when every prayer,*
> *Every prediction, has been turned to stone.*
>
> *There is such life foregathered on these tombs:*
> *A boy depicted with a bird, a flower.*
> *Here, with his documents, a man of power.*
> *A senex here, crutch-lurching to the tomb.*
>
> *My soul, be still, even as you strive and love;*
> *Neither urge onward nor yet hold me back.*
> *It will come soon enough, that stark*
> *Encounter* ˡ *with the certainty of love.*

(p. 900)

Apart from the first and fourth lines of each stanza, which rhyme on the
same word (allowing for *'numbered/unnumbered'* and *'tombs/tomb'*),
the middle pairings, too, have an air of ease, even predictability: *'dread'*
foreshadows *'head'*; *'mouthings'* turn out *'true things'*; *'soothsayer'*
produces *'prayer'*. Even *'flower'*, though semantically unattached, is an
aural augury of *'power'*. Only *'stark'* in the final stanza comes unexpectedly after *'back'*, the half-rhyme perhaps enough of a jolt to evoke the
predestined yet astonishing *'[e]ncounter'* in the last line. This encounter is
predestined precisely because of the rhyme. The consummation of divine
love is exactly as certain as that of the autorhyme. The autorhyme has
come four times already, and by the structure of the poem is bound to
come again. The penultimate line even offers the assurance: *'It will come
soon enough'*. Being bound, the autorhyme seems to bind with it love
itself into returning at the end of life. In the desire for stillness that applies
to both poem and poet, echoes are perceptible (not least in the use of the
same rhyme) between this final stanza (*'My soul, be still, even as you strive
and love* [...] *It will'*) and the final sentence of a poem in *The Book of*

Baruch: 'I do not want this to end but it will; be both transient and still' (*BBGJ* 79, p. 37).[62]

But is this assurance of the end not similar to the facile flexibility with reality, the inadequate interpretation of love, that Larkin observes with subtle irony at the spouses' tomb?

> Time has transfigured them into
> Untruth. The stone fidelity
> They hardly meant has come to be
> Their final blazon, and to prove
> Our almost-instinct almost true:
> What will survive of us is love.[63]

The implication being: whether we like it or not. But it is not only social convention that brings the dead couple into uneasy concord; it is the rhyme. What is 'almost true' is made so by an almost rhyme. The final 'love' strikes a subliminal false note, undercut by the half-rhyme with 'prove'. The rhyme, like most rhymes with 'love' ('moue' and 'proue' being among the examples Hill draws from Campion), is itself dead. The '*love*' in Hill provides its own certainty, rhyming with itself; his poem's 'stone fidelity' consists of '*stone*' perfectly following '*stone*'. The faithfulness is in language itself.

And yet this too is undercut, by a small cut of punctuation in the last line of Hill's poem. It is not '*that stark | Encounter with the certainty of love*' but '*that stark | Encounter ¦ with the certainty of love*'. Logan calls this mark a 'verticule'; but, taking a hint from Hill's *Ludo*, I will augment Logan's diminutive and call it a 'vertical'.[64] It is with the certainty of love's existence that the stark encounter will occur; but the cut of the vertical introduces an ambiguity as to whether that encounter will be with love itself. It is, after all, not for nothing that the 'prominent' anxiety of Hill's life was, in his words, 'about the fate of my own soul'.[65] The vertical here, an obstacle in the line that symbolises the difficult path from earth to Heaven, foreshadows the thirty-fifth poem of *Al Tempo de' Tremuoti*, the penultimate stanza of which faces more bluntly the inevitability not of salvation but of judgement:

> And some will fáll ¦ oút of the hands of God.
> And others not. Yet others wanly fade
> With their own time immoderately made;
> Love's truth still unconfigured to accord.

(p. 902)

The vertical, itself both ascent and descent, gives the line an added meaning: firstly, some will fall out of the hands of God; and, secondly, the fact that some will fall to damnation (because of man's free will, which subject provides the opening meditation of the collection) is out of God's hands.

102 *Geoffrey Hill and the ends of poetry*

The rhyme expresses the pain of the fact in microcosm: it is as natural and straightforward as a full rhyme that some 'made' free by God will freely 'fade' from Him. And it is an uncomfortable discord of reality that God does not reconfigure things according to our idea of harmony – that 'God' does not completely accord with 'accord'. The sounds of words cannot be altered by will; despite the mind's incalculable invention, rhymes (and other accords) cannot, in the end, be desired into existence. The 'God/accord' half-rhyme is as inevitable, and as poignant, as the 'fade/made' full rhyme. The stanza represents not the outward reconciliation of discordances into one transcendent and perfect harmony, but the inward reconciliation of what is perfect with what is not. These rhymes recognise grace in the very midst of gravity.

The first line of the first poem in *Al Tempo de' Tremuoti* offers a 'signal' of what may be the collection's most prominent theme: 'A signal pre-election to free choice' (p. 889). The second and third words present a preliminary ambiguity: 'signal pre-election' could be either noun-and-adjective or adjective-and-noun, either a marked predestinedness or an indication before election. But regardless of one's reading of the line, the subject of predestination – the idea that God has already ordained the fate of souls, whether saved or damned – is hard to miss. In particular, what appears to interest Hill, both in this collection and throughout his late work, is the paradox between this idea and the concomitant Christian doctrine that God has granted man free will, 'free choice'. Ambiguity on this point is heightened later in the same poem: 'Grace condescending to things framed in chance', where there is fruitful doubleness in both 'condescending' (with good or ill will?) and 'framed' (truly or falsely?).

But it should be noted that Hill's interest in the paradox is artistic before it is theological. The rhymes in *Al Tempo de' Tremuoti* are precisely framed in chance. To quote again Charles Tomlinson: 'The chances of rhyme are like the chances of meeting— I In the finding fortuitous, but once found, binding'.[66] This is, as Hill puts it, the sense of being '*held by your own words*' (p. 899). There is a constant play, in *Al Tempo de' Tremuoti*, with the inevitability of rhymes, in that they fall predictably and without exception in the same scheme (ABBA) through ninety-five multi-stanzaed poems, but do so with frequently unfamiliar conjunctions of rhyme-words: the pre-election of the scheme meets, perhaps even seems to enable, the free choice of the rhymes themselves. (Something similar may be behind the description, in *The Book of Baruch*, of 'the genius-struck donkey work of rhyme' (*BBGJ* 65, p. 29).)

Hill's avoidance of the expected rhyme is not necessarily accompanied by a search for the unexpected rhyme. It is not that Hill tasks himself to make every rhyme noticeably peculiar, though some are: 'conjecture/trajectory'

Rhymes   103

(11, pp. 892–93); 'journey/Siena' (31, pp. 900–1); 'seen as/*scenas*' (37, p. 904); '*magma/phlegm*' (43 (f), p. 910); 'discovery/*Convivio*' (56, p. 916); 'arbitrary/nature' (66, p. 920); 'Montale/Ely' (75, p. 924); 'window/leggenda' (78, pp. 925–26); 'arisen/*Úranus*' (85, p. 929); 'mascara/massacre' and 'anarchy/*Monarchia*' (90, p. 933). The pairings here are representative of Hill's unusual, but recurrent, ways of finding rhymes in his late works. In addition to the more straightforward full rhymes and half-rhymes, there are collocations between languages ('seen as/*scenas*'); eye-rhymes of a sort ('*magma/phlegm*'); anagrammish jumbles ('arisen/*Úranus*'); and words already tied by etymology ('anarchy/*Monarchia*'). Nor is it that Hill is attempting in every case to make direct semantic connections between rhyme-words, though many do so – and some make one wonder why one was not expecting them, such as the almost too fitting 'Eden/forbidden' (78, pp. 925–26). It is instead that Hill's inevitable rhymes are performing a more refining function, allowing the expression of new or latent connections by eschewing overfamiliar sound-patterns and, connectedly, overfamiliar thought-patterns.

The last two stanzas of the first poem of *Al Tempo de' Tremuoti* help to illuminate the effect of the collection's rhyme scheme:

> Or in alert idleness build a tower
> Of Fibonacci numbers where each term
> Stands in its self-reflection as the sum
> Of those two that precede it: the sunflower
>
> Head is packed with them, and the pine cone,
> Odd symmetries holding the mind at gaze
> Unlike that solipsism of the maze
> Circling the focus of self will alone.

The Fibonacci numbers invoked here provide a suitable comparison, a rhyme being made up of (at least) two words that are nevertheless distinct from it. It quickly becomes clear that the symmetries of rhyme in this scheme are as inevitable as the numbers that fall one after the next in the Fibonacci sequence. Yet to avoid predictability, these rhymes must be '[o]dd' symmetries, odd enough to hold 'the mind at gaze' at the mysteries of sound–sense conjunction, as traceable and as incomprehensible as the sunflowers' heads.

The ninety-fourth poem of *Al Tempo de' Tremuoti* feeds into the last poem so obviously as to make them seem two parts of a whole. It prepares the ground for conclusion with amusing bluntness: 'I am finished' (p. 935).[67] The relationship between what is given (predetermined) and what is made (chosen freely) is returned to: 'Genius | Thriving on various expediencies, | Like Petrarch's shattered and sustaining column, || Transforms bare

104   *Geoffrey Hill and the ends of poetry*

reflex into rhapsody'. The strictures of Hill's chosen poetic form are again mentioned, with an allusion to twin halves that recalls not only Hardy's jarring consummation but the collection's own rhyme scheme: 'Forcing this verse | Apart is like forcing apart hemispheres'.[68] The rhyming counterpart of 'verse', 'worse', is necessarily forced apart from it by the intervening two lines ending 'hemispheres/air-pressures'. The pressures put on the rhyming pairs of the final two stanzas provide their own transformations of 'reflex into rhapsody':

> But there I rest my case. Vico knew neither
> Neptune nor Úranus. Eddington, paranoid,
> With darkening brilliance informed the Void
> Of his conclusion; took God for his great Other.
>
> We will get there, finding old Henry Moore's
> *Inexplicable jumps* explicable
> Additions to the Fibonacci Table;
> Reality itself grounded in our metaphors.

There is something seemingly fated about the rhyme-pair 'neither/Other', which hovers between affirming and denying its own relation (and that of rhymes in general), the cancellation-in-advance of 'neither' rebutted and completed by the capitalised majesty and mystery of 'Other'. This Other meets also the inner rhyme-workings of the stanza, 'paranoid/Void', which, presenting an ominous majuscule of their own, follow from the broad negativity of 'neither'. Knowing that Giambattista Vico (1668–1744) was an Italian philosopher, and Arthur Stanley Eddington (1882–1944) an English astronomer, informs further doublings: the enfolding of astronomical and philosophical senses in 'the Void'; and of logical and mortal senses in 'conclusion'.

Again, there is a statement of inevitability to open the final stanza: 'We will get there'. But where? The Void? Conclusion? God? Or something Other? The last option appeals for sonic reasons, 'there' being a finessed tail-end of 'Other', but Hill is satisfied to leave the casually vague truism as it is. Then Hill performs an apparently inexplicable jump to a quotation from Henry Moore. Except that it is not quite from Henry Moore, who instead wrote of 'unexplainable jumps'.[69] These 'jumps' express a connection already implicit in the rhyme: the semantic movement from 'explicable' to 'Fibonacci table', or 'Henry Moore's' to 'metaphors', hinges partly on the inexplicable coincidences of sonic likeness.

For Hill, the mystery goes even deeper than that: 'Reality itself grounded in our metaphors.' After a jump, one is inevitably grounded; but where one is grounded depends entirely on the jump. 'Reality itself', then, is said to depend on the jump made in a metaphor or a rhyme, both forgers of

Rhymes 105

connection. A reprised reference to the Fibonacci sequence strengthens the reality-as-relationality thesis, continuing seamlessly (sequentially) into the collection's last poem (pp. 935–36):

> Reality so made: it is like fiction;
> Like Brunelleschi's dome proportionate
> Both to the thrustings of the city-state
> And to the golden straddler, his perfection:
>
> Quattrocento masters knowing them-
> selves imbued practitioners of their scope
> In fallen matter, in the mundane scape,
> The bode of majesty their signal theme.

Reality is given, but it is also 'made'; one is reminded again of R. P. Blackmur's characterisation of poetry as adding to the 'stock of available reality'.[70] Every rhyme in these stanzas is a telling half-rhyme. The meeting of 'fiction' and 'perfection', despite Hill's lauding of Brunelleschi's art, is slightly, inescapably askew: what fallen man makes of nature cannot be without fault. Between these are paired 'proportionate' and 'city-state' (the difference here primarily in stress rather than vowel sound), again bringing together the ideal and the real, and subtly acknowledging another ineluctable distance from right order: that of human government.[71] At the same time, counterpointing the rhymes, there is the erotic but non-rhyming combination of 'thrustings' and 'straddler', which in context is a fecund friction of the imaginative artist with and against the contingencies and necessities of life.

The next stanza, and its rhymes 'them-/theme' and 'scope/scape', pick up on these concerns. The 'scope' of the artist looks to be almost the same as the 'mundane scape', the world as it presents itself, but the changing of a vowel, like the changing of a lens, affords this scope the ability to perceive what is smaller or larger than the world-scape. The rhymes 'them-' and 'theme' at the stanza's ends again present a question of artistic scope: the Quattrocento masters' theme is not *themselves*, a word split in two by the line break; but it is related to 'them', both as artists and as men paying homage to God. 'The bode of majesty their signal theme'. Brunelleschi's famous Dome, part of the masterpiece that is Florence Cathedral, is a bode of divine majesty that is simultaneously a bode of human majesty. It appears to be, implausibly, a 'proportionate' rhyme-like response to the majesty of the God it is designed to house. But the stanza's most significant rhyme-response, which arrives with the inevitability of predestination, is the word 'signal'. The collection has not quite travelled in a circle; this is not the same 'signal' as that in the first poem of *Al Tempo de' Tremuoti*, caught between adjectival and nounal senses. But this quiet, clever autorhyme between the collection's first and last poems is itself a kind of signal sent, an antiphony of its two interwoven 'signal theme[s]': the paradoxical coexistence of pre-election and free will; and the 'bode of majesty'. Both themes resound primarily in an artistic sense, but, through this, also in a theological sense.

Art and theology remain focal points in the final two stanzas of the poem (and of *Broken Hierarchies*). Hill has shifted focus from Brunelleschi to his colleague and rival Donatello, evidently going from the outside to the inside of Florence Cathedral. Having described several Biblical scenes portrayed in sculpture, and having initially ascribed them to Donatello, Hill writes:

> Perhaps not Donatello; one stands bemused.
> That much would be in keeping. Error is,
> And is endemic, and speaks mysteries;
> Yahweh himself not wholly disabused
>
> Of procreation. Time is the demiurge
> For which our impotence cannot atone.
> Nothing so fatal as creation's clone.
> The stars asunder, gibbering, on the verge

It is fitting that Hill, discoverer of so many late muses, should stand 'bemused'. One thinks again of Pope, whose use is cited in the *OED* (sense 2, '*humorously*'): 'When those incorrigible things, Poets, are once irrecoverably Be-Mus'd'.[72] If the Muse, a useful shorthand for the meeting-place between the artistic and the theological, is being punningly invoked here, then it is one of three deities in these stanzas, followed by 'Yahweh' and 'the demiurge' (gnostic god of all matter). A connection is made between gods and artists, but it is simultaneously held at arm's length. Is art 'creation's clone'? Again, one may say that it is instead a kind of inevitable rhyme, a necessary but inexact imitation of divine creation. Rhyme itself is surely a meeting of siblings more than clones.

'Yahweh' is said to be 'not wholly disabused ‖ Of procreation', a tongue-in-cheek reference to the Incarnation that gives Christ's entrance into the world as an example of what 'Error is'. In its context, the suggestion is not blasphemous; it may sound like an error on Hill's part because he is celebrating error, which is, etymologically, a wandering before it is a blundering. That the phrase 'Error is' rhymes with 'mysteries' is illuminative: error is a mystery of the fallen world; and it is also, by its nature, productive of mysteries (both divine and artistic).[73] Hill captures this in the double-speak of 'speaks': error indicates mysteries (as in *speaks volumes*) and also utters them. Christ's Incarnation is a wandering into the world of error; when Hill, earlier in the poem, notes the sculpture of 'Virgin, Babe, ‖ Playing nosy-on-facy', there is something of awe in the juxtaposition of God becoming an infant and experiencing the linguistic errancy of childhood.

Rhymes 107

The game of 'nosy-on-facy' between Mother and Child is among other things a very human play with words.

Hill's summoning of deities is not the only indication that he senses the unavoidable end. Though the will to 'atone' is denied, its echoes of consummation resound into the last, unconsummated words of the poem ('on the verge'); similarly, the word 'fatal' signals that the voice that 'speaks' here is about to be silenced. Hill's turn to full rhymes in the last stanza is another conclusive gesture.

In the essay 'Rhetorics of Value and Intrinsic Value', first delivered in the year 2000 as one of the Tanner Lectures on Human Values, having reached the end of a lengthy argument for the ultimate inseparability of 'intrinsic' and 'mediated' value, Hill writes:

> The rest is paradox. For the poem to engage justly with our imperfection, so much the more must the poem approach the nature of its own perfection. [...] I am left with no other course but to say that the great poem moves us to assent as much by the integrity of its final imperfection as by the amazing grace of its detailed perfection. (*CCW*, p. 447)

What I am calling the inevitable rhyme is, here, complemented by the rhetoric of inevitability: Hill is 'left with no other course' than to admit the dual power of imperfection and perfection. One may say that according to Hill, while imperfection is inevitable, perfection is, without the external aid of 'grace', impossible. But with grace, perfection is not only possible but actual, and it resides in the details of the 'great poem'. This is why the detail of rhyme, with its relatives the pun and the paradox, provides such rich ground for the emergence of this 'amazing grace'. At its best, rhyme's bringing together of words, rendering them 'mystically espoused', is a consummation of detail that allows the poem to 'approach the nature of its own perfection'. Even the (great) poem's 'final imperfection' Hill describes as having 'integrity', a noble wholeness, in spite of unavoidable corruption.

Hill's rhyme represents, in the eye-rhyming words of the fifty-third poem of *Al Tempo de' Tremuoti*, the 'nuptial mysteries of those unwed | Aptly consenting, with an end bestowed | Some painter reaches out for' (p. 915). The inevitable rhyme in Hill is not the same as Stevens's 'expected' rhyme or even Kenner's 'predictable' rhyme; nor can it be happily aligned with Eliot's liberated rhyme, used when 'wanted for some special effect'. (As this chapter's epigraph has it: 'Ye shall offer no | Strange incense-effect'.) Hill's inevitable rhyme is wilfully unpredictable, even when strictly patterned, because it 'reaches out for', and attempts to reveal, the action of grace, the unexpected collision with the divine. The 'special effect' in Hill's rhyme does not belong to him, but is an 'end bestowed', an 'end' that his impossible rhyme appears to consider lost.

108   *Geoffrey Hill and the ends of poetry*

Equities

The insistence on rhyme in Hill's late work, despite its known imperfections, is illuminated by Hill's understanding of faith in *The Triumph of Love*: 'So what is faith if it is not | inescapable endurance?' (*TL* CXXI, p. 275). The grace of the question subsists in a pun. The 'endurance' here is that of both the faith itself and the one who has it. Like a rhyme, it is both worked at and effortlessly bestowed; it is both free gift and hard-earned reward. The section immediately preceding this in *The Triumph of Love*, meditating on Shakespeare, bestows further back-light:

> As with the Gospels, which it is allowed to resemble,
> in *Measure for Measure* moral uplift
> is not the issue. Scrupulosity, diffidence,
> shrill spirituality, conviction, free expression,
> come off as poorly as deceit or lust.
> The ethical *motiv* is—so we may hazard—
> opportunism, redemptive and redeemed;
> case-hardened on case-law, casuistry's
> own redemption; the general temper
> a caustic equity.
>
> (*TL* CXX, p. 275)

To present Hill's rhyme, finally, in the light of these insights might be in danger of undermining the significance of words being 'mystically espoused' ('moral uplift | is not the issue'); but the above poem's concerns indicate the hard practical reality of the poet's task. Rhyme – in this respect a metonym for the creation of poetry in general – is a 'case-hardened' exemplification of 'opportunism, redemptive and redeemed'; the poet may notice how two words seem peculiarly drawn to each other, but it is the poet's 'hazard' to bring them into impossible and inevitable harmony, a harmony that reveals the words' bond and makes the poem. In such a case, the poem ends, as this one does, in 'caustic equity'.

Equity is one of the quintessential Hillian words; it is in one sense a word of hard edges, a legal, political, worldly word. In another sense, it is 'a beautiful word, too beautiful for its own good, possibly'; it 'exists in two modes; it is at once an indicator, an emblem in itself, of a mode of justice that partakes of the divine; and a semantic ploy enabling us to get the better of our opponent in casuistical argument'.[74] Hill's sermon at Great St Mary's, Cambridge, in 2011 demonstrated his knowledge (enhanced, one presumes, by the *OED*) of just about every significant use of the word in English literary history. Words, as he said there, 'are not equitable'; they are, 'even in the hands of a master, [...] impregnated by strait and circumstance; even those straits that they preen themselves on having avoided,

Rhymes 109

even those circumstances they appear most gloriously to transcend'.[75] The third epigraph of *Broken Hierarchies*, from Ezra Pound's *Ta Hio*, a version of Confucius, ends: 'equity is the treasure of states' (*BH*, p. vii). It is also the treasure that Hill's rhyme, in its governance of the poem, seeks. It is necessarily a 'caustic equity': the inequitable words burn each other and themselves in their meeting; yet a balance is forged. Perhaps this is why Hill is drawn to 'ponder rhyme late'. It presents an abrasive paradox, 'a hard-won knowledge of what wears us down' (*OS* LXVI, p. 416); and it persists in a struggle for grace at once 'caustic' and 'redemptive'.

4

Syntaxes

Ordering disorders

'Order Romantic and disorder Classic' (*O* 136: *Welsh apotheosis* (I),
p. 786). The syntax of the sentence catches it between indicative and imperative moods, which suggest opposite meanings: either order is Romantic
and disorder is Classic; or the Romantic is to be ordered and the Classic is
to be disordered. A sentence marked by its bluntness becomes an instrument
of surprising entanglements. Hill's predominating sense of order and the
'ORDERING ENERGY OF SYNTAX' (as he writes in an early notebook)
is imbued with an awareness, by turns painful and playful, of unavoidable
disorder.[1] Even late claims about words' right arrangement are set in such
intricate, awkward syntax as to suggest imminent collapse: 'Ordered re-
appearance of ideas from chaos: motto-phrase for poiesis of my declared
period but not since' (*BBGJ* 142, p. 76). At times, the order of words and
sentences in Hill's poems is a disordering, a reordering, or a blunt heckling,
of the eye's and the ear's expectations. Hill finds ends, and the means to
them, in unpredicted places; places that invite readerly revision – and, in
some cases, writerly revision.

For instance, what becomes an intermezzo of sorts in the final version
of *A Treatise of Civil Power* begins, in the Clutag edition, as a finale of
sorts:

> Intermezzo of sorts, something to do with gifts.
> In plainer style, or sweeter, some figment
> of gratitude and reconciliation
> with the near things, with remnancy and love.
> I show you the ownerless, serene, eighteenth-
> century tombstones set about like ashlar;
> I give you the great, storm-severed head
> of a sunflower, blazing in mire of hail.
> ....
> CETERA DESUNT[2]

Syntaxes   111

This is the forty-second and last section of 'A Treatise of Civil Power', a poem found in Clutag's 2005 publication of *A Treatise of Civil Power*, but not in the 2007 or any subsequent edition. The loud majuscules of 'CETERA DESUNT', or *the rest are missing*, usually found as a scholarly annotation on incomplete manuscripts, constitute a jarring end to the sequence, which had already reached a perfect cadence in the two anaphoric clauses of the exuberant concluding sentence.[3] But Hill is fond of tonal disruption, often at such ecstatic or epiphanic moments. Disruption, however, is not the end of the matter. Hill's acknowledgement of disorder, or incompletion, particularly in the later work, is key to the attainment of a less tightly controlled, more self-reconciled ordering. As in *kintsugi*, the Japanese art of remaking broken pottery with gold-dusted lacquer, for Hill the consummate forming of a poem is often a conspicuous repairing of deformed language. (The difference might be that on occasion Hill finds he wishes first to break the pots himself.)

This last section of 'A Treatise of Civil Power', along with seven others, is revised and becomes a poem in its own right in the 2007 version collected in *Broken Hierarchies*.[4] The revised poem, though it is now presented in the midst of the collection, presents a fragmentary ending of its own: its title is 'Before Senility', and is subtitled 'dum possum volo', or *while I can, I want to*. The end in this case is an imagined but realistic one, an end to the possession of faculties and competences; the poem becomes the notation of a last 'figment', a last significant vision to be saved and held onto in times to come, in the 'mire of hail':

> Intermezzo of sorts, something to do with gifts.
> In plainer style, or sweeter, some figment
> of gratitude and reconciliation
> with the near things, with remnancy and love:
>
> to measure the ownerless, worn, eighteenth-
> century tombstones realigned like ashlar;
> encompass the stark storm-severed head
> of a sunflower blazing in mire of hail.
>
> (TCP, p. 594)

The pronouns of the first version have been lost in the hail, but not the sunflower, which Hill orders himself to 'encompass' in verse. Numerous reorderings take place in this revision. The poetic offerings 'I show you' and 'I give you' have become more or less impersonal verbs (one full infinitive and one imperative); the 'near things' here, under the title's shadow, seem markedly further away from the speaker. The tombstones, 'set about' in the original, find themselves 'realigned' here; and the lines themselves are realigned, from a block of eight (plus the coda) into two equal stanzas

112   *Geoffrey Hill and the ends of poetry*

of four. The sunflower's 'storm-severed head', once a 'great' monument like the stones, is now 'stark'; and the rhythm of the final line has been quickened by the omission of the comma.[5]

In the balance of a collection, the final poem bears a certain weight of expectation. At the ending of any poem, the reader might reasonably (though not necessarily consciously) expect a gratifying sense of conclusion, even reconciliation; in a similar way, with a group of poems, one might presume that the last will be '[i]n plainer style, or sweeter, some figment | of gratitude and reconciliation | with the near things, with remnancy and love'. With the old ending of *A Treatise of Civil Power* (2005) remade and repositioned in the 2007 edition, a greater weight (particularly for anyone who had read the first version) falls on the final work of the revision. In the case of the 2007 edition, the final work is three poems, all of them advertised as addenda: the antepenultimate poem is titled 'Coda', which is followed by 'Lyric Fragment' and finally 'Nachwort', German for *afterword*.[6] And this last poem is an afterword, not only on the group of poems that precedes it but on the conceptions and uses of syntax – the focus of this chapter – in Hill's work as a whole:

> Sometime, with a near-helpless cry, I shall
> wrench out of this. I don't much have
> the patience, now, of the artificer
> that so enthralls itself, impels
> mass, energy, deep, the stubborn line,
> the line that is that quickens to delay.
>
> —Urge to unmake
> all wrought finalities, become a babbler
> in the crowd's face
>
>   (*TCP*, p. 601)

Between its two irregular stanzas, this poem implicitly connects the end of life with the perfect completion (or not) of a poem. The 'wrench' of the first stanza recalls 'the pitiless wrench between | truth and metre' in the earlier 'Citations II' (*TCP*, p. 561). But this poem presents even more strongly the syntactical wrench, the onerous pull to-and-fro between opposite poles, that is a feature not only of this collection or of its relation to the first version, but of Hill's poetry in general. In the earlier version of the collection, the 'pitiless wrench' is instead 'the unending tug between | syntax and sentiment'.[7] The phrase was wisely revised; but it shows the significance of syntax (mentioned explicitly twice elsewhere in the early edition's title poem) in Hill's stylistic and broader poetic quandaries.[8] The revision also suggests that, despite the clear dissimilarities between the pairings 'truth

Syntaxes 113

and metre' and 'syntax and sentiment', one can accurately speak of the wrench in Hill's poetry between 'truth' and 'syntax' (and also between metre and syntax).

The syntactical wrench is distilled in the last stanza of 'Nachwort': it is the '[u]rge to unmake | all wrought finalities'. The irony of this, the poem's after-afterword, the fragment without grammatical subject or full stop, is clear: it is itself the 'wrought' finality of the collection. As elsewhere in *A Treatise of Civil Power* (one example being the reference to 'plainer style' in 'Before Senility'), Hill points to his own artifice, alluding to the change of style, lately attempted, from that of the patient 'artificer' to 'a kind of ecstatic commonplaceness'.[9] The wrench between the urge to 'unmake | all wrought finalities' on one hand, and the urge to make them on the other, is inseparable from the push and pull of Hill's poetic syntaxes.[10]

That conspicuous plural, 'syntaxes', is justified most clearly in 'Nachwort'. The first stanza is a carefully, tightly knit construction: its second and longer sentence, in its 'mass' of clauses, makes Hill's point by losing its 'energy' along the way; it is an exercise in atrophy ('I'd | swear myself blind atrophy's not the word | but that invention reinvents itself | every so often in the line of death').[11] It is a 'stubborn line', a laborious sentence. It is one 'that quickens to delay', that both enlivens and stunts the work. The syntax of 'Nachwort' is accordingly stuck in this paradox. With the long second sentence gradually rendering itself inert, Hill is exaggerating and mocking the effort of the 'artificer' – an undeniable side of his own poetic self – and at the same time proving the difficulty of unmaking the artifice, of helping 'truth' to win over 'metre'.

The 'babbler | in the crowd's face' appears to evoke Pound's 'faces in the crowd; | Petals on a wet, black bough'.[12] But Hill's phrase retains an ambiguity: the babbler is in, among, the wide face of the crowd, but he is also in its face, speaking to it, confronting it, becoming a disturbance. It is only in the later work, from *Canaan* (1996) onwards but with *Speech! Speech!* (2000) as a particular turning point, that Hill becomes convinced that the '[u]rge to unmake | all wrought finalities' comes from the deeper urge to make them, and ought to be included in that grand task. Whether in the maker's or the unmaker's mask, Hill, in a certain sense, always seeks to be a 'babbler', uttering a language familiar enough that the crowd may understand but unfamiliar enough that the crowd may (or may not) want to understand. With babbling, one returns to the unsteady, uncluttered syntax of the infant's emergence from muteness (as discussed in the second chapter). There is an innocence, a sinlessness, in such utterance, not dissimilar to the seeming transcendence of a madman's babbling. The change in the '[u]rge' of Hill's syntax is a new

114   *Geoffrey Hill and the ends of poetry*

way of seeking the same end: to speak to, and in, 'the crowd's face', and yet beyond it.

In a provoking essay on the endings of Donne's poems, Ricks writes of how Donne employs an 'insinuatingly interrogative syntax, plaiting it and plighting it even in the prospect of rupture'.[13] For Hill, rupture is not a prospect but a reality with which the syntax must contend. Looking at Donne, Ricks observes 'how unhealthily the poems end'; 'the success of the ending', he writes, 'is the failing of the poem, since it demeans'. Ricks even frustratedly asserts that '[t]he better the best things in his poem, the more Donne is driven to rend it with his ending'.[14] None of this can be said of Hill, despite his urge 'to unmake'. The breaking of syntax, which often occurs at poems' ends and is especially a feature of Hill's later work, is a reaction not to the preceding truth-claims of the poem but to the confronting 'truth' outside it. The syntax, as well as the metre, is engaged in a struggle to express reality; Hill, over the course of his poetic corpus, becomes increasingly inclined to display its fallings and failings.

In the essay 'Redeeming the Time', examining a long and convoluted sentence in a letter from Gerard Manley Hopkins to Robert Bridges (having cited Hopkins elsewhere remarking to Bridges that 'this Victorian English is a bad business'), Hill writes: '[Hopkins's] own syntax, in the letter of 6 November 1887, is a bad business; it is, to apply one of his own terms, "jaded"' (*CCW*, p. 99). The syntax of the first stanza of 'Nachwort' is similarly jaded, the mark of a style apparently 'so near the end of its tether' (*CCW*, p. 99) – but not quite the mark of 'unwilled dereliction' Hill finds in the late writings of Eliot (*CCW*, p. 564). This jadedness is, at first look, a fair distance from the seeming optimism of Hill's first collected essay, 'Poetry as "Menace" and "Atonement"':

> Ideally, as I have already implied, my theme would be simple; simply this: that the technical perfecting of a poem is an act of atonement, in the radical etymological sense – an act of at-one-ment, a setting at one, a bringing into concord, a reconciling, a uniting in harmony; and that this act of atonement is described with beautiful finality by two modern poets: by W. B. Yeats when he writes in a letter of September 1935, to Dorothy Wellesley, that 'a poem comes right with a click like a closing box' and by T. S. Eliot in his essay of 1953, 'The Three Voices of Poetry':
>
> > when the words are finally arranged in the right way—or in what he comes to accept as the best arrangement he can find—[the poet] may experience a moment of exhaustion, of appeasement, of absolution, and of something very near annihilation, which is in itself indescribable. (*CCW*, p. 4)

Syntaxes 115

The adverbial preface to all of this is crucial: 'Ideally'. As the title of the essay implies, the 'effort of writing a good bit of verse' is not undertaken in ideal circumstances.[15] The 'menace' of human error, guilt, and anxiety, and the menace of language that slips unbeknownst out of its 'setting' and its 'concord', are ever-present. Ricks notes 'an unremarked irreconcilability' in the passage above, namely that one can 'imagine a poet's instinctive assent to one or other of [Yeats's and Eliot's] statements, but not to both'.[16] I would argue instead that the 'irreconcilability' Ricks discovers is in the deferred weight of '[i]deally', which is never properly picked up again in Hill's essay. The banner above the 'reconciling' and the 'absolution' is a word that fatally undermines their reality. There is no corresponding passage in the essay that begins: 'But since such reconciliations are not possible, here is what the poet must do.' Hill simply states the impossible ideal of atonement; there is no contingency plan. What the poet must do is make do. ('Make do with cogent if austere finale' (*TCP*, p. 584).)

This, Hill later finds, can mean undoing: upsetting the sought reconciliation as a different, more visibly flawed reconciliation of its own kind. The 'beautiful finality' achieved by Yeats and Eliot, like Hill's 'wrought finalities', is plagued by that undoing menace. As Hill's later poetry especially shows, it is a strong urge, one that competes with, and in so doing augments, the 'instinctive' urge to make. The second stanza of 'Nachwort' – with its urgent opening em dash – finds the syntax revivified with the spirit of interruption, the uncivil persistence of the pest.

The end of syntax in Hill's poems, as I have suggested, is an equilibrium of contradictory urges: that to make wrought finalities; and that to unmake them. Hill's poetic syntax is itself, to the degree of its success, an atonement of 'menace' and 'atonement'.[17] The syntactical labour of atonement in a poem like 'Coda', the first and longest of the three tailpiece poems in *A Treatise of Civil Power*, is, as in 'Nachwort', finally undone by a tonal incongruity, a demotic interruption. But does it compete with, or in fact complete, the foregoing meditation?

> 5
> Write that I saw how much is gift-entailed,
> great grandson, and son, of defeated men,
> in my childhood, that is; even so I hope—
> not believe, hope—our variously laboured
> ways notwithstanding—we shall accountably
> launch into death on a broad arc; our dark
> abrupt spirit with fourth day constellations
> that stood assembled to its first unknowing—

116   *Geoffrey Hill and the ends of poetry*

                                6
which is an abashed way invoking light,
the beatific vision, a species of heaven,
the presence of the first mover and all that,
great grandfather and Dante's *Paradiso*
understanding each other straight-on, to perfection.
I fear to wander in unbroken darkness
even with those I love. I know that sounds
a wicked thing to say.

                                        (*TCP*, p. 600)

The wrought finality here, syntactically and rhetorically, is the extended first
sentence, stretched from the beginning of the fifth section to the fifth line of
the final section, which ends with the word 'perfection'. This, as one might
anticipate, is too perfect an ending. The long sentence is, as Hill writes within
it, 'an abashed way invoking light' (note the lack of *of* after 'way'); the syntax
is suitably abashed and bashed, pulling and twisting through commas, em
dashes, semicolons (though not brackets).[18] Some segments of its 'laboured'
journey are difficult to track. The phrase 'even so I hope' is obscure in origin
('notwithstanding' that 'even so' repeats the final sentence of the poem's
fourth section (*TCP*, p. 599)) and obstructed in continuation. It is not clear
why seeing 'how much is gift-entailed [...] of defeated men' is in principle
contrary to the 'hope' of launching 'into death on a broad arc'; the perception and the desire seem insufficiently related, either verbally or semantically.
The elision of Hill, his 'great grandson, and son', into one 'dark | abrupt
spirit' is a further unaccounted-for jump. It might also be asked, in scrutiny
of the poem's indeterminate joinings-up, why 'great grandson', 'fourth day',
and 'great grandfather' are unhyphenated. (One can even imagine 'variously
laboured' with a hyphen, in keeping with Hill's typical use.)

   The dramatis personae of 'Coda' are somewhat clearer. Hill is the
'great grandfather', understanding Dante's *Paradiso* 'straight-on, to perfection'. There is an understated humour in this fantasy: it is not Heaven
itself that Hill hopes to understand rightly but Dante's written version of
it, as though *Paradiso* were the real paradise to which Hill aspires.[19] The
characters of 'Coda' are all familial but distanced: Hill's own great grandfather, 'a Welsh iron-puddler' (p. 599), mentioned in the second and
fourth sections, is known only by 'the census'; and the 'great grandson,
and son' (who could be either biological or poetic heirs, real or imagined)
are addressed only to be withdrawn from again. This may be partly why
the poem's final two short sentences, which follow and unsettle the long
invocation of 'the beatific vision', are ineffective. The many hesitations
in that long sentence, never fully committed to the vision it presents,
give no sense of surprise to his 'fear to wander in unbroken darkness',

Syntaxes 117

while no readerly attachment to 'those I love' has been made possible. Those whom the speaker loves are made less important, at the level of syntax, than the speaker himself, whose 'I' ends the penultimate sentence and is the only figure in the last. The coda to 'Coda', these final two sentences, represent an unmaking of what was never distinctly made, because the wrought finality of the preceding long sentence is already syntactically broken, wandering, halting. The clangingly uncomfortable last three words of 'the presence of the first mover and all that', their unsure footing, are enough to put into question the premise of the long sentence and undermine its vision. They also diminish the power of the last sentences' withdrawal from such a vision. The syntax is involuted long before the closing turn.

In 'Coda', as in Eliot's 'East Coker', there is an 'intolerable wrestle' with words, a struggle to find them and then to find proper places for them.[20] At one point a place was found for 'damn-fool' instead of 'wicked' in the last sentence: 'I know that sounds | a wicked thing to say.' In the 2005 version of *A Treatise of Civil Power*, the line reads as it does here in *Broken Hierarchies*; it was in the 2007 publication that the adjective temporarily changed.[21] Hill's repeated tinkering with the line suggests that its casual unmaking was in fact a particularly frustrating finality to work, a 'hammered threnos' (p. 599) that refused to be beaten into adequate shape. Hill knows it does not sound right, but whether that is because it is 'wicked' or 'damn-fool' is disputable. I refer to 'East Coker' because 'Coda' also seems to owe Eliot's poem a debt. 'Coda', 'invoking light' in the face of a feared 'unbroken darkness', not only calls upon Eliot's poetic hero Dante ('So here I am, in the middle way' being the first line of the fifth section of 'East Coker') but is an example of the 'folly' of (damn-fool) old men approaching 'dark dark dark', their 'fear of fear and frenzy, their fear of possession, | Of belonging to another, or to others, or to God'.[22] In addition, Hill's metanoia, his return upon himself in the line 'which is an abashed way invoking light', recalls Eliot's more explicit self-criticism in 'East Coker': 'That was a way of putting it – not very satisfactory'.[23] Both Hill's and Eliot's are syntactically interruptive remarks following protracted sentences that present visions of the end (of the world in Eliot's case and of life in Hill's, though such ends may be considered inseparable). But while Hill's way is 'abashed', his syntax uncertain of itself from the start, Eliot's successfully discordant metanoia follows a vision of ten fast-paced and verb-heavy lines that is, until its terminating full stop, unpunctuated (a run of lines that would require punctuation according to the conventional grammar reintroduced immediately after it).

A happier dissonance of syntaxes occurs in many of the other later poems. The penultimate section of *Scenes from Comus*, written in 2005, the same year as the early version of *A Treatise of Civil Power*, is able to have (if not raise) a laugh about the struggle of the writer:

> Nothing is unforgettable but guilt.
> Guilt of the moment to be made eternal.
> Reading immortal literature's a curse.
>
> Beatrice in *The Changeling* makes me sweat
> even more than Faustus' Helen. Recompose
> Marlowe's off-stage blasphemous fun with words
>
> or Pound's last words to silence. Well,
> let well alone. The gadgetry of nice
> determinism makes, breaks, comedians.
>
> All the better if you go mad like Pound
> (*grillo*, a cricket; *grido*, a cry from the fields).
> The grief of comedy you have to laugh.
>
> <div align="right">(<i>SC</i> 3. 19, p. 480)</div>

One 'can repent and be absolved of a sin, but there is no canonical repentance for a mistake'.[24] The menace of the potential mistake, the '[g]uilt of the moment to be made eternal', concerns this poem, but does not haunt it. The syntax, effortfully artless, manages to reconcile its 'moment' with the 'eternal', the menace with atonement, by bearing so lightly the weight, the '*pondus*', of such a task.[25] Instead, as throughout *Scenes from Comus*, Hill treats the whole exercise as 'off-stage blasphemous fun with words' more than 'last words to silence'.[26] This is unusual. It does not seem to atone with the tone of 'Poetry as "Menace" and "Atonement"', in which a humorous quotation of Katherine Whitehorn is, to its credit, given, but is also given the charge of unseriousness:

> A knitting editor once said 'if I make a mistake there are jerseys all over England with one arm longer than the other'. Set that beside Nadezhda Mandelstam's account of the life and death of her husband, the Russian poet Osip Mandelstam, and one can scarcely hope to be taken seriously. [...] And yet one must, however barely, hope to be taken seriously. (*CCW*, p. 9)

Must one? 'All the better if you go mad like Pound' begs to differ. It might be better to go mad if only not to have to worry about being taken seriously. In *Scenes from Comus* one arm longer than the other is cheerfully attributed to the author's own incapacities; take for example the last, foreshortened line of the collection, a gesture towards senility, and a blunt joke at the futility of everything preceding it: 'WHAT DID YOU SAY?' (*SC* 3. 20, p. 480).

It is, Hill acknowledges, a 'grief' to 'have to laugh' at the gap, not only between menace and atonement, but between his own work and 'immortal

Syntaxes   119

literature'. There is a grammatical and syntactical gap in the last line that gives a subtle sense of the writer's painful but necessary conclusion. 'The grief of comedy you have to laugh' provides an intransitive verb in a sentence that demands a final transitive verb. *The grief of comedy is that you have to laugh*, or *The grief of comedy you have to laugh at*, or even a phonetic adjustment of the last word from 'laugh' to *love*, would work at fixing the line's meaning – but instead, without even a punctuation mark to distinguish the two irreconcilable clauses, it remains an unmade wrought finality. Its ambiguity, its unfinishedness, are carefully worked: they are tools in the 'gadgetry of nice I determinism' that 'makes, breaks' poets as well as comedians. That sneaked-in adjective 'nice' is a nexus of this kind of semantic complexity fixed in place by the syntax: the obsolete sense, the first listed in the *OED* (second edition), 'Foolish, stupid, senseless' (1), ghosts the meaning; but so do '[w]anton' (2), 'elegant' (2d), '[f]astidious in matters of literary taste' (7c), 'punctilious, scrupulous, sensitive' (7d), '[r]equiring or involving great precision, accuracy, or minuteness' (8), 'demanding close consideration or thought' (9a), '[f]inely discriminative' (12c), and the more common '[a]greeable; that one derives pleasure or satisfaction from; delightful' (15a).[27] Hill's determinedly unmade syntax plays with the same niceties of such polyvalent words, which can be to the poems' detriment, turning them towards vague rather than precise ambiguities. The success of 'nice' here lies in its relation to 'determinism': determinism can credibly be called '[f]oolish', 'elegant', '[f]inely discrimina-tive', even '[a]greeable'; but there is an irony in the stubborn indeterminacy of 'nice', which undermines the very word it aptly describes.

The sentences of the poem above, like many others in Hill's late work, lose the sense of their address; pronouns become blurry (though, evidently, '[b]lurring sharpens' (*OS* XXX, p. 380)). The *I* is concealed as impera-tives come to the fore, despite the fact that Hill appears to be ordering himself: 'Recompose I Marlowe's off-stage blasphemous fun'; 'Well, I let well alone'. In addition, fragments emerge ('Guilt of the moment to be made eternal', as well as the last line); and *you* is used in the demotic general sense ('All the better if you go mad like Pound', and again the last line). Nevertheless, there is a feeling of conclusion in the final line. Two factors contribute to this. The first is that the parenthesis that leads up to it, '(*grillo*, a cricket; *grido*, a cry from the fields)', is metrically imbal-anced and, at twelve syllables, overlong; its syntax, too, that of an Italian phrasebook, sets up a question to be answered. The second factor is that the line itself, 'The grief of comedy you have to laugh', does answer and resolve its precursor, first of all in the ear: it is a perfect iambic pentameter, the clearest in the poem. As Barbara Herrnstein Smith writes: 'Metrical regularity at the end of a poem, especially when accompanied by monosyl-labic diction, has closural effects [...]. [I]t is a re-establishment of the norm,

120   *Geoffrey Hill and the ends of poetry*

the most probable and therefore the most stable arrangement of stresses.
[...] [I]t suggests control, authority, and, in both senses, dependability.'[28]
This final line in *Scenes from Comus* 3. 19, with its predominantly monosyllabic diction, slows and settles the jaunty caesurae that have led up to
it, a settling bolstered by the line's semantic force, which presents a gently
authoritative, though equivocal, resolution: 'you have to laugh'.

'On Reading *Blake: Prophet Against Empire*', in *A Treatise of Civil
Power*, offers a more grimly comic disjunction of syntax at its end:

> VIII
> One dies dutifully, of fearful exhaustion,
> or of *one's wrathful self*, self's baffle-plates
> contrived with the dexterity of a lifetime.
> Nobody listens or contradicts the screen;
> though, homeward-bound, some find combustious
> sights to be stepped aside from—an old body
>
> IX
> its mouth working.
>
> (*TCP*, p. 570)

This 'contrived' death is equally an unmaking and a wrought finality. Ricks
writes: 'Everything about this is working except a mouth capable of voicing
the movement across IX.'[29] Not only the voice but the syntax is disturbed
by the roman numeral, which comes to function grammatically, together
with the line and section breaks, as a comma. And yet it is not a comma. It is
an 'I' alongside a cross-shape (not quite a crossed-out *I* but close). The 'its'
of 'its mouth working' marks a further distance from personhood and adds
to the horror of the image. The 'old body' is spatially split apart, decom-
posed between the sections. It 'dies dutifully' as the disruptive, unexpected,
and (in the double sense) arbitrary arrival of the 'IX' prompts it. The body's
death, here, is also dictated by the death of the poem's body: both its being
broken down mid-sentence and its coming to an end. The poem, like many
of Hill's, gestures to its own end; 'homeward-bound' in the third-last line is
an especially artful hint.[30]

In turn, and in a startling example of how Hill's syntax can work at the
level of whole collections, linking one poem to the next, the beginning of
'On Reading *Blake: Prophet Against Empire*' is audibly cued by the final
words of the poem that precedes it, 'Harmonia Sacra'. Except for the
intervening title, 'Everything swings with the times' is read immediately
after '*I sing of times trans-shifting* were his words' (*TCP*, pp. 568–69).

The words in question in this latter line are Robert Herrick's. They come
from 'The Argument of his Book', the cataloguing prologue to *Hesperides*.
These are the sonnet's last six lines:

Syntaxes   121

I sing of *Times trans-shifting*; and I write
How *Roses* first came *Red*, and *Lillies White*.
I write of *Groves*, of *Twilights*, and I sing
The Court of *Mab*, and of the *Fairie-King*.
I write of *Hell*; I sing (and ever shall)
Of *Heaven*, and hope to have it after all.[31]

In the same iambic pentameters, Hill's 'Harmonia Sacra' ends: 'This sounds like Herrick though without his grace. | *I sing of times trans-shifting* were his words' (*TCP*, p. 568). While Hill's poem signals its end with this self-evaluating turn, Herrick's begins and ends as self-evaluation. Since the subjects Herrick mentions singing and writing about do not follow a discernible pattern, the movement towards the poem's end has to be audible and syntactical ('No connection—you catch it all in the syntax', Hill writes in the 2005 version of 'A Treatise of Civil Power').[32] Accordingly, in Herrick's poem, the parenthesis '(and ever shall)', the strong caesura after '*Heaven*', and finally the use of a new verb, 'hope', in the final line, arrest the eye and the ear in preparation for the quiet but effective pun that finishes the poem ('after all' meaning both *despite it all* and *when everything is finished*).[33]

'The Argument of his Book' is a vivid example of what Hill avowedly wishes to attain in his poems' syntax. In fulfilling the demands of the sonnet's structure, and in setting up a sense of conclusion, Herrick makes an ordered and wrought finality; and yet the syntax of the poem as a whole is an unpicking, an unpacking, laying bare (in the bare verbs 'I sing' and 'I write') its own composition and that of poetry in general. Its making is its unmaking. One of Herrick's best-known works, 'Delight in Disorder', takes the erotic overtones of the same process and plays them at concert pitch:

A sweet disorder in the dresse
Kindles in cloathes a wantonnesse:
A Lawne about the shoulders thrown
Into a fine distraction:
An erring Lace, which here and there
Enthralls the Crimson Stomacher:
A Cuffe neglectfull, and thereby
Ribbands to flow confusedly:
A winning wave (deserving Note)
In the tempestuous petticote:
A careless shooe-string, in whose tye
I see a wilde civility:
Doe more bewitch me, then when Art
Is too precise in every part.[34]

122 *Geoffrey Hill and the ends of poetry*

The metaphor of undress for artlessness is at least as old as Cicero. In *Orator ad M. Brutum*, he writes: 'there is such a thing even as a careful negligence. Just as some women are said to be handsomer when unadorned—this very lack of ornament becomes them—so this plain style gives pleasure even when unembellished: there is something in both cases which lends greater charm, but without showing itself.'[35] Herrick's poem is an extremely careful negligence. The whole work is one sentence, in which the main verb is delayed until the penultimate line: 'Doe more bewitch me'. The verb '[k]indles', which kindles the movement of the poem, allows the sentence to finish at the end of the second line; but each measured couplet that follows hangs on that set-up, and at length awaits the completion of the verb 'bewitch'. It takes the form of an argument: the opening couplet is the declarative statement; the middle couplets provide substantiating examples; and the final couplet concludes the case. The difference here is that there is no argument. Herrick is not especially interested in convincing the reader; his long list of examples instead constitutes a luxuriating in the relative undress both of women and of words (or at least the idea of such undress), the intoxicating force of which luxuriating might be enough to persuade the reader by proxy. His conclusion is that of a personal meditation: it is not that the 'erring Lace' and 'Cuffe neglectfull' are bewitching as such; but that they 'more bewitch' the speaker than an overwrought finality. Like 'The Argument of his Book', 'Delight in Disorder' does not seem to fret over finding its end. For such a long sentence, the pace is slow; it is not of utmost import that the reader remembers each subordinate clause to which '[d]oe more bewitch me' applies. The gentle connecting colons between each couplet are consummately 'carelesse' and easy. The poem is fourteen lines of iambic tetrameter: a shorter, looser kind of sonnet, one with its shoestrings untied.

Herrick's 'wilde civility' is a kind of inversion of what *Civil Power* signifies for Hill. Herrick's phrase suggests an alluringly disordered order; Hill's (and originally Milton's) suggests the agreeable ordering of a potential disorder (i.e., power).[36] The 'pitiless wrench between | truth and metre' (*TCP*, p. 561) expresses the same tension. Not merely the urge but also the expression of the '[u]rge to unmake | all wrought finalities' in Hill's poetry are part of its civility, its overarching desire to be rightly ordered. In 'G. F. Handel, Opus 6' the phrase 'civil power' appears as Hill contends that repetitions of theme are like 'figures in harmony with their right consorts',

each of itself a treatise of civil power,
every phrase instinct with deliberation
both upon power and towards civility.

(*TCP*, p. 585)

Syntaxes 123

The chief function of the word 'instinct' here (the stress falling on the second syllable) is as an adjective ('[i]mbued or charged *with* something, as a moving or animating force or principle' (*OED, adj.*, sense 3)). The *OED*'s first two citations for the sense are from the Baptist minister and essayist John Foster, who writes that '[Edmund] Burke's sentences are pointed at the end,—instinct with pungent sense to the last syllable'; and Shelley's *Queen Mab*, which describes Ianthe's soul as '[i]nstinct with inexpressible beauty and grace'. These appeal to different instincts; one imagines that the notion of sentences 'pointed at the end' might have been striking to Hill. What every phrase must be charged with, in Hill's vision of syntax, is this double 'deliberation': 'upon power', not merely governmental but chiefly poetic; and 'towards civility', not merely formal correctness but formal perfection. The word 'instinct' also plays on its nounal meaning, which makes of 'instinct with deliberation' another parallel: this 'phrase' too could be a dancing pair of wild power with civility.

If Hill is a 'hobbyist of his own rage' (*TCP*, p. 588) it is because the desire of his syntax is to direct the destructive impulse of poetic power 'towards civility'. Near-synonyms for 'civil power', readable as an oxymoron but also denoting a natural and necessary balance of forces, can be found all over Hill's poetry and prose. The syntax, the 'clause upon clause' of the second poem in *Canaan*, 'That Man as a Rational Animal Desires the Knowledge Which Is His Perfection' (p. 172), deliberates on and instantiates this balance of forces.[37] (One aspect of the balance is between this heavy title and what comes after it; Peter McDonald notes that the poem 'contrives to jump clear of the fetters' of its title.[38]) The poem, like 'Delight in Disorder', and like others in *Canaan*, which this chapter will go on to discuss, is an abbreviated sonnet; lacking rhyme, metre, and conventional punctuation, its unmaking is nevertheless the wrought atonement of 'reason and desire', of 'sensuous intelligence', of the wild power of 'singing' (on one half) and (on the other) the ordered civility of 'getting it right':

Abiding provenance I would have said
the question stands
                    even in adoration
clause upon clause
                    with or without assent
reason and desire on the same loop—
I imagine singing I imagine

getting it right—the knowledge
of sensuous intelligence
                    entering into the work—
spontaneous happiness as it was once
given our sleeping nature to awake by
                    and know
innocence of first inscription

124   *Geoffrey Hill and the ends of poetry*

Limited punctuations

Syntactically, *Canaan* is not so much a turning point as an edifying cul-de-sac. To see the workings of syntax in *Canaan*, one must attend closely to the unusual punctuation. Especially in poems as intricately constructed as Hill's, punctuation has a major governing influence on syntax. Hill occasionally stresses the point himself: 'To dispense, with justice; or, to dispense I with justice' (*MCCP* 6, p. 148).[39]

Only the early drafts of *Odi Barbare*, the fifth of *The Daybooks*, repeat *Canaan*'s eschewals of punctuational convention.[40] Of the thirty-nine poems in *Canaan*, only nine end without a full stop or question mark, and only three are lacking any punctuation; and yet the impression of the collection's lack of punctuation is pervasive and abiding.[41] The unpunctuated poems are preceded in Hill's oeuvre only by 'A Prayer to the Sun', the second of 'Four Poems Regarding the Endurance of Poets' (*KL*, pp. 55–58 (p. 56)); and 'The Pentecost Castle' (*T*, pp. 115–20).[42] In work after *Canaan*, excluding early versions of poems, only 'The Oath' (*TCP*, p. 598) is entirely unpunctuated. This makes a total of just six poems without punctuation in Hill's corpus as he presents it.

But this count excludes a poem like 'Sobieski's Shield', the second part of which, though it ends with a full stop, makes its 'abashed way' to 'unbroken darkness' without punctuated signposts:

> Brusque as the year
>   purple garish-brown
> aster chrysanthemum
>   signally restored
> to a subsistence of scant light
> as one might assert
>   Justice Equity
> or Sobieski's Shield even
>   the names
> and what they have about them dark to dark.
>
>   (C, p. 173)

If this were a piece of music, its key would be ambiguous until the last note. Only the repetition of 'dark' at the end could be said to prepare the reader for conclusion; otherwise the syntax seems to meander and makes grammatical and semantic connections less clear than the prepositions and conjunctions 'to', 'of', 'as', 'or', and 'and' might suggest. Poems like this, and the one immediately before it ('That Man as a Rational Animal [...]'), though not completely lacking punctuation, are examples of the kind of limited punctuation that obtains in much of *Canaan*.

Syntaxes 125

Punctuation and Hill have often been connected. His scrupulosity, his fine-tuning, his attention to attentiveness, give a preliminary sense that the punctuation in Hill's poems matters – and more than in most poetry. One of Ricks's three major essays on Hill is chiefly a disquisition on the hyphen in his poems; another chiefly on brackets; and the last is distracted at length from its focus on a suffix (*-ble*) by Hill's varying use of majuscules and of arabic and roman numbering.[43] In *Geoffrey Hill and his Contexts*, an essay by Charles Lock entitled 'Beside the Point: A Diligence of Accidentals' goes so far as to propose 'a theology of punctuation'.[44] Hill's fastidiousness is contagious.

My approach to Hill's punctuation, before looking at the excess of markings in the early poem 'Two Formal Elegies', and the changes of punctuation from drafts of the late work *Odi Barbare*, will begin by going through the poems of limited punctuation in *Canaan*, particularly those that share with the last poem in *Broken Hierarchies* the unusual characteristic of finishing without a full stop, question mark, or exclamation mark.[45] To end a poem with a dash, or without any mark, raises a question about whether the poem might be intended to dismiss, or transcend, the notion of its conclusiveness. A poem is not a treatise, nor an argument, though it may involve elements of both. Sometimes, instead of offering an expected sense of ending, the poem gets 'in the crowd's face' (*TCP*, p. 601). It is difficult to argue that Hill's poetry resides in the realm of what Leonard B. Meyer calls '*anti-teleological* art'; and yet it is marked with failed reconciliations and unreached ends.[46] There is in general the feeling of an attainable end in each of Hill's poems, both syntactically and narratively; sometimes the apparent ends not attained nonetheless produce effective poetic closes. What is surprising, then, is that for poems that seem not to reach a satisfactory end, one must look elsewhere than the nine in *Canaan* that lack an ending mark.

I will come to looking elsewhere. But the ways in which these nine poems in *Canaan* reach their ends are instructive places to begin when considering punctuation's part in Hill's syntactical searches for consummation. The six of the nine poems that employ punctuation at all use only two marks: the em dash and the colon. Four of them, which are presented consecutively, share another feature: they each have twenty-one lines, split into three equal stanzas of seven lines.

The first of these is 'Of Coming into Being and Passing Away'. Like several poems in *Canaan*, it comes into being with a blooming plant. Here is the opening stanza:

126 *Geoffrey Hill and the ends of poetry*

> Rosa sericea: its red
> spurs
>   blooded with amber
> each lit and holy grain
> the sun
>   makes much of
> as of all our shadows—
>   (p. 174)

April is the cruellest month. In the very germination of Rosa sericea (or the silky rose), immediately after the colon by which it introduces itself to the poem, it is cut by 'spurs', a word on its own line, split from 'blooded', which naturally proceeds from it. Its moment of being 'lit and holy' is short; before the stanza ends it has been lumped in with 'all our shadows'. The dash could be its being dashed, as suddenly as it lived; but the reader is led on, and into circuitous syntax:

> prodigal ever returning
> darkness that in such circuits
> reflects diuturnity
>   to itself
> and to our selves
>   yields nothing
> finally—

The indentations, frequent even in the poems of *Canaan* that use punctuation more conventionally, constantly present wrong turns (a hint threaded through 'ever returning', 'circuits', and the pun within 'diuturnity') to the reader. What might be a noun, 'prodigal' (denoting the subject of Jesus's parable in Luke 15), in the stanza's first line turns out to be an adjective describing 'darkness'. The fifth line, 'and to our selves', seems to refer back to the third line's verb, 'reflects', but soon yields more to 'yields nothing'. The irony of the stanza is that, 'finally', despite its syntactical acrobatics, it yields next to nothing semantically. The first four lines are involuted 'circuits' of stating variously that darkness always comes back; and the last three lines assert the vacuity of the first four. Such, it appears, is the long death (*diuturnity* meaning 'lastingness' (*OED*)) after the short life (the almost nothing between 'Coming into Being and Passing Away'). But 'finally' is not the final word, and the dash directs the eye and ear again, this time to another kind of return: a volta, a 'but':

Syntaxes   127

        but by occasion
visions of truth or dreams
as they arise—
            to terms of grace
where grace has surprised us—
the unsustaining
           wondrously sustained

Is the image of the rose 'blooded with amber' in the first stanza one of the 'visions of truth' mentioned here? Are the first three lines of this third stanza parenthetical between the dashes, so that there is a kind of syntactical continuity before and after ('darkness [...] yields nothing | finally [...] to terms of grace')? Such questions are unanswerable, because the syntax has been pushed just beyond perfect comprehensibility. The 'terms of grace' are unclear because this line is one of the places 'where grace has surprised us'. Grace, as Hill seems to suggest in the context of death's diuturnity, is always an unexpected word, an uncontextualised thing. Yet the context of Hill's prose might help: 'If I were to consider undertaking a theology of language, this would be one of a number of possible points of departure for such an exploration: the abrupt, unlooked-for semantic recognition understood as corresponding to an act of mercy or grace' (*CCW*, p. 404).

The saving grace of the poem is, as the volta line puts it, the unlooked-for 'occasion': the unpremeditated 'dreams | as they arise' that, by inexplicable and unseen turns, offer moments of 'recognition', new semantic understandings, that transcend the dependable sentence of death. The words are arranged as occasion suggests; grammatical expectations get, as it were, dashed. The epiphanic turnaround in the final two lines is a clear ending – a joyful one – and its surprise is playfully prefigured by 'surprised' in the previous line. In this past participle, and in the final past participle, 'sustained', there is a sense of assured knowledge that counterbalances the second stanza's present-tense certainty of death. It is a declaration of trust that depends on a recollection of how that trust was earned; in this it resembles the declaration quoted by Hill from the ninetieth Psalm (in a larger reference to its musical setting by Charles Ives) in *Speech! Speech!*: 'LORD | | THOU HAST BEEN OUR DWELLING PLACE—FROM ONE | GENERATION | TO ANOTHER' (*SS* 52, p. 314). It is not that grace surprises us but that 'grace has surprised us'; and what sustained earlier generations can be relied on for the 'unsustaining' present. The poem, accordingly, is sustained into the space beyond a final full stop.

In 'De Anima', syntactical ambiguities complicate the foregoing poem's parabola of life discovered to be fruitless and revived by grace. The suggestion is that the soul cannot be wholly passive in response to grace, and must become watchful of, and newly responsible for, its movements:

Geoffrey Hill and the ends of poetry

                    Salutation: it is as though
                    effortlessly—to reprise—
                                    the unsung spirit
                    gestures of no account
                    become accountable
                                    such matters arising
                    whatever it is that is sought

                                        (C, p. 175)

Like the previous poem, 'De Anima' begins with an ungrammatical statement of its ostensible subject, followed by a colon; this time, instead of 'Rosa sericea', the subject is '[s]alutation'. The word might be read initially as a mock-formal greeting to the reader; but it soon becomes apparent that salutation itself is the poem's subject, and that what is at issue in the poem springs from the arrival of grace described in 'Of Coming into Being and Passing Away' (the clue in this stanza being the parenthetical 'to reprise'). How is the poet to salute such grace? The minutiae of syntax – in thoughts, 'spirit | gestures', as in words – once held 'of no account', 'become accountable'. The play on *account* is solidly a favourite for Hill.[47] His syntax, like his metre, is an often visible process of counting (of beats, syllables, constituent parts of a thought, sentence, line, stanza) and accounting (for what is not said, what is said imperfectly, and one's own imperfections).

Having summed the cost, the second and third stanzas consider how the poet subsequently might attain 'whatever it is that is sought':

                            through metaphysics
                research into angelic song
                ending as praise itself
                the absolute yet again
                atoned with the contingent—
                                        typology
                incarnate—Bethlehem the open field—

                still to conceive no otherwise: an
                aphasia of staring wisdom
                the soul's images glassily exposed
                                    fading to silverpoint
                still to be at the last
                ourselves and masters of all
                                    humility—

It is humility, though a playful sort, for a poet to deem 'angelic song' so beyond his competence that the best he can hope to do is conduct 'research into' it. Nonetheless, the very mention of 'metaphysics' as something to be

Syntaxes 129

worked 'through' indicates that lofty ambitions are not outside this poem's scope (nor, by its account, the scope of poetry in general). The poet's relationship to these ambitions, however, is obfuscated. Again, the sparsely punctuated syntax is instrumental in the poem's forging of illuminating ambiguities. For instance, in the lines 'research into angelic song | ending as praise itself', is it the research or the angelic song that ends as praise itself? The next line, 'the absolute yet again', appears at first to comment self-referentially and disparagingly on the absoluteness of the locution 'praise itself'; but it too is soon resolved with a succeeding verb: 'atoned with the contingent'.

The final word, sticking out its tongue of a dash, is another surprise finish, subverting a different absolutism, that of 'masters of all'; 'humility' undercuts a lofty (but worldly) ambition with an aspiration towards the soil (if the etymology of *humility* is taken seriously). A death of self is the loftier ambition of 'humility', a poet's acknowledgement of the 'wisdom' in 'aphasia' (a medical term for speechlessness or inability to comprehend speech). Aphasia is the result of angelic contact as far back as the second poem, and one of the earliest written, in Hill's first collection, 'God's Little Mountain':

I saw the angels lifted like pale straws;
I could not stand before those winnowing eyes

And fell, until I found the world again.
Now I lack grace to tell what I have seen;
For though the head frames words the tongue has none.
And who will prove the surgeon to this stone?

(*U*, p. 5)[48]

As with the aphasia in 'De Anima', this is a speechlessness that seems to require medical remedy, here a 'surgeon'. Significantly, the reason attributed to the muteness provides a link to the unexpected keystone in 'Of Coming into Being and Passing Away': 'Now I lack grace to tell what I have seen'. Humility, then, is the necessary virtue to cultivate in the presence of angels and their song – or of Christ, the Word, who is the 'typology incarnate' of 'De Anima', with 'Bethlehem the open field'. The descent of God into humanity's field of time and space is the prime example of the absolute being 'atoned with the contingent'. Bethlehem is the 'open field' because it is where the metaphysical fence between God and man, between the Word and the world, is strangely and powerfully absent. Hill's syntax in 'De Anima', researching this field, seeks to imitate that field's openness by allowing its own lack of directing punctuation to leave ambiguities 'glassily exposed | fading to silverpoint'. The poem's syntax appears appropriately sketchy, its dash

130   *Geoffrey Hill and the ends of poetry*

like an artist's flourish 'pointed at the end', as Foster writes of Burke's sentences.

This dash after 'humility', ending with the discovery of a starting point in virtue, invites the question of the next poem's title: 'Whether the Virtues are Emotions'. And the dashes, quickening both the emotion and the pace, carry over to this poem's opening:

> Overnight—overnight—
>   the inmost
> self made outcast: here
> plighting annihilations
>   unfinished
> business of eros
>   the common numen
>   (C, p. 176)

The first, repeated words in particular invite a comparison that seems to have been latent all along this punctuational line:

> Wild nights—Wild nights!
> Were I with thee
> Wild nights should be
> Our luxury!
>
> Futile—the winds—
> To a Heart in port—
> Done with the Compass—
> Done with the Chart!
>
> Rowing in Eden—
> Ah—the Sea!
> Might I but moor—tonight—
> In thee![49]

The 'unfinished | business of eros' (that universal divinity or 'common numen') is more plainly dealt with here than in Hill's poem. Dickinson's limited punctuation, like that found in *Canaan*, has no time for full stops and abounds in fast dashes; but instead of the colon used in *Canaan* there is the exclamation mark. While Dickinson's exclamation mark signifies increased emotion, a raised pitch, Hill's colon, throughout *Canaan*, is a mark of increased concentration, of emotion held back or distilled into meditation.

The dashes in 'Overnight—overnight—', the first line of 'Whether the Virtues are Emotions', are the only ones in the poem. The emotion is perceptibly allayed in the focusing colons, both preceding 'here' in the first stanza and throughout the second stanza:

of waking
        reverie where you had dreamt
to be absolved:
                and with the day
forsakenness
        the new bride brought forth:
carnal desuetude

It is not the 'Heart in port' here but the body, seeking a 'carnal' absolution, a fulfilment of eros, but finding only 'desuetude', a state of disuse. The moving, lively dashes are gone; the pace has been controlled and slowed. By the third stanza the eye of the storm has been reached, all marks of motion stripped away:

her mystic equity
her nature's ripped hardihood
the radiant
        windrows where a storm
emptied its creels
thrusting ailanthus that is called
        the Tree of Heaven

Once again, a strange epiphany, and an unanticipated sense of balance, occur in the last stanza of this poem. The 'new bride' of 'carnal desuetude' gains, instantly and astoundingly, a 'mystic equity', whose sense of daring, or 'hardihood', is 'ripped', and in the process transfigured into the erotic vigour of an observed storm. A final concentration occurs without a colon to accompany it: the speaker's eye closes in on the ailanthus, which the virile storm is 'thrusting' in the air. The plant, in another, consummating transformation, becomes what its name means, 'the Tree of Heaven', standing alone with its bold capital letters; and suddenly the 'ripped hardihood' of the bodily forsaken speaker is lent a 'radiant' new aspect.

Distilling the syntactical and thematic turns of the previous three poems, 'Whether Moral Virtue Comes by Habituation', the last in this quartet in *Canaan*, further illustrates the punctuational distinction of concentration and emotion. Its first stanza employs five dashes and ends with a colon; the second uses a further colon; and the last, again, sheds all punctuation:

It is said that sometimes even fear
drops away—
        exhausted—I would not
deny that: self
expression—you could argue—the first to go—
immolated
        selfhood the last:

132   *Geoffrey Hill and the ends of poetry*

> deprivation therefore
>   dereliction even
> become the things we rise to:
> ethereal conjecture
>   taking on
> humankind's heaviness of purchase
> the moral nebulae
>
>   common as lichen
> the entire corpus of ruinous sagesse
> moved by some rite
>   and pace of being
> as by earth in her slow
>   approaches to withdrawal
> the processionals of seared array
>
>   (C, p. 177)

The 'taking on' of 'humankind's heaviness of purchase' (in which 'purchase' puns on the notion of Christ's redeeming purchase of all humanity on the Cross) and the attendant 'moral nebulae', quandaries of interstellar vastness, throughout these four consecutive poems in *Canaan* would presumably render anyone 'exhausted'. The conversational tone of the opening stanza ('It is said that [...] I would not I deny [...] you could argue'), admittedly a distinctly Hillian and academic kind of conversation, allows the dashes to shift and pivot in argument, or else to jolt the thought forward, as though a debate is taking place between the aforementioned pronouns.

But if it is a debate, as the inquisitive title suggests, it is soon reconciled into an agreed and disagreeable thesis. The second stanza, recalling the discovery of 'humility' in 'De Anima', names 'deprivation' and 'dereliction' as 'the things we rise to'. (This dubious ascent is the end of another thread between these four poems, the first and second of which find places for 'arise' and 'arising', and the third of which involves 'waking'.) The 'ethereal conjecture' that has shaped the syntax of these poems is posited as 'taking on' (both bearing and confronting) 'humankind's heaviness of purchase' (the last word also signifying grip, resistance). An unresolvable situation, a held suspense, is the sure result. The remainder of the poem, the third stanza, seems dedicated to defining that situation in order to find an ending that is secure at least in its known deferment. Yet this unpunctuated stasis accompanies a depiction of movement. The 'corpus of ruinous sagesse' ('ruinous' meaning at once destroyed and destructive), like a demonic sister of Solomon's personified Wisdom (see, e.g., Proverbs from 1.20), is 'moved by some rite I and pace of being'; Hill's syntax in these poems, moved at its own pace, exhibits similarly obscure and formal gestures. Wisdom itself has been obscured into the archaic 'sagesse' by the poet's ruinous cleverness.[50]

Syntaxes   133

The body of sagesse's 'slow | approaches to withdrawal' are 'the procession-als of seared array'. This ending, the least epiphanic in these four poems, is nevertheless secured by the repeated pinning-down of ambiguities, most notably in this last pair of two-word oppositions: 'approaches to with-drawal' and 'seared array'. The poet's, and humanity's, wisdom, drawing near and turning away, is reliably unreliable. It is 'seared' by corruption; yet it still represents an 'array', an ordered, even a beautiful, display. (*Array* can be described as a distant calque for *syntax*, both signifying an arrangement or putting into order.[51])

The corruption of representation is a repeated theme, and is seen as something repetitious, in Hill's poetry. What is described at the end of 'Whether Moral Virtue Comes by Habituation' is not, after all, a stasis but a cycle: a natural and syntactical cycle, of approaching and withdrawing, blossoming and withering, giving and taking back. There is another 'Cycle' in *Canaan*; it is one of the three poems lacking even the limited punctuation found elsewhere. Its subtitle is '*William Arrowsmith, 1924–1992*', remem-bering the American classicist who had worked at Boston University (Hill's employer at the time of writing) and who died in Brookline, Massachusetts (Hill's residence at the time of writing). A cycle, as of life and death, as of nature, constantly determines an end; but the syntax of this poem in five parts appears at first to be as free as its free verse:

<blockquote>
1
Natural strange beatitudes
         the leafless tints
of spring touch red through brimstone
what do you mean   praise and lament
it is the willow
      first then
larch or alder
</blockquote>

(C, p. 206)

Where 'Of Coming into Being and Passing Away' sees the 'red spurs' of mortality in burgeoning life, the red touches here are 'tints | of spring' on 'leafless' – nearly but not quite lifeless – trees. As 'seared array' is both 'praise and lament', the earthly cycle Hill pictures is caught between visions of Heaven and of Hell. The phrase 'praise and lament', repeated in the fifth section, accounts for two aspects of this poem in memoriam: eulogy and elegy. It also broadly follows the pattern of '*laus et vituperatio*', praise and blame, in which Hill is profoundly interested.[52] The many words in Hill's poems that poise on the boundary between praise and blame share with the 'beatitudes', namely Christ's on the Mount (Matthew 5.3–11), an awareness of oxymoron: in what appears to be a curse is proclaimed a blessing, a supposed weakness counted a strength. The 'beatitudes' in this

134 *Geoffrey Hill and the ends of poetry*

poem are closely followed by the threat of 'brimstone'. Such juxtapositions are indeed '[n]atural strange'. A deathly decay of the syntax seems to be at work. The semblance of the sentence is at a greater distance in this poem than in any other by Hill.

As the fifth and final section of the poem demonstrates, though, there is a stranger order in the arrangement of these words:

> Larch or alder
> > first
> then willow
> > leafless tints
> of spring touch red through brimstone
>
> praise and lament
> praise and lament
>
> what do you mean
> > praise
> lament
> > praise and lament
> what do you mean
> > do you mean
> beatitudes

(p. 207)

This is not (as it may appear) a strict or even broad reversal of the first part of 'Cycle', but a strained attempt to bring it to order. None of the words used here is absent from the first part. The repetitions, those within this section itself, are not sonically or semantically emphatic; if a poem is, as Don Paterson says, 'a little machine for remembering itself', the final part of 'Cycle' is a faulty machine, struggling and finally failing to remember itself.[53] It cannot reproduce in a more ordered and sense-making fashion the syntactical bits and pieces of the first section. In the end, this machine's scrupulosity reduces these bits even further, coming to its halt with an enquiry that, in its redundancy, casts doubt on the transcendent epiphanies that occasion the poem in the first place: 'do you mean | beatitudes'. The multiplied interruptions of 'what do you mean', questions without question marks, are difficult to place – who is addressing and who being addressed? – and, if put to a difficult poet like Hill by a critic, might be difficult to hear.

The 'you' and the unvoiced *I* in 'what do you mean' are only briefly and speculatively reconciled to 'we' in the penultimate section of 'Cycle'. This section is also an unmarked question. The only two words from the first part that are not repeated in the last ('[n]atural strange') find themselves strangely transposed:

Syntaxes   135

```
Are we not moved by
                 'savage
indignation' or whatever
strange
           natürlich
dance with antlers
paces over and
                 over the same
ground
```
(p. 207)

Is the estrangement of 'natural', becoming here the German 'natürlich' (which can mean either *natural* or *naturally*), a recovery of the 'strange' appearance of nature, anticipating the 'dance with antlers' in the next line? This dance is a ritual aggression, which 'paces over and | over the same | ground' as the fifth section is about to do, an instinctive and inevitable conflict in nature. So, the poem and its syntax suggest, is human nature 'moved by some rite' against itself, heavenly against hellish impulse; its moves are of '"savage | indignation"'. The quotation is from Yeats:

> Swift has sailed into his rest;
> Savage indignation there
> Cannot lacerate his Breast.[54]

Is savage indignation, then, what sustains life, even as it lacerates it like antlers? The torn-apart syntax of 'Cycle', though its energy drains at last, sustains itself until its uncertain final 'beatitudes'. But tearing apart relinquishes a degree of control from the poet. The clash of registers that results from the play with the demotic sense in 'or whatever', which hangs on the line after Hill's quotation, is a misstep: the note of a teenage shrug does not belong in the poem. The 'and' that holds up an unrinsed cliché ('over and | over') marks another questionable line break.[55] But the general syntactical urge behind the poem's unresolved fragmentation moves a long way towards annulling these quibbles.

To Hill, the 'Cycle' is a way in which the syntax might make 'visions of truth' (*C*, p. 174), or '[n]atural strange beatitudes', recognised; but it is also the case that, for Hill, the circularity of words, things, is a truth in itself.

> Rivers bring down. The sea
> Brings away;
> Voids, sucks back, its pearls and auguries.

(*U*, p. 29)

This is from the second part of 'The Death of Shelley', itself the third in a sequence entitled 'Of Commerce and Society', in Hill's first collection.

136   *Geoffrey Hill and the ends of poetry*

Vincent Sherry writes of this passage: 'Hill is led to undermine the whole principle of material progress. The poem is an epitaph for the millennialism that led Shelley, in youth, to envision a gradual refinement of man's natural condition.'[56] Hill is inclined to write an epitaph for this ambition of refinement because he understands it: his constant struggle is to refine his own language, to clarify his syntax. Man is refined only in isolated instances in Hill; man's fixed, inexorable, and 'natural condition' is that of original sin.

Throughout his early poetry, the weight of this condition on the very effort to represent it amounts to a heavy load, not least in terms of punctuation. And one result of this sin-prone condition, namely the weight of 'abused | Bodies', is difficult for speech to bear in the second of 'Two Formal Elegies' (their dedicatory subtitle being '*For the Jews in Europe*'):

> Is it good to remind them, on a brief screen,
> Of what they have witnessed and not seen?
> (Deaths of the city that persistently dies...?)
> (To put up stones ensures some sacrifice.)
> (Sufficient men confer, carry their weight.)
> (At whose door does the sacrifice stand or start?)
>
> (*U*, p. 17)

The four separately bracketed lines that conclude the poem constitute an overt surfeit of punctuation. Like the reappearance of 'wicked' after a revisionary intermission of 'damn-fool' in 'Coda''s 'I know that sounds | a wicked thing to say' (*TCP*, p. 600), these brackets have variously disappeared before finally being presented as they appeared originally. The first publication, which provided all four sets of brackets, was in *Paris Review* in 1959.[57] Collected in *For the Unfallen* in the same year, it had lost two sets, the middle pair, which left only the two questions bracketed.[58] As late as 2009, in the paperback edition of Yale's *Selected Poems*, the final four lines retained only these two sets of brackets.[59] In *Broken Hierarchies* (2013), however, the four sets return. Ricks, who discusses the poem at some length, would not have welcomed them:

> Hill was right to think that his is a poetic gift which must be profoundly and variously alive to what simple brackets can do. He had been wrong to think that he could command to favourable judgment a concatenation of four lines, each bracketed, without his poem's indurating itself into mannerism and self-attention, a sequence of self-containednesses such as then seals the poem into self-congratulation. By removing the brackets from both the antepenultimate and the penultimate lines, he not only removed the oppression of paralysing self-consciousness, but also tautened the arc of the poem. For, unlike the first poem, the second has at last gravitated to couplets; against which there is now played a beautiful and complementary chiasmus, *a/b/b/a*, in the sombre punctuation alone.[60]

Syntaxes 137

This is an exaggeration. The 'oppression of paralysing self-consciousness' is especially overstated. The punctuation of the poem as it first and last appears is indeed 'sombre', none more so than these lines of brackets; but their induration is not 'into self-congratulation'. Rather, it is a defensive hardening, like pairs of arms raised protectively over heads. To remove two of the sets of brackets is to remove the impression the brackets give of memorials set up, cairns or gravestones, witnessing insufficiently but enduringly to those whom they honour. The four lines, each bracketed, respond more vividly to the couplet that precedes them: 'Is it good to remind them, on a brief screen, | Of what they have witnessed and not seen?' The subsequent brackets are, like cinema screens, frames of vision, consciously narrow. They are placed as fragile shelters for the words, in case they say too much; in case they presume to say what they cannot; in case they self-condemn, coming from a speaker who, like every late onlooker, has merely 'witnessed and not seen'. To isolate each of the four lines in this way, too, shelters them from one another, purports to deny syntactical relations between them. Like the poems from *Canaan* examined above, the lines (full of folded ambiguities) are made fragmentary; but unlike those poems, whose syntactical and semantic borders are fluid, traversable, these lines lock themselves in punctuation. The more unsure they are, the more scrupulous or elaborate their markings: '(Deaths of the city that persistently dies...?)'. This, looking up at the 'brief screen' in the line above, alludes to the repeated films at memorial sites and museums that seem to bring about anew each time the destruction of civilisation ('the city'). The first and last lines are questions; and the middle two forbiddingly vague: the reader shifts at the unpersoned infinitive and the 'some' of '(To put up stones ensures some sacrifice.)'; and at the uncertain balance and setting of '(Sufficient men confer, carry their weight.)'.[61] The sense of a terrible and weighty bodily toll hangs over both.

Where Ricks finds 'self-congratulation' in these lines' excessive punctuation is not clear to me; but 'self-attention' is justified. But the poem too is justified in its self-attention. It obtains not in the two extra sets of brackets but in the ambiguities of the final line, '(At whose door does the sacrifice stand or start?)'. These words, remembering Keats's question 'Who are these coming to the sacrifice?' and also the description of the Passover in Exodus, are resonantly self-reflexive.[62] As in Keats's ode, Hill is considering art's capacity to attend properly to 'sacrifice', how well it might 'stand', and where it might 'start'. It is also wondering aloud, guiltily, where the artist's sacrifice is; and whether such an offering could be to any extent redeeming or propitiatory. The brackets of what is probably the most discussed stanza in Hill's oeuvre, the third stanza of 'September Song', help the reader retrospectively to interpret the character of those that end 'Two Formal Elegies':

138   *Geoffrey Hill and the ends of poetry*

(I have made
an elegy for myself it
is true)

              (*KL*, p. 44)

This admission of 'self-attention' is shamed into its brackets. In the same way, the last line of 'Two Formal Elegies', too aware of its reflection back onto the artist, retains its apologetic parentheses. Ricks sells short the punctuation's ambiguous 'mannerism and self-attention' when he charges it also with self-praise; the opposite reading rings truer.

'Two Formal Elegies', despite its neat closing set of four lines, each a bracketed sentence, ends with a profound lack of consummation. Hill's revision of the punctuation in these lines suggests the accompanying struggle to communicate a lack of consummation consummately (or at least well); and it suggests too the weight Hill places on his punctuation in this struggle. In the next section, I look at the revisions in *Odi Barbare*, which are visible between the poems published in journals and magazines from 2009 to 2012, the Clutag edition of the collection in 2012, and finally the version in *Broken Hierarchies* in 2013. They show a convoluted and self-entangled syntax with highly unconventional punctuation gradually clarified by the introduction of more grammatically orthodox punctuation.[63]

Forms of trust

Hill's implied desire, quoted above in 'Before Senility', to write in 'plainer style'; his stated desire for 'ambiguity in plain speaking' (*TCP*, pp. 594, 597); and the earlier statement 'I'm | ordered to speak plainly, let what is | speak for itself' (*OS* XVIII, p. 368), in which 'ordered' emphasises the significance of right arrangement (both syntactically and metrically) in Hill's pursuit of plain speaking, find peculiar expression in the punctuational development of *Odi Barbare*.[64]

Odi Barbare is not an obvious example of 'plain speaking'. It is written in sapphics: four-line stanzas, the first three lines having eleven syllables and the fourth five syllables. Its syntax is so condensed that even with the more conventional punctuation in *Broken Hierarchies* the reader's mind often cannot help but lag well behind the mouth:

Briefed at hazard scamble the brittle crystal
Bough from saltmine Stendhal has made so much of.
Titan arum's rotten Sumatran splendour
        Passion of substance.

              (*OB* XXIX, p. 863)

Syntaxes 139

The stanza appeared in *Standpoint*, in 2010, thus:

Briefed at hazard scramble the brittle crystal
Bough from saltmine Stendhal has made so much of
Titan arum rotten Sumatran splendour
Passion of substance[65]

Because, in the earlier *Standpoint* version, the first two lines are enjambed, it is unclear whether the third and fourth lines are intended to follow their sense. The *Broken Hierarchies* version's full stop separates the thoughts and gives a clearer idea of why they might be presented together in the stanza. The first two lines allude to Stendhal's concept of crystallisation, which, arguing that someone infatuated tends to 'overrate' his beloved, uses the metaphor of a 'leafless wintry bough' thrown into a salt mine and later found 'studded with a galaxy of scintillating diamonds'; the latter two lines, considering the weak leafless bough, hold up the titan arum, a gigantic flowering plant also called the *corpse flower* due to its putrescent aroma, as a sturdier and altogether more virile metaphor, one not for 'brittle' passion but '[p]assion of substance'.[66] Without punctuation, the comparison seems closer to free association, to a hazardous 'scramble' (or indeed, as it later became, 'scamble'); the insertion of a single full stop (together with the amendment of 'arum' to 'arum's') lends visible structure to the stanza and digs out the thought's path far more clearly.[67]

The early published versions of poems from *Odi Barbare* reveal Hill determined to avoid punctuation, or at any rate conventional punctuation. The manifest vigour of the titan arum (or *Amorphophallus titanum*, to give it its improper proper name) is an apposite symbol for the syntax in these early versions of the work; the poems have a relentless and restless energy, forbidding on first reading. In this they resemble *Speech! Speech!*, about which Hill said in an interview: 'It is odd when you think of the way society runs on energy – or rather, a *vis inertiae*. When energy is presented to them they recoil from it in horror.'[68] With limited punctuation, the early *Odi Barbare* poems shift quickly from line to line, thought to thought, in a different manner from the graceful piecing of broken lines in *Canaan*, and again closer to the whiplashing movement of *Speech! Speech!*, of which he writes elsewhere: '*Speech! Speech!* is not a book to be slowly pondered; it is meant to be taken, at least on first reading, at a cracking pace'.[69] The energy of *Odi Barbare* is not drained away by the changes in punctuation seen in *Broken Hierarchies*, but distilled, focused.

One of the focuses of *Odi Barbare*'s energy, in this instance an angry energy, is what he calls, in his inaugural Professor of Poetry lecture at Oxford, 'the bankers' scam', in reference to the worldwide financial crisis of 2007–2008.[70] The thirteenth poem of *Odi Barbare* was first published in

140   *Geoffrey Hill and the ends of poetry*

The Baffler in 2012. Here are its second stanza and final two stanzas:

> Herod rants ¦ pageants on their wooden tractions
> Cannot hold him · Now he is in the shambles
> Butchers Row · Come back you old wakeman ¦ watch us
>   Cartwheel to ruin
>
> [...]
>
> Shall they break us twice in unbroken cycle
> Lords of our time ¦ losers of others' livings
> Negative life equity left our children
>   With a bone ploughshare
>
> Who are these restless in the darkened kingdom
> Apprehension memory clamour spectral
> Turn in conned sleep murmurous vexing nation
>   Now and regardless[71]

And here are those stanzas as they appear in *Broken Hierarchies*:

> Herod rants; pageants on their wooden tractions
> Cannot hold him. Now he is in the shambles,
> Butchers Row. Come back, you old wakeman, watch us
>   Cartwheel to ruin.
>
> [...]
>
> Shall they break us twice in unbroken cycle,
> Lords of our time, losers of others' livings,
> Negative life equity left our children
>   With a bone ploughshare?
>
> Who are these restless in the darkened kingdom?
> Apprehension, memory, clamour spectral.
> Turn in conned sleep, murmurous vexing nation,
>   Now and regardless.
>
>   (*OB* XIII, p. 847)

The verticals and dots in the second stanza of the *Baffler* version, Hill seems to realise, are doing the jobs of more familiar punctuation marks; and so they are replaced by a semicolon, commas, and full stops. But, reading each of the stanzas above, it is clear that these marks are not doing the same jobs. The rhythms of the earlier poem are noticeably looser; as Hill says of *Speech! Speech!*, it appears to be designed to be read more quickly.[72] Its lines, mostly lacking punctuation, take on a more impatiently hostile tone, a ranting quality, tamed in the regularised syntax and cadences of the *Broken Hierarchies* version. The earlier poem's limited punctuation allows

Syntaxes   141

the reader more interpretative leeway as to sound and tempo, but also as to meaning. For example, in the early version, the stanza beginning 'Shall they break us' is conceivable as two sentences, the first a question spanning the first two lines, and the second a statement. *Broken Hierarchies* resolves this ambiguity by rendering the stanza as one longer question. Similarly, the possibility of an enjambed 'spectral | Turn' between the second and third lines of the last stanza, following the ghostly apparitions '[a]pprehension memory clamour', is closed in *Broken Hierarchies* by the addition of a full stop. Hill, in these late amendments, finds in favour of increased directness, '[p]assion of substance' rather than spectral turns. The change in *Odi Barbare*'s punctuation is a sacrifice, less than expected for many critics of Hill, of ambiguity for communicability.

'I am happy to make my work as generally accessible as I honestly can', Hill writes, using a word he decries (insofar as it is used in relation to poetry) on several other occasions. 'But this is less often than many professional and amateur readers consider right and proper.'[73] It may be fair to censure Hill for his own positive use of 'accessible' here; as applied to literature, it is a clumsy word that elides a question of style with one of perceived propriety (what 'readers consider right and proper'); the formulation of the statement as a concession ('I am happy to') does not do Hill any service either, savouring of condescension and aesthetic compromise at once.

Or is this a little harsh? Might Hill simply have Arnold's implicit warning in mind?

Shakspeare is the great poet he is from his skill in discerning and firmly conceiving an excellent action, from his power of intensely feeling a situation, of intimately associating himself with a character; not from his gift of expression, which rather even leads him astray, degenerating sometimes into a fondness for curiosity of expression, into an irritability of fancy, which seems to make it impossible for him to say a thing plainly, even when the press of action demands the very directest language, or its level of character the very simplest. Mr. Hallam, than whom it is impossible to find a saner and more judicious critic, has had the courage (for at the present day it needs courage) to remark, how extremely and faultily difficult Shakspeare's language often is. It is so: you may find main scenes in some of his greatest tragedies, *King Lear* for instance, where the language is so artificial, so curiously tortured, and so difficult, that every speech has to be read two or three times before its meaning can be comprehended. This overcuriousness of expression is indeed excessive employment of a wonderful gift – of the power of saying a thing in a happier way than any other man; nevertheless, it is carried so far that one understands what M. Guizot meant, when he said that Shakspeare appears in his language to have tried all styles except that of simplicity.[74]

142   *Geoffrey Hill and the ends of poetry*

Hill is capable of simplicity, and willing 'to say a thing plainly' – but, as he writes, 'less often' than many think 'right and proper'. Arnold's 'excessive employment of a wonderful gift' finds an almost direct response in the first poem of *Speech! Speech!*: 'Some believe I we over-employ our gifts' (p. 289). (And, by reason of this Arnoldian allusion, it is possible that Hill's 'we', already a tongue-in-cheek pronoun that evokes the royal *we*, is intended to stand for *Shakespeare and I.*)

The changing punctuation of *Odi Barbare* may be the result of Hill's awareness, in the verticals and dots of its early published poems, of 'a fondness for curiosity of expression', or an 'overcuriousness of expression', that was already present in the syntax. The final stanzas of the first poem of *Odi Barbare* reflect, as poems in *The Daybooks* are wont to do, on the work's own form; and again recall Arnold's words on excessively employed gifts:

> Measure loss re-cadencing Sidney's sapphics
> Not as words fall but as they rise to meaning.
> Laurels withheld, fractured the noble column;
>   Alien torsos
>
> Too much gifted. Angular backlit miners'
> Profiles. Build up roofing and side supports, quote
> Axioms, blast access to unsuspected
>   Caverns of fluorspar.
>
> (p. 835)

The 'roofing and side supports' that shape the syntax of the sapphic stanza are metrical as well as punctuational: the first stanza here begins with the word 'Measure'; the notion of words falling and rising suggests ictus, the movement of stressed and unstressed syllables; the fracturing and angularity Hill writes of may be found in the metrical make-up of the sapphic stanza itself. But, from another angle, the 'noble column' of the sapphic is purposely 'fractured' by Hill with awkward syntax, as though, at the time of writing, any poetic evocation of nobility would not be 'right and proper'. 'Too much gifted' is double-ended: 'Sidney's sapphics' are more laden with poetic gifts than the current age deserves; and so the age is given Hill's sapphics, '[a]lien torsos', which are more laden with poetic gifts than the current age can perceive. At the same time, however, the phrase is an admission on Hill's part of difficulty; difficulty that can be fairly seen as unnecessary, but that is almost impossible for him to avoid without diminishing his own effort to write what is 'sound and true', to infuse into his poetry 'soul and matter'.[75]

'Syntax so confusing I encodes its own message before your name I is put to it' (*HOLC* 19, p. 167). The struggle between systems of punctuation in

Odi Barbare is emblematic of the larger conflict between syntaxes in Hill's poetry, the 'pitiless wrench between | truth and metre' (p. 561). Avoidance of a language that is 'extremely and faultily difficult' is in the mind of Hill's late syntax. It fears to be 'so confusing' that it frustrates its own pursuit of ordered precision. It is right to fear this; and sometimes the clutter and awkwardness of the syntax harms rather than assists both 'truth and metre'. 'To say this awkwardly or not at all', explains a (grammatically but not semantically incomplete) sentence in *The Book of Baruch* (47, p. 22). And yet, when the words fall in place easily and fluently, Hill, much more often than he delights in what Arnold calls 'the power of saying a thing in a happier way than any other man', is suspicious and asks himself:

> Why does this never falter? I say we múst
> Túrn and be broken, even as metre holds—
> Let's mean by that, *progresses* and *enfolds*—
> Moving the syntax to a form of trust.
>
> (TT 49, p. 913)

Syntax and metre are here bound up together – both in the prosodic sense and by Hill's terminological conflation. The verse does not 'falter', partly because the poet's skill is consummate; but also because the patterns of both metre and syntax have become so easily, almost automatically, found, which Hill has a habit of worrying about. Even when Yeats's 'click' is found at the end of a poem, Hill says in his last reading, it is found 'somehow too self-satisfied, too self-admiring'.[76] But Hill's trust, as in *Canaan*'s poems of limited punctuation, is in the 'things of grace' that unexpectedly visit the work, albeit snagged by the brokenness of human nature ('Parentalia' ('Go your ways'), C, p. 209). Syntax, as Hill writes of metre, '*progresses* and *enfolds*' language; in the wrong hands, and with the wrong ends, it is a kind of abduction. This is why trust, for Hill, is so 'curiously tortured' (*torture* from the Latin meaning *to twist*), why it entails such irritable difficulty. To trust in the unpredictable, often dubious movements of language is to some extent, as Hill writes of memory, to 'let it go as rain | streams on half-visible clatter of the wind | lapsing and rising' ('Sorrel', C, p. 208). This 'let it go' might have Empson's poem of that title in mind, which utters a danger of such release to syntax: 'The talk would talk and go so far aslant.'[77]

But Hill finally refuses to follow Empson in giving primacy to ambiguity.[78] Hill's trust in syntax, evident in the allusive meanderings of his late poetry (particularly *The Daybooks*, as the diaristic title implies, and *The Book of Baruch*, 'more a daybook than *The Daybooks* ever were' (*BBGJ* 186, p. 102)), is undeterred by the thought of going aslant, as long as it goes divertingly. The decision to adapt the punctuation, and consequently the syntax, of *Odi Barbare* appears to bespeak a lack of trust in language's

144   *Geoffrey Hill and the ends of poetry*

difficulty, its ambiguity. Indeed, though the abundance of accurately ambiguous puns remains, the stress shifts in the syntax of the late poems, as here from one draft to another, from a trust in language's difficulty to a trust in its potential simplicity.

> *I can see someone walking there, a girl,*
> And she is you, old love. Edging the meadow
> The may-tree is all light and all shadow.
> Coming and going are the things eternal.
>
> (*TT* 88 (f), p. 932)

Could this shadowy but lucid stanza appear, in the last book of *Broken Hierarchies*, if not for such a trust? This is not the tyrannous simplification of language of which Hill warns; but the finding again of a syntax moved towards simplicity, moved 'to a form of trust'.[79] There is a shimmer of King James grandeur in the reversed adjective of 'things eternal'; but otherwise the stanza is, even for Hill's late work, unusually self-reconciled and unusually plain-spoken.[80] Even 'all light and all shadow', which could sound enormous in its scope, is quiet, quietened not only by the *sh* of 'shadow' but by the casual, painterly broadness of its generalities: the may-tree is simply characterised by light as strongly as by shadow. This stanza, the second and last in this last of 'Sei Madrigali' or *Six Madrigals*, finds a consummating end, unsurprisingly doubled, in its vision of the tree. 'Coming and going are the things eternal': at once, the poem is resigned to transience – *coming to be and passing away are what occur continually* – and alive to transcendence – *eternal things are momentarily appearing*. This latter possibility in the last line enlarges again the vision of the penultimate line: perhaps it really is, somehow, 'all' light and 'all' shadow that are seen or foreseen in the may-tree.

A trust in syntax, which deepens throughout Hill's late work, from the unpunctuated conclusions of *Canaan* to the self-persuading assertions of *The Book of Baruch*, is finally a trust in language's capacity for expressive consummation. 'If this is going to be your testament', Hill tells himself in the latter work, 'best press on with it. Trust that its true being is song' (*BBGJ* 47, p. 22). This implies that the work, as it first appears or sounds, is not 'song', not euphonious or beautiful; but that its 'true', as yet unrevealed, nature is 'song'. Whether or not 'song' is expected to emerge in the course of the work, and whether or not Hill expects it to emerge by his own skill, by grace, by chance, or otherwise, are left unclear. But the trust is in itself significant. Hill instructs himself, seemingly successfully, to 'press on' (though not regardless) and believe that the end of consummate articulation – both beautiful (as 'song') and lastingly true (as 'testament') – will be achieved.[81] What is mistrusted is a '[s]yntax so confusing' that it 'encodes its own message'; language is, for Hill, not to be so trusted that it can be allowed to get away from the poet, from deliberation, from struggle. 'O language, my allergy, my bloody colleague!' (*BBGJ* 190, §3, p. 104). The ordering influence of the familiar punctuation in *Odi Barbare*'s final version reveals a faith placed in the poem's (not merely the poet's) 'message', one that is not so much fretted over as expressed with greater, and riskier, directness. Just before ending the forty-fifth poem of *Odi Barbare* (p. 879) with one of the collection's most luxuriously final flourishes, 'Adamantine age set to melt in flames of | Absolute longing', Hill exhorts himself: 'Be a fool and say so'.[82]

5

Forms

Ideal finesses

The ideal is an idea of the end. It is a vision held out in front, a destination that, illusory or not, gives direction. Hill's use of *ideally* is more colloquial than Platonic; but it is nonetheless concerned with ends. The previous chapter of this book quotes the first of Hill's *Collected Critical Writings*: 'Ideally, as I have already implied, my theme would be simple; simply this: that the technical perfecting of a poem is an act of atonement' (*CCW*, p. 4). In 2008, conversing with Rowan Williams, then Archbishop of Canterbury, Hill uses the adverb again, picking up on two of the themes of my discussion of syntax, namely difficulty and epiphany:

> What I see ideally in the poem – in a difficult poem – is difficulties on the way, leading up to a kind of semantic epiphany, or a semantic annunciation, which will incandescently take up into itself the difficulties en route and burn off any impurities, and present them in a kind of final seraphic light. That is why I am impatient with those passages in Eliot's *Four Quartets* which, in a kind of formal and sophisticated mumble, proclaim difficulties in a manner which, in a rather low-grade way, is extremely fluent nonetheless. To me the difficulty and the resolution have to be much more a thing encountered within the semantic body. I don't like pensées. I don't think poetry has much to do with pensées, and *Four Quartets* is full of pensées about things, but I don't find that it engages me with the real struggle in the way that much less well-known poetry does. I have a great admiration for the American poet Richard Eberhart, and those Kierkegaardian poems that Eberhart wrote. There's a poem of Eberhart's which ends with a sudden line: 'Where stays ǀ The abrupt essence and the final shield?' And, to me, that last, wonderfully luminous, clarifying line – when I say 'luminous' and 'clarifying', I'd be hard put to say what are '[t]he abrupt essence and the final shield', except I know '[t]he abrupt essence and the final shield' is something that the semantic and metrical issues of the poem had inevitably to arrive at. And the epiphany, so to speak, is in that wonderful, mysterious last line which doesn't, at one level, connect with what has gone before, but which, at a deeper level, is the only

Forms

thing he could have said after the Kierkegaardian paradoxes which he has hitherto engaged in.[1]

Between these two ideals, Hill's subject remains the 'technical perfecting of a poem'. It is unusual to find Hill portraying the 'formal' in a negative light, as where he speaks of the 'formal and sophisticated mumble' of *Four Quartets*. (His finding fault with that work is less unusual; his complaint that it fails to engage him 'with the real struggle' ignores the fact that the work engaged him in a lifelong critical struggle.[2]) Hill contrasts this Eliotic formality, understood narrowly in this context as though it were as vacuous as the correct tying of a cravat, with the 'semantic epiphany' present in the final lines of poems such as the Eberhart he cites.[3] This 'semantic epiphany', quickly given the alternative appellation 'semantic annunciation', must be 'encountered within the semantic body'; and must be, finally, 'something that the semantic and metrical issues of the poem had inevitably to arrive at'.[4] Only with 'metrical' does Hill begin to acknowledge again the importance of the formal in a poem's final perfecting.

Hill's emphasis on the poem's ending is striking. The ideal poem's difficulties are a 'leading up to' a final epiphany, a 'last, wonderfully luminous, clarifying line'. In his own last appearance to his 'subterranean' readership, at Emmanuel College, Cambridge, Hill augmented his readings of three poems by discussing the 'essential' word of each, what he called 'the sounding note'; 'you must train yourself', he said, 'to have an ear to catch it'.[5] What distinguishes each of these words is that they all occur in the final lines of their respective poems. During his discussion of 'pinnacled', the penultimate word in the early poem 'Merlin', Hill said:

> Can you see how poems have almost a valve-like action? They open out to receive new sustenance, which is the raw energy of language. They then close in upon that raw energy, as if one's life depended on finding the necessary shape; and as if the necessary shape could be governed by the discovery, somewhere in the back of one's mind, of a word like 'pinnacled', to go with 'corn'.[6]

And then later, having read 'Requiem for the Plantagenet Kings', with its final phrase 'evacuates its dead':

> Just as 'pinnacled' was essential to the click – what was it Yeats said? – the poem comes together with a click like a closing box. One is looking for words that click the poem together like a closing box. And then one regrets it of course; because the click is somehow too self-satisfied, too self-admiring. But as 'pinnacled' does something to the terrain, the verbal terrain of 'Merlin', so 'evacuates' has to carry within it that double sense of being shepherded to safety; and filth. If there is any power, that is the power it has. And I cannot see how the poem could have satisfied myself – which I admit it does... quite

148 *Geoffrey Hill and the ends of poetry*

a number of my poems actually satisfy me, and I'm terribly sorry to have to tell you that.[7]

Finally, on the subject of these 'closing' words, he said:

> It's on that very shaky foundation that I build my ridiculous hypothesis of the necessary closure that has to take place in a poem before the plethora of possible meanings is finessed – 'finessed'?! – finessed to a statement which some intelligent people will read and think 'ah, yes'.[8]

The word 'finessed', which gives Hill pause here, is itself a word of consummation, of bringing to a desired (and final) state: etymologically, *finesse* is a contraction of *fineness*; *fine*, in turn, is a word historically related to ends or limits of things.[9] (There is also Sidney on the Euphuists: 'well may they obtain an opinion of a seeming fineness, but persuade few, which should be the end of their fineness.'[10])

Hill's idea of 'closure' agrees with another critical 'statement', Smith's in *Poetic Closure*: 'the sense of closure is a function of the perception of structure'.[11] In this chapter, I examine the relationship between structure and closure in Hill's poems, and I do so by treating four poetic forms, four 'necessary shape[s]' that Hill finesses to their ends: unrhymed sonnets (as in the eight sections of *King Log*'s 'Funeral Music'); versets (as in *Mercian Hymns*); clavics (a form of Hill's own devising, presented in his book of the same name); and sapphics (as in *Odi Barbare*). The former two of these are from Hill's early work (1968–1971), the latter two from his late work (2007–2012). Although discussions of Hill's use of rhymed sonnets, quatrains, and the peculiar twenty-one-line stanzas of *Liber Illustrium Virorum* would be thoroughly worthwhile, I concentrate on the four forms above because it seems to me that, though all of them can be traced back to earlier writers, these are the forms that Hill most convincingly makes his own.

The formal characteristics of a poem are attended by connotations and expectations: these connotations might be lexical, syntactical, thematic, stylistic, even visual – and often they are all of these.[12] The boundaries between the definitions of *form* and *genre* are indefinite. In Michael D. Hurley and Michael O'Neill's *Poetic Form: An Introduction*, chapters of which are headed 'Lyric', 'Elegy', and 'Epic', there is an acknowledgement that the word *form* has been necessarily expanded to include concerns of genre.[13] I intend to follow this practice here. An investigation concentrated strictly and exclusively on the formal elements of Hill's unrhymed sonnets or sapphics would not have the natural or sufficient scope to attend to their relationships with the 'semantic epiphany', the satisfying 'click', the 'necessary closure'. Hill's own reflections imply that his engagement with the poetic forms he works in is end-focused. That the ending he seeks is in a 'kind of final seraphic light' indicates that 'shape' and 'metrical issues' are not of sole or first importance to his poetic ideal. This chapter aims to ascertain how his poems' structures 'open out' to 'close in'; how and to what extent they function by 'leading up to' their closures. Such questions move the reader into, but also beyond, formal considerations.

Unrhymed sonnets: Lowell and 'Funeral Music'

Hill's first book of poetry was published in 1959, the same year that saw Robert Lowell's *Life Studies*. Hill's book is strongly influenced by both Lowell and one of Lowell's poetic mentors, Allen Tate; its title, *For the Unfallen*, provides a counter to Lowell's poem 'For the Union Dead', which itself responds to Tate's 'Ode to the Confederate Dead'.[14] But while Lowell, in *Life Studies*, was moving on stylistically, Hill was attached to the earlier Lowell, the Lowell who displays his mastery of conventional poetic forms, particularly in *Lord Weary's Castle* (1946). In his ninth lecture as Professor of Poetry at Oxford, Hill claimed that this, 'Lowell's second book, produced largely under Tate's aegis, is one of the finest verse collections since the work of Yeats's final decade.'[15]

Stephen James has illuminatingly charted the influence of early Lowell on early Hill (including unpublished poems, one of which, 'An Ark on the Flood', draws from Lowell more obviously than the poems in *For the Unfallen*).[16] One can spot further parallels repeatedly. To take only a couple of examples, there is the prevalence of the word 'dead', especially as the terminal word in a line, in both Hill's and Lowell's first collections.[17] Then there is the pairing of 'God' with 'blood' in the first poem of Hill's *For the Unfallen*, 'Genesis'; the pair is repeated in 'Doctor Faustus' (twice: once as an end-rhyme and once as an internal rhyme) and in 'Ovid in the Third Reich'; it is earlier used by Lowell as the final rhyme in 'New Year's Day' and as an internal rhyme in the sonnet 'France'.[18]

Lowell's influence on Hill's poetic forms can be observed even in Hill's late work: the unusual form of Lowell's twenty-one-line poem 'Rebellion', from *Lord Weary's Castle* (p. 32), is used precisely and exclusively in the fifty-four poems of Hill's *Liber Illustrium Virorum* (2007–2012).[19] The nine-line stanza of *Oraclau | Oracles* (2007–2012), borrowed ultimately from Donne's 'A nocturnall upon S. Lucies day', is also a favourite of Lowell in *Lord Weary's Castle*: see 'The Ghost' (pp. 52–54) and 'Mr Edwards and the Spider' (pp. 59–60).

The purpose of this section, however, is to trace not influence but an illuminating likeness in the use of form. Between 1968 and 1973, unrhymed sonnets were all Lowell wrote; and one of the most significant sequences

150 *Geoffrey Hill and the ends of poetry*

in Hill's early writing, published in 1968, is a group of eight unrhymed sonnets entitled 'Funeral Music'.[20] In the six years that culminated in the three simultaneous publications of *History*, *For Lizzie and Harriet*, and *The Dolphin*, Lowell wrote startlingly many unrhymed sonnets: of the 539 poems or sections collected in these books, all but a handful are blank-verse quatorzains (and those in the handful are unfinished or over-finished sonnets, having too few or too many lines).

Some poetic forms provide more to compete with than others. Though there are notable exceptions, the unrhymed sonnet does not have the distinguished ancestry of its rhymed sibling. Christopher Ricks lists Blake's 'To the Evening Star', Keats's 'Oh thou whose face hath felt the Winter's wind', and Thomas Lovell Beddoes's 'A Crocodile' as Lowell's most significant forerunners in the form.[21] (There are also Lowell's own unconventional sonnets in 1961's *Imitations*.[22]) Ricks also cites the opinion of Eliot on Samuel Johnson's play *Irene*: 'the phrasing is admirable, the style elevated and correct, but each line cries out for a companion to rhyme with it'.[23] For Eliot here, the line crying out represents an unwanted lack of effect; but I argue here that, in unrhymed sonnets such as Lowell's and Hill's, the line that 'cries out for a companion' is both an effect entirely necessary to the poems' designed unfinishedness and a component of poems that, without the local reconciliations of rhyme, search (recurrently, at times tormentedly) for other sorts of gatherings, completions, endings.

The first sonnet in Lowell's *The Dolphin*, entitled 'Fishnet', gathers fourteen lines (though it did not always); the sense of companionship between them rises and falls and again rises.[24] 'Fishnet' can be read as an apologia for the unrhymed sonnet itself:

> Any clear thing that blinds us with surprise,
> your wandering silences and bright trouvailles,
> dolphin let loose to catch the flashing fish...
> saying too little, then too much.
> Poets die adolescents, their beat embalms them,
> the archetypal voices sing offkey;
> the old actor cannot read his friends,
> and nevertheless he reads himself aloud,
> genius hums the auditorium dead.
> The line must terminate.
> Yet my heart rises, I know I've gladdened a lifetime
> knotting, undoing a fishnet of tarred rope;
> the net will hang on the wall when the fish are eaten,
> nailed like illegible bronze on the futureless future.
>
> (*The Dolphin*, p. 645)

Forms   151

Is this what Hill calls a torso poem? 'I'm all for torsos. I think poetic torsos are good. Long poems that finish with three hapless dots. Very very interesting, and very very vital to the health of poetry, these torso poems, whether nineteenth-century or Romantic.'[25] This seems to exclude Lowell's poem on a few counts. And yet it sounds as though Hill, if not thinking about unrhymed sonnets, is at least thinking about poems in blank verse; to be like torsos, one presumes, poems cannot be broken up into stanzas and must have a certain consistency of line length, which pentameter guarantees (aurally, if not also visually). Hill's reference to the nineteenth century recalls what Eliot writes immediately after his comment on Johnson's *Irene*: 'Indeed, it is only with labour, or by occasional inspiration, or by submission to the influence of the older dramatists, that the blank verse of the nineteenth century succeeds in making the absence of rhyme inevitable and right, with the rightness of Milton.'[26]

In 'Fishnet', Lowell makes the absence of rhyme inevitable and right (though comparison with Milton would not be right). Yet still it does not appear to be one of Hill's '[l]ong' torso poems. How can something as short as a sonnet be a torso poem, unless it is Rilke's 'Archäischer Torso Apollos'? Nevertheless, though broken like Apollo's, 'Fishnet' is a kind of torso poem as Hill describes it. It is a haul of lines that starts, stops, starts, and inconclusively stops at last. Its 'three hapless dots' do not finish it, but they do (in the original version especially, from which I now quote) finish its beginning:

> Any clear thing that blinds us with surprise,
> your wandering silences and bright trouvailles,
> dolphin let loose to catch the flashing fish ....[27]

These are, one may reasonably argue, not three but four hapless dots. John Lennard, in his *Poetry Handbook*, writes: 'Poets may also, like scholars, distinguish "internal" ellipsis from a "terminal" four-dot form comprising ellipsis + full stop, as Lowell did "To Speak of Woe That is In Marriage".'[28] Lennard then quotes that (rhymed) sonnet's seventh line, 'Oh the monotonous meanness of his lust ....'; though, in the poem's initial appearance in *Life Studies*, the 'terminal' form falls not in the seventh line but only in the antepenultimate line: 'Each night now I tie | ten dollars and his car key to my thigh ....' (p. 190). Hill's 'three hapless dots' are a kind of tic in Lowell's poetry, occurring from his first works to his last, ending thoughts without concluding, coming to dead ends, or junctions alive with too much possibility. Without imputing any faults, moral or stylistic, one might paraphrase Shakespeare's Julius Caesar and say that, with so many ellipses, Lowell's poems die many times before their deaths. Above, in 'Fishnet', the terminal ellipsis marks not only an early volta, but a false start: the optimism of its

152 *Geoffrey Hill and the ends of poetry*

'clear thing that blinds us with surprise', its 'bright trouvailles', is 'let loose', allowed to trail off and be forgotten.[29] The next lines start the poem again: 'Poets die adolescents, their beat embalms them, I the archetypal voices sing offkey'. This sonnet, unrhymed and therefore full of 'offkey' endings, hopes to be embalmed by what it retains of the rhymed sonnet: its 'beat'.

It also retains, as I have said, the volta. There are two in this sonnet; or, seen another way, there are three endings. The first volta follows the third line's ellipsis; the second follows the tenth line, 'The line must terminate', which cleverly cuts itself off, its trimeter restricting even the 'beat' of the sonnet. And, having terminated, the metre starts beating once again:

> Yet my heart rises, I know I've gladdened a lifetime
> knotting, undoing a fishnet of tarred rope;
> the net will hang on the wall when the fish are eaten,
> nailed like illegible bronze on the futureless future.

The sonnet gives itself away in its end-words: though they do not rhyme in sound ('surprise' and 'trouvailles' an exception), they regularly share some semantic or connotative chime. The eighth and ninth lines' final words are 'dead' and 'terminate'; the volta line (after '[y]et', 'heart', 'rises', and 'gladdened') ends with 'lifetime'. Lowell's unrhymed sonnet is caught, to some degree willingly, in a stylistic net: it is 'let loose', but it 'must terminate'; it is engaged in both 'knotting' and 'undoing'. The tension animates the closing oxymoron, 'futureless future'. Is this, as Hill says of Richard Eberhart, 'the only thing he could have said after the Kierkegaardian paradoxes he has hitherto engaged in'? In a sense, yes; it is 'something that the semantic and metrical issues of the poem had inevitably to arrive at'. But this, in Lowell's 'Fishnet' at least, eliminates the sense of an 'epiphany'; there is, at the end, no 'clear thing that blinds us with surprise'.

There is, however, a confronting question. It comes in the penultimate significant pair of words: 'illegible bronze'. The poem's stated hope for itself is to be visible and lasting, perhaps like bronze to have a sort of faded lustre; the possibility of its being understood is dismissed. Is this a surprise or does the poem lead up to it? Is this part of an explanation for the apparently arbitrary commingling, during the span of *History*'s 368 sonnets, of the world's history with Lowell's own? In such a conflation, there is a nihilism about the 'futureless future' of poetry; if histories (poetic and other) are to become 'illegible bronze', as incomprehensible as the details of one man's life, of what value would their shaping into form be, their undeniable visibility?

There is an answer a few lines before the end: 'I've gladdened a lifetime I knotting, undoing a fishnet'. One might jump to thinking this a self-absorbed motivation for writing, but it is possible that the 'lifetime', blurred into history, is not (or is more than) Lowell's own; it could refer to a family

Forms 153

member or a lover, or be an abstracted figure of the reader. Considering Lowell in the title poem of the 2005 edition of *A Treatise of Civil Power*, Hill writes: 'Dramatic ambiguities were his forte; | and final lines'.[30]

An unexpected passing claim aside ('*The Dolphin* may be spared', *Clavics*, 25, p. 815), it is, as I have noted, the early Lowell, recent Catholic convert and protégé of Allen Tate at Kenyon College, and not the later sonneteer who appealed most to Hill. In the same Professor of Poetry lecture from which I quote above, entitled 'A deep dynastic wound' (a quotation from John Crowe Ransom's poem 'Dead Boy'), a lecture concerned with literary inheritance, Hill commented at length on Lowell's 'For the Union Dead' as a '*Meistersinger* challenge' to Tate's 'Ode to the Confederate Dead'. Lowell's *Imitations* (1961) is, Hill states in a review for *Essays in Criticism*, an 'impressive, disturbing work' of 'beautifully-finished artefacts' and 'the proper consummation of the first twenty years' of Lowell's poetic career.[31] The same emphasis on finishing is found in the stanza about Lowell in the 2005 edition of *A Treatise of Civil Power* ('and final lines').[32] Less impressed is the single reference to Lowell in Hill's *Collected Critical Writings*: 'There is no genuine parity between, say, Wordsworth's sense, in and around 1800, that he had an obligation to engage social injustice in poems such as "The Female Vagrant" or "Resolution and Independence" and Robert Lowell's compulsion to batten on the suffering of his wife and daughter for *Notebooks* and *The Dolphin*' (CCW, p. 401). (Hill uncharacteristically errs in pluralising *Notebook*, though it helps in proving his disdain.) There may be an additional concealed rebuke in this to Lowell's comparison, in 'After Enjoying Six or Seven Essays on Me', of his life's work to Wordsworth's *Prelude*.[33]

It would be difficult to name any of Hill's odes to the dead as a '*Meistersinger* challenge' to Lowell or to Tate. But 'Funeral Music', like Tate's 'Ode' and Lowell's 'For the Union Dead', constitutes a sustained meditation on those fallen in battle and on the suffering of wives, daughters, and sons. Hill describes it in his accompanying essaylet in *King Log* as 'a commination and an alleluia for the period popularly but inexactly known as the Wars of the Roses'. 'Without attempting factual detail', Hill writes, 'I had in mind the Battle of Towton, fought on Palm Sunday, 1461'.[34] (It may also be noted that Lowell has two unrhymed sonnets that discuss the Wars of the Roses, the second of which mentions the Battle of Towton: 'Bosworth Field', in *History*, p. 457; and 'Dream', in *The Dolphin*, p. 664.)

'Funeral Music' comprises eight numbered unrhymed sonnets. The form, whether or not taken up from Lowell's work in *Imitations*, is significant in Hill's oeuvre. *Canaan* (1996) is haunted by it: twenty poems or sections in that collection, none of which has a rhyme scheme and all of which have irregular metres, are made up of fourteen lines.[35] In Hill's notebooks for

154   *Geoffrey Hill and the ends of poetry*

Canaan, it is clear that this is no accident; many incomplete drafts include marginal countings of fourteen lines.[36] Other collections also yield several kinds of unrhymed and quasi-sonnets.[37] 'Funeral Music' (along with *Canaan*'s 'De Jure Belli ac Pacis', pp. 198–205) represents the joint-longest run of unrhymed sonnets in *Broken Hierarchies*; and, like Lowell's 'The Dolphin', each of the eight sonnets' endings is in some sense a negation and a paradox ('futureless future').

This negation and paradox derive from what Vincent Sherry calls 'the creative riddle of strength through renunciation' that forms one of the poem's main themes.[38] An obvious but interesting renunciation in these sonnets is that of rhyme. The clinching final rhyme of a conventional sonnet, whether in a couplet or as part of an interlocking sestet, affords an aural conclusiveness that can be either reinforced or played against semantically and syntactically. The unrhymed sonnet relies far more heavily on its rhetorical and syntactic momentum to arrive, or fail to arrive, at an ending. Of 'Funeral Music', Sherry writes that 'all the sonnets (except the fourth) conclude with expressions of an ascetic contempt for the flesh'.[39] I would argue that all of the sonnets, including the fourth, conclude with reflections on the soul's separation from flesh. The first sonnet, having depicted the beheading of John Tiptoft, Earl of Worcester, in 1470, ends with

> Creatures of such rampant state, vacuous
> Ceremony of possession, restless
> Habitation, no man's dwelling place.
>
> *(KL, p. 47)*

The second sonnet concludes with 'darkness over the human mire' (p. 48). In the third, 'the most delicate souls | Tup in their marriage-blood, gasping "Jesus"' (p. 49). The fourth contemplates Averroës's philosophy of monopsychism: that there exists only one soul, and therefore one intellect (classically considered a faculty of the soul), in which each person participates. Such a sharing necessitates a separation of body from soul, of individual bodies from the one soul; this explains the bodilessness of the 'unpeopled region | Of ever new-fallen snow' Hill imagines at the fourth sonnet's end, 'a palace blazing | With perpetual silence as with torches' (p. 50).[40] The fifth finishes with those '[r]acked on articulate looms' who show 'a flagrant | Tenderness of the damned for their own flesh' (p. 51). This tenderness of the 'damned', clinging (as it were) onto their bodiliness rather than nobly giving it up, is the exact opposite of Sherry's idea of 'ascetic contempt for the flesh'. The sixth ends: 'I believe in my | Abandonment, since it is what I have' (p. 52), where 'my | Abandonment' means, on one level, my abandonment of myself, my dissociating soul from body. The seventh recounts at its close: 'carrion birds | Strutted upon the armour of the dead' (p. 53); and the eighth

Forms

155

completes the set with a reference to 'anyone | Dragged half-unnerved out of this worldly place, | Crying to the end 'I have not finished'' (p. 54).

In this sense, all eight sonnets reach a clear end. But the fact that it is the same end is a problem. Why the need to revisit the idea seven times if the first conclusion is satisfactory? As Sherry also notes, the beginning of each sonnet marks a definite shift in pitch or perspective from the end of the preceding sonnet. 'Thus, while the first poem concludes with the Platonist's image of physical vacancy, the second opens with the lusty rhythms of a soldiers' chorus'.[41] And after the brutal closing vision of '[t]hose righteously-accused those vengeful' being tortured to death in the fifth sonnet, the sixth's opening line is: 'My little son, when you could command marvels' (pp. 51, 52). There are no conventional voltas within the sonnets, but these could be viewed as voltas between them.

Each sonnet's end in 'Funeral Music' is a compacted clash of ends (in the double sense of *closures* and *purposes*). There is a clash between the imagined end and the actual; between the bodily end and the spiritual. Separations of souls from bodies – deaths – are the result in each sonnet, despite their various beginnings. Each time, the ideal is defeated by the real. But what is a defeat for the body may be a triumph for the soul; the ideal may yet be achieved, despite contrary appearances ('Not as we are but as we must appear', p. 54); and this unearthly possibility is the itch that keeps the poem turning on itself.

The end, then, is ever-present in 'Funeral Music'. The regularity of end-related words and phrases throughout the sonnets is immediately conspicuous: 'dying', 'reconciled', '[u]ltimate recompense' (p. 48); 'atonement', 'rest', 'consummate | Justice' (p. 51); 'composed', '[a]nd so it ends', 'reconciled' (p. 52); 'timeless', 'forever', 'eternity', 'end', 'finished' (p. 54). The sense of the great End, the apocalypse, is never far away. The notion of 'consummate | Justice', combined with the repeated separations of soul from body in 'Funeral Music', call to mind a rightly famed passage in Frank Kermode's *The Sense of an Ending*:

> Already in St. Paul and St. John there is a tendency to conceive of the End as happening at every moment; this is the moment when the modern concept of *crisis* was born – St. John puns on the Greek word, which means both 'judgment' and 'separation.' Increasingly the present as 'time-between' came to mean not the time between one's moment and the *parousia*, but between one's moment and one's death. This throws the weight of 'End-feeling' on to the moment, the crisis [...]. No longer imminent, the End is immanent. So that it is not merely the remnant of time that has eschatological import; the whole of history, and the progress of the individual life, have it also, as a benefaction from the End, now immanent. History and eschatology, as Collingwood observed, are then the same thing.[42]

156 *Geoffrey Hill and the ends of poetry*

It may be useful here to make a brief return to Lowell. The scattered vignettes of his *History* attempt to take in 'the whole of history'; they also take in 'the progress of the individual life'; they may seem less concerned with the *parousia* (a Greek word for the Second Coming that happens to generate an extra pun in the Kermode passage, since its literal meaning is *being present*) than Hill's unrhymed sonnets in 'Funeral Music'. In the latter sequence, history and eschatology are, if not the same thing, very closely entwined. But in another sense Lowell's *History* sonnets are full of the dead's stories, full of their personal ends; they could be described as 368 rehearsals of the author's own death. Each sonnet details and to some extent embodies a 'crisis', in what Kermode describes as St John's punning sense, engaged in 'judgment' of the historical figure's life and hindered by 'separation' from it across time and the boundary of death. The separations of bodies from souls at the ends of poems in *History* sometimes express what Sherry calls 'contempt for the flesh' but rarely in an 'ascetic' sense:

> So calm perhaps will be our final change,
> won from the least desire to have what is.
>
>   ('Solomon, the Rich Man in State', p. 425)

> A grave was what he wanted. Death alone
> shows us what tedious things our bodies are.
>
>   ('Xerxes and Alexander', p. 436)

> for the moment, he is king; he is the king
> saying: *it's better to have lived, than live.*
>
>   ('Bosworth Field', p. 457)

> there was no hilt left for my hand to try.
> Everything ached, and told me I must die.
>
>   ('Spain Lost', p. 465)

> the rumors we leave behind us, our small choice ...
> it is sweet to destroy my mind, and drown in this sea.
>
>   ('Leopardi, The Infinite', p. 478)

> God, how hatefully bitter it is to die,
> how snugly one lives in this snug earthly nest!
>
>   ('Heine Dying in Paris 2', p. 481)

These last lines, from a relatively small chunk of *History*, give nonetheless a representative account of reactions to death among Lowell's cast of characters. Going backwards from the last excerpt, there is something of Hill's '[f]lagrant | Tenderness of the damned of their own flesh' in 'Heine Dying in Paris 2'; a longing for mental more than corporal oblivion in 'Leopardi, The Infinite'; a high-minded resignation in 'Spain Lost'; a desire for death

Forms   157

arising from indignation with life in 'Bosworth Field'; more strongly, in
'Xerxes and Alexander', a detachment from the body born of disgust at the
soul's slavery to it; and in 'Solomon, the Rich Man in State' a dwindling
(but not quite extinguishing) of bodily desire that is the result of age rather
than character. Highly unusually for these sonnets, 'Spain Lost' involves
some end-rhyme, including in the quoted final lines. The rhyme 'try/die' is
the mark of a suicide pact, a bitter reconciliation, as the speaker attempts
to recover personal nobility in the shadow of his vanquished country. The
repetitions elsewhere, often approaching rhyme, of 'snugly' and 'snug',
'*lived*' and '*live*', 'king' and 'king', especially in the Heine poem, are comfort
blankets, though ineffectual. The sonic parallels in the last line of the
Leopardi poem provide a similar though more haunting lull: the beginning
and end of the line are faint but distinct echoes ('it is sweet', 'in this sea'); the
middle is softly submerged in alliteration ('destroy my mind, and drown').
As in 'Spain Lost', the assonance of 'choice' and 'destroy' finds harmony
only in self-annihilation. The 'judgment', at such moments of separation, is
often directed at death itself, which denies the companions to which a life
grows familiar; suitably, Lowell's sonnets in *History* deny language its final
reassuring harmonies.

The eighth and last sonnet of Hill's 'Funeral Music' is also a Johannine
crisis. In a poem of such 'immanent' ending, the terrible realisation at its
close is that one's life may not be leading up to a final reconciliation, and
that 'the end', for all human concern about it, has (in Lowell's words) 'no
outcome', no meaning:

> Not as we are but as we must appear,
> Contractual ghosts of pity; not as we
> Desire life but as they would have us live,
> Set apart in timeless colloquy.
> So it is required; so we bear witness,
> Despite ourselves, to what is beyond us,
> Each distant sphere of harmony forever
> Poised, unanswerable. If it is without
> Consequence when we vaunt and suffer, or
> If it is not, all echoes are the same
> In such eternity. Then tell me, love,
> How that should comfort us— or anyone
> Dragged half-unnerved out of this worldly place,
> Crying to the end 'I have not finished'.

(p. 54)

The syntax here is, '[d]espite' itself, an effortful fight for meaningful
structure. Following the seventh sonnet's vision, '[a]t noon, | As the armies
met, each mirrored the other' (p. 53), this sonnet's first sentence attempts

more sedate, logical parallels: 'Not as we [*a*] but as [*b*], [*explanation of b*]; not as we [*c*] but as [*d*], [*explanation of d*].' The sentence's remote abstractions, paired with the sudden proliferation of the pronoun 'we' (who are evidently all the living, with 'they' signifying the memorialised, '[s]et apart' dead), appear to be preparation for a grand philosophical conclusion. This impression is strengthened as the poem progresses. The positive frame of the second sentence's clauses ('So [...]; so [...]') contrast with the repeated negatives of the first. The third sentence provides the *prima facie* conclusion: 'If it is [...], or | If it is not [...], [*this is the result in either case*]'. It is in the fourth and final sentence that Hill's unrhymed sonnet comes into its own. After the conditional conjunctions of the previous sentence, both capitalised, the opening 'Then' catches the eye as a possible answer to the quandary (though it is already provisionally answered, with an implied *then*, by 'all echoes are the same | In such eternity'). But instead the sentence marks a volta, an unexpected break from argument to personal address: 'Then tell me, love'. The sentence proceeds to undermine the significance of the logic that has come before it: 'tell me, love, | How that should comfort us'. It is not merely a 'worldly' comfort in the speaker's mind, but one of 'eternity'. If the sonnet's logic suggests that, 'beyond us', there is no ultimate logic, no final 'sphere of harmony', then it only adds to what we 'suffer' – and so what is its use? Lacking rhyme, especially a terminal, clinching rhyme, the unrhymed sonnet is caught between completion and incompletion. It too ends '[c]rying to the end "I have not finished"'. In one sense, it cries until its end that it is not finished, until it is; in another sense, it cries to death, and to the cosmic End, that it is not exhausted by either and not finally 'without | Consequence'.

The final two lines, in Hill's first printed draft of the poem, appear thus in one of his notebooks:

> *Dragged* Torn [s̶o̶] askance from any human place,
> *Protesting* [A̶n̶d̶ ̶c̶r̶y̶i̶n̶g̶] to the end "I have not finished".[43]

'Dragged half-unnerved out of this worldly place' is a major improvement on any of the possible permutations of the first of these lines. In death one is 'half-unnerved' because, though the soul is severed like a nerve, the body and all the components that made it live remain. At the same time, though dying with a higher purpose in mind, 'in honorem Trinitatis' in Tiptoft's case (p. 47), one might be at least 'half-unnerved', disconcerted, by the physical realities of death one is made to face. While 'askance' and '[p]rotesting' in the draft lend an air of haughty, deprecatory warning to the final four words, 'half-unnerved' and 'crying' emphasise instead the desperateness of the speaker's situation. There is a gulf in self-possession between protesting and crying. The End may be immanent – there may have been seven similar endings in the poem already – but that does not make the imminent personal end any more comfortable.

The unrhymed sonnet ends crying its lack of rhyme, its lack of concord, its unfinishedness; but it does so with such a consummate paradox ('I have not finished') that it seals the satisfyingly paradoxical close for the poem. If in eternity 'all echoes are the same', then the absence of rhyme's particular echo in these sonnets should be unimportant; but, after allowing that 'the phrasing is admirable, the style elevated and correct', to repeat Eliot's words on *Irene*, can one say that in the eighth sonnet of 'Funeral Music' 'each line cries out for a companion to rhyme with it'? Curiously, if one strains the eye and ear a little, the sonnet already sounds as though it has end-rhymes: 'appear/forever/or'; 'not as we/colloquy'; 'bear witness/beyond us'; 'live/love'. What could be said to cry out most loudly for a companion, appropriately, is the last word, 'finished'. It finds dull local echoes, though only within the lines: 'Dragged'; 'half-unnerved'; 'end'. This is nonetheless an unrhymed sonnet: there is no rhyme scheme; and the repeated sounds, though some fall at the ends of lines, are not in fact rhymes, that is by Žirmunskij's definition, because they have no 'organising function in the metrical composition of the poem'.[44]

Without rhyme, then, the weight of organisation in a blank-verse sonnet falls on metre and syntax. Examining the last line of Eberhart's '"Where are those high and haunting skies"', Hill speaks of it as 'something that the semantic and metrical issues of the poem had inevitably to arrive at'. Nearing the last line of the eighth sonnet of 'Funeral Music', the voice of the academic breaks into the voice of the lover, the hindering semicolons give way to quicker commas and a dash. The rhythm of the last line has an urgency unique in the poem:

> [...] all echoes are the same
> In such eternity. Then tell me, love,
> How that should comfort us— or anyone
> Dragged half-unnerved out of this worldly place,
> Crying to the end 'I have not finished'.

The sudden trochee 'Crying' disrupts the steady beat established in the lines leading to it (in a way that neither 'Protesting' nor 'And crying' would have achieved). The last line is trochaic pentameter rather than iambic:

> /   x / x /   x/   x / x
> Crying to the end 'I have not finished'.

The line is ten neat syllables, but unlike an iambic line, it fails to finish with the resounding emphasis of a strong syllable. In 'finished', the ineffectual dangle of an unstressed syllable, like a not quite decapitated head, remains,

160 *Geoffrey Hill and the ends of poetry*

as though to spoil the satisfaction of an overly clean conclusion. The soft
tangle of unvoiced consonants in that final syllable of 'finished' prolongs,
poignantly because only briefly, the sense of not being finished.

In contrast, the first sonnet of 'Funeral Music' fails to render Tiptoft's
beheading with similarly judicious consideration of 'semantic and metrical
issues':

> 'In honorem Trinitatis'. Crash. The head
> Struck down into a meaty conduit of blood.
>
> (p. 47)

There may be here, particularly in the juxtaposition of Christian language
with the earthy description of (brutal) death, a debt to Lowell's 'The Soldier',
who 'drowned face downward in his blood' (*Lord Weary's Castle*, p. 38).
The grim human deterioration in 'France', the dead speaker's 'groined
eyeballs' and 'blackened skull and eyes' (*Lord Weary's Castle*, p. 42), may
also have an influence on Hill here. Hill's lines, though, are less effective.
'Crash' is too familiarly comic to achieve any gruesome onomatopoeia
(for which the next sentence's 'meaty conduit of blood' attempts to make
redress). The bathetic drop of the single-word sentence, placed mundanely
in the middle of the trochaic line, is shallower than it ought to be; it lessens
any shock or disgust the succeeding image may provoke.

But the semantic and the metrical are justly measured and well married
in the sixth unrhymed sonnet:

> My little son, when you could command marvels
> Without mercy, outstare the wearisome
> Dragon of sleep, I rejoiced above all—
> A stranger well-received in your kingdom.
> On those pristine fields I saw humankind
> As it was named by the Father; fabulous
> Beasts rearing in stillness to be blessed.
> The world's real cries reached there, turbulence
> From remote storms, rumour of solitudes,
> A composed mystery. And so it ends.
> Some parch for what they were; others are made
> Blind to all but one vision, their necessity
> To be reconciled. I believe in my
> Abandonment, since it is what I have.
>
> (p. 52)

This is a sonnet of stoical despair. The first nine and a half lines, in which
the speaker, the poet-soldier, contemplates the world of his son's imagination, are fluent and compelling blank verse. The images and scenes of the
son's 'fabulous' dream-world, its dragons and 'remote storms', are morally

neutral; and it gradually becomes clear that the speaker, looking back on them, sees more truth, more of the 'world's real cries', in their plain practicality than in any 'vision' of ultimate justice and reconciliation. There is a blunt volta in the tenth line: 'A composed mystery. And so it ends.' The sonnet, as well as the dream-world, has been a composed mystery up to this point. 'And so it ends' appears to mean *and so the dream-world must come to an end*; but, having already identified this world with the actual world, it signifies rather the end of investigation into the world's meaning. The mystery of existence is composed too well, too tightly, for one to be able to read anything into it.

After the volta, the speaker regards others' endeavours to square their past with their present, or themselves with their circumstances. The hint of self-preserving arrogance in 'I believe in my | Abandonment, since it is what I have', in which 'Abandonment' finds itself capitalised like a theological virtue, subtly undermines its integrity as a conclusion.[45] This is appropriate, seeing that this sonnet is not the end of the poem, just as 'And so it ends' is not the end of this sonnet. The reader cannot help but perceive in the speaker, as also throughout Hill's poetry, both of the yearnings he attributes to others: if some 'parch for what they were', so does the speaker, who has spent ten lines reflecting on the imagination of his child; and if others are blinded by 'their necessity | To be reconciled', so is the speaker, struggling to make his own sense of the 'world's real cries'. The last line of the sonnet recovers metrical regularity, strengthening the sense of ending; but it is trotted out in miserable resignation.[46] The sentence it completes is tautological, a repeated paradox, in which the speaker doubles his claim to possession of a predicament characterised by not possessing: it is 'my' abandonment, he says, and 'it is what I have'. In itself this conclusion, despite its steady construction of iambs, is a yearning, a desperate reaching to possess, if nothing else, the speaker's own relinquishment.

Like Lowell's unrhymed sonnets in *History*, the two longest sets of unrhymed sonnets in Hill's work, 'Funeral Music' and 'De Jure Belli ac Pacis' (subtitled '*i.m. Hans-Bernd von Haeften, 1905–1944*'), are efforts to bring forward the 'real cries' of history; to forge between the sufferings of past and present a verbally alive understanding.[47] The sonnet, a form that has generated innumerable grand conclusions, is stripped of its rhyming power and asked to bring its reduced endings, semantic and metrical, to what is finally inconclusive. One of Lowell's statements on writing, with which Hill would likely have disagreed and with which his poetry would too, though with a little more difficulty, suggests why the frame of the unrhymed sonnet held Lowell's poetry for so long: 'I think in the end, there is no end, the thread frays rather than is cut, or if it is cut suddenly, it usually hurtingly frays before it is cut. No perfected end, but a lot of meat

162   *Geoffrey Hill and the ends of poetry*

and drink along the way.'[48] This is a hedonist's end; a reaction against the idea of 'dying | To satisfy fat Caritas' ('Funeral Music', 2, *KL*, p. 48).[49]

Lowell's *History* also begins in dying. The first sonnet, which is given the same title as the collection, includes, like the sixth sonnet in 'Funeral Music', a look back at childhood in its review of the broader past. Coming near to death, Lowell agrees, unsettles the ideals even of a 'skeptic'.[50] Crying out for rhyming companions, and for renewed innocence, all of the last nine lines exceed the pentameter:

> History has to live with what was here,
> clutching and close to fumbling all we had—
> it is so dull and gruesome how we die,
> unlike writing, life never finishes.
> Abel was finished; death is not remote,
> a flash-in-the-pan electrifies the skeptic,
> his cows crowding like skulls against high-voltage wire,
> his baby crying all night like a new machine.
> As in our Bibles, white-faced, predatory,
> the beautiful, mist-drunken hunter's moon ascends—
> a child could give it a face: two holes, two holes,
> my eyes, my mouth, between them a skull's no-nose—
> O there's a terrifying innocence in my face
> drenched with the silver salvage of the mornfrost.

The metaphor of the cows 'crowding like skulls against high-voltage wire' is a vision not of the past but of the possible future: the cows' end is foreseen but not certain to come by the 'wire'. Similarly, the 'flash-in-the-pan', a phrase arising from the mechanics of ballistic weapons, and denoting the reaction 'when the priming powder is kindled without igniting the charge' (*OED*, 'flash', sense 5c), is a near-miss with death, a not-quite-ending that nonetheless prefigures the end. Though the flash does not result in a shot, it still 'electrifies'. Surprisingly, the connection between cows, the flash-in-the-pan, and the end of time is repeated in Lowell's 'The Day', not a sonnet (*Day to Day*, p. 763).[51]

Without rhyme's familiar or unfamiliar squarings, these sonnets of Lowell and Hill gravitate towards the strange and unreconciled phenomena of death, doubt, open-endedness. Even the metaphor, in 'History' above, of the moon as a child's drawing of a face is quickly transformed, like the cows' heads in the poem's imagination, into the memento mori of a skull. The playground autorhyme of 'two holes, two holes' becomes warped into the more sinister jingle of 'no-nose'. These internally rhyming representations of vacuity, of something lacking, are characteristic of these sonnets. They poignantly cry out, at every turn of a line, for a companion to rhyme with; and the hollow chime that follows – 'Abandonment', 'the futureless

Forms 163

future', 'I have not finished' – serves only as a reminding echo of what cannot be answered.

Versets: *Mercian Hymns*

> You are eager to hear next how language without metre is made to resemble a beautiful poem or lyric, and how a poem or song is made similar to beautiful prose.[52]

Mercian Hymns, like the sixth sonnet in 'Funeral Music', is both a history and a childhood dream-world. Its thirty hymns are doublings in numerous other ways, which I will touch on; but the most important with which to begin is the hymns' doubled form. Dionysius above is interested in the resemblances between literary forms, firstly in 'language without metre': the phrase might be a fitting description for the unmetrical *Mercian Hymns*, looking both ways at verse and prose. Hill describes the hymns to John Haffenden thus:

> They're versets of rhythmical prose. The rhythm and cadence are far more of a pitched and tuned chant than I think one normally associates with the prose poem. I designed the appearance on the page in the form of versets. The reason they take the form they do is because at a very early stage the words and phrases began to group themselves in this way.[53]

A very early stage perhaps, but not at first: one of the notebooks shows that Hill was playing with (rhymed) sonnets at least for some sections in *Mercian Hymns*, including an 'Offa's Dynasty' poem.[54] Later in the same notebook, there is a 'NOTE FOR MYSELF 28/6/70. I'm not at all happy, now, about the idea for a sequence of love-sonnets. It seems much too much like going over the same ground, ground that I've already [gone over] better in "The Songbook of Seb. Arr.["]'. And on the reverse of this page there is the bewildered scribble 'SYLLABICS??'.[55] All of this goes against the implication in Hill's comment that the form of the verset arrived with ease.

Even to call the hymns 'versets of rhythmical prose' requires consider-able forethought. Whether or not the unusual form arrived with ease, there is a difficulty in the form's given name, in the doubling of 'versets' with 'prose'. The *OED* gives two senses for *verset*: the first directly equates it with *versicle*: '*Liturg*. One of a series of short sentences, usually taken from the Psalms and of a precatory nature, said or sung antiphonally in divine service'; the second is: 'A little or short verse, esp. one of the Bible or similar book; a short piece of verse.'[56] In his second, and far longer, book of versets, *The Book of Baruch by the Gnostic Justin*, Hill gives a somewhat obscure

164   *Geoffrey Hill and the ends of poetry*

reflection on the form's character: 'Such a verset is about the bearable extent of a particular line of wit; its posited capacity to pass without detriment to the sign' (*BBGJ* 243, p. 131).[57]

In the wry scholarly endnotes (ends of a different sort) to *Mercian Hymns*, strongly influenced by those to *The Waste Land*, Hill mentions two general sources for the work, which, like the others Hill mentions, are (as Knottenbelt observes) by no means recherché but standard reference books that would have been read by any Oxford student of English in the early 1950s.[58]

> The title of the sequence is a suggestion taken from *Sweet's Anglo-Saxon Reader* (1950 edn), pp. 170–80. A less-immediate precedent is provided by the Latin prose-hymns or canticles of the early Christian Church. See Frederick Brittain, ed., *The Penguin Book of Latin Verse* (1962), pp. xvii, lv.[59]

Brittain's book, at the latter of the pages Hill refers to, describes the unusual proximity of prose and verse in early Christian hymns, which indicates the kind of form-doubling at which Hill's hymns are aiming:

> When Greek ceased to be the language of the majority of Christians in western Europe, prose hymns of the same type – called canticles today, to distinguish them from hymns in verse – continued to be written in Latin. The finest example of these is the 'Te Deum', written probably in the latter half of the fourth century. Parallelism is a striking feature in it, as is also the introduction of rhythmical endings to its prose clauses.
>
> The next step – to hymns in verse – was therefore but a short one.[60]

Hill's hymns are poised on this next step to verse.

Before examining what at the beginning of this section I call doublings in *Mercian Hymns*, conflations of disparate or opposed words, ideas, and stories, which emerge towards the ends of many of the hymns, more distant pairings ought to be considered. Like the canticles described by Brittain, versets or versicles, 'said or sung antiphonally in divine service', also lend themselves to parallelism. Antiphony and dialogue pervade *Mercian Hymns*, from the concluding comment of Offa in the first hymn ('"I liked that", said Offa, "sing it again"' (p. 83)) to the 'broken utterance' in the seventeenth hymn (p. 99), which is both a radio-play heard in the car and a remembrance of the speaker's own childhood, his 'timid father's protective bellow'. Slightly earlier in his introduction Brittain describes the Hebrew psalter as 'a collection of religious poems in prose, unsurpassed in beauty to this day'. He goes on: 'They had neither metre nor rhyme; but each verse was divided into two parts linked to each other by parallelism of thought. The second half of each verse emphasized or amplified the thought expressed in the first half or repeated it in different words, or answered a question contained in it.'[61] In *Mercian*

Hymns, there are some similar syntactical parallels: 'Today I name them; tomorrow I shall express the new | law' (VIII, p. 90); 'They brewed | and pissed amid splendour; their latrine seethed | its estuary through nettles' (XII, p. 94); 'The sword is in the king's hands; the crux a crafts- | man's triumph' (XVI, p. 98); 'Processes of generation; deeds of settlement [...] urge to marry well; wit to invest [...] Hearthstones; charred | lullabies' (XXVIII, p. 110).

Here and there the antiphony takes a catechetical form, asking rhetorical questions, sometimes dubiously answering them: 'What should a man make of remorse, that it might | profit his soul?' (X, p. 92); 'What is carried over? The | Frankish gift, two-edged, regaled with slaughter' (XVI, p. 98); 'What is | borne amongst them? Too much or too little' (XVI, p. 98); 'Where best to stand?' (XXIV, p. 106).

The questions are a symptom of Hill's excavatory intelligence in *Mercian Hymns*, seeking both past and future. The fourth hymn names this crucial pairing:

> I was invested in mother-earth, the crypt of roots
> and endings. Child's-play. I abode there, bided my
> time: where the mole
>
> shouldered the clogged wheel, his gold solidus; where
> dry-dust badgers thronged the Roman flues, the
> long-unlooked-for mansions of our tribe.

(p. 86)

Hill wishes to reopen that 'crypt of roots and endings', which, as the linguistic terms suggest, is primarily a word-crypt. Reopening it would be in hope to enact a resurrection of 'dead language'.[62] This is a tricky business. Hill's '[c]hild's-play' with 'abode' and 'bided', a complex dirt-tangle of etymology, syntax, and sound; or the unusually immediate chime of 'mole ‖ shouldered', in which the shouldered shape of the new stanza bolsters the effect, are impromptu experiments, clumsily striking attempts to reconstitute the dug-up bits of language, discovered in the 'long-unlooked-for mansions' of its history.

Roots and endings are also, in a metaphorical sense, relevant to cultural politics (to further the application of 'tricky business'): where the roots of a 'tribe' inhere; whether it will last; what its final values are.[63] The atonement of cultures with different roots, like that of words, could be presumed an undertaking without a fixed end. Enoch Powell, whose allusion to Virgil in his most hotly debated speech is modified and cited in *Mercian Hymns*, contends that the opposite is true.[64] Powell is the subject of numerous newspaper cuttings in one of Hill's notebooks for *Mercian Hymns*; the below is from one marked 'TIMES, 24/4/69':

166   *Geoffrey Hill and the ends of poetry*

Mr. Powell has said about his famous immigration speech at Birmingham that 'it was something which had to be done. I have always had the sense of doing things because there is no alternative. When you write a Latin sentence there is no alternative to the Latin ending. When you write verse there is no alternative to the arrangement of the words'. There is a kind of inevitability about the process by which poetry works out the paradoxes of the inner life. In politics Mr. Powell moves with the certainty of the poet.[65]

The poet can have certainty about the existence of uncertainties and be reconciled to particular irreconcilabilities. The verset has an unfixed form: there is no metrical limit and no limit to the number of syllables, lines, or stanzas. Despite this, the relative uniformity of the stanzas' shapes lends them an appearance of '[e]xactness of design' (*MH* XI, p. 93). 'There is a kind of inevitability about the process by which poetry works out the paradoxes of the inner life'; in the case of *Mercian Hymns*, that 'process' is Hill's use of the malleable structure of the verset to work out, with difficulty, its own paradoxes.

Some of the hymns end with the difficulty rather than the working out. The tenth's last sentence is: 'He wept, attempting to mas- | ter *ancilla* and *servus*' (p. 92). The child, Offa and Hill, cannot master the Latin language, here exemplified by the words for *maid-servant* and *servant*; the suggestion is that Offa's capacity for naming, richly demonstrated in the first two hymns (pp. 83–84), will not extend to his governance, or to an understanding of proper political authority. He is eager to 'mas- | ter' (even though the very attempt involves a severing in half), to rule over, but does not have a sufficient understanding of the subjects over whom he rules and, consequently, cannot grasp the concepts of right order or just leadership. These are the broken hierarchies Offa lives with, and which Hill, for his part, struggles to restore.

The twenty-eighth hymn, which immediately succeeds the description of Offa's funeral, returns to this theme. Its syntactical extremity is a sign of the sequence coming to a close; there is a sense of summation.

> Processes of generation; deeds of settlement. The
>   urge to marry well; wit to invest in the proper-
>   ties of healing-springs. Our children and our
>   children's children, o my masters.
>
> Tracks of ancient occupation. Frail ironworks rust-
>   ing in the thorn-thicket. Hearthstones; charred
>   lullabies. A solitary axe-blow that is the echo
>   of a lost sound.
>
> Tumult recedes as though into the long rain. Groves
>   of legendary holly; silverdark the ridged gleam.

(p. 110)

Forms 167

The only complete sentence here is the penultimate. Otherwise the poem is a series of fragments, common to these paratactic hymns but unusually frequent here. The excitement of the opening hymns' lists has been replaced by loss and resignation. Offa, speaking (as, in one sense, throughout the sequence) from beyond the grave, has discovered, and wishes to pass on, something of civilisation and hierarchy; but he understands them only in terms of mundane expediency. The roots and endings of his childhood, exploring in the lively dirt, have become cold '[p]rocesses of generation'. Thinking of legacy, of children and 'children's children', Offa turns to social expectation. Once 'invested in mother-earth', now investments (financial and other) in what are seen to be the right properties become his 'proper- | ties'.

The sentences are fragmented because the meaningful connections have been missed: 'Our children and our children's children, o my masters'. This is a tired and unfinished rhetorical appeal to others' desire for legacy, with a small 'o' for added pathos (as in 'o my heart' in the early version of 'The Pentecost Castle').[66] The polite, meaningless words are recited, lacking the weight of grammatical coherence. Such words have become Offa's 'masters'. Meanwhile, around him, the desolate landscape also refuses to make sense. The 'solitary axe-blow' can only be 'the echo | of a lost sound': like '*ancilla* and *servus*', it can be heard but not interpreted.

This axe-blow, along with the poem's one complete sentence that follows it – 'Tumult recedes as though into the long rain' – recalls the kinds of death and indecipherable sound that occur in 'Funeral Music'. 'So these dispose themselves to receive each | Pentecostal blow from axe or seraph' (1, *KL*, p. 47). 'A field | After battle utters its own sound | Which is like nothing on earth, but is earth' (3, p. 49). 'I made no sound, but once | I stiffened as though a remote cry | Had heralded my name. It was nothing ...' (7, p. 53). Suffering of this kind cannot be reconciled with its surrounding reality. Hill, as well as Offa, can only make it sit beside the rest of experienced life, unsettling as it may be (but these are the 'deeds of settlement'; see also the ending of the ninth hymn (p. 91): 'You had | lived long enough to see things "nicely settled"'). The conclusions of the hymns, however, do reach for reconciliations, even if only in the way of 'natural min- | utiae' (XIV, p. 96). In the example of the twenty-eighth hymn above, though the sentence reverts to incompleteness ('Groves | of legendary holly; silverdark the ridged gleam'), there is the Anglo-Saxon, unhyphened, oxymoronic conflation of 'silverdark', a literal silver lining to finish the poem, and a 'settlement' in the paradoxes of nature.

The final word of the thirteenth hymn is an even clearer illustration of this conflation, a reduction of prolonged parallels to a single doubling ('with a click like a closing box'). Here is the poem in full:

168   *Geoffrey Hill and the ends of poetry*

> Trim the lamp; polish the lens; draw, one by one, rare
> coins to the light. Ringed by its own lustre, the
> masterful head emerges, kempt and jutting, out
> of England's well. Far from his underkingdom of crin-
> oid and crayfish, the rune-stone's province, *Rex
> Totius Anglorum Patriae*, coiffured and ageless,
> portrays the self-possession of his possession,
> cushioned on a legend.
>
> (p. 95)

The similarities between numismatist, studier of coins, and poet, studier of words, can be traced throughout. Both are also studying King Offa, as a man and as a face on his coins. They do so by drawing him 'to the light', '[f]ar from his underkingdom', out of the darkness of what is lost in 'England's well', materially and culturally. Again, the struggle with mastery 'emerges' with the 'masterful head'; the first sense of 'masterful' in the *OED* is 'accustomed to or insisting upon having one's own way; imperious, wilful, overbearing' (sense 1a). As in the eleventh hymn ('Exactness of design' (p. 93)), there is an emphasis on enclosure, on a sealing that is both restrictive and essential to formal perfection: 'Trim'; 'polish'; 'Ringed'; 'kempt'; 'coiffured'; 'self-possession'. In a short article on the different layout of *Mercian Hymns* in Penguin's *Selected Poems* (2006), Thomas Day describes the verset as 'short paragraphs justified at both margins, with the first line of each "outdented", slightly overhanging the left margin – like the effigy of Offa's coins as described in hymn XIII, at once "kempt and jutting"'.[67] *The Book of Baruch* puts it simply: 'I am found amid rough paragraphs' (*BBGJ* 25, p. 11).

The last four words, set on their own line, and supported by the preceding double 'self-possession of his possession', complete the design with a clinching (or clinking) half-rhyme: 'cushioned on a legend'. In one of Hill's notebooks for *Mercian Hymns*, there is a printed cutting of these words with added marks of stress and conclusion: 'cúshióñed óñ a légènd. (FÍNÌS)'.[68] It is unclear precisely what the marks signify; and also whether Hill imagined the parenthetical 'FINIS' to be included at the end of the poem. What can be said with confidence is that Hill wishes to accentuate strongly the impression of conclusion at the end of the thirteenth hymn. The puns do the doubling work, particularly the latter: Offa's head is presented as though cushioned on the inscription, or legend, that the coin bears: '*Offa Rex*'. (The eleventh hymn (p. 93) states this as the motto; '*Rex | Totius Anglorum Patriae*', in the thirteenth, is a separate title not inscribed on the coins.)[69] At the same time, Offa's reputation is cushioned on a legend in that it relies on spurious myth. The 'self-possession of his possession' is an artifice, too perfectly ringed like the coins; it is the artifice of

Forms   169

autobiography, which reaches the author of *Mercian Hymns*.[70] What Offa is cushioning on coins, and what Hill is inscribing in poems, is the same as what the 'mob' at Offa's funeral receives: 'memorial vouch- | ers and signs' (XXVII, p. 109). They are, at least on one level, memorialising themselves in advance. With the signs of consummately sculpted coins and poems, they are vouching for having lived.

The death that these signs are created against is omnipresent in *Mercian Hymns*. Corruption, putrefaction, mortality abound; if nature was once 'kempt' in the walled garden of Eden, it has now been brought 'to the place without the | walls: spoil-heaps of chrysanths dead in their | plastic macs' (IX, p. 91). The hymns too, though appearing to be within well-formed walls, are in fluid, unprotected prose, desperately seeking their own closures. The rotted Eden of Hill's Mercia is a '[p]rimeval heathland spattered with the bones of mice | and birds' (XX, p. 102), not far from the arena of human execution in the first sonnet of 'Funeral Music', with axes '[s]pattering block-straw with mortal residue' (*KL*, p. 47).

Such proximity to the beginning of creation, in this world of oxymorons, implies the imminence (not merely the immanence) of the apocalypse. This particular sense of consummation enters the hymns late and subtly. Here is the twenty-third hymn:

> In tapestries, in dreams, they gathered, as it was en-
> acted, the return, the re-entry of transcendence
> into this sublunary world. *Opus Anglicanum*, their
> stringent mystery riddled by needles: the silver
> veining, the gold leaf, voluted grape-vine, master-
> works of treacherous thread.
>
> They trudged out of the dark, scraping their boots
> free from lime-splodges and phlegm. They munched
> cold bacon. The lamps grew plump with oily re-
> liable light.
>
> (p. 105)

The tapestry resembles the verset: framed but sprawling; tending towards narrative and analogy; prone to unpicking ('treacherous thread'). Just as the verset is designed and used by Hill to transcend the singularity of history, here transcendence re-enters the world of medieval England through worked tapestries that represent the historical Christian 'mystery'. This is the figurative sense of transcendence. But 'in dreams', and 'riddled' in the Old English tradition, this 're-entry' is also a vision of the physical return of transcendence that is the Second Coming of Christ.

The workers who trudge 'out of the dark' in the second stanza are like the virgins in the parable from the Gospel of Matthew, their 'lamps'

Geoffrey Hill and the ends of poetry

growing 'plump with oily re- | liable light' (Matthew 25.1–13). The wise virgins' lamps are reliable; to the foolish virgins, their exhausted lamps are a liability, showing them responsible for fault. The break in 're- | liable' in the twenty-third hymn rests on this fault-line. The parable, spoken by Jesus, is apocalyptic: when He is to come again to consummate the world, some lamps will be found 'plump', and others gone out. The wise virgins, Jesus says, 'trimmed their lampes': is this why the thirteenth hymn begins with the imperative 'Trim the lamp'? The 'sublunary' weavers, working through the night, in Hill's vision, are wise and hard labourers. The story ends, for them, with the word 'light'.

The following hymn, the twenty-fourth, moves from tapestry to architecture; the masterful but unmastering Offa is now a 'master-mason' (p. 106). The palimpsest of stone envisaged by Hill, with Offa, back from a European pilgrimage, overlaying the cultic images of pagan Britain with Christian figures and motifs, is another lens on the form of *Mercian Hymns*. The reliefs, like tapestries, and like the 'rhythmical prose' of the hymns, are designed for storytelling. The verset also is a doubled palimpsest: firstly in its modernisation of the Latin canticle; and secondly in its overlaying Offa's story with Hill's own. The mood of apocalypse, meanwhile, intensifies:

> Itinerant through numerous domains, of his lord's retinue, to Compostela. Then home for a lifetime amid West Mercia this master-mason as I envisage him, intent to pester upon tympanum and chancel-arch his moody testament, confusing warrior with lion, dragon-coils, tendrils of the stony vine.
>
> Where best to stand? Easter sunrays catch the oblique face of Adam scrumping through leaves; pale spree of evangelists and, there, a cross Christ mumming child Adam out of Hell
>
> ('Et exspecto resurrectionem mortuorum' dust in the eyes, on clawing wings, and lips).
>
> (p. 106)

The versets, their lines being pushed to both margins, resemble inscribed stones; and they offer the same variability of interpretation as the architecture here ('Where best to stand?'). Even the sunrays by which the 'stony' apocalyptic images are viewed are 'Easter sunrays'. Offa's, and the viewer's, vision of myth has been reawakened by Christianity; but it is an alarming new vision. If the atmosphere of a ruined Eden was present in the twentieth hymn's '[p]rimeval heathland spattered with the bones of mice | and birds' (p. 102), here the grumpy, childish Adam, banished from Eden and 'scrumping through leaves', finds himself in immediate proximity to eternal

Forms 171

death (in 'Hell'). What comes between Adam's (man's) beginning and his end, in the stone-reliefs, is Christ. As well as being angered at sin and crucified for it, Christ is 'cross' in other, archaic senses (see *OED*, 'cross, *adj.*', senses 1a, 1b, and 3): He is contrary (to Adam and his sin); intersecting (as to human history); and transverse (in that He extends through time, from Genesis to Revelation). Accordingly, one might look forward from this hymn's stone to that of a much later poem, regarding Christian alchemy: 'Momentous instauration—all is One. | But time has crossed its arrow on the stone' (*O* 35: *to Thomas Vaughan* (v), p. 752).[71]

The final, bracketed stanza of the hymn, which is its own 'ob- | lique' commentary on the above, examines the 'dust in the | eyes, on clawing wings, and lips'. This dust from the stone is the dust of all artistic ambition: its visions; its stubborn efforts to ascend; its communications. Since it is the dust of which man is made, it might also represent the vacuity of religious hope; yet the hope persists in the phrase, from the Niceno-Constantinopolitan Creed, that is finally on the 'lips': 'Et exspecto resurrectionem mortuorum' (*And I look forward to the resurrection of the dead*). Hill acknowledges, in the notes, 'a debt to Olivier Messiaen', the French composer whose piece with the Latin title above, a notebook reveals, was heard in All Saints' Church in Hill's hometown of Bromsgrove during the writing of *Mercian Hymns*.[72]

Such expectation of the end – as well as such beginning in medias res, with an *And* – informs the final hymn. It is the shortest of the thirty:

And it seemed, while we waited, he began to walk to-
    wards us   he vanished

he left behind coins, for his lodging, and traces of
    red mud.

(p. 112)

As Knottenbelt observes, the gap in the first stanza is 'the only instance in the hymns where Hill might be said to be imitating the "look" of Old English verse'.[73] But it is a very modern lacuna into which Offa vanishes: it is one of those left by the fragmentation, the forgetfulness, of modernity. In contrast to the twenty-third and twenty-fourth hymns, this last, punctured by its empty spaces, approaches the appearance of rubble (or damaged parchment) rather than tablets. Waited-for, wished-for, communion is denied (as in 'The Hollow Men': 'Lips that would kiss | Form prayers to broken stone').[74] Nevertheless, in the unpunctuated break between the stanzas, a different kind of consummation seems to become visible. A doubled legacy is perceived in the two sorts of object 'left behind' by Offa. The 'coins, for his lodging', are a poignant touch: those coins brought into being by Offa, and made of Mercia's earth, are now his payment to that earth, which accommodates his body; and his viaticum for the next journey.

172 *Geoffrey Hill and the ends of poetry*

They are Offa's last offer. In another sense, *Mercian Hymns* picks up with gratitude the left-behind linguistic coinages from Offa's time, its 'crypt of roots and endings'.

The 'traces of red mud' are variants of the Adamic 'dust' of the twenty-fourth hymn (also present in the twenty-fifth: 'In dawn-light the troughed water | floated a damson-bloom of dust || not to be shaken by posthumous clamour' (p. 107)). The traces of Offa are red with his blood and the blood of others on his hands. While the notion of Adam's dust being red is common, and derives from the senses and connotations of the Hebrew word אדם (or Adam) itself, the emphasis on the 'traces' in this ending evokes a beginning, a single-line fragment by Beddoes: 'Like the red outline of beginning Adam'.[75] Offa becomes, and is now, no more than a red outline.

As to mud, like words in stone and like versets, it can be shaped and reshaped; in Penguin's *Selected Poems* (2006) the mud-sculpture of the hymns, in terms of their line breaks, is altered. Whether or not this was intentional on Hill's part, *Broken Hierarchies* (2013) sees the vast majority of the original shapes restored.[76] This shows that there is a design, which perhaps became more conscious upon revision, to the broken ends of *Mercian Hymns*' lines. The conclusion of the narrative sequence is 'open-ended', but not completely so.[77] All humanity seems involved in the fraught anticipation of 'we waited'; this too is apocalyptic, since it is not only Offa's return that is expected ('*Et exspecto*') but Christ's.

The final doubling I wish to point out precedes the hymns. It is the epigraph, from C. H. Sisson:

> The conduct of government rests upon the same foundation and encounters the same difficulties as the conduct of private persons: that is, as to its object and justification, for as to its methods, or technical part, there is all the difference which separates the person from the group, the man acting on behalf of himself from the man acting on behalf of many. The technical part, in government as in private conduct, is now the only one which is publicly or at any rate generally recognised, as if by this evasion the more difficult part of the subject, which relates to ends, could be avoided. Upon 'the law of nature and the law of revelation', Blackstone said, 'depend all human laws.' This quaint language, which would at once be derided if it were introduced now into public discussion, conceals a difficulty which is no less ours than it was our ancestors'.[78]

Here, before any poems, Offa as overseeing king and fallen man, Hill as overseeing poet and fallen man, are already brought together with 'difficulty'. This epigraph, like the hymns, is a block of stone (though, lacking the longer initial line, not a 'jutting' one); it is also a commentary on words meant to be definitive: human and divine laws. These designate endpoints, lines not to be crossed. The epigraph is already concerning the work-to-be-read with 'ends': not only legacies but purposes, ultimate destinations.

Forms 173

(Knottenbelt, succinctly: 'The *Mercian Hymns* are about "roots and endings", but especially about ends'.[79])

Clavics

> Rose-cheekt *Lawra*, come
> Sing thou smoothly with thy beawties
> Silent musick, either other
>   Sweetely gracing.
>
> Louely formes do flowe
> From concent deuinely framed;
> Heau'n is musick, and thy beawties
>   Birth is heauenly.
>
> These dull notes we sing
> Discords neede for helps to grace them;
> Only beawty purely louing
>   Knowes no discord,
>
> But still mooues delight,
> Like cleare springs renu'd by flowing,
> Euer perfet, euer in them-
>   selues eternall.[80]

This poem, one of Thomas Campion's '*Ditties*', reads like a manifesto for Hill's work. Its '[s]ilent musick' echoes in the second sonnet of 'Funeral Music': 'Suppose all reconciled | By silent music; imagine the future | Flashed back at us [...] Ultimate recompense' (*KL*, p. 48). Its vision of form, as in Hill's hymns, is of something fluid ('Louely formes do flowe') but 'deuinely framed'. Campion's poem pertains especially to Hill's *Clavics*, which emphasises the same relation between 'beawty' and '[d]iscords', 'dull notes' and the 'helps to grace them'.

In Hill's late work, several forms emerge. Like the *Mercian Hymns*, they tend to be palimpsestic: that is, they use the frameworks of forms successfully employed by other poets – especially the rhythmic, metrical, and rhyming patterns such forms may have – and write over them, often introducing elements of discord in the syntax and diction. For instance, *Pindarics*, originally included in the collection *Without Title* (2006), and which later appeared, much revised and expanded, in *Broken Hierarchies*, there dated '2005–2012', is a series of odes drawing on Pindar as well as Allen Tate (and, through Tate, Abraham Cowley).[81] Elsewhere, *Oraclau | Oracles*, the third of *The Daybooks* ('2007–2012'), uses the stanza of Donne's 'A nocturnall upon S. Lucies Day'.[82] In these final two sections of

174   *Geoffrey Hill and the ends of poetry*

the chapter I examine the forms of the fourth and fifth *Daybooks*: *Clavics* and *Odi Barbare*. As with *Oraclau | Oracles*, *Clavics* looks to the metaphysical poets of the seventeenth century, while *Odi Barbare* goes further back to Sidney's sapphics.

The clavic of *Clavics* is a composite form: it is a doubling of two sections, divided by a printer's ornament, the first of which utilises the form of Henry Vaughan's 'The Morning-watch' (not, as some commentators have averred, that of Herbert's 'The Altar'), and the second of which borrows the form of Herbert's 'Easter-wings' (though only one pair of wings appears in each).[83] I refer to these as the clavics' (or the poems') Vaughan sections and Herbert sections. These two sections together form, Michael Robbins writes, 'more or less, the shape of a key'.[84] Robbins's approximation is a precise one; Hill is inducing his reader to squint to see such a key, just as his syntax, rhymes, and puns in *Clavics* often amount to 'a dissonance to make them wince' (*Cl.* 23, p. 813).[85] In the first published version, the twentieth Herbert section begins and ends with a reflection on its shape: 'Side-on spread wings, upright an hour-glass | Better if egg-timer [...] Herbert times and twists text hereby: | Balanced glass wit let-tipple into Grace'.[86]

Clavics was published first by Enitharmon Press in 2011; there it had thirty-two poems. In the revised version, which appears in *Broken Hierarchies*, one clavic is entirely omitted, eleven new clavics included, and several others subjected to reorderings and rewordings.[87] The several paratexts from the first edition – the bogus *OED* entry, the epigraphs, the drawing and intaglio – disappear in *Broken Hierarchies*.[88] But the doubling shapes remain. As in *Mercian Hymns*, so remain the doublings of people; in the case of *Clavics*, there are two sets of brothers (the latter set twin brothers) who take the stage: Henry and William Lawes; and Henry and Thomas Vaughan. All were seventeenth-century Royalists, and all may have been present at the Battle of Rowton Heath, on 24 September 1645, during the first English Civil War.[89] William Lawes is the book's dedicatee, a great composer (and one of the King's) who was killed at the battle.

The potential intersection at Rowton Heath of such important figures in the history of English art mirrors the intersections of past and present in the replicated shapes of *Clavics*. Again as in *Mercian Hymns*, these poems are attempts to negotiate a historical poetic terrain with the incongruous tools of modern-day language. In *Clavics*, the clash of times and words is more aggressive and frantic, at times to the point of jarring syntactical abbreviation. The first poem announces itself in a mad rush: 'Bring torch for Cabbalah brand new treatise, | Numerology also makes much sense, | O *Astraea*!' (1, p. 791). The poem continues in self-exposition (which, as elsewhere in *Clavics*, can be wilfully indecent – '(Shit) it can peg out,

Forms 175

cathetered high art' (40, p. 830)) before its Herbert section brings the poem
to a close with a playfully stilted proposal to the reader:

> Intensive prayer is intensive care
>   Herbert says. I take it stress marks
>   Convey less care than flair
>   Shewing the works
>   As here
>   But if
>   Distressed attire
>   Be mere affect of clef
>   Dump my clavic books in the mire
> And yes bid me strut myself off a cliff.
>
> (p. 791)

Marcus Waithe notes that this poem 'has attracted some harsh commentary,
aimed at the closing conditional offer [...], where the cliff edge is the poem's
pronounced outer edge. It makes a sort of sense, I think, as a parody of staged
Cavalier exasperation, its lack of finesse deliberately incongruous, rather
than inept'.[90] The same could be said of *Clavics* as a whole. Hill, in manu-
facturing his self-consciously clumsy clavic, a form of '[d]istressed attire',
suspects himself of too much 'flair' and not enough 'care', a '[s]hewing' off of
archaic forms (as the spelling hints) rather than a patient working with them.
The flair and care of Hill's clavics take turns in outweighing each other;
it is a precarious balancing act. Poems that inhabit the forms of Herbert
and Vaughan advertise their own riskiness. The struggle to hold together
meaning and metre, as well as the two, sometimes tenuously related, sections
of each clavic, is staged with an inevitably variable degree of success. As in
the last line of the first clavic above, Hill's progress through the clavic's
metre is a purposely unseemly 'strut'; his assurance in his technical ability
may, he admits, be ill-founded (leading him off the 'cliff' of his own poetic
shapings), but it will be retained in any case.

The first line of the Herbert section above, 'Intensive prayer [...]', with
its intensive local rhyming, less recalls Herbert's 'Easter-wings' than it does
the reference to prayer's harmonising efficacy in his 'Prayer (I)': 'A kinde of
tune, which all things heare and fear'.[91] 'The Morning-watch', the formal
source of the Vaughan sections, sounds attuned to the same line:

> Thus all is hurl'd
> In sacred *Hymnes*, and *Order*, The great *Chime*
> And *Symphony* of nature. Prayer is
>   The world in tune,
>   A spirit-voyce,
>   And vocall joyes
>   Whose *Eccho is* heav'ns blisse.[92]

176 *Geoffrey Hill and the ends of poetry*

Such symphony and attunement find their echoes distorted in *Clavics*. Nevertheless, the very employment of formal elements of 'The Morning-watch' implies a yearning to hurl poetic subjects into order and chiming symphony. In *Clavics*, as throughout *The Daybooks*, Hill sees bringing contrarieties into close contact as the surest way to poetic order and integral tunefulness. In this he follows the example of the unusually chromatic music of Lawes.

The third clavic, which considers the death of Charles I, clarifies the intention to make harmony of discord, with its dissonant atonement of 'poetic craft', musical craft, and statecraft.[93] (In the fortieth clavic (p. 830), Lawes's music 'Bravely refines | Music's harsh concord with the laws of state'.) Here is a passage from the third clavic's Vaughan section, followed by its Herbert section in full:

> The grace of music is its dissonance
> Unresolved beneath resolution
>   Of flow and stance:
>   Our epic work —
>   Cadenced nation —
>   Figuration
>   Running staidly amok,
>   Discord made dance.

>   [...]

> Take the old issue with chromatic tunes,
>   False relation, dishabitude
>   Of polity, dead loans
>   Anarchs beside
>   Lost thrones
>   A m e n d
>   Our sovran maims.
>   Be to love as well-found.
> Drive slow instauration of themes.
> Grant fidelity to heterophones.
>   (p. 793)

Fidelity to heterophones is as close as one is likely to get to a perfect summation of Hill's poetics. (It says something of his politics too: it demands a place for the 'antiphonal voice of the heckler' (*CCW*, p. 94); it perceives the adversarial discussion as the most, perhaps the only, productive discussion.) Hill's puns, repeating figures, rhymes, and syntactical and formal collisions are all grantings of fidelity to heterophones. The restoration of words' fidelities, their 'slow instauration', is almost certainly related to Francis Bacon's *Instauratio magna*, or *Great Instauration*, an unfinished project of books, the stated aim of which was to see how '*the commerce between the Mind and Things* [...] *could be entirely restored, or at least put on a better footing'.*[94] The same word may not be a reflection of the Christian vision *'instaurare omnes in Christo'*; but there is a similar sense of eschatology about it.[95] How can words be restored to a preternatural fidelity (to one another; to true communication or communion) in a linguistically fallen world? Would they not require the divine Word's consummating intervention in order to be restored? The word 'Amend', above, is stretched out almost so far as to require its own restoration.

The yearning for verbal fidelity is also, in a distinctly Hillian sense, erotic. 'Eros is the power that can be felt in language when a word or half-finished phrase awaits its consummation. Eros is so palpably evident in rhyming verse that at times it seems like a parody of itself' (*CCW*, p. 548). Lines that rhyme 'loans', 'thrones', and 'heterophones' do not amount to self-parody, except perhaps in that their congruity is, on the face of it, a foolish congruity. Hill is acting as what Christopher Middleton, in an interview, calls 'the literary figure [...] as clown, as jester, as simpleton [...], someone who takes everyone by surprise, by having a different interpretation of reality and a distinct one for which he is prepared to fight and die'.[96] The strange fidelity of 'loans/thrones/heterophones' provides a steady, dissonant 'descant' to the linguistic 'mêlée' of 'the times' (*Cl.* 24, p. 814). In contemporary use, a descant is an independent countermelody 'added above an existing melody' (see *OED*, 'descant, *n.*', sense 2). The harmonies Hill looks for in the late work are like harmonics: ethereal, unfamiliar, sounding above and beyond the accompanying music ('Not harmonies—harmonics, astral whisperings | light-years above the stave' ('De Jure Belli ac Pacis', §V, C, p. 202)). They are designed to unsettle harmonic habits, and to unlock ('The science or alchemy of keys') a loftier purpose for poetry's music: 'Discordant harmony as praise' (*O* 113, p. 778).

Rhyme is a significant element in the structure of the clavic; another, particularly in the Herbert sections, is metrical transformation. The second of Herbert's 'Easter-wings' reflects on its own reduction and expansion; as in the first stanza, or pair of wings, the 'thinne' middle lines are the locus of the rhetorical turn:

My tender age in sorrow did beginne:
  And still with sicknesses and shame
    Thou didst so punish sinne,
      That I became
       Most thinne.
       With thee
     Let me combine
   And feel this day thy victorie:
  For, if I imp my wing on thine,
Affliction shall advance the flight in me.[97]

178 *Geoffrey Hill and the ends of poetry*

In Hill's third Herbert section above, 'Amend' is the word that begins to amend the broken-down metre from its single metrical foot. For Herbert, it is man's involution, his circling inward, the 'My' and 'I' of the first four lines, that reduces his expression and renders it '[m]ost thinne'; it is, the poem suggests, the imping, or grafting, of God's expressiveness onto his own that allows Herbert to rebuild his verse to the full and proper length of the pentameter.

In Herbert's case, this shaped stanza is a radical transformation of the courtly 'figure' Puttenham describes as the 'Tricquet displayed', a 'halfe square [...] parted vpon the crosse angles':

> A certaine great Sultan of Persia called *Ribuska*, entertaynes in love the Lady *Selamour*, sent her this triquet reue[r]st pitiously bemoning his estate, all set in merquetry with letters of blew Saphire and Topas artificially cut and entermingled. [...] To which *Selamour* to make the match egall, and the figure entire, answered in a standing Triquet richly engrauen with letters of like stuffe.[98]

In Herbert's 'Easter-wings', as well as the upper halves being 'answered' by the lower, and the speaker beginning the second stanza 'pitiously bemoning his estate', there is an echo (in 'Let me combine' and 'if I imp my wing') of the collage effect Puttenham describes ('set in merquetry'; 'artificially cut and entermingled'; 'richly engrauen'). Yet Herbert's poem is obviously unconcerned with the trivialities of courtly romance and deals instead with the relationship between God and the individual. Such a 'match' cannot be made 'egall', since one restores the other; God's power, which generates the poem, is the same power that turns it to its completion, despite human, writerly reduction.

And despite its metaphysical obscurities, the Herbert section of Hill's twenty-ninth clavic verges on such a turn, alluding to its own form, and alluding also, in its final line, to the word 'advance' in the last line of 'Easter-wings':

> In strife of certitudes to be outstared.
>   Let me urge for myself virtues
>   Of the skald as hit-man
>   Things narrow thus
>   C h a o s
>   Or chess
>   T o   h a r r o w   u s
>   Go swanning through skidpan
>   As a freelance virtuoso
> Other means of advancement undeclared.

(p. 819)

Forms 179

'Things narrow thus' appears to eschew a Herbertian personal responsibility for the poem's reduction; but if the 'skald', the poet, aspires to the virtues of the 'hit-man' it may be little wonder that poetic 'Chaos' ensues.[99] Immediately, on the turning point of the section, this chaos offers to arrange itself into a logical 'chess'; but finally reverts to a reckless sense of 'advancement', 'swanning through skidpan | As a freelance virtuoso', which echoes the 'strut' of the first clavic.

Hill's Herbert sections are neither amatory triquets nor Easter-wings; but, in their contraction and expansion, strive ('In strife of certitudes') in various ways towards restoration (with a suggestion, in view of the collection's four Royalist tutelary spirits, of longing for political Restoration), while often doubting the possibility of its arrival and subverting the logic of the metre. In the Herbert section of the ninth clavic, the contraction of lines marks a concentration of divine praise, underwhelmingly exploded (in the etymological sense, driven off stage) in the second half.[100] Put another way, the metre works in precise contrary motion to the pitch: as the rhetoric swells to include the singing courts of Heaven, the lines shrink; and then, as the lines are built back up, the rhetoric is deflated:

Listen to and make music while you can
　Pray *Mater ora Filium*
　　Cry *Spem in Alium*
　　　God is made man
　　　　Choric
　　　　Lyric
　　　Heaven receives
　　Impartial these tributes.
　Creation call it that believes
Even to blasphemy in our ranged throats.

(p. 799)

Rather than a wing or an egg timer, this is a ranged (and re-arranged) throat. At that crucial, central junction, the chorus worshipping God becomes at once, in the shift from 'Choric' to 'Lyric', a single voice. Arnold Bax's *Mater ora Filium* is arranged for double choir, eight voices; Thomas Tallis's *Spem in alium* is written for forty. These works represent the chorus writ large as well as the grand ambition of the artist. The flipside of sacred music, even that of sublime quality, is the indifference of Heaven (singular, '[l]yric | Heaven') to its merit. Conversely, and worse still, humanity ('Creation call it that') gives too much credit to the beauty of its own creation, puts too much stock in the sounds of 'ranged throats'. What man 'believes' in is not God but his own extolling of Him; the belief and even the extolling are so disordered as to be blasphemous.

180   *Geoffrey Hill and the ends of poetry*

A more orderly sounding of praise, which is at the same time a description of one, marks the end of the twelfth clavic. Its Vaughan section begins with a temporary migration to the clavic's chronological birthplace: 'What constitutes Metaphysics: you are | A revived soul like the spirit of Donne?' (12, p. 802).[101] The section goes on questioning, self-recriminating ('My fault my fault'), and worrying over its own tone ('Not to desire | Sentiment on such track is difficult'). The beginning of the Herbert section is an assured turn, tonally and rhetorically:

> I detect something false in that disquiet;
>   So let's mark time as it remains.
>   Fiction may find itself
>   Compatible
>   With truth
>   Like Ruth
>   In the Bible;
>   In a bright simple clef;
>   *Sul ponte*, bearing on the strains;
>   Break C minor to C major at LIGHT.

The sense of a nearing end here, in 'let's mark time as it remains', recalls the ninth Herbert section's 'make music while you can'. Both in turn obliquely recall Herrick's 'To the Virgins, to make much of Time' ('Gather ye Rosebuds'), which was set to music by Lawes.[102] In making music, one marks time; one notates time and, in a sense, captures, gathers it by doing so.[103] In *Clavics*, it is a wintry gathering, a gathering against time's last ravages: 'Consort like winter sky' (3, p. 793); 'So the sun's aurora in deep winter [...] I think we are past Epiphany now' (4, p. 794); 'Calling to witness here the Winter Queen' (24, p. 814); 'Shadows long wintering beneath the flare' (27, p. 817). *Clavics* plays the sounds of its own time discordantly against the political, cultural, and poetic textures of Lawes's time ('Lawes makes his way in grinding the textures | Of harmony' (15, p. 805)). Again, there is an allusion to harmonics: '*Sul ponte*' is a musical direction to bow a stringed instrument near the bridge, producing a glassier sound that emphasises the harmonics, the overtones, at the expense of the fundamental tone. One might have to 'wince' to hear this sort of harmony.

Not all of the Herbert sections exhibit a perfectly symmetrical rhyme scheme (as the 'Easter-wings' do not); but the twelfth, above, does.[104] The 'fiction', the governing artifice, of the form is stressed by the pronounced rhymes and rhythms, particularly in the central lines' chiming iambs ('With truth | Like Ruth'). The 'strains' of the form, forcing uncomfortable pairings, forcing a struggle to make the verse 'compatible' with truth, can gain the poem a certain 'mystical | And eccentric' insight (8, p. 798). Unexpected epiphanies dawn, as in the last line. 'Break C minor to C major

Forms 181

at LIGHT' is a description of an epiphany in music that has its own verbal epiphanic power. Its source is not Caroline consort music but Haydn's *The Creation*, the text of which was published (in German and English) in 1800. In the second section of the first part of the oratorio, the chorus recites from the first chapter of Genesis: 'and God said, Let there be light; and there was light'.[105] At the moment that this second 'light' is sung, the music modulates dramatically from C minor to C major. It is a beginning that is its own perfect ending: the sudden and complete banishment of chaos, followed immediately by the procession of order. It is a '[b]reak': a relief, as well as an irrevocable change. Hill's Herbert sections find relief, and their ends, in such dramatic shifts, closings-in, openings-out.

In the only poem from the initial publication of *Clavics* that is completely omitted in *Broken Hierarchies*, the opening lines of each section seem, respectively, to dismiss the idea of a satisfactory end and advance that of a mere all-encompassing finality: 'Even less able to approach or end'; 'Set yourself as finality avails'.[106] In the latter, one expects not 'avails' but *prevails*. How, after all, does finality 'afford help' (*OED*, 'avail, *v.*', sense 1a)? The preceding words in the line serve to answer the question: if the command is '[s]et yourself', the knowledge of finality, of death, might reasonably 'have force or efficacy for the accomplishment' (*OED*, 'avail, *v.*', sense 1a) of such a purpose. 'Set yourself' implies that, facing the end, one should not merely hold firm or grin and bear it but order oneself, make personal reconciliations, in expectation of a greater, incorporating order.

Perhaps, then, as *Clavics* finally sees it, somewhere there is such an ordered kingdom. There may be, too, certain earthly intimations of it: in the technical accomplishments of the artist, and also in what the artist (for one) observes. At the end of the twenty-eighth clavic's Vaughan section Hill, after Nabokov (mentioned in the fourteenth clavic (p. 804)), looks to lepidoptera:

The butterflies, high flyers on high winds;
Invisible to us they plane and soar
        Beyond our minds'
Troubled conventioning and do not err.

(p. 818)

The unambiguous artifice, the '[t]roubled conventioning', of the clavic as a form seeks to imitate the transcendent, 'high', '[i]nvisible' patterns of the natural world ('Creation call it that'). The modulation in Haydn's *Creation*, breaking through vague disorder with new, discernible, and harmonious convention, represents a similar aspiration. As Campion's ditty puts it: 'Louely formes do flowe | From concent deuinely framed'.[107] The 'butterflies, high flyers on high winds', operate in a divinely framed

182   *Geoffrey Hill and the ends of poetry*

consent, an order not humanly understood, but that the forms of art strive towards – all the while, in *Clavics*' case, suspecting themselves ('Are we slid cant | Wishing to end well?' (42, p. 832)). There is a beautiful and achieved restraint in the half-rhyme 'soar/err' because of its implicit acknowledgement of failure and its ambition to 'soar' and go '[b]eyond' the error of its connection. 'Between dissatisfaction and finish | Is where it goes wrong' (16, p. 806); but it is also where the clavic goes right. The minute, constant, instinctively fitting and precise intricacies of flora and fauna, exemplified by the motions of Hill's butterflies, are conventions that 'do not err'; the way in which these words finish the intricately worked Vaughan section of this clavic lends it, too, an air of unlikely impeccability.

Sapphics: Sidney and *Odi Barbare*

During his last public appearance, Geoffrey Hill read one poem in sapphics, a poem brought about by a reading of another poem in sapphics. The latter is spoken by Cleophila in Sidney's *Old Arcadia* (of which Hill read the fifth stanza, which became the second epigraph of *Odi Barbare*). Here is Sidney's poem in full:

> If mine eyes can speake to doo harty errande,
> Or mine eyes' language she doo hap to judge of,
> So that eyes' message be of her receaved,
>   Hope we do live yet.
>
> But if eyes faile then, when I most doo need them,
> Or if eyes' language be not unto her knowne,
> So that eyes' message doo returne rejected,
>   Hope we doo both dye.
>
> Yet dying, and dead, doo we sing her honour;
> So become our tombes monuments of her praise;
> So becomes our losse the triumph of her gayne;
>   Hers be the glory.
>
> If the sencelesse spheares doo yet hold a musique,
> If the Swanne's sweet voice be not heard, but at death,
> If the mute timber when it hath the life lost,
>   Yeldeth a lute's tune,
>
> Are then humane mindes priviledg'd so meanly,
> As that hatefull death can abridge them of powre,
> With the voyce of truth to recorde to all worldes,
>   That we be her spoiles?

Forms 183

Thus not ending, endes the due praise of her praise;
Fleshly vaile consumes; but a soule hath his life,
Which is helde in love, love it is, that hath joynde
    Life to this our soule.

But if eyes can speake to doo harty errande,
Or mine eyes' language she doo hap to judge of,
So that eyes' message be of her receaved,
    Hope we doo live yet.[108]

Two words that are important in the context of Hill's poetry come to mind on reading Sidney's poem: communication and consummation. In this poem, whether one is to hope for life or death depends on the correctly interpreted language of eyes: 'So that eyes' message be of her receaved'. (Hill, one suspects, would have appreciated the slight emendation to the repeated stanza, 'If mine eyes can speake' in the first becoming 'But if eyes can speake' in the last.) This language is a wooing language (and the word *woo*, which does not appear, could just about become expected as a rhyme with the repeated 'doo's). It seeks erotic, aesthetic, and spiritual consummations.

It also evokes them linguistically, even in the midst of doubt. 'If the mute timber when it hath the life lost, | Yeldeth a lute's tune': the first word may be a conditional, but the play of the language achieves the described transformation almost without its speaker's permission. The 'mute' timber is brought to sounding life by its rhyme with 'lute'. The rhyme itself is an analogue of the wood's manufacture into a musical instrument; rhyme is a poet's tool for the vivifying sculpture of words, and the poem is their newly made music. There is an echo of Christ's parable in Sidney's timber, dead but full of potential: 'Uerely, verely, I say vnto you, Except a corne of wheat fall into the ground, and die, it abideth alone: but if it die, it bringeth forth much fruit' (John 12.24).

In a lecture given at Trinity College, Cambridge, Gavin Alexander spoke of Sidney 'overdetermining' and 'stuffing' his poems that are in classical forms, such as sapphics, with rhetorical devices.[109] Cleophila's poem is a clear example. Without looking for long, one finds various examples of repetition, not including the near-complete replication of the first stanza in the last: anaphora ('eyes' and 'Hope we do [or 'doo']' in the first, second, and last stanzas; 'So' in the third; 'If the' in the fourth); conduplication ('praise' in the sixth); polyptoton ('dye […] dying, and dead'; 'become […] becomes'; 'ending, endes'); and chiasmus ('soule […] life […] love, love […] Life […] soule'). The poem's structure, also, is characterised by metanoia, with Cleophila repeatedly turning and questioning the argument in a spirit of self-judgement; two stanzas begin with the word 'But' and another with 'Yet'.

184   *Geoffrey Hill and the ends of poetry*

Such a rhetorically classical style recalls what has been written of Sappho herself. For instance, Demetrius writes: 'There is obvious charm from the use of figures, preeminently in Sappho, for example the use of repetition [...]. Sometimes too she makes attractive use of anaphora [...]. There is a kind of charm from a change of direction which is peculiarly characteristic of Sappho. She will say something and then change direction, as though changing her mind.'[110] It is plausible that Demetrius is thinking about the sapphic stanza here, which, in terms of metre, repeats its first line twice before changing direction with a final line of half the length.

Christopher Middleton remarks on the power of such a style in Sidney's poem: 'Form can be something we don't want but at the same time, if there is not some of it there—a kind of recurrence of sounds, a kind of circularity, a kind of ritualization of language—then there is a flattening and a diminution of the forces or of the flavours of words.'[111] The notion of writing in Sidneian sapphics seems to have come to Hill by way of Middleton. In a short memoir of Hill, Marius Kociejowski, referring to his own published conversation with Middleton (from which I have just quoted), entitled *Palavers*, writes: 'I sent a copy to Geoffrey and so deeply moved he was by its arguments that he wrote *Odi Barbare* as a response to it and he even adopted the form of Edmund Spenser's poem which Christopher had quoted in full.'[112] The misattribution is an unfortunate gaffe; he means to refer to Sidney's poem. But the claim Kociejowski makes is justified by Hill's own words. At his last public reading, Hill said:

> I will read one poem from a book called *Odi Barbare*, which happens to be based on Christopher Middleton's reading of Sidney's sapphic ode, which ends 'Are then humane mindes [Hill reads the rest of the stanza]'. Wonderful poem, written in strict sapphics; some of the stressing is illicit; that is to say, you occasionally find *the* being given a strong stress. And I decided I would write a book in which I – entirely in sapphic metres – in which you didn't get these occasional misplacings of stress. Didn't work, of course; but I was no worse than Sidney.[113]

The poem Hill went on to read, the twenty-eighth in *Odi Barbare*, will be an important subject in this section. It is significant that Hill describes his decision to write *Odi Barbare* as motivated by the pursuit of one aspect of formal perfection ('I would write a book [...] in which you didn't get these occasional misplacings of stress'). There is also the sense of competing with Sidney to better fulfil the formal exigencies of the sapphic stanza. Hill, too, makes an error, and a telling one. Sidney's poem does not end, as Hill says it does, with the stanza beginning 'Are then humane mindes'. The strictness of the sapphic form, which Hill emphasises, seems to put Hill in mind, as though by reflex, of reconcilings and ends.

Similarly, the last poem in *Speech! Speech!* includes a reference to sapphics, which is followed by a reference to death: 'English Limper | after the English Sapphic. This | has to be seen. But what a way to go' (*SS* 120, p. 348).[114] Hill is making a subtle prosodic joke here. The final word of the first line, 'This', is a limping addition to ('after') the hendecasyllabic line (of two trochees, a dactyl, and two trochees), three of which would make three quarters of a sapphic stanza. Aware that this metatextual play might appear pompous, Hill weaves in an extra, self-deprecating pun: he is regarding himself with his walking stick when he writes 'English Limper'. And the metrical licentiousness is not the only kind: though near death, Hill pictures himself limping 'after' an unnamed, fantastic poetess, 'the English Sapphic'.[115]

In the nineteenth poem of *Odi Barbare*, Hill alludes to the sapphic metres of another figure of literary antiquity:

> *Carmen saeculare* I might have called this;
> Now am too far in. In a way much better
> Done as not doting on mellifluousness.
>   You know me better.
>
>   (*OB* XIX, p. 853)

Carmen Saeculare, or *Hymn for a New Age*, is a poem in sapphics by Horace.[116] Hill's metanoia, half-wishing aloud to change the work's title, is a trope he employs earlier in *The Orchards of Syon*.[117] The mock-arrogance, also, is hardly new; here Hill calls *Odi Barbare* 'much better | Done' but the comparison is deliberately unclear: is it better done than if it were called *Carmen saeculare*, or better done than Horace (as well as 'no worse than Sidney')? The rest of the stanza summarises Hill's defence for his late work's harsher harmonies, and for his sapphics; and ends with an impish wink to the reader, punningly repeating 'better'.

The poetic line, which in *Clavics* is subjected to a tight set of fluctuating metres, and often shrunk to one or two feet, opens out in *Odi Barbare* to three longer lines of eleven syllables, followed by a useful condensing coda (or, as above, an aside) of five syllables (a dactyl and a trochee), in ancient Greek prosody called the adonic.[118] Though the rhythmic pattern Hill imposes on his sapphics is stringent, the longer lines allow Hill, when he wishes, to give extended descriptions (of nature, of works of art); to wonder aloud, as in the stanza quoted above; to shape his words largely rather than compactly; to write with a greater lyric fluency, as found more frequently in *Oraclau | Oracles* and *Al Tempo de' Tremuoti*, yet 'not doting on mellifluousness'.

In the history of English poetry, perhaps no one has been oftener said to dote on mellifluousness than Swinburne.[119] And yet, in one important respect, Hill is following Swinburne, who, also taking up Sidney's mantle, wrote a poem of twenty sapphic stanzas, entitled 'Sapphics'. It is a simple but perfectly apt title for what is an encomium of Sappho, her mastery of metre, and, by extension, metre itself. Swinburne describes Sappho looking upon her fellow residents of Lesbos and perceiving in their midst a vision of her own poetic work as she makes it. She has already made the nine Muses weep at her song; in the fourteenth and fifteenth stanzas, Swinburne writes that Sappho, not seeing Aphrodite calling on her,

> Only saw the beautiful lips and fingers,
> Full of songs and kisses and little whispers,
> Full of music; only beheld among them
>   Soar, as a bird soars
>
> Newly fledged, her visible song, a marvel,
> Made of perfect sound and exceeding passion,
> Sweetly shapen, terrible, full of thunders,
>   Clothed with the wind's wings.[120]

Sappho's passion, like Swinburne's, may be 'exceeding' but it does not exceed the 'visible' form of the '[s]weetly shapen' stanza. The five-syllable adonics of the stanzas channel and direct the momentum they have built up: in the first stanza, the narrowed line, its rhythm quickly changing, its first and last words inexactly mirroring each other, itself imitates a bird's soaring flight; and in the second stanza, the avian image returns, and the alliteration and assonance ('with the wind's wings') afford the shorter line a neatly summative effect, as well as doing homage to the 'perfect sound' of Sappho's own verse.

The final stanza of 'Sapphics' begins, like the adonic of the fifteenth, with the word 'Clothed'. As in much of Swinburne's poetry, this stanza is clothed with layers of repeated words and polyptoton. Sappho has been finally abandoned by all hearers, except the ghosts 'of outcast women' who return,

> Clothed about with flame and with tears, and singing
> Songs that move the heart of the shaken heaven,
> Songs that break the heart of the earth with pity,
>   Hearing, to hear them.[121]

Compare the last stanza of the fortieth poem in *Odi Barbare*:

> Hendre Fechan, hearth of our hearts' indwelling,
> Giving song hearth-room and the harp's thrilled diction,
> Deep penillion woven to snow's curled measures
>   Heard past unhearing.

(p. 874)

Forms   187

Hill's 'diction' has to some degree been 'thrilled', it appears, by Swinburne's. While in Swinburne, 'heart' breaks to 'Hearing' and 'hear', Hill's 'hearth' gives room to 'hearts'' and 'harp's' before it too settles on auditory variations, 'Heard' and 'unhearing'. There are further possible parallels in the references to song and to clothing ('woven').[122] In both, too, the adonics suggest that what 'song' contains is so '[d]eep', has such capacity to 'move' and 'break' the heart, that one almost wishes not to have heard it.

Hill's sapphics use their adonics effectively, often beautifully. These short lines, like Swinburne's, sometimes reflect on their own shaping and power, though usually obliquely. Like the soaring bird in 'Sapphics', these short lines are, as one in the eleventh poem of *Odi Barbare* has it, '[h]eld by momentum' (p. 845). They '[t]ighten the grammar' (XLI, p. 875). In the fiftieth poem they are 'Precious detritus' and a 'Terse apparition' (p. 884). Two other short lines accentuate themselves: 'Mind if I stress this?' (XXVII, p. 861); 'Stressed and in order' (XXXII, p. 866). Another, which could serve as 'motto-phrase' (*BBGJ* 142, p. 76) for much of the late work, signals its brevity: 'Metric makes gnomic' (XX, p. 854). The endings of the eighth poem's stanzas seem especially self-aware: 'Pitch me *vox clamans*'; 'Twixt porch and altar'; 'let us imagine purpose, | Poverty married in the way conceit's made | Hostage to metrum'; 'Bide me my pardon, enigmatic cadence | Cracked and repaired thus' (p. 842). The last line of the sapphic stanza can be a crack and a repair. The first poem ends: 'blast access to unsuspected | Caverns of fluorspar' (p. 835), in which the last line feels like a narrow blasted passage in a cavern, an 'unsuspected' rhythmic discovery.[123] At other times, the short line is more akin to a crack in memory; it has a fleeting quality, as if it were a long line, like the others, but suddenly forgotten in midstream:

> How the sea-lightning with a flash at hazard
> Cleft the lanterned yard into pelting angles.
> Had we been there, had you then turned towards me,
>   By this remembered ...
>
>   (IV, p. 838)

Elsewhere, the line is a comic cut-off: 'Who denies this I would expect the Queen to | Rise up and smite him' (VI, p. 840). Elsewhere still, it is a counterpoint to the foregoing stanza, as in the second in the thirty-fourth poem, in which three long lines, all questions, precede a child's eager rejoinder: 'Ask me another' (p. 868).

The twenty-eighth poem of *Odi Barbare*, the last poem Hill recited during his final reading, begins with the pairing and breaking of a kiss. This probably has little to do with Swinburne's kisses ('Ravaged with kisses'; 'Full of songs and kisses'); but this first stanza might owe something to

188   *Geoffrey Hill and the ends of poetry*

the juncture between the eighth and ninth stanzas of 'Sapphics': 'Laurel by laurel, ‖ Faded all their crowns'.[124]

> Broken that first kiss by the race to shelter,
> Scratchy brisk rain irritable as tinder;
> Hearing light thrum faintly the chords of laurel
>   Taller than we were.
>
>   (p. 862)

'Taller' falls elegantly from the vowel-sounds of 'laurel'; and there are end-line echoes between 'shelter', 'tinder', and 'we were'. 'Taller than we were' looks up at the three taller lines above it. The pronoun 'we' is delayed until the last moment, making the couple sound and look small; the three leisurely lines of description that precede it provide the couple's bulky 'shelter', as the laurel from the rain.

Alluding to Hill's 'Eros is the power that can be felt in language when a word or half-finished phrase awaits its consummation' (*CCW*, p. 548), in a discussion of the poem 'A Cloud in Aquila' (*TCP*, p. 576), Ratcliffe writes: 'Drawing on the power of the 'half-finished phrase', Hill's use of enjambment, and the curtailed final line of each verse, seems to enact the notion of a 'shared life aborted', and a longing for union'.[125] Batchelor relates this remark to Hill's sapphic stanza: its adonic, he proposes, is 'like an afterthought that calls the reader back, detaining us a little longer'; a 'gesture of yearning seems implicit in the form'.[126]

On this thought of yearning, it is worth taking a step sideways from the twenty-eighth poem in *Odi Barbare* to consider a few remarks in and around Hill's essays on F. H. Bradley and Eliot. Here is the first, from 'Word Value in F. H. Bradley and T. S. Eliot': 'Eliot's self-laceration in *Four Quartets* [...] gives not so much a syntax of self-recognition as a stasis of yearning, a yearning which is the negative correlative of a Schopenhauerian and Nietzschean exaltation of music as the supreme art' (*CCW*, pp. 545–46). For Hill, the Eliot of *Four Quartets* does not fruitfully fight with, or even fruitfully resign himself to, the difficulties of consummation; instead, he smoothes over them. Eliot's 'yearning', in this understanding, is a lacklustre sort, empty of the proper vigour of thoughts and words, and ready to accept even a weak kind of aesthetic satisfaction; what Hill is looking for is a 'syntax', poetry defined by the hard-wrought, coiled logic of the sentence, a logic that will not settle for less than truthful reconcilements. What Hill is looking for, in other words, is eros, as he understands it: the linguistic effort made in pursuit of 'real' consummations, the thoughtfully and fully acted-on yearning of word for word, or love for love.[127] 'I am claiming for the writing of major poetry', Hill writes in a late essay, 'the necessity of something I can do no better than call an erotic impulse. The element of

Forms 189

eros need not stray outside the semantic field' (*CCW*, p. 571). (Note the suggestion of rhythmic genesis in 'impulse'.)

The second remark I wish to highlight is the first epigraph of *Without Title* (2006), a book that is roughly contemporaneous with the writing of Hill's essays on Bradley and Eliot. It is from Bradley; it could be brought into conversation with the epigraphs of 'The Pentecost Castle', from Yeats and Weil:

> Here to my mind is the objection to taking love as ultimate. There is no higher form of unity, I can agree. But we do not know love as the complete union of individuals, such that we can predicate of it the entirety of what belongs to them. And if we extend the sense of love and make it higher than what we experience, I do not see myself that we are sure of preserving that amount of self-existence in the individuals which seems necessary for love. (*BH*, p. 481)[128]

Surely, one might object, Hill's poetry does take 'love as ultimate'. I would argue that it does, but that the question lies in the definition of that *love* for which the 'self' yearns.[129] Hill's 'self-laceration' and 'self-recognition' find another mirror in Bradley's 'self-existence'. Bradley appears to be saying that human love, the love of two people, cannot be taken as ultimate; that is, as the final end of existence. A love 'higher than what we experience', which to Bradley represents an extension of the sense of the word, would be a true and complete fulfilment, a perfect reconciling, of the 'self' that is hyphenated into contingent unions by both Hill and Bradley ('self-recognition', 'self-existence'). 'Broken that first kiss by the race to shelter': the human union is unconsummated, interrupted by the natural (though fallen) instincts of the 'individuals'. It is a 'race' to shelter, as though suddenly the lovers, faced with the condition of the world and their own condition, find themselves in competition with one another.

But compare this with the quotation from Bradley in the essay 'Eros in F. H. Bradley and T. S. Eliot': 'We may be told that the End, because it is that which thought aims at, is therefore itself (mere) thought. This assumes that thought cannot desire a consummation in which it is lost. But does not the river run into the sea, and the self lose itself in love?' (*CCW*, p. 548). It may be tempting to dismiss this as a fanciful lyric turn; but it makes clear that, for Bradley, love as involving the loss of self is a consummation, an 'End'.

In human, 'real' terms, such love is never easy. The forty-first poem of *Odi Barbare* begins with a hope of self-enclosed reconciliation: 'God who holds our memories reft at pre-birth, | I would trust, intended their restitution' (p. 875). The third, fourth, and fifth stanzas present two erotic stories, one reft by the other. The first is the myth of Orpheus and Eurydice, split by death, and split again, later, by Orpheus's lack of faith that Eurydice's spirit

190   *Geoffrey Hill and the ends of poetry*

is following him out of the underworld. After Orpheus's death, the musician's head is removed by the Muses so that it may continue to entertain with its song.[130] The second story, which in Hill's poem comes in the midst of the first, is that of Paolo and Francesca, in part a true story but that took on mythical proportions after its telling in Dante's *Inferno*. Paolo and Francesca, both married but not to one another, have a long affair and are killed when found *in flagrante delicto* by Paolo's lame brother (to whom Francesca is married). The story moves Dante the Pilgrim to tears and even fainting.[131] Here is Hill's double-retelling:

> Lamentation's triumph, rejoicing Orpheus:
> His detached head that can be tuned to pleasure.
> Speculate these opera cast the shades by
>   Lucent obstruction.
>
> (Strange to each other in that intimacy
> Purgatory, even, can learn to weep at.
> Paolo I am not nor are you Francesca;
>   No such temptation.)
>
> This is no rare dogma confiding why such
> Acts encrypt endings. Let us reap the darkness,
> Take to ourselves limping Eurydice's cry
>   New to abandon.
>
>   (p. 875)

The stories are indeed '[s]trange to each other in that intimacy', an intimacy both suggested and denied by the brackets that close one story off from the other. The lovers, too, in both stories, are made strange to each other by their own fallenness. Yet there are hidden comings-together. 'Let us reap the darkness, | Take to ourselves limping Eurydice's cry': the lameness of Paolo's brother in the story from *Inferno* is transposed into the Orphean myth; in the ambiguous tangle of the syntax, it could be 'ourselves' or Eurydice limping. 'Speculate these opera cast the shades by | Lucent obstruction': even though Orpheus has died, his music continues to give 'pleasure', so much so that Hill imagines his musical works (his 'opera', punning on the musical genre, numerous examples of which have been devoted to the myth of Orpheus) as constituting a dispelling 'obstruction' to the 'shades', to the encroachment on the present of past tragedy.

There is an allusion to the dramatic performances of these myths in the penultimate sentence above: 'This is no rare dogma confiding why such | Acts encrypt endings'. Staged 'Acts' can be inferred here; but the principal meaning of the word is less obvious. Following the reference to 'temptation' in the previous (though bracketed) stanza, one can assume that sexual acts, possibly sinful, are meant. The 'rare dogma', which Hill simultaneously propounds

Forms 191

and renounces, is that acts – sexual, sinful, dramatic – have their endings, and therefore their meanings, already written in them, encrypted. The poem, being no such 'dogma', throws off this concern and proclaims: 'Let us reap the darkness', which, especially as followed by 'Take to ourselves', 'cry', and 'abandon', sounds like an invitation to do as the aforementioned lovers did.

The sapphic stanza, here, has a fluency about it, though not quite a 'mellifluousness' (XIX, p. 853). The final words of each stanza, all of them amphibrachs, even establish a sense of half-rhyme (as well as an illuminating narrative arc mirroring the story in Dante): 'obstruction / temptation / abandon'. The rhythm and the enjambment (the way 'by' hangs placidly in 'cast the shades by'; the line-beginning, sentence-ending power of 'Acts encrypt endings') threaten to glide the poem away from 'obstruction[s]' to erotic and poetic consummation. The final stanza corrects any such blurred vision. Though 'Let us reap the darkness' is a proposal that one embrace mystery, the next stanza begins: 'Lunar fallibilities; eyes adjusting' (p. 875). Hill has caught himself moonstruck.

No such 'stasis of yearning', as Hill finds in *Four Quartets*, is permitted in *Odi Barbare*'s twenty-eighth poem (to which I return at last).[132] In the place of stasis, it is not exactly a 'syntax of self-recognition' that prevails but a syntax of interrogation. The fifth stanza of Sidney's 'Cleophila' sapphics, *Odi Barbare*'s second epigraph, hovers amid Hill's questions: 'Are then humane mindes priviledg'd so meanly [...]?' 'Answer one question, this is all I need', Hill requests, before asking two. In the stanza stating the first of these questions, the epanaleptic adonic 'Laurel by laurel' in Swinburne's 'Sapphics', already verbally present in 'the chords of laurel' from the first stanza, appears to be imitated:

> Ancient question haunting the Platonist: can
> Spirit ransom body, and if so could I
> Rise again in presence of your devoting
>   Sorrow to sorrow?
>
> (p. 862)

It is a question of eternal ends; a question arising from what Hill calls 'an anxiety about the fate of my soul'.[133] The body itself is in need of final, transcendent 'ransom'. The stanza is enjambed to a degree unusual in *Odi Barbare*. Its urgency is made more explicit in the next stanza, which abbreviates the question:

> Quick, is love's truth seriously immortal?
> Would you might think so and not be this other
> Finally known only through affirmation's
>   Failing induction.
>
> (p. 862)

192 *Geoffrey Hill and the ends of poetry*

The end of life is near, which is why the answer has to be '[q]uick'. The next sentence begins like another question: 'Would you [...]'. But it is an archaising use expressing desire.[134] The phrase 'affirmation's | Failing induction' is apposite to a discussion of the syntax of this and the final two stanzas of the poem; as 'Would you might' indicates, the remainder of the poem's discourse is hedged on every side by conditionals, preemptively removing the means by which affirmations might gain purchase. Nevertheless, somehow, the poem ends in revelation:

> What though, wedded, we would have had annulment's
> Consummation early, and though in darkness
> I could see that glimmerous rim of folly
> Lave our condition,
>
> Had we not so stumbled on grace betimely
> In that chanced day brief as the sun's arising
> Preternaturally without a shadow
> Cast in its presence.

(p. 862)

Though the stanzas commence as though to ask questions ('What though'; 'Had we not'), the long sentence finds itself having 'stumbled', after all, on affirmation. The syntax is convoluted; but it sounds as though the thought, rather than the sapphic metre, is what is causing the complications. Middleton's comments on Cleophila's fourth and fifth stanzas are pertinent here: 'It's *grand*, that. It's also obscure. You don't figure out what on earth it means to start with. It has a sort of luminous, blinding, dazzling splendour about it.'[135] Middleton sees the Sidney stanzas as simultaneously 'obscure' and 'luminous'. The 'shades' and '[l]ucent obstruction' of the forty-first poem of *Odi Barbare* come to mind; but above, too, there are exchanges of darkness and light. Where in the forty-first poem the existing 'shades' are 'cast' out, here, by 'grace' and chance, and despite the 'darkness' of the previous stanza, the sun's light is '[p]reternaturally' preserved from the onset of shadow.[136] This is a 'brief' moment, but also a 'blinding, dazzling' one.

It is a moment in which consummation is glimpsed as a 'glimmerous rim of folly'. In the last of Hill's collected essays, he again cites Bradley: 'We have the idea of perfection—there is no doubt as to that—and the question is whether perfection also actually exists.'[137] Of the parenthesis here, Hill writes: 'This is flatter than a flat assertion, and yet a brief flicker lights up the flatness; the momentary uncertainty as to whether "no doubt" goes with "perfection" or with "idea"' (*CCW*, p. 571). This brief flicker, this 'shivelight', as in Hill's reference to Hopkins in the same essay (p. 570), is a kind of visitation of 'grace betimely'. *Betimely* (*OED*;

Forms   193

'*Obsolete. rare*') means early.[138] '[W]e would have had annulment's |
Consummation early'.[139] The final stanza, an enjambed and scarcely
punctuated haze of unshadowed sun, is a prevention of grace, in Eliot's
archaic sense; a coming-before.[140] In this preternatural moment, even the
human 'condition' of the couple is washed away, as by baptism; or as,
perhaps, by death. The early rise of the sun, here, is a punning remembrance of the Cross; it is also a prevision of a perfect end. It is not merely
what Bradley calls 'the idea of perfection' but perfection's real 'presence',
a word doubled in the twenty-eighth poem of *Odi Barbare*. It comes
early, like the 'half-finished' end of each sapphic stanza; and yet it comes
from outside time.

Concluding-problems

Hill's poems are end-directed even when they are pointedly open-ended.
Ends and endings are continually made manifest, including by their conspicuous absence.

In *Canaan*'s poems of limited punctuation and frequent marginal indents,
as in unpunctuated poems such as 'The Pentecost Castle', the loosened free
verse seems to invite a freer approach to thoughts of spiritual and erotic
reconciliation, of unexpected consummations (devoutly wished if not actu-
alised). The unbounded line of the verset and unrestricted number of poems
in *The Book of Baruch by the Gnostic Justin* affords a similar liberation,
particularly in contemplating political ends (that is, objectives), even those
current at the time of writing. This re-found form, it seems, is so freeing to
Hill that he not only declares his voting intentions in the referendum on
Britain's proposed exit from the European Union – 'I shall vote to remain'
(*BBGJ* 240, p. 129) – but even backs a candidate for the leadership of the
Labour party: 'Corbyn must win' (*BBGJ* 186, p. 102). Hill's expression of
and meditation on these desired ends, already at my time of writing long
dashed and gone, are not limited to the short quotations above. Compared
with the other ends meditated on in the poetry – loss, sexual love, death,
apocalypse – such declarations appear remarkably flimsy. Why should
a reader new to Hill care that he intended to vote to remain, or backed
Corbyn? Many years from now, will a reader who has no recollection of
or concern about these fleeting political events value Hill's stated opinions
of them – and value them as poetry? What is it about these moments that
could exempt them from Hill's injunction that a poem not be 'a naive
vehicle for the transmission of political opinions and sentiments'?[141] And,
more to my point here, is the expansiveness of the verset to blame for this
unsuccessful foray?

194   *Geoffrey Hill and the ends of poetry*

Yes and no. The verset of *Mercian Hymns* is employed differently by Hill, not only with a keener sense of ends but with a keener sense of limits. The title *The Book of Baruch by the Gnostic Justin* gives adequate suggestion of the formal latitude of its kind of verset. This by itself is no fault, and indeed almost always yields good things; but on a few occasions, particularly towards the end of the book, Hill seems encouraged by the form's latitude to indulge himself with bland statements of political opinion such as those above, statements of no poetic effect or final value. One may argue that *Canaan*, also formally loose, is similarly engaged with contemporary British politics (though in a far more subdued way, with no names named). But *Canaan*'s sleek, sinewy free verse embodies the sinister 'slither-frisk' of the politicians it rebukes; no bland statements on statesmen in sight.[142]

The story of the relationship between Hill's end-directed use of forms and their success as consummate, finished, poems is not straightforward or linear. Firstly, it is not that Hill's poems begin formally strict and end up loose, or vice versa; experiments with restrictive forms recur throughout his career. It is clear enough that *Canaan* marks the arrival of free verse in Hill's corpus; but both *Canaan* and *The Triumph of Love*, which follows it, are repeatedly visited (as are the prose-poems of *Mercian Hymns*) by the ghosts of form, especially sonnet form. Secondly, it is not that Hill is clearly more successful in the use of either one form or another; or in either earlier or later uses of a given form; or even in the use of either generally looser or more binding forms. The best work, for many critics of Hill and for me, is found scattered (liberally) from the earliest poems to the latest; in poems both metrically bound and unbound; rhymed and unrhymed. Thirdly, the presence of a formal characteristic in one place does not entail its exact replication when it is found elsewhere. The tightness of the forms (and of the syntax and diction) in *For the Unfallen* is a different tightness to that of the forms, syntax, and diction in *Clavics*. In shorthand, the former collection's tightness is of a closely fitting suit while the latter's is of a suit with various joints poking through it.

For all these objections to a Hillian narrative of form, there are certain concluding observations that can be made on considering the four forms discussed in this chapter. The two forms examined from the early work, unrhymed sonnets and versets, have strong and evident connections with the various thematic ends inherent in the poems. In both examples, too, the ends of poems and collections strongly emphasise, by formal as well as other means, a sense of incompletion that is in some measure their own. The unrhymed sonnets of 'Funeral Music' are marked by the closures of death but also by the lack of resolution; the sonnets' form carries the transferred expectations of its rhymed sibling and is met continually with endings that seem, and feel, unfinished. Yet Hill's exploitation of the unrhymed sonnet's

Forms 195

natural unfinishedness is artistically consummate and consummating. The versets of *Mercian Hymns* are end-directed in their very appearance, resembling monumental inscriptions; but, at the end, the form visibly falls into stony fragments like its coins and traces of mud.

The two forms examined from the late work, clavics and sapphics, are also strongly end-directed but do not have such immediate and obvious ties to their poems' thematic ends. The clavic's double-stack of poetic models provides two formal conclusions in every poem, the Vaughan sections gaining conclusive momentum from rhyme, the Herbert sections from shape, and both from metre; while the sapphic stanza's adonic draws constant attention, syntactically, metrically, and visually, to final lines. But the texture of poems in both *Clavics* and *Odi Barbare*, as with much of the late work, is so much more variegated that the end-related themes emerge sporadically, unpredictably. In addition, these works are so much further removed from a sense of narrative, at the level of the poem as well as of the collection, that the forms' unfinishedness is not something that is led up to. Instead it is, as it were, disseminated throughout, and felt from the beginning. When a collection begins 'Bring torch for Cabbalah brand new treatise, | Numerology also makes much sense, | O *Astraea*!' (*Cl.* 1, p. 791), there is a sense that the reader is joining this 'brand new treatise' halfway through.

In *The Book of Baruch*, there are numerous meditations on the nature of the poem (including some funny comparisons beginning 'Poem as […]'). Among these is an explanation, decidedly unfunny, of the unfinished quality of many of Hill's own poems. 'It is the rare poem that reaches full term' (*BBGJ* 250, p. 135). If this is true for Hill, even as an exaggeration of the truth, it may provide a way of understanding the end-directedness of his poems – and how the character of this end-directedness differs between earlier and later work. To take again the poems already discussed in this chapter as examples, the 'Funeral Music' and *Mercian Hymns* sequences, obsessive over endings and the lack of satisfactory conclusions, are at pains to resist the irresolutions of life that they confront; even when what they present is incoherence, they strive to do so with a consummate artistic and aesthetic coherence. The clavics and sapphics are no less concerned with consummate artistry, but the ways in which the forms are employed indicate a different attitude towards the goal of the poem's internal unity and finishedness. It is an attitude that is both more resigned and more relaxed. The agonised wrestle with irresolution is not abandoned but newly construed, perhaps as a (still somewhat pained) dance.[143] In Hill's late collections, the beginning of the first poem and the end of the last poem seem equally *in medias res*; but ends and endings appear throughout, simmer under the surface everywhere, are immanent.

The 'gnomic' nature of much of the late work, particularly *The Book of Baruch*, is itself a kind of answer to the inevitable incompleteness of the poetic endeavour.[144] These are the fragments Hill has shored against his ruins; local perfections, prized before (though not to the exclusion of) the perfected unity of the whole.[145] (*OED*, 'end, *n*.', sense 5a: 'A piece broken, cut off, or left; a fragment, remnant.') In his first collected essay, Hill cites Edward Mendelson's defence of Auden's late work: 'as he grew older Auden became increasingly determined to write poems that were not breathtaking but truthtelling[.] [T]he local vividness of a line or passage can blind the reader into missing a poem's overall shape'.[146] Hill suggests instead that 'the poet's craft is precisely the ability to effect an at-one-ment between the "local vividness" and "the overall shape", and that this is his truthtelling' (*CCW*, p. 12). One may say that the approach to truthtelling in Hill's late work is in contrary motion to that described by Mendelson. Is there an 'overall shape' to *The Book of Baruch*? The work itself does not seem hopeful: 'Poem as shapeless form in a sack' (*BBGJ* 212, p. 116). But, if there is a formal coherence in the work, it is trusted to subsist in the unity of desire for conclusive form that pervades it.

According to the 229th poem of *The Book of Baruch* (p. 123), a good end is hard to find: 'Poem as form found in a citadel of the mind if not exiled therefrom [...] Poem as problem for the 'concluding-problem': in this sequence a current theme.' What is the 'concluding-problem'; and why does Hill place quotation marks around it? The hyphenation suggests that the phrase is in fact Hill's; and that the quotation marks are scare quotes, which Hill employs with unusual regularity in *The Book of Baruch* (including around the word 'closure' (144, p. 77)).[147] Hill thus places the 'concluding-problem' at some indiscernible distance from his own voice, which also means refusing to verify or deny the proposition. In any case, what is the 'concluding-problem'? The hyphen seems to rule out any sense that it is the final problem; instead, it is a problem of or surrounding concluding. More confusingly, what could it mean for the poem to be 'problem for the "concluding-problem"'? On one hand, the poem is the source of the concluding-problem's problem. By this reading, the poem is by its nature averse to conclusion. This concurs with Agamben in 'The End of the Poem': 'For if poetry is defined precisely by the possibility of enjambment, it follows that the last verse of a poem is not a verse. [...] [H]ere there lies something like a decisive crisis for the poem [...]. As if the poem as a formal structure would not and could not end'.[148] On the other hand, and seemingly in complete contradiction, the poem presents a problem to the 'concluding-problem': that is, the poem unsettles, or even resolves, what one may perceive as the problem of concluding. Every finished poem, after all, ends. Perhaps it is not, or not always, a problem.

Forms 197

But then there is the conclusion of Hill's sentence: 'in this sequence a current theme'. It is harder to argue that a river ends. A sequence may have a natural or planned end; *The Book of Baruch* has the former only in the most literal sense. If the 'concluding-problem' is a 'current theme' of the sequence, it moves continually through it; the end is always present to it. The problem of ends is not only a theme running through the last, unconcluding (and yet concluded) sequence of Hill's poetry but also an essential, animating, formative force throughout.

End notes

I

In its expanding view of the poem from its smallest prosodic ends to its largest framing ones, this book intends to build an understanding of the ends of poetry in what seems the most intuitive way, at least (as I understand it) from the poet's perspective. A joiner, and in this case I mean a manual labourer, must first achieve the smallest elements of construction; otherwise arrival at the total finished product will not be possible. Nevertheless, the image of this finished product must always be in mind as a guiding spirit. Similarly, the individual joints of poetry, from those within a word, to those between identical, similar, and different words, should be – and in Hill's poetry are – constantly minded of the joined-up, completed poem (an entity that, while the poem is being composed, is only ever potential). The end is something integral to every moment of a poem's composition, the honings of thought and word by which speech comes to be. This does not, as has been shown, preclude the leaving-open of windows and doors; the acknowledgement that certain bricks are for whatever reason missing; or the warning that the foundations are unavoidably unstable.

Muldoon, in his Oxford lectures, picks up on Agamben picking up on Dante, who calls the stanza 'a capacious storehouse or receptacle for the art in its entirety'.[1] Describing the larger passage from which this quotation comes, Agamben writes that Dante 'opposes *cantio* as unit of sense (*sententia*) to *stantiae* as purely metrical units'. The poem is the joining-point of myriad ends: ends of sense with ends of sound; ends of 'truth' with ends of 'metre'; thoughts of conclusion with thoughts of intention.

The analysis of poetic technique in this book only begins, and more by example than by systematic explication, to gesture towards a way of perceiving an end-directedness that is immanent throughout the writer's making, and subsequently throughout the reader's experiencing, of a poem.

End notes 199

II

Kenneth Haynes, at the beginning of the editorial notes that comprise the final pages of *The Book of Baruch by the Gnostic Justin*, writes that Hill 'planned [it] as a posthumous work, to consist of as many poems as he would live to complete' (*BBGJ*, p. 147). This is striking and telling. Hill did not know that *The Book of Baruch* would be his last work: he made sure of it. In one sense this indicates Hill's particular kind of mania for completion, for ending: there were to be no loose ends; no other kinds of poems to be written (as far as I know) than those intended to end up in this final volume. By default, *The Book of Baruch* is not unfinished, because it was designed to finish arbitrarily, to be complete whenever Hill could write no more. Every poem, therefore, in *The Book of Baruch* is potentially its last, and Hill's last, in a fully intentional way that the book makes explicit.

At the same time, another interpretation of the design of this posthumous book written as a posthumous book suggests itself: it may be for Hill a reconciled and final relinquishment of his poetry's end, in several key senses. Control over what would be his last poem is given up.[2] Control over the final appearance of the book, editorial decisions, and so on, are given up. In a late notebook that includes Hill's plan for his own funeral service, there is a passage for a poem marked 'IV', presumably intended as a section of the original long poem *A Treatise of Civil Power* (2005). The passage illustrates a doubled desire at once to maintain control over the end and to let go of it:

> I shall attend
> my own funeral service. [...]
> and my ashes
> to be scattered on the grave of my grandmother
> the site of which is forgotten, there is to be no marker.[3]

On one hand, there is a controlling precision in this language of a last will and testament; beyond the slightly surreal smirk of the first sentence here, beyond even the possible sense of it that suggests a living death (or perhaps a writing death), Hill appears to be insisting, albeit indirectly, on his body's presence at his funeral (the corpus this time physical rather than textual).[4] On the other, as in his choice of a lost burial plot, never to be marked, so much is left to chance, guesswork, silence. This is, at least in part, a nod to the inexorable and obvious: that the end is unknown, and the moment of its arrival unexpected, until the moment comes: 'ye know neither the day, nor the houre'.[5] Seventeen years before *The Book of Baruch*, there was already an oxymoronic sense of impending surprise (a sense bound up, too, with the poet's intended ends): 'Last days, last things, loom on: I write | to astonish myself' (*OS* XXIII, p. 373).[6] The poet's ability to dictate and animate ends can be a noble imitation (or a hubristic parody) of divinity; but, still bound by the limits of concupiscence, vanity, weathering, the imperfection of the poet's ends is as real as the ends themselves. The 'concluding-problem' may be that the poet is not God. The poet's authority over ends is not absolute. And yet the poem is a 'problem' to the 'concluding-problem' precisely because it is end-directed.

In the year after the first publication of *A Treatise of Civil Power*, Hill published the collection *Without Title*. Its two last poems suggest that the doubled desire to bind and yet to loose the endings of both life and poetry ('[t]he consummation held and set apart') is enfolded also in the question of poetry's final purpose for Hill.[7] The first of these poems, 'Luxe, Calme et Volupté' (the title of Matisse's seminal painting, itself filched from a poem by Baudelaire), offers a darker vision of the end than its title seems to promise. It is an end found in the painfully unrequited, consummation, once again, in the unconsummated:

> Lost is not vanished; nor is it finished;
> more like a haunting from the ghosted future
> that was not ours and cannot now be called
> through into being by too late consent.
> Motions towards life are not living
> except abstractly I am moved to say.
> Both of us here conjoined in epitaph
> > awaiting stone.
>
> > > (*WT*, p. 518)

Hill's poetry, what he is 'moved to say', is figured as an abstraction of life, a motion towards life but 'not living'. Yet 'except' is also *except that*. A door is left open to the sixth line's meaning *except that abstractly I am moved to say*. This saying is its own way of life and its own end; but the other of its ends is to reconcile what cannot otherwise be brought together. 'Both of us here conjoined': only here, in the poem, but here nonetheless.

The next and last poem in *Without Title*, 'Improvisation on "Warum ist uns das Licht gegeben?"', ends with these lines: 'Against survival something that endures: | win, lose, the paid-up quiet death' (p. 519). This is the mystery of an ending that lasts. The end is held to by releasing it. How already quiet 'paid-up' is. (Cockeram's 1623 Dictionary: '*Atonement*. Quietnesse.'[8]) The word 'paid-up' is Hill's own 'betimely' *consummatum est*: what was owed has been given; what needed to be done has been done. Here, as in the death of Jesus, what is emphasised as lasting is not the memories of a life or even the thought of a life to come; it is instead, paradoxically and truly, the paid-up quiet death itself, the perfection of that end, that 'endures'.

Notes

Introduction

1 Both the French original and the English translation are found in Wallace Fowlie, *Age of Surrealism* (Bloomington, IN: Indiana University Press, 1972), p. 51. The second epigraph of the book is from 'The Annuntiation and Passion', in *The Poems of John Donne*, ed. by Herbert J. C. Grierson, 2 vols (Oxford: Oxford University Press, 1912), I, 335.

2 The poem continues: 'So to misspeak my friend Desnos, so there | To float equity for all that it's now worth | On the exchanges' (*EV* 2, p. 630). See also 'Domaine Public', the third of 'Four Poems Regarding the Endurance of Poets', *KL*, pp. 55–58 (p. 57), the subtitle of which is: '*i.m. Robert Desnos, died Terezin Camp, 1945*'; *SS* 21, p. 299: 'See if Í care | any less than did Desnos, but he cannot | now be recovered'.

3 Fowlie, *Age of Surrealism*, pp. 51–53. The notebook in which this quotation is found is in the Geoffrey Hill Archive at the Special Collections, Brotherton Library, University of Leeds. It is labelled 'Notebook 2: Images', BC MS 20c Hill/2/1/2, and is on both sides of leaf 18 and on the recto of leaf 19. Hereafter, references to the Geoffrey Hill Archive will comprise the name of the notebook, the manuscript reference, and the page or leaf number. Where a manuscript or notebook is numbered by the leaf, references will use 'fol.' (*folio*) to signify the leaf number, followed by a superscript 'r' or 'v' to indicate recto or verso (e.g., fols 18ʳ–19ʳ).

4 *The Collected Works of Gerard Manley Hopkins*, ed. by Leslie Higgins and Michael F. Suarez, S.J. (Oxford: Oxford University Press, 2006–), III: *Diaries, Journals, & Notebooks*, ed. by Leslie Higgins (2015), C.I.47, p. 126.

5 *The Tragedie of King Lear the Folio Text*, II. 2. 1333–35, in *The Oxford Shakespeare: The Complete Works: Original-Spelling Edition*, ed. by Stanley Wells and others (Oxford: Oxford University Press, 1987), p. 1080.

6 Charles Péguy, *Oeuvres en prose complètes*, ed. by Robert Burac, 3 vols (Paris: Gallimard, 1987–1992), I (1987), 414. My translation: 'Before the beginning will be the Word'.

7 Isaiah 34.4: 'And all the hoste of heauen shalbe dissolued, and the heauens shalbe rouled together as a scrole: and all their hoste shall fall downe as the

202 *Notes*

leafe falleth off from the Uine, and as a falling figge from the figge tree.' See also, among many other examples, Matthew 24.29, Revelation 6.13.

8 Matthew 19.6 (cf. Mark 10.9): 'What therefore God hath ioyned together, let not man put asunder.'

9 The five new books in *Broken Hierarchies* are: *Pindarics* (2005–2012), some of which was originally published in *Without Title* (London: Penguin, 2006); *Ludo* (2011), *Expostulations on the Volcano* (2007–2012), *Liber Illustrium Virorum* (2007–2012), and *Al Tempo de' Tremuoti* (2007–2012). The book greatly expanded is *Hymns to Our Lady of Chartres* (1982–2012).

10 See, e.g., the analysis of the hyphen and its syntactical importance in Christopher Ricks's '"Tenebrae" and at-one-ment', in *EW*, pp. 62–85 (pp. 67–85); Vincent Sherry's references to syntax in poems from *For the Unfallen* in *The Uncommon Tongue: The Poetry and Criticism of Geoffrey Hill* (Ann Arbor, MI: University of Michigan Press, 1987), pp. 62–64; the scrutiny of form and formal allusion in poems from *For the Unfallen*, *Mercian Hymns*, and *Tenebrae* in E. M. Knottenbelt, *Passionate Intelligence: The Poetry of Geoffrey Hill* (Amsterdam and Atlanta, GA: Rodopi, 1990), pp. 35–41, 151–54, 206–8; Sperling's comparison of Hill's and Newman's syntax in *Visionary Philology* (Oxford: Oxford University Press, 2014), pp. 140–41, 158; Stephen James's examination of the syntactical confusions of *Clavics* in 'The Nature of Hill's Later Poetry', in *Strangeness and Power: Essays on the Poetry of Geoffrey Hill*, ed. by Andrew Michael Roberts (Swindon: Shearsman Books, 2020), pp. 39–63 (pp. 54–58); Martin Dodsworth's discussion of Hill's 'appositional' syntax in 'Geoffrey Hill's Difficulties', in *Strangeness and Power*, pp. 174–202 (pp. 179–80); the formal considerations of Edward Reiss's unpublished doctoral thesis 'Geoffrey Hill: Poet of Sequences' (University of Leeds, 2021); the thoughts on formal and other endings in Christopher Ricks, 'Geoffrey Hill's Grievous Heroes', in *Along Heroic Lines*, pp. 225–56; and the discussion of end-directed revision in David Isaacs, '"Unfinished to perfection": Geoffrey Hill, Revision, and the Poetics of Stone', *Textual Practice*, 36.7 (2022), 1071–95.

11 Christopher Ricks, *The Force of Poetry* (Oxford: Clarendon Press, 1984), pp. 285–368.

12 Christopher Ricks, 'Cliché as "Responsible Speech": Geoffrey Hill', *London Magazine*, 8 (1964), 97–98.

13 Ricks, '"Tenebrae" and at-one-ment', p. 64.

14 Christopher Ricks, 'Hill's Unrelenting, Unreconciling Mind', in *ELW*, pp. 6–31. Ricks's later essay 'Geoffrey Hill's Grievous Heroes', in *Along Heroic Lines* (pp. 225–56), is a revision and expansion of this work.

15 Matthew Sperling, review of John Lyon and Peter McDonald, eds, *Geoffrey Hill: Essays on his Later Work* (2012), *The Review of English Studies*, New Series, 64 (2013), 730–31 (p. 730).

16 See, e.g., Henry Hart, *The Poetry of Geoffrey Hill* (Carbondale, IL: Southern Illinois University Press, 1986); Sherry, *The Uncommon Tongue* (1987); Knottenbelt, *Passionate Intelligence* (1990); W. S. Milne, *An Introduction to*

Geoffrey Hill (London: Bellew, 1998); Andrew Michael Roberts, *Geoffrey Hill* (Tavistock: Northcote House, 2004); Jeffrey Wainwright, *Acceptable Words: Essays on the Poetry of Geoffrey Hill* (Manchester: Manchester University Press, 2005).

17 Sperling, *Visionary Philology*, p. 2.

18 See, e.g., David Annwn, *Inhabited Voices: Myth and History in the Poetry of Geoffrey Hill, Seamus Heaney and George Mackay Brown* (Frome: Bran's Head Books, 1984); Eleanor J. McNess, *Eucharistic Poetry* (Lewisburg, PA: Bucknell University Press, 1992); Peter McDonald, *Serious Poetry: Form and Authority from Yeats to Hill* (Oxford: Clarendon Press, 2002); Antony Rowland, *Holocaust Poetry* (Edinburgh: Edinburgh University Press, 2005); Stephen James, *Shades of Authority: The Poetry of Lowell, Hill and Heaney* (Liverpool: Liverpool University Press, 2007); Jean Ward, *Christian Poetry in the Post-Christian Day: Geoffrey Hill, R. S. Thomas, Elizabeth Jennings* (Frankfurt a.M.: Peter Lang, 2009); David-Antoine Williams, *Defending Poetry* (Oxford: Oxford University Press, 2010); Natalie Pollard, *Speaking to You: Contemporary Poetry and Public Address* (Oxford: Oxford University Press, 2012); William Wootten, *The Alvarez Generation* (Liverpool: Liverpool University Press, 2015); A. V. C. Schmidt, *Passion and Precision* (Newcastle upon Tyne: Cambridge Scholars Publishing, 2015); Kevin Hart, *Poetry and Revelation: For a Phenomenology of Religious Poetry* (London: Bloomsbury, 2017); Peter O'Leary, *Thick and Dazzling Darkness: Religious Poetry in a Secular Age* (New York: Columbia University Press, 2017); Davide Castiglione, *Difficulty in Poetry: A Stylistic Model* (Cham: Palgrave Macmillan, 2019); Antony Rowland, *Metamodernism and Contemporary British Poetry* (Cambridge: Cambridge University Press, 2021); Bridget Vincent, *Moral Authority in Seamus Heaney and Geoffrey Hill* (Oxford: Oxford University Press, 2022); Elizabeth S. Dodd, *The Lyric Voice in English Theology* (London: Bloomsbury, 2023); Kevin Hart, *Lands of Likeness: For a Poetics of Contemplation* (Chicago: University of Chicago Press, 2023).

19 Peter Robinson, ed., *Geoffrey Hill: Essays on his Work* (Milton Keynes: Open University Press, 1985); Harold Bloom, ed., *Geoffrey Hill* (New York: Chelsea House, 1986); Piers Pennington and Matthew Sperling, eds, *Geoffrey Hill and his Contexts* (Bern: Peter Lang, 2011); John Lyon and Peter McDonald, eds, *Geoffrey Hill: Essays on his Later Work* (Oxford: Oxford University Press, 2012); Roberts, ed., *Strangeness and Power* (2020).

20 Kathryn Murphy, 'In My Opinion, Having Read These Things', *PN Review*, 191 (2010), www.pnreview.co.uk/cgi-bin/scribe?item_id=5981. All webpages last accessed 20 November 2023.

21 Kathryn Murphy, 'Geoffrey Hill and Confession', in *ELW*, pp. 127–42 (p. 137). Murphy is quoting from Hill's essay 'Language, Suffering, and Silence' (*CCW*, p. 400).

22 Murphy, 'In My Opinion'.

23 For Hill's remarkably high praise of, and intense engagement with, the *OED*, see Sperling, *Visionary Philology*, pp. 7–39.

204   *Notes*

24 There are also separate *OED* entries for 'endable' ('That admits of being ended; terminable'); 'end-all'; and 'end-day' ('The last day; the day of one's death').

25 There should also be room in the definition of 'end' as *attained perfection or good* for the *OED*'s sense 1d(b), '*U.S. slang* (esp. *Jazz slang*). A term of extreme approbation: the best, the ultimate', the first illustrative quotation being, from the magazine *Neurotica* in 1950, 'Senor this shit [*sc.* narcotic] is the end!'

26 Reiss argues that Hill's tendency, especially in later poetry, to work in sequences, means that his poetry 'escapes the aesthetic of the short lyric, the well-wrought urn or two inches of ivory, whose ideal is to be finished, flawless, compressed, intense, exquisite, polished, self-contained. Most of Hill's poetry, and nearly all his later poetry is written as poetic sequence: open-ended, imperfect, expansive, extensive, awkward, rough-surfaced, and composed of inter-relating sections'. Reiss, 'Geoffrey Hill: Poet of Sequences', p. 1.

27 The double-sidedness of the word *consummation* is significant to the consummations in and of Hill's poetry, which can be characterised by its doublings of words and thoughts. See the *OED*'s etymology: 'process of adding together, accumulation [...] destruction (Vulgate)'.

28 *OED*, 'finished', sense 2.

29 Modern commentators have called Aristotle 'the most teleological of all thinkers' and 'the arch teleologist'; one claims that the 'intuitive notion of functions and what they explain is basically Aristotelian'. See Monte Ransome Johnson, *Aristotle on Teleology* (Oxford: Oxford University Press, 2005), p. 1, n. 3 (and also n. 1 for a brief survey of Aristotle's numerous references to ends).

30 Mariska Leunissen notes that Aristotle's view, as opposed to Plato's, is that 'the teleology of art is itself ontologically dependent on the teleology of nature'. Mariska Leunissen, *Explanation and Teleology in Aristotle's Science of Nature* (Cambridge: Cambridge University Press, 2010), p. 16, n. 19.

31 Aristotle, *Physics, Volume I: Books 1–4*, trans. by P. H. Wicksteed and F. M. Cornford (Cambridge, MA: Harvard University Press, 1957), II.ii.194a–b, pp. 123, 125.

32 The connections between Aristotle's notions of God and of teleology are helpfully traced in Christopher V. Mirus, 'The Metaphysical Roots of Aristotle's Teleology', *The Review of Metaphysics*, 57.4 (2004), 699–724.

33 CCW, pp. 146–69 (p. 146): 'Sir Philip Sidney, as shrewd as he was magnanimous, evidently had it in mind to keep poetry out of the courts: "Now for the *Poet*, he nothing affirmeth, and therefore never lieth".' The essay ends with an end of poetry in Pound (p. 169): 'If we seek the *mot juste*, it was no more and no less than poetic justice. "And when one has the mot juste", as Pound observed, "one is finished with the subject."'

34 Philip Sidney, *The Defence of Poesie* (London: William Ponsonby, 1595), sigs C2[r–v].

35 Sidney, *Defence*, sig. C2[v]. Sidney also mentions Aristotle in sigs E1[r], E3[v], E4[v], H3[v], I2[r], K1[r], K3[r], L2[v]. Cf. Samuel Johnson: 'The end of writing is to instruct;

Notes

205

the end of poetry is to instruct by pleasing.' *Johnson on Shakespeare*, ed. by Walter Raleigh (Oxford: Oxford University Press, 1908), p. 16.

36 Sidney, *Defence*, sig. C4^v.

37 Sidney, *Defence*, sigs C4^v–D1^r.

38 The idea of poetry as a capping endeavour among all others suggests the crowning virtue of charity in, e.g., Colossians 3.14: 'And aboue all these things put on charitie: which is the bond of perfectnesse.'

39 Sidney, *Defence*, sig. G3^r. Hill does not quote this passage but does quote Thomas Hobbes, who, some decades after Sidney, writes in his treatise of *Humane Nature*: '*Ratio* now is but *Oratio*' (*CCW*, p. 193).

40 Sidney, *Defence*, sig. K4^r.

41 Hill's lavish praise of Williams as Archbishop of Canterbury in 2011 suggests more than a passing acquaintance with Williams's scholarly (as well as his ministerial) work. See Geoffrey Hill, 'Orderly Damned, Disorderly Saved', University Sermon preached at Great St Mary's, Cambridge, 16 October 2011, www.yumpu.com/en/document/read/5084440/geoffrey-hill-16-october-2011-great-st-marys-church: 'But in sacramental, eschatological time, all is well. Voices in that dimension are raised in wonder and praise. In my inadequate transcript they speak somewhat as follows: "At the start of the twenty-first century, what gifts of faith and of imagination that strange Anglican Communion must have possessed: to have perceived in one of their ordained scholars, a man greatly gifted but not ostentatious of those gifts, qualities of mind, heart, spirit, and sanctified purpose; and to have had the grace, the wit, to raise him to the see of Canterbury; at a time of division and perplexity and incoherent false accord; a man who could reconcile by means of the 'clear bounding line' (as Blake would say) and not by emotional fudging; who single-mindedly and full-heartedly translated the corporate mind of the Church from chaos into equity; and who redeemed equity from its own corrupt shadow.["]'

Williams, for his part, has written about Hill many times, not least as a contributor to the book *Geoffrey Hill: Essays on his Later Work* in 2012 (Rowan Williams, 'The Standing of Poetry', in *ELW*, pp. 55–69). A public conversation between the two was held at Hill's alma mater, Keble College, Oxford, in 2008; eight years later, Williams delivered the sermon at Hill's funeral at Emmanuel College, Cambridge.

42 Rowan Williams, *Grace and Necessity: Reflections on Art and Love* (London: Continuum, 2005), pp. 10–11.

43 Williams, *Grace and Necessity*, pp. 21, 22.

44 Williams, *Grace and Necessity*, p. 42.

45 Sidney, *Defence*, sigs C1^r, C2^r. See Williams, *Grace and Necessity*, p. 60: 'The artwork is indeed, as Gill put it, an extension of "nature"; but it is so by the thoroughness of the transmutation of given nature into another material reality that reflects it and in so doing alters it and displays the hidden "more than it is".'

46 For Thomas Aquinas's eudaimonistic (or happiness-oriented) ethics, see, e.g., Robert Pasnau, 'Thomas Aquinas' (esp. §8.1, 'Happiness'), in *The Stanford*

206 *Notes*

Encyclopedia of Philosophy, ed. by Edward N. Zalta and Uri Nodelman, https://plato.stanford.edu/archives/spr2023/entries/aquinas/.

47 David Jones, 'Art and Sacrament', *Epoch and Artist* (London: Faber and Faber, 1959), pp. 148, 150–51.

48 The impression of Jones's visual art on Hill is evident in two references to Jones's paintings in *Al Tempo de' Tremuoti* (7, p. 891; 62, pp. 918–19). Hill's lecture 'War and Poetry', delivered at Wolfson College, Oxford, discusses Jones at some length, naming the dedication of *In Parenthesis* as 'even by itself [...] one of the greatest utterances to come out of the Great War' (https://podcasts.ox.ac.uk/war-and-civilization-series-lecture-2-war-and-poetry). See Paul Robichaud, '"Some Wayward Art": David Jones and the Later Work of Geoffrey Hill', in *David Jones: A Christian Modernist?*, ed. by Jamie Callison, Paul S. Fiddes, Anna Johnson, and Erik Tonning (Leiden and Boston: Brill, 2018), pp. 153–66; Hilary Davies, '"The Castaway of Drowned Remorse, the World's Atonement on the Hill"[:] History, Language and Theopoetics: Geoffrey Hill's Dialogue with David Jones in "Mercian Hymns" and "Tenebrae"', *Études anglaises*, 71–72 (2018), 154–67.

49 Paul Muldoon, *The End of the Poem: Oxford Lectures in Poetry* (London: Faber and Faber, 2006), p. 6.

50 Muldoon, *The End of the Poem*, pp. 27, 32, 58, 115, 366 (from the first, second, third, fifth, and fourteenth lectures). Muldoon cites the *OED*'s fifteenth sense of 'end' (an 'object for which a thing exists') in the twelfth lecture (p. 298), but this sense obtains also in the sixth, seventh, thirteenth, and fifteenth lectures (see pp. 141, 169, 325, 374). The *end* as limit and as terminus are the other most common senses drawn on by Muldoon. Some of Muldoon's other *ends* that coincide with this book's concerns are: 'the delineation of where verse ends and prose begins' (p. 84, fourth lecture); the question of 'the *"latest full effort"* of a poet in respect of his or her poem' (p. 115, fifth lecture); 'revision, the process by which the poet attempts to determine when a poem is finished, to determine, for the moment, when it has come to an end' (p. 246, tenth lecture); and the poem as 'solution to a problem only it has raised' (p. 374, fifteenth lecture).

For Hill's suggestions that his posthumous *Book of Baruch* may be seen as an 'epilogue', presumably to his own body of work and even his life, see *BBGJ* 190, §3, p. 104 ('Must admit, favoured dodgy epilogue not now or ever hugely in vogue'); 202, p. 111 ('plan a dream epilogue').

51 Giorgio Agamben, *The End of the Poem: Studies in Poetics*, trans. by Daniel Heller-Roazen (Stanford, CA: Stanford University Press, 1999). Muldoon makes fruitful use of Agamben's philosophical thoughts, such as that verse 'defines itself only at the point at which it ends' (Muldoon, *The End of the Poem*, p. 145; Agamben, *The End of the Poem*, p. 111).

52 The *OED* is much fussier and messier in defining the 'poem': 'A piece of writing or an oral composition, often characterized by a metrical structure, in which the expression of feelings, ideas, etc., is typically given intensity or flavour by distinctive diction, rhythm, imagery, etc.; a composition in poetry or verse' (sense 1).

Notes 207

53 See: 'Funeral Music', §5, *KL*, p. 51; 'Tenebrae', §5, *T*, p. 139; 'De Jure Belli ac Pacis', §VI, *C*, p. 203; *OS* XLV, p. 395; *L* 64, p. 623; *O* 39, p. 753; *OB* XXV, p. 859; XXVIII, p. 862; *TT* 17, p. 895; 69: *i.m. R. B. Kitaj*, p. 922; *CCW*, pp. 27, 63, 152, 159, 256, 323, 374, 413, 547, 557; *The Orchards of Syon* (Washington, DC: Counterpoint, 2002), LXVIII, p. 69 (in lines not replicated in *Broken Hierarchies*).

54 Hart, *The Poetry of Geoffrey Hill*, p. 125.

55 'The Absolute Reasonableness of Robert Southwell' and 'Language, Suffering, and Silence', *CCW*, pp. 21–40, 394–406.

56 'Lachrimae Verae', §1, 'Lachrimae', *T*, p. 121. Contrast the bitter vision of solipsistic self-sacrifice in 'An Order of Service', *KL*, p. 45: 'Let a man sacrifice himself, concede | His mortality and have done with it; | There is no end to that sublime appeal.'

Chapter 1

1 The epigraph is from 'In Memoriam: Ernst Barlach', *TCP*, p. 597.

2 Eleanor Cook, 'Paronomasia', in *The Princeton Encyclopedia of Poetry and Poetics*, ed. by Roland Greene, 4th edn (Princeton, NJ: Princeton University Press, 2012), pp. 1003–4 (p. 1003).

3 Cook, 'Paronomasia', p. 1004.

4 For other uses of 'pun' and its relatives in Hill's criticism, see *CCW*, pp. 40, 62, 167, 187, 200, 310, 313, 322, 388, 425, 646, 700.

5 See *CCW*, pp. 178, 199 (the connection to Peacham found here), 201, 314, 646 (notes beginning 'a figure…away' and 'Puttenham').

6 'All art constantly aspires towards the condition of music.' Walter Pater, 'The School of Giorgione', *Studies in the History of the Renaissance* (New York: Oxford University Press, 2010), p. 124.

7 See, for many examples, *Puns and Pundits: Word Play in the Hebrew Bible and Ancient Near Eastern Literature*, ed. by Scott B. Noegel (Bethesda, MD: CDL Press, 2000).

8 *SS* 91, p. 334 ('A pun, then, *arms?*'); *SC* 3. 18, p. 479 ('Roman theology | hits us with *culpa*, though that's not a coup | except to unwary punsters'); *P* 13, p. 535; *O* 127: *Marwnad William Phylip, Hendre Fechan* (I), p. 783; 139: *Welsh apotheosis* (IV), p. 787 ('That this is so we owe to more | Than to indentured pun or quibble'); *OB* XXXVII, p. 871 ('Though Petrarca punned on that name more roundly'); *BBGJ* 55, p. 25 ('If truth's told, to flake out while punning that, at worst, is like panning for lost gold'); 79, p. 37 ('Be as good as the *Sun* once was with a headline pun').

9 'September Song' (*KL*, p. 44); 'An Order of Service': 'There is no end to that sublime appeal' (*KL*, p. 45); 'Tristia: 1891–1938' (subtitled 'A Valediction to Osip Mandelstam' and the last of 'Four Poems Regarding the Endurance of Poets'): 'hard summer sky | Feasting on this, reaching its own end' (*KL*, p. 58).

208 *Notes*

10 There are similar verses at Matthew 25.29; Mark 4.25; Luke 8.18; Luke 19.26; John 15.2.

11 'Notebook 67: Without Title', BC MS 20c Hill/2/1/67, fol. 9^r. The second quotation is from Ricks, 'Cliché as "Responsible Speech"', p. 97.

12 'The quotation-marks around 'menace' and 'atonement' look a bit like raised eyebrows' ('Poetry as 'Menace' and 'Atonement'', *CCW*, p. 3).

13 The parenthetical quotation is from O 123: *Hiraeth* (v), p. 781.

14 The allusion to Coleridge is noted in Ann Hassan, *Annotations to Geoffrey Hill's 'Speech! Speech!'* (New York: Glossator Special Editions, 2012), p. 200.

15 Somewhat inevitably, Hill hears the lingering pun in '*de excessu*': '"Excessus" signifies "ecstasy"'. The 'tormented and the ecstatic soul' (*CCW*, p. 38) are atoned in the word.

16 William Empson, *Seven Types of Ambiguity*, 3rd edn (London: Chatto and Windus, 1953), pp. ix–x.

17 Jeffrey Wainwright appears to miss the point that for Hill the ambiguity resides in the 'plain speaking' when he writes: '*Glowery* is indeed, simply in its sound, "a mighty word" [...], but if such power involves "plain speaking" and by this is meant speech without ambiguity, then for all his extolling of it Hill cannot but fall – perhaps cravenly – into searching out different meanings.' Jeffrey Wainwright, 'The Impossibility of Death', *ELW*, pp. 89–111 (pp. 96–97).

18 Empson, *Seven Types of Ambiguity*, p. 1. Cited in *OED*, 'ambiguity', sense 3b.

19 John Haffenden, *Viewpoints: Poets in Conversation with John Haffenden* (London: Faber and Faber, 1981), p. 90.

20 Hill does, however, praise the 'pedantry' of Jonson and of Fulke Greville: 'each is prepared to risk appearing over-scrupulous in the attempt to define true goodness' (*CCW*, p. 55).

21 Hill in an interview with Carl Phillips, 'The Art of Poetry LXXX: An Interview with Geoffrey Hill', *Paris Review*, 154 (2000), pp. 272–99 (p. 275). As Hill concedes, this thought owes much to the 'German classicist and Kierkegaardian scholar' Theodor Haecker, who, Hill says, 'went into what was called "inner exile" in the Nazi period'. See also *OS* VIII, p. 358: 'language of inner exile'.

22 'Preface to the Penguin Edition', in Henrik Ibsen, *Brand: A Version for the Stage*, trans. by Geoffrey Hill, 3rd edn (Harmondsworth: Penguin, 1996), p. xi.

23 Hill is no stranger to French–English puns and rhymes. Eleanor Cook points out that each of the ten sections of Hill's *The Mystery of the Charity of Charles Péguy* includes French–English rhymes; see Eleanor Cook, *Against Coercion: Games Poets Play* (Stanford, CA: Stanford University Press, 1998), p. 29.

24 *Private Passions*, BBC Radio 3, 25 April 2004. Cited in David-Antoine Williams, *Defending Poetry*, p. 166.

25 Geoffrey Hill, 'I know thee not, old man, fall to thy prayers', Professor of Poetry lecture, University of Oxford, 5 May 2015, http://media.podcasts.ox.ac.uk/engfac/poetry/2015-05-05_engfac_hill.mp3.

Notes 209

26 Geoffrey Hill, *Clavics* (London: Enitharmon Press, 2011), 30, p. 40.

27 '"Arbitrary" itself can mean either discretionary or despotic' (*CCW*, p. 563). 'The arbitrary, by a long process of semantic conglomeration, is at once freedom of will and the will obdurate in itself and subject to, and in service to, a greater obduracy ("difficulty is our plough")' (*CCW*, p. 573). Hill's 1963 review of T. S. Eliot's *Collected Poems* is titled 'The Poet as Arbiter' (*Yorkshire Post*, 3 October 1963, p. 4); this is noted in Sperling, *Visionary Philology*, p. 66.

28 Simone Weil, *The Need for Roots*, trans. by Arthur Wills (Boston, MA: Beacon, 1952), p. 207. Cited in *CCW*, p. 573. See also Geoffrey Hill, 'Civil Polity and the Confessing State', *The Warwick Review*, 2 (2008), 7–20 (p. 11); '"The Conscious Mind's Intelligible Structure": A Debate', *Agenda*, 9.4–10.1 (1971–1972), 14–23 (pp. 14–15).

29 Weil, *The Need for Roots*, pp. 70, 74.

30 For an examination of the meanings of work in Hill's poetry, see Peter McDonald, '"But to my Task": Work, Truth, and Metre in Later Hill', in *ELW*, pp. 143–169.

31 Thomas Hobbes, *Humane nature* (London: T. Newcomb, 1649), pp. 50–51. Cited in *CCW*, p. 193.

32 Tony Tanner, *Adultery in the Novel* (Baltimore, MD: Johns Hopkins University Press, 1979), p. 335. Cited in Walter Redfern, *Puns* (Oxford: Basil Blackwell, 1984), p. 11.

33 Ernest B. Gilman, *The Curious Perspective: Literary and Pictorial Wit in the Seventeenth Century* (New Haven, CT: Yale University Press, 1978), p. 234. Cited in Redfern, *Puns*, p. 5.

34 Haffenden, *Viewpoints*, p. 83. Hill quotes the Yeats in *CCW*, p. 4.

35 For the theme of the labours of the months, see, e.g., Bridget Ann Henisch, *The Medieval Calendar Year* (University Park, PA: Pennsylvania State University Press, 1999).

36 On this vision of language, see, e.g., *CCW*, p. 19, which remarks on the 'irredeemable error in the very substance and texture of one's craft and pride'.

37 The word seems to gain philosophical meaning in Hill's later poetry: 'Partaking of both | fact and recognition, it ['*Intrinsic value*'] must be, therefore, | in effect, at once agent and predicate' (*TL* LXX, p. 259); 'mortal self-recognition' (*SS* 24, p. 300); 'self-making otherness by recognition | even as I describe it' (with possible additional pun on 'even'; *SS* 79, p. 328); 'get together for shared únrecognition' (*SS* 82, p. 329); 'Recognition turning upon cognition' (*OB* XI, p. 845); 'The self self-knowing in the Other-seeing. || These metaphysics blind you suddenly | With recognition' (*TT* 40, p. 906); 'Let's pretend that we demand recognition rather than spooked emotion at a tragedy's end' (*BBGJ* 164, p. 88). The square brackets in the first quotation above are my own. For other 'recognition's see *HOLC* 19, p. 167; *TL* CX, p. 271; *SS* 75, p. 326; 101, p. 339; *OS* LXI, p. 411; 'Lyric Fragment', *TCP*, p. 601.

38 'Index Cards: Clark Lectures "Supplementary"', BC MS 20c Hill/4/12/1. Cited in Sperling, *Visionary Philology*, p. 76.

210 Notes

39 T. S. Eliot, 'Little Gidding', §II, *Four Quartets*, in *The Poems of T. S. Eliot*, ed. by Christopher Ricks and Jim McCue, 2 vols (London: Faber and Faber, 2015), I: *Collected and Uncollected Poems*, pp. 203–4. Hereafter the abbreviation '*Poems of T. S. Eliot*' refers to this first volume.

40 'Little Gidding', §II, *Poems of T. S. Eliot*, p. 204. See Helen Gardner, *The Composition of 'Four Quartets'* (London: Faber and Faber, 1978), p. 174. The episode with ser Brunetto occurs in the fifteenth canto of *Inferno*. See Dante Alighieri, *The Divine Comedy: Inferno, Purgatorio, Paradiso*, trans. by Robin Kirkpatrick (London: Penguin, 2012), pp. 66–69.

41 'Little Gidding', §II, *Poems of T. S. Eliot*, p. 204.

42 Geoffrey Hill, 'Milton as Muse', lecture delivered at Christ's College, Cambridge, 29 October 2008, www.youtube.com/watch?v=r40eTgLwceU. Cited in Matthew Paskins, 'Hill and Gillian Rose', in *GHC*, pp. 171–85 (p. 179).

43 For a scrutiny of Aristotelian *anagnorisis* and its relevance to poetic and dramatic fiction, see Terence Cave, *Recognitions: A Study in Poetics* (Oxford: Clarendon Press, 1988).

44 Kathy Eden, *Poetic and Legal Fiction in the Aristotelian Tradition* (Princeton, NJ: Princeton University Press, 1986), pp. 7–24. According to Eden, Aristotle's discussion of *anagnorisis* 'enjoyed the status of a poetic law' (p. 10). See also Marcus Waithe, 'Empson's Legal Fiction', *Essays in Criticism*, 62 (2012), 279–301, which cites Hill on Empson's poem 'Legal Fiction' (p. 295). Hill refers to Waithe's essay and to Empson's poem in the eighth of his Professor of Poetry lectures at the University of Oxford, '"Legal Fiction" and legal fiction', 5 March 2013, http://media.podcasts.ox.ac.uk/engfac/poetry/2013-03-21-engfac-poetry-hill-2.mp3.

45 Eden, *Poetic and Legal Fiction*, p. 10.

46 Geoffrey Hill, 'The Eloquence of Sober Truth', *TLS*, 11 June 1999, pp. 7–12 (p. 11). Cited at greater length in McDonald, *Serious Poetry*, p. 213. See also *BBGJ* 242, §3, p. 131: 'Bless rather than curse according to revised fable.'

47 Christopher Ricks, *True Friendship* (New Haven, CT: Yale University Press, 2010), p. 150.

48 'Notebook 6: King Log', BC MS 20c Hill/2/1/6, p. 36.

49 See the entry for Edita Polláková in the Holocaust.cz database of victims, www.holocaust.cz/en/database-of-victims/victim/114716-edita-pollakova/.

50 Yet another pain may reside in the fact that 'September Song' has fourteen lines, albeit that the irregular metre and stanza length draw it away from the conventions of the sonnet; the forging of connection with this historically romantic poetic form is (I think intentionally) disconcerting. More generally, its fourteen lines remind the reader, who perhaps would rather not be reminded, of the poem's awareness of itself as a poem; and of its conscious response to its poetic ancestry, both of which strike one as somehow distasteful in a poem that addresses such a subject.

51 Here, with a few surrounding sentences: 'Even the most extreme consciousness of doom threatens to degenerate into idle chatter. Cultural criticism finds itself faced with the final stage of the dialectic of culture and barbarism. To write

Notes
211

poetry after Auschwitz is barbaric. [...] Critical intelligence cannot be equal to this challenge as long as it confines itself to self-satisfied contemplation' (Theodor W. Adorno, 'Cultural Criticism and Society', *Prisms*, trans. by Samuel and Shierry Weber (London: Neville Spearman, 1967), p. 34). See also Antony Rowland, 'Re-reading "Impossibility" and "Barbarism": Adorno and Post-Holocaust Poetics', *Critical Survey*, 9 (1997), 57–69.

52 Matthew Arnold, 'Preface', *Poems* (London: Longman, Brown, Green, and Longmans, 1853), p. viii. Cited in Knottenbelt, *Passionate Intelligence*, p. 64, n. 12.

53 Derek Attridge reads the stanza otherwise, noting the 'assertiveness of "I have made" as a single segment', and the 'strongly felt insistence on the truth of the poet's art that emerges from the division of "it" and "is true"' (*Moving Words: Forms of English Poetry* (Oxford: Oxford University Press, 2013), p. 219).

54 Hill invokes the rose, the symbolic flower of England, as a closing image elsewhere also: most notably in the final stanza of the antepenultimate poem of *Broken Hierarchies*, *TT* 93 (p. 934): 'Such troubling of the senses I recall, | Such red as when a singular, fissured, rose | Turbined the still air to equipose, | No colour more unearthly or more real'; and in the very last sentence (to be presented as complete) of *The Book of Baruch* (*BBGJ*, 271, p. 145): 'Even so, the power of stout roses has risen watt by watt against the afterglow of each brief thunder-shower.'

55 In a reading concerned with Hill's endings, Isaacs points out that the last line of 'September Song' in Hill's first draft was '"I have not finished"', later transferred to the end of 'Funeral Music' (Isaacs, '"Unfinished to perfection"', 1074).

56 Cf. the first complete sentence in *Scenes from Comus*: 'The tragedy of things is not conclusive' (*SC* 1. 2, p. 421); and, from 'In Memoriam: Gillian Rose', §14, *TCP*, p. 591: 'This ending is not the end'.

57 Sidney, *Defence*, sig. C2ᵛ.

58 This poem begins: 'When all else fails CORINTHIANS will be read | by a man in too-tight shoes.' Hill recalls the reference in *The Book of Baruch*: '"Tight shoes" I would still have entitled every trim announcer; or even "cherry bum", the term borrowed from a nickname of the Crimean lancer—though by no means the same as "lackey of the régime"; perhaps more like dispatchful jockey: such would be my theme' (*BBGJ* 14, p. 7). For 'love' in *Al Tempo de' Tremuoti*, see *TT* 1, 2, 4, 9, 11, 17, 23, 30, 35, 36, 37, 40, 47, 56, 65, 70, 77, 78, 81, 84, 88 (d), 88 (e), 88 (f), 91, pp. 889–933.

59 John 15.4: 'Abide in me, and in you: As the branch cannot beare fruit of itselfe, except it abide in the vine: no more can ye, except ye abide in me', etc.; John 17.21–23: 'That they all may be one, as thou Father art in mee, and I in thee, that they also may bee one in vs: that the world may beleeue that thou hast sent mee. And the glory which thou gauest me, I haue giuen them: that they may be one, euen as we are one: I in them, and thou in mee, that they may bee made perfect in one, and that the world may know that thou hast sent me, and hast loued them, as thou hast loued me.' See also *O* 120: *Hiraeth* (II), p. 780: 'Tell me, what is mý sense of *abiding*'.

212 *Notes*

60 Charles Tomlinson, 'The Chances of Rhyme', *The Way of a World* (Oxford: Oxford University Press, 1969), p. 59. The title is taken up by Donald Wesling in his useful study *The Chances of Rhyme* (Berkeley, CA: University of California Press, 1980).

61 John Henry Newman, *Apologia Pro Vita Sua*, ed. by Martin J. Svaglic (Oxford: Clarendon Press, 1967), pp. 217–18. Cited in *CCW*, pp. 279, 331, 400, 475, 479; and in *TT* 67, p. 921.

62 Sophie Ratcliffe discusses Hill and physical awkwardness in 'On Being "a man of the world": Geoffrey Hill and Physicality', in *ELW*, pp. 70–88.

63 This fact pertains even in earlier poems in which Hill eschews the affirmations of Christian language, such as 'Annunciations' (*KL*, p. 40), of which he writes (in the note accompanying the poem in *The Penguin Book of Contemporary Verse*, p. 392):

> By using an emotive cliché like 'The Word' I try to believe in an idea I want to believe in; that poetry makes its world from the known world; that it has a transcendence; that it is something other than the conspicuous consumption (the banquet) that it seems to be.
>
> What I say *in* the section is, I think, that I don't believe in The Word. The fact that I make the poem at all means that I still believe in words.

64 J. L. Austin's *How to Do Things with Words: The William James Lectures delivered at Harvard University in 1955*, ed. by J. O. Urmson (Oxford: Clarendon Press, 1962) is especially relevant to the idea of words' actions. See Hill's essay on Austin, 'Our Word Is Our Bond', *CCW*, pp. 146–69.

65 Locke himself may be borrowing the phrase 'bare preservation' from Thomas Hobbes's *Leviathan*. See John Locke, *Two Treatises of Government* (London: printed for Awnsham Churchill, 1690), 2. 6, p. 222; Thomas Hobbes, *Leviathan* (London: printed for Andrew Crooke, 1651), 2. 30, p. 175. See also *SC* 3. 5, p. 473: 'Bare preservation is the speaking power.'

66 But then one should also point out that the word *travesty* ('travesties' appearing, in slightly different phrasings, in both the first and last lines here) has its semantic origins in cross-dressing and disguise. In this sense it could be, for Empson at least, a figure for the pun, so often seen as an unbecoming dressing-up of language. Coleridge writes: 'There sometimes occurs an apparent *Play* on words, which not only to the Moralizer, but even to the philosophical Etymologist, appears more than a mere Play. Thus in the double sense of the word, *become*. I have known persons so anxious to have their dress *become* them [...] as to convert it at length into their proper self, and thus actually to become the Dress' (*The Collected Works of Samuel Taylor Coleridge*, ed. by Kathleen Coburn and others, 16 vols (Princeton, NJ: Princeton University Press, 1969–2001), ix, 60). Cited in David-Antoine Williams, '"All corruptible things": Geoffrey Hill's Etymological Crux', *Modern Philology*, 112.3 (2015), 522–53 (p. 547). For more of Hill's travesties, see 'A Pre-Raphaelite Notebook', *T*, p. 133 ('Salvation's travesty ‖ a deathless metaphor'); *HOLC* 10, p. 162; *TL* XCVIII, p. 267; *P* 14, p. 536; *LIV* IX, p. 693; *O* 65: *Ty-tryst* (IV), p. 762; *TT* 3, p. 890; 43 (a), p. 908; *BBGJ* 5, p. 4.

Notes 213

67 *O* 20, p. 747 ('Rimbaud's infernal | Provocations of alchemic-carnal'); 28, p. 750 ('Alchemic-carnal, such the earth remains | In winter'). Stephen James elaborates helpfully on the word in 'The Nature of Hill's Later Poetry', pp. 48–52.

68 The first reference to alchemy in Hill's poetry comes as late as *Canaan*, significantly in a poem about the Last Judgement; the theme's intensity grows as Hill's oeuvre continues. For uses of 'alchemy' and its relatives in Hill's poetry, see 'Psalms of Assize', §VII, *C*, p. 229; *TL* CXII, p. 272; *OS* XXIII, p. 373 ('this calls for matching alchemies to make | gold out of loss in the dead season'); 'In the Valley of the Arrow', §1, *WT*, p. 509; *EV* 40, p. 668 ('alchemical retorts'); *O* 20, p. 747; 28, p. 750; 35, p. 752; 42, p. 754 ('Clavics, the alchemy of keys: | As lacking something so I have made art'); 73, p. 765; 74, p. 765; 118, p. 780 ('I mate sobriety with délire | Privy to alchemists'); *Cl.* 4, p. 794; 26, p. 816 ('Alchemical desires: stars and stones, | Compassioning embraces'); 27, p. 817 ('It may – | Virtú from mother earth – | Be alchemy […] Tom Vaughan an alchemist of the Cross'); *OB* L, p. 884; *TT* 37, p. 904 ('linguistic alchemy, | Vicarious redemption by the word'); 80, p. 926; 93, p. 934; *BBGJ* 91, p. 42; 123, §3, p. 64; 150, §3, p. 82. Hill uses the word 'alchemical' only three times in his critical prose: once quoting Donne; then quickly again in the same discussion; and elsewhere quoting Pound: see *CCW*, pp. 216, 217, 256.

69 There is a punning edge to 'primal' here as elsewhere in Hill: the *prime*, particularly the idea of *materia prima* or the primordial matter of the universe, is important to alchemical texts from the thirteenth century onwards (*OED*, 'materia prima'). For other uses of 'prime' and its relatives in Hill's poetry, see *SS* 81, p. 329 ('Sun-glanced […] immaterial reflection beautifully | primed'); *OS* II, p. 352; 'To Lucien Richard: On Suffering', *WT*, p. 494; 'Improvisations for Jimi Hendrix', §2, *WT*, p. 503; 'On the Sophoclean Moment in English Poetry', *WT*, p. 508; 'In the Valley of the Arrow', §1, *WT*, p. 509 ('Now here's real alchemy—the gorse […], spectator of its own prime'); 'Broken Hierarchies', *WT*, p. 516; *P* 4, p. 526 ('Darkly a primed sun works to expose grand chill'); 8, p. 530; 12, p. 534; 'A Précis or Memorandum of Civil Power', §VI, *TCP*, p. 584; *L* 43, p. 617; *EV* 41, p. 669; *LIV* XXXVI, p. 720; XL, p. 724; XLII, p. 726; *O* 99: *Welsh apocalypse* (XII), p. 773; *Cl.* 19, p. 809; *OB* L, p. 884 (two instances); *TT* 2, p. 889; *BBGJ* 111, §2, p. 56; 123, §3, p. 64; 150, §3, p. 82.

70 For extensive studies of alchemy and other occult practices in Renaissance literature, see, e.g., Charles Nicholl, *The Chemical Theatre* (London: Routledge & Kegan Paul, 1980); John S. Mebane, *Renaissance Magic and the Return of the Golden Age* (Lincoln, NE: University of Nebraska Press, 1989).

71 For Dorn's *coniunctio*, Carl Jung's interpretation of Dorn, and the relation of the *coniunctio* to Jung's alchemical psychology, see Jeffrey Raff, *Jung and the Alchemical Imagination* (Berwick, ME: Nicolas-Hays, 2000), pp. 84–86.

72 In a poem that also mentions Marsilio Ficino, one of the most important early figures to write about the theological and other implications of alchemy, Hill remarks on a '[h]appy conjunction for a lyric flow' (*TT* 8, p. 891). For other uses of 'conjunction' in Hill, see *LIV* V, p. 689; *OB* XX, p. 854; *CCW*, pp. 168,

214   *Notes*

292, 400, 433, 514, 580, 604. Hill, in an interview with the French poet Anne Mouric, published in French, speaks of 'une conjonction magique de mots', adding, 'La conjonction est heureuse ou ne l'est pas. C'est cette magie qui fait les grands poètes': Anne Mounic, 'Le poème, "moulin mystique": Entretien avec Geoffrey Hill', *Temporel*, 28 September 2008.

73 Thomas Vaughan, *Lumen de lumine, or, A new magicall light discovered and communicated to the world by Eugenius Philalethes* (London: printed for H. Blunden, 1651), p. 8. In the passage from which this quotation comes, Vaughan is describing a dream in which he meets a woman of 'divine *Beauty*' who calls herself Thalia. Thalia takes Vaughan to the 'mountains *of the* Moone' and shows him a strange '*viscous*' substance that turns out to be the *materia prima* (pp. 4–8). 'When I had viewd and search'd it well, it appear'd somewhat *spermatic*, and in very Truth it was *obscene* to the *sight*, but much more to the *Touch*. Hereupon *Thalia* told me, it was the *first Matter*, and the very Naturall, true *Sperm* of the *great World*' (p. 8).

74 For the 'Black Sun', especially as it relates to Jungian psychology, see Stanton Marlan, *The Black Sun: The Alchemy and Art of Darkness* (College Station, TX: Texas A&M University Press, 2005).

75 Vaughan, *Lumen de lumine*, p. 7.

76 *OED*, 'character', *n.*, sense 1a. *Paradise Regained*, in *The Poetical Works of John Milton*, ed. by Helen Darbishire and others, 8 vols (Oxford: Oxford University Press, 1963–2012), II, ed. by Helen Darbishire (1963), IV. 383–85, p. 50.

77 'A nocturnall upon S. Lucies day, Being the shortest day', *Poems of John Donne*, I, 44–45. The rhyme scheme of Donne's poem is ABBACCCDD, the first two lines of each stanza in iambic pentameter, the next two in tetrameter, the fifth in trimeter, and the remaining four in pentameter. The stanzas of *Oraclau* | *Oracles* replicate Donne's exactly, except for 3, 5, 10, 11, 15, 17, 18, 20, 21, 25, 27, 34–37, 62–74, 76, 79, 106, 109, 110, 126, 129–133, and 137–140, all of which have ABBACDCDD rhyme schemes, and in which lines 1–4 have become alternating tetrameter and pentameter, the trimeter of line 5 tetrameter, and the pentameter of line 6 trimeter. This alternative structure reduces the numbers of each stanza by a foot.

78 *Poems of John Donne*, I, 44.

79 Elsewhere, of Donne's third verse-letter to Henry Wotton, Hill writes: 'Donne engineers a conceit out of the curve-necked alchemical vessels, the "crooked lymbecks", to argue that the morally crooked world may be made to retort upon itself, may be the means of the soul's self-purification. [...] Donne perceives that the medium of language must itself be conceived as a "crooked lymbeck"' (*CCW*, p. 216).

80 *Poems of John Donne*, I, 44.

81 Ceri Richards, letter to Gerhard Adler, 2 August 1968, cited in Richard Burns, *Keys to Transformation: Ceri Richards & Dylan Thomas* (London: Enitharmon Press, 1981), p. 63.

82 William Bloomfield, quoted in *Theatrum Chemicum Britannicum. Containing Severall Poeticall Pieces of our Famous English Philosophers*, ed. by

Notes 215

Elias Ashmole (London: J. Grismond, 1652), p. 313. Cited in Nicholl, *Chemical Theatre*, pp. 3–4.

83 Richards, cited in Burns, *Keys to Transformation*, p. 63.

84 Dylan Thomas, quoted in Constantine Fitzgibbon, *The Life of Dylan Thomas* (London: J. M. Dent, 1975), p. 241. Cited in Burns, *Keys to Transformation*, p. 60.

85 'Of Education', *The Complete Prose Works of John Milton*, ed. by Don M. Wolfe and others, 8 vols (New Haven, CT: Yale University Press, 1953–1982), II: *1643–1648*, ed. by Ernest Sirluck (1959), 357–415 (p. 403). Hill first uses the phrase in his poetry in 'A Short History of British India (III)' (*T*, p. 128) and in his critical writings discusses each word in detail, especially 'sensuous' (often distinguishing it from 'sensual'): see *CCW*, pp. 148, 274, 313, 353, 485, 512, 521. As Michael Molan points out in his essay 'Milton and Eliot in the Work of Geoffrey Hill', in *GHC*, pp. 81–105 (pp. 85–86), Coleridge was enamoured with the phrase first, and Hill acknowledges in an interview that Milton's words 'were rediscovered and developed by Coleridge' (Phillips, 'The Art of Poetry LXXX', p. 277).

86 Sidney, *Defence*, sigs B4^v–C1^r.

87 R. P. Blackmur, 'Three Notes', *Language as Gesture* (New York: Harcourt, Brace, 1952), p. 364. Hill quoted the passage in his inaugural Professor of Poetry lecture at the University of Oxford, entitled 'How ill white hairs become a fool and jester', 30 November 2010, http://media.podcasts.ox.ac.uk/kebl/general/2010-11-30-hill-poetry-keble.mp3. 'My God,' Hill remarked after quoting it, 'if only I could have written that.' John Berryman felt so similarly that he did write it into a poem, 'Olympus', noting after the quotation, 'I was never altogether the same man after *that*' (John Berryman, 'Olympus', *Collected Poems 1937–1971* (New York: Farrar, Straus, and Giroux, 1989), p. 179).

88 F. H. Bradley, *Appearance and Reality* (Oxford: Oxford University Press, 1930), p. 127. Cited in *CCW*, p. 532.

Chapter 2

1 'NEPTUNE THE MYSTIC', 'Early Poems – [Booklet 2]', BC MS 20c Hill 2/2/1, p. 19. Judging from another undated draft of a poem entitled 'SEVENTEENTH BIRTHDAY' (BC MS 20c Hill 2/2/2, loose sheets), the poem quoted may be from Hill's mid- to late-teenage years.

2 'Notebook 11: Mercian Hymns', BC MS 20c Hill/2/1/11, p. 76^r.

3 I would name as the other *'errata'* poems: *TL* XLI, p. 250; XLVIII, p. 252; LXIV, p. 257; LXXIV, p. 260 ('For Cinna the Poet, see under *errata*'); LXXV, pp. 260–61; XCVIII, p. 267; CV, p. 269.

4 See Jeremy Reed, *Heartbreak Hotel* (London: Orion, 2002). I say 'probably unknowingly' because during his last reading in 2016, before quoting (with great admiration) the last lines of Jeremy Reed's 'Hart Crane', Hill said that

216 *Notes*

he had known of Reed's name but not been familiar with his work until very recently; and that he had only read the poem for the first time a few weeks earlier, having picked up by chance *Conductors of Chaos*, ed. by Iain Sinclair (London: Picador, 1996), in which the poem is anthologised (pp. 365–66).

5 Cf. T. S. Eliot, 'Milton I', *On Poetry and Poets* (London: Faber and Faber, 1957), p. 141: 'Milton writes English like a dead language. The criticism has been made with regard to his involved syntax.' See also the last line of the last ode of Coventry Patmore's *The Unknown Eros*, entitled 'Dead language': 'Alas, and is not mine a language dead?' (*The Unknown Eros and Other Poems* (London: George Bell and Sons, 1877), p. 120). Hill quotes a passage from the end of this poem in his review of Grevel Lindop's biography of Charles Williams (Geoffrey Hill, 'Mightier and darker', *TLS*, 23 March 2016, www.the-tls.co.uk/articles/public/mightier-and-darker/).

6 Kathryn Murphy, 'Hill's Conversions', in *GHC*, pp. 61–80; Sperling, *Visionary Philology*, pp. 142–48. Hill's translation of Luther's phrase is 'mankind turned, or bent, inwards upon itself'; he offered it during a Remembrance Day sermon at Balliol College, Oxford, on 11 November 2007. The sermon was printed in the *Balliol College Annual Record* (2008), pp. 24–27 (pp. 24–25). Hill also suggests the possible origin of a similar Lutheran phrase, '*cor corvum in se ipsum*, the heart bent inwards upon itself' in his essay 'Language, Suffering, and Silence': he writes that it is 'a trope perhaps derived from Augustine's *detortae in infirma voluntatis*' (*CCW*, p. 400). The word 'trope' here is an etymological pun, since it derives from one of the Greek words for *turn*.

7 Hill makes much of this etymology. See 'Dark-Land' ('Are these last things reduced'), *C*, p. 219; *SS* 24, p. 300; *OS* LXVI, p. 416; *SC* 1. 15, p. 428; *CCW*, pp. 273–74, 267. See also Sperling, *Visionary Philology*, pp. 45–48.

8 The first line of *Al Tempo de' Tremuoti*, to take one example, is: 'A signal pre-election to free choice' (p. 889). See also the related list of quotations in the third section of the previous chapter (in the paragraph beginning 'The paradox, struck repeatedly').

9 The phrase 'gredie to do euell' is William Tyndale's. See Hill's note at *CCW*, p. 673.

10 The final words in Hill's 'draft additional verses' to the final poem of *The Book of Baruch* also bear some verbal relation: 'How do I rate? Anything disordinate in that?' (*BBGJ*, p. 148).

11 *The Economist*, 'Poems should be beautiful', video interview with Geoffrey Hill, 2 December 2011, www.economist.com/prospero/2011/12/02/poems-should-be-beautiful.

12 In the first publication of the poem, there is an added address to one of the three imaginary critics – Croker, MacSikker, and O'Shem – to whom the collection refers: 'It's a Plutarchan twist: even our foes | further us, though against their will and purpose (*up | yours, O'Shem*)' (Geoffrey Hill, *The Triumph of Love* (London: Penguin, 1998), p. 76). Earlier in the poem there is another of these asides: 'All things by that argument are bound | to the nature of disordinance (*eat | shit, MacSikker*)' (Hill, *The Triumph of Love* (1998), p. 75). Less advertised

Notes 217

than the pun is the doubling-back of editing already published works; Hill silently removes these parenthetical remarks and makes several other changes to this poem in *Broken Hierarchies*. For Hill's disapproval of the poetic revisions of John Crowe Ransom, see *CCW*, pp. 127–145; Murphy, 'Hill's Conversions', p. 66.

13 Plutarch, *Moralia*, ed. by H. Cherniss and W. C. Hermbold, 16 vols (Cambridge, MA: Harvard University Press, 1927–2004), II, trans. by Frank Cole Babbitt (1928), pp. 4–5.

14 As Murphy notes in 'Hill's Conversions', in *GHC*, p. 73, Hill uses an example of anadiplosis (that Hill appears to identify as metanoia) from Keats's 'Ode to a Nightingale' to illustrate the 'return upon oneself': 'Of perilous seas in faery lands forlorn. ‖ Forlorn! The very word is like a bell' (*CCW*, p. 7). In *Scenes from Comus* Hill's use of the rhetorical figure is turned into a self-aware joke: 'The charge ǀ is *anadiplosis* and the sentence ǀ the sentence here handed down' (*SC* 2. 54, p. 457). The figure recurs elsewhere in this collection: see *SC* 2. 13, p. 437 ('Yes, Comus, about time; about time ǀ and justification'); 3. 16, p. 478 ('Here's a beginning ‖ beginning at the end').

15 Regarding another example of anadiplosis, Hill does indeed find himself 'the enemy'. 'Requiem for the Plantagenet Kings' (*U*, p. 15) includes the lines: 'With well-dressed alabaster and proved spurs ǀ They lie; they lie'. Hill at his last reading expressed regret at this repetition, saying: 'That's a mistake. I shouldn't have repeated "they lie". Because the implications of *lying* as supine and *lying* as telling a manifest untruth about the nature of power is [sic] already sufficient in the one "they lie". The repeated "they lie" is cheap. Not all that cheap, but cheap. Yeah, pretty cheap. And I – fifty years since I wrote this – I still cringe.' This and subsequent quotations from the reading at Emmanuel College, Cambridge, on 28 April 2016 are my transcriptions taken from my own audio recording.

16 See also *SS* 82, p. 329: 'Plutarchan parallels to special order. ǀ End of a calendar year. The double ǀ lives of veterans haunt me.'

17 *P* 33, p. 555: 'Look at yourself; it makes no difference ǀ the mirror is upside down.'

18 Maritain criticises Cartesian philosophy by accusing it of angelism; see Jacques Maritain, *Three Reformers: Luther, Descartes, Rousseau* (New York: Scribner, 1929), pp. 77, 86. See also Richard Fafara, 'Angelism and Culture', in *Understanding Maritain: Philosopher and Friend*, ed. by Deal Wyatt Hudson and Matthew J. Mancini (Macon, GA: Mercer University Press, 1987), pp. 171–80. Allen Tate charges Edgar Allan Poe with angelism in the essay 'The Angelic Imagination', in *The Forlorn Demon* (Chicago: Regnery, 1953), pp. 56–78.

19 F. H. Bradley, *Essays on Truth and Reality* (Oxford: Clarendon Press, 1914), p. 265. See *CCW*, pp. 561, 568.

20 In his final lecture as Professor of Poetry at the University of Oxford, Hill quoted with approval the choreographer Mark Morris's statement, 'I'm not interested in self-expression but in expressiveness'. Hill, 'I know thee not', 5 May 2015.

218   *Notes*

21 As Sperling observes (in *Visionary Philology*, p. 144), this also hearkens back to *Speech! Speech!* 20, p. 298, which twists a phrase famously attributed to Luther, '*Ich kann nicht anders*', or 'I can do no other', out of context.

22 Following the etymology of *lógos* with Hill's end in mind is interesting: '*lógos* (from *légo*, "speaking to a conclusion")—a *word*, being the expression of a thought'; '*légo* (originally "lay down to sleep," used later of "laying an *argument* to rest," i.e. bringing a message to closure; see Curtius, Thayer)—properly, to *say* (speak), moving to a *conclusion*' (https://biblehub.com/greek/3056.htm and https://biblehub.com/greek/3004.htm). *Lógos* and its derivatives occur 331 times in the New Testament, *légo* and its derivatives 2267 times.

23 Geoffrey Hill, 'A deep dynastic wound', Professor of Poetry lecture, University of Oxford, 30 April 2013, http://media.podcasts.ox.ac.uk/engfac/poetry/2013-04-30-engfac-hill.mp3. See also *L* 36, p. 615; *TT* 69, p. 922 ('The common *techne* that our wits engage ‖ Even when they engage nothing').

24 See Hill's interview with Anne Mounic, in which Hill discusses at some length the idea of the spiritual vertical and mundane horizontal: 'Si vous imaginez notre existence dans le monde comme une ligne horizontale, la verticale de la spiritualité coupe cette horizontale de notre existence inéluctable' (Mounic, 'Le poème'). And elsewhere: 'If certain events, in the Hebrew Bible as much as in the New Testament, exist for us in two dimensions of time, so also do certain words, and equity is one of them. By two dimensions of time, I intend to suggest eschatological time, as if in a geometric diagram intersecting common linear time at an angle of ninety degrees': Hill, 'Orderly Damned, Disorderly Saved'. Relatedly, in his essay on Southwell, Hill quotes Christopher Devlin: 'the Jesuit discipline, in the design of St Ignatius, sets up an interior tension which can only be resolved by crucifixion' (*CCW*, p. 39).

25 *Orthodoxy*, in *The Collected Works of G. K. Chesterton*, ed. by David Dooley and others, 37 vols (San Francisco: Ignatius Press, 1986–2012), I: *Heretics, Orthodoxy, The Blatchford Controversies*, ed. by David Dooley (1986), p. 303. Chesterton writes of 'the μέσον or balance of Aristotle' (p. 296), though a more literal definition of *meson* would be *midpoint* or *mean*.

26 Dodsworth, 'Geoffrey Hill's Difficulties', pp. 183–84.

27 Ransom, as it happens, shadows these lines: 'there is somewhere a final equation' seems to remember 'Somewhere Is Such a Kingdom', the title of a Ransom poem. Hill uses the title for a collection of his first three books of poetry, his first American publication (Geoffrey Hill, *Somewhere Is Such a Kingdom* (New York: Houghton Mifflin, 1975)). See Steven Matthews, 'Geoffrey Hill's Complex Affinities with American Agrarian Poetry', *The Cambridge Quarterly*, 44 (2015), 321–40 (p. 327).

28 See also *SS* 93, p. 335; 101, p. 339; *OS* XXV, p. 375; XXXVIII, p. 387; LVIII, p. 408 ('I pitch | and check, balanced against hazard, | self-sustained, credulous; well on the way | to hit by accident a coup de grâce'); 'Holbein', §1, *TCP*, p. 565; *L* 60, p. 622; *EV* 25, p. 653; *LIV* XLV: TO TONY HARRISON, p. 729; *O* 36, p. 752; 71: *Bollingen, May 1958 (Afal du Brogŵyr)*, p. 764; 109, p. 777; *OB* XXV, p. 859 ('How the blood's tempered in its modulation | balanced

Notes

219

impulsive'); *CCW*, pp. 15, 20, 27, 47, 61, 73, 128–32, 188, 197, 224, 307, 337, 360, 370, 408, 415, 430, 437, 446, 504, 539.

29 From the Greek μετα- (in this instance, 'change') and νόος ('mind'); see *OED*, 'metanoia'. See also Murphy, 'Hill's Conversions', p. 62.

30 Hill notes the distinction between this and an unhealthy kind of self-involvement: '"Recoil" from the self should [...] be distinguished from that "return upon the self" which may be defined at the transformation of mere reflex into an "act of attention", a "disinterested concentration of purpose" upon one's own preconceived notions, prejudices, self-contradictions and errors' (*CCW*, pp. 164–65). See also *CCW*, pp. 7, 83, 167, 189, 195, 214, 218, 274, 356, 372, 443, 505, 545.

31 The operative word here, 'anticipate', is in a sense intrinsically end-directed, as a poem from *The Orchards of Syon* suggests: 'Begin with golden curtains; helps to anticipate THE END' (*OS* XI, p. 361).

32 See, e.g., Psalms 7.10, 15.2, 32.11, 37.37 ('Marke the vpright man, and beholde the iust: for the end of *that* man *is* peace'), 64.10, 97.11; Proverbs 2.7, 2.21, 10.9, 11.3–5; Habakkuk 2.4.

33 *Paradise Lost*, in *Poetical Works of John Milton*, I, ed. by Helen Darbishire (1963), III. 99, p. 56. There are 108 other occurrences of the word 'stood', as well as forty-two occurrences of 'stand' and six of 'standing', in *Paradise Lost*. See also *Paradise Regained*, in *Poetical Works of John Milton*, II, IV. 551–54, p. 54: 'There stand, if thou wilt stand; to stand upright I Will ask thee skill'.

34 The quotation comes from an unlikely source: Francis W. Hirst's *The Stock Exchange* (Oxford: Oxford University Press, 1948), p. 9.

35 Ewan James Jones, *Coleridge and the Philosophy of Poetic Form* (Cambridge: Cambridge University Press, 2014), p. 147. For such a genealogy, see pp. 148–51.

36 Sol Saporta, 'On Meaningful Tautologies', *Anthropological Linguistics*, 28 (1986), 509–11 (p. 509).

37 See Jones, *Coleridge and the Philosophy of Poetic Form*, p. 149; Saporta, 'On Meaningful Tautologies', p. 509. This figure is sometimes called *diaphora*.

38 *OED*, 'tautology', sense 1, cites William and Thomas Gouge, *A learned and very useful commentary on the whole epistle to the Hebrewes* (1655): 'To shew that there is no tautology, no vain repetition of one and the same thing therein'.

39 Kant: 'Such is, for example, the tautological proposition, *Man is man*. For if I know nothing else of man than that he is man, I know nothing else of him at all' (*Logic*, trans. by Robert S. Hartman and Wolfgang Schwarz (New York: Dover, 1974), p. 118). Cited in Jones, *Coleridge and the Philosophy of Poetic Form*, p. 150.

40 The quote from 'cranky old Barnes', that is, William Barnes, has its punctuation shuffled by Hill (in addition to the accent-marks Hill adds). The line, which concludes 'The Hill-Shade', is: 'But, oh, our people; where are they?' (in *The Oxford Book of English Verse*, ed. by Christopher Ricks (Oxford: Oxford University Press, 1999), p. 413). Hill, after quoting Barnes, writes: 'And I could I not answer, but left him there in silence.'

41 This, referring to John Clare, is the last in a short series of similar formulae: 'Whitbread, house of Whitbread' (twice: *BBGJ* 8, p. 5; 11, p. 6); 'Coke, house of

220 *Notes*

Coke' (34, p. 14). While these name apparent lords of (literary or other) manors, there is also, later, the mysterious tautology 'Unshakeable lord | unshakeable lord' (217, p. 118).

42 The word 'repeat' and its relatives, particularly in phrases such as 'I repeat', 'let me repeat', and 'repeat after me', are themselves repeated in *BBGJ* (17, p. 8; 38, p. 18; 94, p. 43; 105, p. 51; 181, p. 96; 182, §2, p. 98; 199, p. 110; 220, p. 119; 248, p. 134; 261, p. 140). See also *HOLC* 20, p. 167; *TL* CXXV, p. 276; *OS* XV, p. 365; XXXIX, p. 389; LI, p. 401; *SC* 3. 16, p. 478; *P* 6, p. 528; 25, p. 547; 28, p. 550; 'G. F. Handel, Opus 6', *TCP*, p. 585; *EV* 27, p. 655; 52, p. 680; *LIV* LIV, p. 738; *O* 126, p. 782; 135, p. 785; *TT* 36, p. 903; 43 (c), p. 909.

43 See also 'Language, Suffering, and Silence', *CCW*, pp. 394–406; and, on the silence of another Jesuit, Southwell, under torture, *CCW*, p. 29.

44 *In Memoriam A. H. H.*, §LIV, *The Poems of Tennyson*, ed. by Christopher Ricks, 2nd edn, 3 vols (Harlow: Longman, 1987), II, 370. Hill offers a double-sided appraisal of Tennyson in *The Book of Baruch* (69, p. 32): 'I love this atmosphere-laden afternoon as I do Tennyson. | Intelligence matters. Even *In Memoriam* is an emotional scam drawn on the pieties of our social betters, including high-collared men on science and letters. | There is a strong lyric charge in each song from *The Princess*. What I miss is some obduracy of the mind's address'.

45 *Poems of Tennyson*, II, 370.

46 Empson suggests that, in the eighteenth and nineteenth centuries, the infant replaced the swain as the figure for the poet in pastoral poetry. See William Empson, *Some Versions of Pastoral* (New York: New Directions, 1974), p. 254. See also D. B. Ruderman, *The Idea of Infancy in Nineteenth-Century British Poetry: Romanticism, Subjectivity, Form* (New York and London: Routledge, 2016).

47 William Blake, 'I want! I want! Plate 9, For the Sexes: The Gates of Paradise', object number P.444–1985, in Fitzwilliam Museum, Cambridge. 'I want! I want!' is not necessarily tautological; the two senses of 'want' could be considered as separate: *I lack! I desire!*

48 Seamus Perry, *Alfred Tennyson* (Tavistock: Northcote House, 2005), p. 32.

49 Words from Marvell's 'A Poem upon the Death of O. C.', which Hill uses as the second of four epigraphs for *Liber Illustrium Virorum*, may be relevant here: 'he, vertue dead, | Revives' (*BH*, p. 683). It is also notable that 'has effectively said' could mean either *has said effectually* or *has all but said*, again humorously inviting doubt as to whether the words are attributable to anyone except Hill.

50 *The Letters of Ezra Pound 1907–1941*, ed. by D. D. Paige (London: Faber and Faber, 1951), p. 366. See *CCW*, p. 165. Hill also repeats the quotation in an interview in the context of defining poetry as 'a form of responsible behaviour': see Haffenden, *Viewpoints*, p. 99.

51 Andrewes is the 'preacher'; Hill is citing the 1622 Christmas Day sermon (Lancelot Andrewes, *XCVI Sermons* (London: Richard Badger, 1632), pp. 139–47 (p. 144)). Andrewes's influence on Eliot's poetry is felt in more than one place; but the most obvious relation in Eliot to 'Christ is no wild-cat' is in

Notes   221

'Gerontion': 'In the juvescence of the year I Came Christ the tiger' (this only appearing to contradict Andrewes but in fact following his sense). The preceding part of the stanza – 'The word within a word, unable to speak a word' – draws from Andrewes's 1618 Christmas Day sermon: '*Verbum infans*, the Word without a *word*; the *eternall* Word not able to speake a *word*' (Andrewes, *Sermons*, p. 112).

52 Matthew 27.50: 'Iesus, when hee had cried againe with a loud voice, yeelded vp the ghost'. Cf. Mark 15.37; Luke 23.46. One may think also of those words from the Cross, which in John's Gospel come directly before 'It is finished' (John 19.30), and that seem to verbalise the helplessness of an infant: 'I thirst' (John 19.28).

53 The last of these, from Traherne's *Centuries of Meditations*, is an epitome of all-encompassing, transcendental evenness, expressed also in its unhurried rhythm: 'Everything was at rest, free, and immortal'.

54 Geoffrey Hill, 'A matter of timing', *The Guardian*, 21 September 2002, www. theguardian.com/books/2002/sep/21/featuresreviews.guardianreview28. I have rendered hyphens as dashes where they are used as such in this article.

55 See also *OS* II, p. 352; V, p. 355; XXI, p. 371; XXXIV, p. 384; XXXV, p. 385; XXXVII, p. 387; XXXVIII, p. 388; XLV, p. 395; XLVI, p. 396 (two occurrences); LIII, p. 403; LIV, p. 404; LX, p. 410; LXVII, p. 417.

56 The entry for 'even' in the second edition of the *OED* (1989) can be accessed online: www.oed.com/oed2/00079014. The entry for 'even' in the third, online edition is completely revised, but not as relevant to the discussion as the previous edition, to which Hill would have referred.

57 Wainwright, *Acceptable Words*, p. 118.

58 See *OS* I, p. 351; XII, p. 362; XIII, p. 363; XVIII, p. 368; XXII, p. 372; XXV, p. 375; XXXII, p. 382; XXXV, p. 385; XXXVIII, p. 388; XLIV, p. 394; XLVII, p. 397; XLIX, p. 399; LIV, p. 404; LX, p. 410; LXVI, p. 416; LXVIII, p. 418.

59 Pedro Calderón de la Barca, *La vida es sueño*, in *La vida es sueño, El alcalde de Zalamea*, ed. by Enrique Rodríguez Cepeda (Madrid: Ediciones Akal, 1999), ll. 2158, 2187, pp. 181, 182.

60 Williams, 'The Standing of Poetry', p. 68. The Spanish phrase appears in *OS* I, p. 351; III, p. 353; XV, p. 365; XXV, p. 375; LVIII, p. 408.

61 Williams, 'The Standing of Poetry', p. 68.

62 See Wittgenstein, *Tractatus Logico-Philosophicus*, trans. by C. K. Ogden (London: Kegan Paul, Trench, Trubner & Co., 1922), Preface, pp. 23–24; 4. 461, p. 53; 5. 142, p. 58; 6. 1, p. 76; 6. 11, p. 77; 6. 1265, p. 81; 6. 127, p. 81; 6. 22, p. 82.

63 *Persever* is the archaic spelling of the word *persevere*. As the notion of the Orchards of Syon is historical and symbolic, the use of 'persever' acquires meaning from its modern equivalent while retaining the connotations of its previous uses. One of these is in Herbert's 'Heaven', full of punning repetitions voiced by an answering 'ECHO': 'Light, joy, and leisure; but shall they persever? I ECHO. Ever.' *The Works of George Herbert*, ed. by F. E. Hutchinson (Oxford: Oxford University Press, 1941), p. 188.

222   *Notes*

64 There are two worded preservations elsewhere in *The Orchards of Syon*: see
    OS II, p. 352; XLIII, p. 393. For Hill's quotation of Locke's *'bare preservation'*,
    see Chapter 1, n. 65. See also *CCW*, p. 567, in which Hill locates (in the cor-
    respondence between Yeats and Margot Ruddock) a 'distinction between inept
    self-expression on the one hand and, on the other, the preservation of formal
    distinctions as a necessary part of self-expression'.
65 Cf. *BBGJ* 36, §6, p. 17: 'If I have ever known a poetics it is this.'
66 Wittgenstein, *Tractatus*, 3. 23, p. 35.
67 Wittgenstein, *Tractatus*, pp. 23–24.
68 In 'Notebook 45: The Triumph of Love', BC MS 20c Hill/2/1/45, fol. 90ʳ, Hill
    writes in a draft for *TL* CXXV:

> 'There ought to be an investigation
> of tautology as echo, echo as tautology
> [there is—ED]' [...]
> 'Wittgenstein, who is powerfully Augustinian,
> relates tautology to an absolute
> state, states, of stated Truth.'

    (In this draft, 'powerfully' is struck through and 'clearly' written above it;
    '['Strewth—ED]' is written in the margin.)
69 Alex Wylie, commenting on the last seven lines of this poem, notes the use of
    will in *Ludo*: 'What's here anarchic and libidinous | Shakespeare names *Will*'
    (19, p. 610); 'Grief is everywhere; [...] it will not grow | with watching; arbitrar-
    ily though law | bends natural justice to accommodate will' (20, p. 610). Alex
    Wylie, *Geoffrey Hill's Later Work: Radiance of Apprehension* (Manchester:
    Manchester University Press, 2019), p. 53.
70 Even the supposed 'will' of a deterministic, ordered 'all right' universe may
    be or seem disrupted by sexual 'will'. I think of Valentine and Chloë in Tom
    Stoppard's *Arcadia* (1993): 'CHLOË: The universe is deterministic all right, just
    like Newton said, I mean it's trying to be, but the only thing going wrong is
    people fancying people who aren't supposed to be in that part of the plan. VAL-
    ENTINE: Ah. The attraction that Newton left out. All the way back to the apple
    in the garden' (Tom Stoppard, *Arcadia*, in *Tom Stoppard: Plays 5* (London:
    Faber and Faber, 1999), 7, p. 104). For another provoked take on Augustine
    several poems earlier, see *TT* 10, p. 892: 'Let Augustine be, and with him the
    inspired | Self-destitution of the zeal-impaired'.
71 Geoffrey Hill, *Scenes from Comus* (London: Penguin, 2005), p. 12. The line
    'Hyphens are not-necessary for things I say', omitted in *Broken Hierarchies*, and
    about which Ricks writes in *True Friendship*, p. 5, is a response to the observa-
    tions about hyphens in Ricks's essay '"Tenebrae" and at-one-ment'.
72 Ricks, *True Friendship*, p. 5.
73 Rowland cleverly connects this with the emphasised 'is' of 'September Song' ('it
    | is true') in *Metamodernisms*, pp. 158–59, n. 68.
74 This recalls again the not wholly reconciled weights of 'neither wisdom | nor
    illusion of wisdom' in OS LXVIII, p. 418, in which it is the very repetition, the

Notes

223

'of wisdom', that unbalances the trochaic rhythms of 'neither wisdom' and 'nor illusion'.

75 Perhaps the most important precedent for Hill is Hopkins's 'That Nature is a Heraclitean Fire and of the Comfort of the Resurrection'. Of that poem's mid-line declaration 'Enough! the Resurrection', Hill writes: 'It is a great moment, one of the greatest grammatical moments in nineteenth-century English poetry' (*CCW*, p. 570).

76 The latter pair is not, as it may seem, an example of polyptoton, because 'restitution' and 'rest' do not share a morphological root; but something of the effect of tautology is shared by both pairs. Quintilian, in the eighth book of his *Institutio Oratoria*, gives 'non solum illud judicium judicii simile, judices, non fuit' as an instance of tautology (*The Orator's Education*, trans. by Donald A. Russell, 5 vols (Cambridge, MA: Harvard University Press, 2001), III, 369). See Jones, *Coleridge and the Philosophy of Poetic Form*, p. 148.

77 Sonnet 66, in *Shakespeare's Sonnets: An Original-Spelling Text*, ed. by Paul Hammond (Oxford: Oxford University Press, 2012), p. 241. Hill begins a note-book for *Without Title* by writing the sonnet by hand ('Notebook 67', fol. 1ʳ). See also *TL* CIV, p. 269: 'Pasternak, for example: *shestdesyat | shestoy*, they shout—give us the sixty- | sixth (sonnet, of Shakespeare). You could say | that to yourself in the darkness before sleep | and perhaps be reconciled.'

78 R. P. Blackmur, 'Irregular Metaphysics', in *Literary Lectures Presented at the Library of Congress* (Washington, DC: Library of Congress, 1973), p. 147. Cited in Hill's lecture 'How ill white hairs'.

79 The connection between the 'unalloyed | unallured TETRAGRAMMATON' (*SS* 62, p. 319) and God's Name as translated into English is not straightforward; there is a Rabbinic and kabbalistic argument that the form translated 'I am' is a con-jugation of the tetragrammaton. See, e.g., G. H. Parke-Taylor, *Yahweh: The Divine Name in the Bible* (Waterloo, Ontario: Wilfrid Laurier University Press, 1975), pp. 79–96.

80 Wittgenstein, *Tractatus*, 3. 03, 3. 031, p. 31.

81 The *OED* lists several senses of 'metaphysical', one of which mentions Wittgenstein (sense 1d); here I am taking advantage of the second sentence of sense 1a: 'Also more generally: transcendental, philosophical'; and sense 4a: 'Designating that which is immaterial, incorporeal, or supersensible'. The passage above from *The Triumph of Love* is also metaphysical in the literary-critical sense (3a), its poetic style being 'characterized by wit, syntactic complex-ity, and the use of elaborate and intricate schemes of imagery to express abstract ideas and emotional states'.

82 Ludwig Wittgenstein, *Philosophical Investigations*, trans. by G. E. M. Anscombe (Oxford: Basil Blackwell, 1963), §371, p. 116ᵉ. See also §373, p. 116ᵉ: 'Grammar tells what kind of object anything is. (Theology as grammar.)' For 'God's grammar' in Hill, see *The Orchards of Syon* (2002), LXVII, p. 68 (a poem omitted from *Broken Hierarchies*); *Cl.* 23, p. 813; *CCW*, p. 263. The last of these reveals that Hill has in mind Donne's use of the phrase in a sermon. See Sperling, *Visionary Philology*, p. 159. For more connections between God and

224 *Notes*

grammar in Hill, see *TL* XXIII, p. 245; CXXV, pp. 276–77; CXXXIX, p. 282; *SS* 18, p. 297; 80, p. 328; *OS* LVIII, p. 408; *EV* 20, p. 648; *O* 24: *Hermeneutics* (I), p. 748; 118, p. 780; *OB* XLI, p. 875; *TT* 18, p. 895; 21, p. 896; 33, p. 901. Hill says in an interview: 'the grammar of the poem decides the grammar of belief' (Daniel Johnson, 'Geoffrey Hill and the Poetry of Ideas', *Standpoint*, June 2014). Cf. *CCW*, p. 263: 'With Donne, style *is* faith.'

83 'Introduction', *Songs of Innocence and of Experience*, in *The Complete Poetry & Prose of William Blake*, ed. by David V. Erdman (New York: Anchor, 1988), p. 7.

84 The poems are 'Holy Thursday' (*U*, p. 6), originally subtitled 'Of William Blake' (see 'Early Poems', BC MS 20c Hill/2/2/3 (loose sheets)); and 'On Reading *Blake: Prophet Against Empire*' (*TCP*, p. 569). The review is in *The Isis*, 4 March 1953, p. 22. Blake's *Jerusalem* also appears in *The Book of Baruch by the Gnostic Justin*, in which another primal 'cry' is figured: 'Approve him according to the likes of Blake's *Jerusalem*. Why? People self-maim, irrespective of injury. The cry you have just uttered has not heard of you, trust me' (*BBGJ* 114, p. 58).

85 In a draft ('Notebook 45', fol. 94ʳ), the poem ends instead with a tautology (though a bad one, since it doubles its meaning twice) – one defined as a meaning of 'silence' – in what could be the voice of God:

> 'Its silence meaning: I am
> before you, and before you.'

86 Elsewhere the Blessed Virgin is described as 'eloquently mute' (*TT* 2, p. 890).

87 Sperling, *Visionary Philology*, p. 169, on *SS* 89 (p. 333): 'the poem instructs itself to identify a *cause*, perhaps with a glance towards the Aristotelian understanding of the several kinds of "cause" as key to a thing's nature—as in the title of Thomas Bradwardine's *De Causa Dei*, or the derivation of French *chose* or Italian *cosa* (a thing, a matter) from Latin *causa*. No causes except in things; and vice versa.'

88 For the origins of this Neoplatonic–Christian idea, see, e.g., E. R. Dodds's commentary in Proclus, *Elements of Theology*, ed. and trans. by E. R. Dodds (Oxford: Clarendon Press, 1963), p. 220; Paul Rorem, *Pseudo-Dionysius* (New York and Oxford: Oxford University Press, 1993), pp. 51, 172–73.

89 See, e.g., Thomas Aquinas, *Summa Theologiae*, trans. by Fathers of the English Dominican Province, 2nd edn, 5 vols (London: Burns Oates and Washbourne, 1920), I, I.3.4: '[...] His essence is His existence'; I.4.3: '[...] God is essential being, whereas other things are beings by participation'.

90 *The Notebooks of Samuel Taylor Coleridge*, ed. by Kathleen Coburn and others, 5 vols (Princeton, NJ: Princeton University Press, 1957–2012), IV, ed. by Kathleen Coburn and Merton Christensen (1990), p. 4832.

91 See *The Notebooks of Samuel Taylor Coleridge*, IV, 4832.

92 Samuel Taylor Coleridge, *Lectures 1808–1819 on Literature*, ed. by R. A. Foakes, 2 vols (London: Routledge & Kegan Paul, 1987), I, 267. Cited in Jones, *Coleridge and the Philosophy of Poetic Form*, p. 159. The 'sublime Tautology' is

Notes 225

in Judges 5.27: 'At her feet he bowed, he fell, he lay downe: at her feet he bowed, he fell; where he bowed, there he fel down dead.'

93 Paul Hamilton, *Coleridge and German Philosophy: The Poet in the Land of Logic* (London: Continuum, 2007), p. 108. Cited in Jones, *Coleridge and the Philosophy of Poetic Form*, pp. 159–60.

94 *The Poetical Works of William Wordsworth*, ed. by Ernest de Selincourt and Helen Darbishire, 5 vols (Oxford: Clarendon Press, 1952–1959), II, ed. by Ernest de Selincourt (1952), p. 513.

95 This is the translation in the 1994 *Catechism of the Catholic Church* (New York: Doubleday, 2003), 102, p. 36. For the original Latin, see Augustine, *Enarrationes in Psalmos*, Psalmum CIII, IV, 1, in *Patrologia Latina*, ed. by Jacques-Paul Migne, 221 vols (Paris: Migne, 1841–1855), XXXVII (1861), col. 1378.

96 The Bradwardine quotation comes from the first epigraph of *The Orchards of Syon* (*BH*, p. 349).

97 In 'The Oath' (*TCP*, p. 598), the innocent and mute are met with mute violence: 'the dumb possessed the barricades en masse | their speechless cry so raggedly proclaimed | the Oath took arms against them street on street [...] in lieu of words the one word fire | blazed from its heart'.

98 Blackmur, 'Irregular Metaphysics', p. 139.

Chapter 3

1 The epigraph is from *EV* 1, p. 629. Cf. *EV* 50, p. 678: 'An altar's worth: ye shall offer no strange | incense thereon.' Exodus 30.1, 9–10: 'And thou shalt make an Altar to burne incense vpon [...] Ye shall offer no strange incense thereon, nor burnt sacrifice, nor meate offering, neither shall ye powre drinke offering thereon. And Aaron shall make an atonement vpon the hornes of it'.

2 Apart from the heckling in *Speech! Speech!*, this is explicit in, for example, 'On Reading *The Essayes or Counsels, Civill and Morall*' (*TCP*, pp. 595–96), which ends: 'I wish I could keep | Baconian counsel, wish I could keep resentment | out of my voice'; or 'Coda' (*TCP*, pp. 599–600), which ends: 'I know that sounds | a wicked thing to say.'

3 See '[Author's Preface on Rhythm]', *The Poetical Works of Gerard Manley Hopkins*, ed. by Norman H. MacKenzie (Oxford: Clarendon Press, 1990), pp. 115–17. For Hill's uses of the word 'counterpoint', see *CCW*, pp. 94, 98, 157, 196; *OS* XXXV, p. 385; *SC* 2. 48, p. 454; *EV* 24, p. 652.

4 See Chesterton, *Orthodoxy*, pp. 296–306. 'Paganism declared that virtue was in a balance; Christianity declared it was in a conflict: the collision of two passions apparently opposite' (p. 297).

5 Pollard, *Speaking to You*, p. 196.

6 Wallace Stevens, letter to Elsie Moll, 19 August 1909, *Letters of Wallace Stevens*, ed. by Holly Stevens (New York: Knopf, 1966), p. 157.

226 *Notes*

7 *Samuel Daniel: A Defence of Ryme; and Thomas Campion: Observations in the Art of English Poesie*, ed. by G. B. Harrison (Edinburgh: Edinburgh University Press, 1966), p. 4.

8 *An Essay on Criticism*, in *The Poems of Alexander Pope*, ed. by John Butt (London: Methuen, 1963), ll. 340–41 and 346–51, p. 154.

9 End-rhyme will be considered the norm; but I acknowledge that rhyme can occur elsewhere in the line. This follows V. M. Žirmunskij, who, in a book Simon Jarvis has called 'perhaps [...] the single most important book ever written about rhyme' (Simon Jarvis, 'Why Rhyme Pleases', *Thinking Verse*, 1 (2011), 17–43 (p. 22)), concedes that because rhyme is not restricted to the line's end, 'any sound repetition that has an organising function in the metrical composition of the poem should be included in the concept of rhyme' (Рифма, Её история и теория [*Rhyme, Its history and theory*] (Petrograd: Academia, 1923), p. 9).

10 George Saintsbury, *A History of English Prosody*, 3 vols (London: Macmillan, 1906–1910), III, 539.

11 *The Princeton Encyclopedia of Poetry and Poetics*, ed. by Roland Greene and others, 4th edn (Princeton, NJ and Oxford: Princeton University Press, 2012), from p. 924 of which comes the quotation, uses 'near rhyme' as the catch-all term, recommending that it be understood to signify rhymes 'close to the narrow band of instances qualifying as canonical end rhyme but outside it, in the wider field of "related but alternative forms of sound correspondence"'. As shall be seen later in this chapter, Hill, in *L* 26, p. 613, uses the word 'half-rhyme'.

12 This will include, for example, what the *Princeton Encyclopedia* categorises separately as 'identical rhyme' (pp. 658–59) and 'rich rhyme' (p. 1199): homophones, which sound the same but differ in spelling and meaning; homographs, which are spelt the same but differ in sound and meaning (as in *L* 59, p. 622, which rhymes 'invalid' (adjective) with 'invalid' (noun)); homonyms, which sound and are spelt alike but differ significantly in meaning; and tautologies, which I regard as autorhymes where they have the same organisational function as other end-rhymes.

13 Jarvis, 'Why Rhyme Pleases', p. 27.

14 Hugh Kenner, 'Rhyme: An Unfinished Monograph', *Common Knowledge*, 10 (2004), 377–425 (p. 394).

15 T. S. Eliot, 'Reflections on Vers Libre', *New Statesman*, 3 March 1917, pp. 518–19.

16 *Collected Works of Gerard Manley Hopkins*, II: *Correspondence 1882–1889*, ed. by R. K. R. Thornton and Catherine Phillips (2013), p. 822. See *CCW*, p. 91.

17 S. Ernest Sprott, *Milton's Art of Prosody* (Oxford: Basil Blackwell, 1953), p. 24. See also Ants Oras, 'Milton's Early Rhyme Schemes and the Structure of "Lycidas"', *Modern Philology*, 52 (1954), 12–22.

18 Allen Tate, 'Narcissus as Narcissus', *Essays of Four Decades* (London: Oxford University Press, 1970), p. 602.

19 Geoffrey Hill, 'Acceptance Speech for the T. S. Eliot Prize', *Image: A Journal of the Arts and Religion*, 28 (2000), 72–77 (p. 75).

Notes

227

20 Hugh Haughton, '"How fit a title...": Title and Authority in the Work of Geoffrey Hill', in *EW*, pp. 129–48 (p. 142).

21 Kenneth Allott, ed., *The Penguin Book of Contemporary Verse: 1918–60* (London: Penguin, 1962), p. 393.

22 The exceptions are the first part of 'The Death of Shelley' (itself part three in 'Of Commerce and Society' (pp. 28–30)) and the last poem, 'To the (Supposed) Patron' (p. 35).

23 As for metre, the twenty-one lines are (generally) six pentameter lines followed by five alternating lines of trimeter and dimeter; then one tetrameter; two pentameter; one trimeter; one dimeter; three trimeter; one dimeter; and a final pentameter.

24 *LIV* I, p. 685; XXIV, p. 708; XXXI, p. 715; XLIV: To Tony Harrison, p. 728; LI, p. 735.

25 The much-quoted opening sentence of 'Funeral Music: An Essay': 'In this sequence I was attempting a florid grim music broken by grunts and shrieks' (Geoffrey Hill, *King Log* (London: André Deutsch, 1968), p. 67). See also *HOLC* 1, p. 157.

26 Namely that poem XXII in the *Collected Poems* is entitled 'Offa's "Second Defense of the English People"' (p. 9), while in *Broken Hierarchies* (p. x) it is the first of four (instead of three) poems entitled 'Opus Anglicanum'.

27 'Notebook 13: Mercian Hymns', BC MS 20c Hill/2/1/13, fol. 5^r.

28 'Notebook 13', fol. 9^r.

29 Add to this the fact that *The Book of Baruch* is so often invested in thoughts of rhyme; see *BBGJ* 65, p. 29; 76, p. 35; 98, p. 46; 147, p. 78; 162, p. 87; 188, p. 103 ('These patterns, here, of internal rhyme are set to do more than mnemonically chime'); 202, p. 111; 221, p. 120; 241, §2, p. 129.

30 The same poet is riffed on later: 'stately irate Yeats' (*BBGJ* 158, p. 85).

31 Though less precious in context: 'They're versets of rhythmical prose. The rhythm and cadence are far more of tuned chant than I think one normally associates with the prose poem. I designed the appearance on the page in the form of versets'. Haffenden, *Viewpoints*, p. 93.

32 G. K. Chesterton, 'The Romance of Rhyme', *The Living Age*, 13 March 1920, pp. 656–65 (p. 664). See also *BBGJ* 49, p. 23: 'In the City the Wren spires seem infinitely variable in the logometrics of time, spiritually intrinsic, the patterns of quickened stone acclaiming suitably, as in a children's rhyme or the one hundred and fiftieth psalm.'

33 Chesterton, 'The Romance of Rhyme', p. 657: 'The whole history of the thing called rhyme can be found between [...] the simple pleasure of rhyming "diddle" to "fiddle", and the more sophisticated pleasure of rhyming "diddle" to "idyll".'

34 Henrik Ibsen, *Brand*, I, in *Peer Gynt and Brand*, trans. by Geoffrey Hill (London: Penguin, 2016), pp. 16–17.

35 Adrian Poole, 'Hill's "Version" of "Brand"', in *EW*, pp. 86–99 (p. 95).

36 Ibsen, *Brand* (2016), v, p. 164.

37 Hill mentions the passage as the last he wrote for *Brand* in Haffenden, *Viewpoints*, p. 84. Cited in Poole, 'Hill's "Version"', pp. 98–99.

228   *Notes*

38 Ibsen, *Brand* (2016), iii, p. 88.
39 Henrik Ibsen, *Brand: A Version for the English Stage*, trans. by Geoffrey Hill (London: Heinemann, 1978), p. 82.
40 Jonathan F. S. Post, *Henry Vaughan: The Unfolding Vision* (Princeton, NJ: Princeton University Press, 1982), p. 209. Cited in *CCW*, p. 326 (note at p. 686).
41 Hill's word choice is unlikely to be without its own meticulous reason. I presume that Hill had in mind the root of the word, the Greek *theorema*, meaning 'spectacle, speculation', as well as the common modern sense of the word as a 'proposition or statement which is not self-evident but is demonstrable by argument' (*OED*, etymology and sense 1).
42 For Fibonacci numbers in *Al Tempo de' Tremuoti*, see 1, p. 889; 5, p. 890; 16, pp. 894–95; 88 (f), p. 932; 94, p. 935.
43 Simone Weil, *Gravity and Grace*, trans. by Emma Crawford and Mario von der Ruhr (London and New York: Routledge & Kegan Paul, 1952), p. 150. The italics are Weil's. Cited in Alexander Freer, '"Love-Runes We Cannot Speak": Sacred and Profane Love in "The Pentecost Castle"', *Literature and Theology*, 26 (2012), 199–213 (p. 199).
44 Robert Macfarlane, 'Gravity and Grace in Geoffrey Hill', *Essays in Criticism*, 58 (2008), 237–56 (p. 241). The two periods would be, first, the poems between *For the Unfallen* (1959) and *Hymns to Our Lady of Chartres* (as it was in 1985); and, second, from *Canaan* (1996) onwards.
45 See Plato, *Symposium*, in *Lysis. Symposium. Gorgias*, trans. by W. R. M. Lamb (Cambridge, MA: Harvard University Press, 1925), 203b–c, pp. 180–81.
46 The effect of a mental echo between revisions of a poet's own work, if intended by the poet, would be hard not to deem self-indulgent (in a way that allusion to another's work, which sets up a similar echo, is not, though it may be plain indulgent); and if not intended, it would be per se unsuccessful because it presumes (or requests the pretending of) a readerly amnesia that has not occurred. One cannot unsee or unhear. In the case of the unintended mental echo, the reader is able to make semantic connections between revisions that the writer has tried to smudge out. The same would be true of an ill-considered rhyme that tells on its unsuspecting author or renders the sense dubious or ridiculous by its inclusion of unwanted connotations.
47 W. K. Wimsatt, 'One Relation of Rhyme to Reason', *Modern Language Quarterly*, 5 (1944), 323–38 (p. 328).
48 Ricks, '"Tenebrae" and at-one-ment'.
49 'Burnt Norton', §V, *Poems of T. S. Eliot*, p. 184.
50 Similar terms emerge at the conclusion of the beautifully epiphanic 'Offertorium: Suffolk, July 2003', *WT*, p. 515: 'Abundant hazards, | being and non-being, every fleck through which | this time affords | unobliterate certainties hidden in light'.
51 Hill, *King Log*, p. 70.
52 Apart from punctuational changes, dismissed by William Logan as 'trivial' and by Paul Batchelor as 'minor' but which for Hill are neither, the only change is that the original final line, 'And a few sprinkled leaves unshook', becomes

Notes 229

'Dead cones upon the alder shook'. Logan: 'the wording of the corrective note is odd, even strikingly odd: Hill seems to say that he is reprinting the poem *because* he dislikes it, a form of penance for having written it'. This last clause is less commentary than it is repetition of Hill's own word 'penitential'. Erica McAlpine follows a similar line, calling the revision 'a form of quasi-religious self-flagellation'. William Logan, 'The Absolute Unreasonableness of Geoffrey Hill', in *Conversant Essays: Contemporary Poets on Poetry*, ed. by James McCorkle (Detroit: Wayne State University Press, 1990), pp. 34–47 (p. 44); Paul Batchelor, 'Weight of the Word, Weight of the World', *Poetry*, July/August 2018, www.poetryfoundation.org/poetrymagazine/articles/147126/weight-of-the-word-weight-of-the-world; Erica McAlpine, *The Poet's Mistake* (Princeton, NJ: Princeton University Press, 2020), p. 209.

53 The impulse to revise survives into even Hill's posthumously published work. See *BBGJ* 265, p. 142: 'I who alter, more than thirty years later, "blood" to "gleet" because the field where he fell was, and remains, sugar beet; and one must align invention with those particular stains?' The alteration is in the last line of *MCCP* 2, p. 144 (and 'he' refers to Péguy). The 'gleet of beetroots' here was the 'blood of beetroots' in the first publication (Geoffrey Hill, *The Mystery of the Charity of Charles Péguy* (London: Agenda Editions and André Deutsch, 1983), p. 12). See also *BBGJ* 268, p. 144: 'Stuprate I got wrong lifelong and will have to rewrite. But barely possible after eighty, I should have thought, despite "blood" to "gleet".' Hill's only previous use of *stuprate* is not, as one might infer, in an early collection, but in *Al Tempo de' Tremuoti* (2, p. 889); he uses the word as an adjective but it is listed only as a verb in the *OED*.

54 The quotation, in *CCW*, p. 139, is from Bradley's *Oxford Lectures on Poetry* (London: Macmillan, 1909), p. 71. More restrained 'intestinal warfare' is apparent in the notes of *CP* (1985): 'I have felt impelled to alter words and phrases here and there. I have changed only those details which have become a burden over the years' (p. 199).

55 Knottenbelt, *Passionate Intelligence*, p. 214.

56 Ovid, *Amores*, in *Heroides. Amores*, trans. by Grant Showerman, rev. by G. P. Goold (Cambridge, MA: Harvard University Press, 1914), p. 507.

57 Ovid, *Amores*, p. 507.

58 Ovid, *Amores*, p. 507.

59 Craig Raine, *My Grandmother's Glass Eye* (London: Atlantic Books, 2016), p. 71. *OS* X, p. 360: 'What a find, | a self-awarded *donnée* if ever | I knew one.'

60 The poem is *MCCP* 5, p. 147. See *CCW*, pp. 13, 17, 21, 30, 53, 83, 88, 117, 154, 184, 201, 234, 240, 254, 300, 356, 374, 388, 399, 463, 470, 480, 482, 487, 497, 539.

61 'Notebook 62: Without Title / A Treatise of Civil Power', BC MS 20c Hill/2/1/62, fol. 77ʳ.

62 See also: 'That line of Melville—"The hemlock shakes in the rafter, the oak in the driving keel"—you can feel the impartial wilfulness of language engage with its nature to be both active and still, and thereby at one with the Divine Will...' (*BBGJ* 145, p. 78).

230 *Notes*

63 Philip Larkin, 'An Arundel Tomb', in *Collected Poems* (London: Faber and Faber, 1988), p. 111.

64 *L* 17 (p. 609):

> Break to the varied disciplines of light,
> of good faith in politics, a dimension,
> a value, equal to that of scansion.
> Havel I have to thank for this insight
>
> expressed as a vertical; not *upright*,
> precisely; *vertical*; intersection
> without disseverance, and without action
> given over wholly to the distraught.

65 *The Economist*, 'Poems should be beautiful'.

66 Tomlinson, *The Way of a World*, p. 59.

67 Naturally, this is not the poem's finish; but it may be in autorhyming communication with, and contradiction of, the last line of Hill's well-known early sequence 'Funeral Music': 'Crying to the end "I have not finished"' (*KL*, p. 54).

68 The final line of 'The Convergence of the Twain': 'And consummation comes, and jars two hemispheres.' *The Variorum Edition of the Complete Poems of Thomas Hardy*, ed. by James Gibson (London: Macmillan, 1979), p. 306.

69 'But if the work is to be more than just a sculptural exercise, unexplainable jumps in the process of thought occur; and the imagination plays its part.' Henry Moore, 'The Sculptor Speaks', in *Listener*, 18 August 1937, pp. 338–40, reproduced in *Henry Moore: Sculptural Process and Public Identity*, Tate Research Publication, 2015, www.tate.org.uk/art/research-publications/henry-moore/henry-moore-the-sculptor-speaks-r1176118.

The quotation as it is in Hill's poem, which sounds like an unintentional tidying-up of Moore's words, is from Max Newman, taking part in a roundtable discussion of artificial intelligence with (among others) Alan Turing, which was broadcast on the BBC Third Programme on 14 January 1952. Newman: 'Henry Moore says about the studies he does for his sculpture, "When the work is more than an exercise, inexplicable jumps occur. This is where the imagination comes in".' Alan Turing, Richard Braithwaite, Geoffrey Jefferson, and Max Newman, 'Can Automatic Calculating Machines Be Said to Think?', in *The Essential Turing*, ed. by B. Jack Copeland (Oxford: Clarendon Press, 2004), pp. 487–506 (p. 505).

Hill turns to Turing elsewhere in his poetry, most notably in 'A Cloud in Aquila' (*A Treatise of Civil Power*, p. 576), which also refers to Eddington (the latter having stimulated Turing's fascination with the quantum mechanical physics of the brain). See also *TL* XVI, p. 243; *TT* 77, p. 925.

70 Blackmur, 'Art and Manufacture', *Language as Gesture*, p. 364. See Chapter 1, n. 87, above.

71 This theme is explored at great length in *The Book of Baruch*. See, e.g., *BBGJ* 2, p. 3: 'debate the good nature of the city-state, that odd creature'.

72 Alexander Pope, *The Correspondence*, ed. by George Sherburn, 5 vols (Oxford: Clarendon Press, 1956), I, 10.

Notes

73 The word 'mysteries' (a near-anagram of 'symmetries', as in Hill's 'odd symmetries'), appears numerous times in Hill's late work. See, for example, *EV 35*, p. 663: 'I am more short-tempered with mysteries | Than I have declared lately'; *LIV* XXV, p. 719: 'I would not rumour these | Confrontations mere mysteries'; XXXIX, p. 723: 'I grant that we are mysteries; I grant | Metrum not tagged exempt from pride of cant'; *O* 41, p. 754: 'Best settle in with a good mystery'; 56: *Marwnad Saunders Lewis* (III), p. 759: 'The first mysteries at length retired | Into themselves'; 73: *Afal du Brogûyr* (II), p. 765: 'Save from mystique the ravaged mysteries'; *Clavics*, epigraph (from Thomas Jordan), p. 789: 'In this Urne there lies | The Master of great Musick's mysteries'; *OB* XXI, p. 855: 'Begging still her pardon I here accept all | Necessary mysteries'; LII, p. 886: 'Tell me a mystery, a | Tale of winter, so I shall love you wisely'; *TT* 53, p. 915: 'The nuptial mysteries of those unwed | Aptly consenting, with an end bestowed'; 89, p. 932–33: 'Eleusinian mysteries'.

74 Hill, 'Orderly Damned, Disorderly Saved'. For other appearances of *equity* in Hill's work, see 'Sobieski's Shield', *C*, p. 173; 'Whether the Virtues are Emotions', *C*, p. 176; 'Concerning Inheritance', *C*, p. 233; 'To the High Court of Parliament', *C*, p. 235; *TL* XL, p. 250; *SS* 104, p. 340; *OS* LXI, p. 411; *LIV* I, p. 685; *OB* XIII, p. 847; *CCW*, pp. 25, 26, 27, 28–29, 32–33, 34, 35, 37, 193, 237, 289, 303, 311, 330, 354, 375–76, 403, 467; *BBGJ* 125, p. 67; 135, p. 72.

75 Hill, 'Orderly Damned, Disorderly Saved'.

Chapter 4

1 'Notebook 12: [Mercian Hymns]', BC MS 20c Hill/2/1/12, fol. 10ʳ. From fols 8ʳ to 10ʳ it can be deduced that Hill, taking notes for a lecture on Yeats, is reading Donald Davie and Charles Tomlinson on syntax: 'p. 1. (Tomlinson) [...] 'his very syntax'; 'p. 98. "natural momentum in the syntax"'; 'p. 90. "powerful + passionate syntax."'; 'p74 of (Davie) [...] 82 ORDERING ENERGY OF SYNTAX'.

2 Geoffrey Hill, 'A Treatise of Civil Power', XLII, *TCP* (2005). The pamphlet lacks page numbers; subsequent citations of this poem will refer to section number.

3 The removal of the 'CETERA DESUNT' in the later version of *A Treatise of Civil Power* frees Hill to make use of the conceit again, which he does in *Ludo*: 'It is not a stunt | [*cetera desunt*]' (*L* 25, p. 612). It is a 'stunt' – both a trick and (by way of the verb) something inhibited – that Hill is keen to show off.

 For other ostensibly unfinished endings, see 'Fantasia on "Horbury"', *KL*, p. 65 (which ends on an ellipsis); 'De Anima', *C*, p. 175; 'Scenes with Harlequins', §I, *C*, p. 184 (also an ellipsis); *TL* LXXV, pp. 260–61 (a straightforward segue: 'But, to continue—'); LXXXIV, p. 263; XCIII, p. 265; *SS* 3, p. 290 ('cut here—'); 104, p. 340 ('forsaken in the telling— | pelagic diasporas [LEAVE UNFINISHED]'); 'Nachwort', *TCP*, p. 601; *LIV* XLIX, p. 733 ('Twi- | natured gerund, | Fleshed magnolia, unfazed entity—'); *TT* 16, pp. 894–95 ('The Fibonacci zeroing as they'); 95, pp. 935–36.

232 *Notes*

4 The other sections to which poems in the later version are indebted are IX, XV, XIX, XXV, XXVII, XXXVII, XL, *TCP* (2005).

5 These revisions occur first in the 2007 edition: see Geoffrey Hill, *A Treatise of Civil Power* (London: Penguin, 2007), p. 41.

6 The idea for a triple-tailed ending might have come from Hopkins's 'That Nature is a Heraclitean Fire and of the Comfort of the Resurrection', which Hill calls 'a triple caudated (or "tailed" or coda-ed) sonnet amounting to twenty-four lines in all' (*CCW*, p. 570).

7 'A Treatise of Civil Power', *TCP* (2005), §XXVII.

8 'A Treatise of Civil Power', *TCP* (2005), §§VII, XLI.

9 Geoffrey Hill, quoted by Benjamin Mullen, 'Hill's "A Treatise of Civil Power"': Two Editions', http://pitchpress.blogspot.com/2010/01/geoffrey-hills-treatise-of-civil-power.html.

10 In *The Book of Baruch* Hill states the connection between poetry and finality in the context of Ezra Pound and with an awareness that *consummation* can mean things' falling apart (see *OED*, 'consummation', etymology): 'Pound, at the end, admitted he had failed. [...] When Ez said "bureaucracy is destruction", he saw eighty years ahead, staked out poetry as finality's diction' (*BBGJ* 111, p. 56).

11 'Citations II', *TCP*, p. 561. See also the end of 'Algabal', *C*, p. 192: 'Your desk is a pure altar; | it is [...] for a vital | scintillant atrophy, | a trophy | of the ageless champion.'

12 Ezra Pound, 'In a Station of the Metro', *Personae: Collected Shorter Poems* (New York: New Directions, 1990), p. 251.

13 Christopher Ricks, 'John Donne: "Farewell to Love"', *Essays in Appreciation* (Oxford: Oxford University Press, 1996), pp. 19–50 (p. 27).

14 Ricks, 'John Donne', pp. 19, 20, 24. Agamben's sense of a poem's ending may be brought to bear here: he begins with the premise that 'if poetry is defined precisely by the possibility of enjambment, it follows that the last verse of a poem is not a verse' (Agamben, *The End of the Poem*, p. 112). The 'decisive crisis' this causes for the poem results in 'the often cheap and even abject quality of the end of the poem' (p. 113). Agamben goes on to cite Proust and Walter Benjamin on supposedly guilty poems by Baudelaire; and describes this phenomenon as the 'disorder of the last verse' (p. 113).

15 The quotation is from Empson, *Seven Types of Ambiguity*, p. ix. Cited in *CCW*, p. 4.

16 Ricks, '"Tenebrae" and at-one-ment', p. 63.

17 Not, as Ricks has it, an 'atonement of atonement and at-one-ment', which, he argues, cannot happen (Ricks, '"Tenebrae" and at-one-ment', p. 64).

18 On that lack of *of*, cf. 'Coda', §8, *TCP* (2005): 'which is an abashed way of saying light'.

19 It is contextually necessary for Hill to write 'Dante's *Paradiso*' because, earlier in the collection, he has already written about Gillian Rose's *Paradiso*. See 'In Memoriam: Gillian Rose', *TCP*, pp. 588–90.

20 'East Coker', §II, *Poems of T. S. Eliot*, p. 187.

Notes

233

21 'Coda', *TCP* (2005); Geoffrey Hill, *A Treatise of Civil Power* (London: Penguin, 2007), p. 50.

22 'East Coker', §§II, III, *Poems of T. S. Eliot*, p. 188. 'So here I am': *Poems of T. S. Eliot*, p. 191. See Dante, *Divine Comedy*, p. 3.

23 'East Coker', §II, *Poems of T. S. Eliot*, p. 187.

24 Helen Waddell, *Peter Abelard* (London: Constable, 1939), pp. 23–24. Cited in *CCW*, p. 9.

25 For *'pondus'*, see *SC* 1. 6, p. 423; 1. 14, p. 427; 1. 17, p. 429.

26 See also *OB* XVI, p. 850: 'Pound attained his rôle as the grillo's compère'.

27 As with 'even', discussed in the second chapter, the entry for 'nice, *adj.* and *adv.*' in the third, online edition is completely revised; but Hill knew the second edition, for which the entry quoted can be found here: www.oed.com/oed2/00157740. Of sense 15, the second edition also notes that in this use *nice* is 'freq. somewhat derisive [...] the precise signification varying to some extent with the nature of the substantive qualified by it'.

28 Barbara Herrnstein Smith, *Poetic Closure: A Study of How Poems End* (Chicago: University of Chicago Press, 1968), p. 160.

29 Ricks, 'Hill's Unrelenting, Unreconciling Mind', p. 24.

30 This sort of gesture, as Smith demonstrates with citations ranging from medieval to modern poetry, is nothing new. 'One of the most obvious ways in which a poem can indicate its own conclusion thematically', she writes, 'is simply to say so. [...] Explicit self-closural references are, in fact, only rarely encountered, but something a little different, closural *allusions*, are extremely common'. Smith, *Poetic Closure*, p. 172 (but see the whole section: pp. 172–82). Hill's work provides copious examples of both explicit references and allusions to closure (too copious to list here).

31 'The Argument of his Book', *The Complete Poetry of Robert Herrick*, ed. by Tom Cain and Ruth Connolly, 2 vols (Oxford: Oxford University Press, 2013), I, 7.

32 'A Treatise of Civil Power', *TCP* (2005), §VII. An almost identical early version of 'Harmonia Sacra' figures as §XXXVII of the same poem.

33 I am indebted here to Smith's discussion of the poem in *Poetic Closure* at pp. 108–9. At p. 109, she writes: 'Closure is also strengthened by the introduction of a new verb, *hope* (previously we had only *sing* and *write*)'. While 'hope' admittedly feels like the first new verb after the repetitions of 'sing' and 'write', the poem's speaker has also already claimed to 'have Accesse | [...] to sing of cleanly-*Wantonnesse*' in lines five and six.

34 *Poetry of Robert Herrick*, I, 28.

35 Cicero, *Orator ad M. Brutum*, 23. 78, in *Brutus. Orator*, trans. by G. L. Hendrickson and H. M. Hubbell (Cambridge, MA: Harvard University Press, 1939), p. 363. Part of a quotation from the Oxford translation (ed. by A. S. Wilkins) of the Cicero is included in the notes to 'Delight in Disorder', *Poetry of Robert Herrick*, I, 28.

36 Though civility itself can mask disorder: 'There is a claw in civility and the civil that plays the very devil' (*BBGJ* 45, p. 21).

234   *Notes*

37 The phrase 'clause upon clause' is especially significant in that *clause* is etymologically inseparable from *close*. See *OED*, 'clause, *n*.', etymology. Each clause is a little closure. See W. K. Wimsatt, *The Verbal Icon: Studies in the Meaning of Poetry* (Lexington, KY: University of Kentucky Press, 1954), p. 45: 'Beginnings and middles can be "ends" too, when they are breaking points of rhythm and syntax.'

38 McDonald, '"But to my Task": Work, Truth, and Metre in Later Hill', p. 149.

39 See also Adorno on the just dispensation of punctuation marks. Theodor W. Adorno, 'Punctuation Marks', trans. by Shierry Weber Nicholsen, *The Antioch Review*, 48.3 (1990), 300–5 (p. 305): 'In every act of punctuation [...] one can sense the difference between a subjective will that brutally demolishes the rules and a tactful sensitivity that allows the rules to echo in the background even where it suspends them.'

40 Poems from *Odi Barbare* published in various journals and magazines between 2009 and 2012, as well as in the 2012 Clutag edition, poems which will be discussed later in this chapter, exhibit systems of unusual and sparse punctuation not replicated in the collection as it appears in *Broken Hierarchies* (2013).

41 The three poems without any punctuation are 'Ritornelli', 'Cycle', and 'Psalms of Assize', pp. 178, 206–7, 223–29. The six others without a full stop are 'That Man as a Rational Animal Desires the Knowledge Which Is His Perfection', 'Of Coming Into Being and Passing Away', 'De Anima', 'Whether the Virtues are Emotions', 'Whether Moral Virtue Comes by Habituation', and 'Of Constancy and Measure', pp. 172, 174, 175, 176, 177, 231.

42 'Te Lucis Ante Terminum', the second of 'Two Chorale-Preludes' (*T*, p. 132), as it was first published, in *Stand*, 15/2 (1974), p. 6, where it was titled 'Poem', had no punctuation (unless one counts the three hyphens; a footnote in Ricks's essay 'Geoffrey Hill 2: At-one-ment', in *The Force of Poetry*, p. 341, n. 45, alerted me to the early version of the poem).

43 See Ricks, *The Force of Poetry*, pp. 285–355; 'Hill's Unrelenting, Unreconciling Mind'.

44 *GHC*, pp. 43–60 (p. 60).

45 See *TT* 95, pp. 935–36.

46 Leonard B. Meyer, 'The End of the Renaissance? Notes on the Radical Empiricism of the Avant-garde', *The Hudson Review*, 16 (1963), 169–85 (p. 173). Cited in Smith, *Poetic Closure*, p. 238.

47 See, e.g., *MH* XI, p. 93; 'Terribilis Est Locus Iste', *T*, p. 134; *SS* 57, p. 317; 83, p. 330; 102, p. 339; *OS* X, p. 360; XXXIII, p. 383; *SC* 1. 5, p. 423; 2. 34, p. 447; *P* 2, p. 524; 'A Précis or Memorandum of Civil Power', §V, *TCP*, p. 583; 'The Peacock at Alderton', *TCP*, p. 587; 'Coda', §5, *TCP*, p. 600; *L* 62, p. 622; *EV* 6, p. 634; 11, p. 639; 34, p. 662; 43, p. 671; 46, p. 674; *LIV* XXXVII, p. 721; *OB* IX, p. 843; *TT* 39, p. 905; *BBGJ* 70, p. 32; 265, p. 142.

48 Sperling cites both 'De Anima' and 'God's Little Mountain' in the section on angels in *Visionary Philology*, p. 167. He goes on to discuss the provenance of the phrase 'research into angelic song', quoting a poem drafted (on 24 July 1966) in one of Hill's notebooks, entitled 'Fauxbordon on a C15th Carol' (pp. 168–69).

Notes 235

See also the fourth chapter ('God's Little Mountains: Young Geoffrey Hill and the Problem of Religious Poetry') of Hart, *Poetry and Revelation*, pp. 63–76.

49 Poem 269, *The Poems of Emily Dickinson: Variorum Edition*, ed. by R. W. Franklin, 3 vols (Cambridge, MA: The Belknap Press of Harvard University Press, 1998), I, 288.

50 The word appears again in *The Book of Baruch*, this time italicised: 'Seventeenth-century statesmen's obituaries are copiously tendentious even when they cite Grotius. | You'll say I am ungenerous to a necessary national *sagesse* of that time and place' (*BBGJ* 236, p. 127).

51 See *OED*, 'array, *v.*', etymology, and 'syntax', etymology.

52 See *TL* XXIII, p. 245; XXVI (twice), pp. 246–47; LXXXIX, p. 265; CXLII, p. 283.

53 Don Paterson, *The Book of Shadows* (London: Picador, 2004), p. 184.

54 'Swift's Epitaph', *The Collected Poems of W. B. Yeats*, ed. by Richard J. Finneran (New York: Macmillan, 1996), p. 245. The phrase 'Savage indignation' translates Swift's own Latin, '*saeva indignatio*'; see Hill, *Canaan* (London: Penguin, 1996), p. 76.

55 The notion of an unrinsed cliché comes from Hill's essay on Ben Jonson, in *CCW*, pp. 48–49.

56 Sherry, *The Uncommon Tongue*, p. 66.

57 Geoffrey Hill, 'Four Poems', *Paris Review*, 21 (1959), 98–100.

58 Geoffrey Hill, *For the Unfallen* (London: André Deutsch, 1959), p. 32.

59 Geoffrey Hill, *Selected Poems* (New Haven, CT: Yale University Press, 2009), p. 11. This is the American edition of the Penguin *Selected Poems* (2006).

60 Ricks, 'Geoffrey Hill 1: "The Tongue's Atrocities"', in *The Force of Poetry*, pp. 292–93.

61 'Sufficient' foreshadows another elegy for a victim of Nazi Germany in 'September Song', from Hill's second collection (*KL*, p. 44): 'As estimated, you died. Things marched, | sufficient, to that end.'

62 'Ode on a Grecian Urn', *Keats: Poetical Works*, ed. by H. W. Garrod (London: Oxford University Press, 1966), pp. 209–10. Exodus 12.7: 'And they shall take of the blood and strike it on the two side postes, and on the vpper doore poste, of the houses wherein they shall eate [the lamb]'. Knottenbelt notes the line's remembrance of Keats in *Passionate Intelligence*, p. 34.

63 Poems from *Odi Barbare* were published in the following: 'Excerpts from a Work in Progress: 6, 12, 18, and 34', *Keble College: The Record 2009* (2009), pp. 52–54 [*OB* VI, XII, XVIII, XXXIV]; 'Excerpts from a Work in Progress: III, IV, V', *Iowa Review*, 40 (2010), 191–93; 'From "Odi Barbare"', *Poetry*, 196 (2010), 410–13 [*OB* XXIV, XXV, XXVI, XXVII]; 'New Poems', *Standpoint*, 24 (2010), pp. 88–91 [along with 'Sei Madrigali' (*TT* 88 (a)–88 (f)) and 'Hiraeth' (*O* 119–24; 144), *OB* I, II, XXIX, XLVII, XLVIII]; 'From "Odi Barbare", XXI–XXIII', *GHC* (2011), pp. 227–29; 'From "The Day Books" IV: ODI BARBARE', *Archipelago*, 6 (2011), 1–5 [*OB* XL, XLI, XLII, XLIII]; 'From "Odi Barbare": VII, VIII, IX', *Christianity and Literature*, 60 (2011), 402–4; 'From "Odi Barbare": XVI and XVII', *The New Criterion*, 30.1 (2011), 81–83;

'From "Odi Barbare"', *The Baffler*, 19 (2012), 21 [*OB* XIII]; *Odi Barbare* (Thame: Clutag Press, 2012).

64 There are other moments in the later work that express this desire to 'let what is | speak for itself'. Perhaps the most striking example is at the end of *BBGJ* 48, p. 22, quoted in part earlier: 'Desire to have things merely be as they are. To say nothing. Insidiousness of metaphor; perception not set free with its remarkable power to see; the unreachable itch in the brain to snatch metaphysical spoil for gain. | The lure of conclusion with no notion where to begin.'

See also *OS* XXIII, p. 373: 'Last days, last things, loom on: I write | to astonish myself. So much for all | plain speaking. Enter | sign under *signum*, I should be so lucky; | false cadence but an ending. Not there yet.' Again, here, the thought of speaking plainly (and consummately) coincides with the thought of ending, of a task finally accomplished.

65 Geoffrey Hill, 'New Poems', *Standpoint*, 24 (2010), p. 91.

66 Stendhal, *Love*, trans. by Gilbert and Suzanne Sale (London: Penguin, 1975), p. 45.

67 Changing, in *Broken Hierarchies*, 'scramble' to 'scamble' might seem counter to a pursuit of 'plain speaking', especially when one considers that of the seven main senses of *scamble* described in the *OED*, only one, the last, is not marked as obsolete or a dialect word. The last use of the word quoted is in 1901 (under sense 4a: 'To make one's way as best one can'). There is also in the *OED*, among this word's 'Derivatives', a quotation from Ruskin's *Praeterita*: 'He went scamble-shambling on, a plague to the end.'

68 Nicholas Lezard, 'A growl in his voice, a twinkle in his eye', *The Independent*, 6 February 2005, www.independent.co.uk/arts-entertainment/books/features/a-growl-in-his-voice-a-twinkle-in-his-eye-758572.html.

69 Geoffrey Hill, in *Don't Ask Me What I Mean: Poets in their Own Words*, ed. by Clare Brown and Don Paterson (London: Picador, 2003), p. 116. On this, Hassan comments (*Annotations*, p. 3): 'Hill may be referring to silent reading; at a 2006 recital, he read stanzas 15, 20 and 88 at a steady pace'. At the Serpentine Galleries' Poetry Marathon in 2009, Hill read poems 92, 93, 94, 96, 114, 115, and 116, also at a steady pace, which strengthens Hassan's conjecture (www.youtube.com/watch?v=SiuMKASXJLU).

70 Hill, 'How ill white hairs'.

71 Geoffrey Hill, 'From "Odi Barbare"', *The Baffler*, 19 (2012), 21.

72 The first of the stanzas quoted above, which begins 'Herod rants', and mentions 'pageants' in an allusion to Medieval dramatic portrayals of the Slaughter of the Holy Innocents, suggests another similarity between *Speech! Speech!* and *Odi Barbare*, since in the former collection there is a like reference: 'Like Herod | raging in the street-pageants, work the crowd' (*SS* 94, p. 335).

73 Hill, in *Don't Ask Me What I Mean*, p. 117. Hill's disapprobation of the notion of poetic accessibility is well documented, so that two examples from the poetry should suffice: 'Take accessible to mean | acceptable, accommodating, openly servile' (*TL* XL, p. 250); 'ACCESSIBLE | traded as DEMOCRATIC' (*SS* 118, p. 347).

Notes

237

74 Matthew Arnold, 'Preface', *Poems*, pp. xxiii–xxiv. Cited in Anthony Hecht, *Melodies Unheard: Essays on the Mysteries of Poetry* (Baltimore, MD: Johns Hopkins University Press, 2003), pp. 285–86.

75 Arnold, 'Preface', p. xxx.

76 Hill, reading on 28 April 2016.

77 William Empson, 'Let It Go', *The Complete Poems* (London: Penguin, 2001), p. 99. Hill comments on the poem in his review of Empson's poetry, 'The Dream of Reason', *Essays in Criticism*, 14 (1964), 91–101 (pp. 95–96). He also quotes Empson's poem 'Courage Means Running' (*The Complete Poems*, pp. 76–77) as the conclusion of the first of his collected essays (*CCW*, p. 20).

78 See, e.g., Empson, 'Preface to the Second Edition', *Seven Types of Ambiguity*, p. xv: '[I]s all good poetry supposed to be ambiguous? I think that it is'; and *Seven Types of Ambiguity*, p. 3: 'the machinations of ambiguity are among the very roots of poetry'.

79 For Hill's warning that 'tyranny requires simplification', see Phillips, 'The Art of Poetry LXXX', p. 275.

80 Cf. *OB XXXIII*, p. 867: 'There are brief seasons to have things eternal; | Death your mentor.'

81 See *OED*, 'press, *v.*', senses 8a, 8c: '*to press on regardless: colloquial* (originally *Military slang*) to persevere despite dangers or difficulties' (8c).

82 This '[a]damantine age' seems to be prompted by the 'adamantine tendernesses' of G. K. Chesterton. Hill quotes Chesterton's phrase in the essay 'Gurney's Hobby' (*CCW*, p. 446).

Chapter 5

1 The conversation marked the opening of a two-day conference at Keble College, Oxford, entitled 'Geoffrey Hill and his Contexts', which took place in early July 2008. Cited in 'Introduction', *GHC*, pp. 1–2. Italics for emphasis and for familiar phrases from French have been removed from the original quotation, and in a few places punctuation has been amended.

2 It may also be notable that, regarding Hill's dislike of 'pensées' and their supposed proliferation in *Four Quartets*, Hill's archives include an early handwritten document entitled 'Pensées', in which Hill reflects on the initial critical reception of his work, and which also involves a number of salient comments about his ideas of form and finishedness: 'it is only by a long and arduous process of fashioning that I am able to justify the final poem in my own eyes […]. But I [line scored out] cannot believe that form, seen as an end in itself, can have any positive value. I cannot consider a poem great solely because of its exquisite use of sibilant or judicious ringing-of-changes in vowel sounds. Thought […] must be in the poem. […] [I]f the imagery is conceived with sincere artistry, the poem will be good + true' ('Letter from Oxford / Pensées', BC MS 20c Hill/4/1).

3 Richard Eberhart, '"Where are those high and haunting skies"', *Collected Poems 1930–1976* (London: Chatto and Windus, 1976), p. 17.

Notes

4 As with Hill's rhymes, one may trace here a meeting of the impossible and the inevitable. What happens in the poem 'ideally' is a divine irruption ('epiphany', 'annunciation'), which is beyond the poet's power of manufacture; and yet it is something that the poem 'had inevitably to arrive at'.

5 Hill refers to his 'subterranean' readership in an interview by Alexandra Bell, Rebecca Rosen, and Edmund White, 'Strongholds of the Imagination', *The Oxonian Review*, 9.4 (2009): 'When I see my half-yearly royalties statements I seem not to have a readership at all. [...] There are obviously devoted readers, but it's all rather subterranean, a bit like wartime resistance.' The other quotations are from Hill, reading on 28 April 2016.

6 Hill, reading on 28 April 2016.

7 Hill, reading on 28 April 2016. The ellipsis denotes the pause in Hill's incomplete sentence, and not omitted text. Hill's solecistic use of the reflexive pronoun ('how the poem could have satisfied myself') implies his deep, grammatical identification of himself with his poem.

8 Hill, reading on 28 April 2016. I present the parenthetical 'finessed' with question and exclamation marks to suggest the 'voice of the antiphonal heckler' that Hill adopted here, as elsewhere in the reading; he said the word *sotto voce* and with feigned incredulity. The word 'finesse' and its relatives begin to appear only in Hill's late poetry; see *HOLC* 10, p. 162; *P* 29, p. 551; *EV* 7, p. 635; *LIV* XXVIII, p. 712; *Cl.* 38, p. 828; *OB* X, p. 844; *OB* XXI, p. 855. In Hill's critical prose the word appears from the earliest to the latest essays; see *CCW*, pp. 157, 204, 211, 286, 356, 363, 495, 512, 544.

9 See *OED*, 'finesse, *v.*', sense 2a; 'finesse, *n.*', esp. etymology; 'fine, *adj.*, *adv.*, and *n.2*', etymology ('the semantic development was probably from 'furthermost, extreme' [...] to 'complete' and 'best'); 'fine, *n.1*', sense 1a: 'A cessation, termination, end, or conclusion of something'.

10 Philip Sidney, *An Apologie for Poetrie* (Cambridge: Cambridge University Press, 1891), p. 58. (This sentence is not included in the 1595 edition.)

11 Smith, *Poetic Closure*, p. 4.

12 See *Princeton Encyclopedia*, 'Genre', p. 551: 'Writers' tendencies and readers' expectations regarding the identifying features of a particular genre [...] are highly variable [...]. Genres insist on horizons of meaning and expectations, but they also give rise, through each act of reading, to dialectics and questions. [...] The modern aestheticization of the sapphic fragment as "lyric," for instance, has its origins in the ancient reification of the emotional timbre of the poet Sappho's voice.' (Abbreviations are expanded and references omitted in this quotation.)

13 'Form [...] manifests its presence in local details connected with such matters as prosody, image, diction and allusion, and it also reveals itself in the poem's relationship to genre. [...] *Genre* refers to the poem's type or kind, whether it can be classified as a lyric or epic, for example; genres compose forms that prompt, inhere in and enable further works. Hence our decision to include genres in a discussion of form and under the rubric of form.' Michael D. Hurley and Michael O'Neill, 'Introduction', in *Poetic Form: An Introduction* (Cambridge: Cambridge University Press, 2012), p. 2.

Notes 239

14 Tate's poem is central to Hill's poetic development. See Hill, 'Acceptance Speech', p. 75.

15 Hill, 'A deep dynastic wound'.

16 James, *Shades of Authority*, pp. 106–26.

17 In the thirty-five pages of *For the Unfallen*, there are thirty-three occurrences of the word 'dead' and its conjugates (i.e., 'death', 'deaths', 'die', 'died', 'dies', 'dying'). In the sixty pages of *Lord Weary's Castle*, there are sixty-one occurrences.

18 *KL*, p. 39. Robert Lowell, 'New Year's Day', 'France' (from *Lord Weary's Castle* [1946]), in *Collected Poems* (London: Faber and Faber, 2003), pp. 13, 42. Unless stated otherwise, subsequent citations of Lowell's poetic works refer to *Collected Poems*.

19 This is noted by Karl O'Hanlon in '"A final clarifying": Form, Error, and Alchemy in Geoffrey Hill's "Ludo" and "The Daybooks"', *Études anglaises*, 71.2 (2018), 207–21 (p. 207).

20 See the 'Note' in Robert Lowell, *History* (London: Faber and Faber, 1973), p. 9; see also Robert B. Shaw, 'Lowell in the Seventies', *Contemporary Literature*, 23 (1982), 515–27 (p. 515).

21 Ricks, *True Friendship*, p. 160.

22 The end-rhymes in Lowell's group of eight sonnets entitled 'Eighteen-Seventy' (pp. 264–68), all translation–versions of Rimbaud, are largely irregular; there are many unrhymed lines. The fourth, 'On the Road' (pp. 265–66), has no rhyming lines. The seventh and eighth (pp. 267–68) rhyme throughout. The sonnets 'Helen' and 'The Cadet Picture of My Father' (pp. 272, 275), after Valéry and Rilke respectively, also feature several unrhymed lines.

23 T. S. Eliot, 'Milton II', *On Poetry and Poets* (London: Faber and Faber, 1957), p. 158. Cited in Ricks, *True Friendship*, p. 161.

24 In its initial publication, the poem had only thirteen lines. See Robert Lowell, *The Dolphin* (London: Faber and Faber, 1973), p. 15.

25 Geoffrey Hill, reading at Emmanuel College, 28 April 2016.

26 Eliot, 'Milton II', pp. 158–59.

27 Lowell, *The Dolphin*, p. 15.

28 John Lennard, *The Poetry Handbook*, 2nd edn (Oxford: Oxford University Press, 2006), p. 134.

29 Regarding these 'bright trouvailles': Hill too puts faith in lucky finds and wishes not to lose them. *OB* XX (p. 854): 'Diligence too might be a shade alarmist | Exorcising trouvailles'.

30 Geoffrey Hill, 'A Treatise of Civil Power', *TCP* (2005), §XVI.

31 Geoffrey Hill, 'Robert Lowell: "Contrasts and Repetitions"', *Essays in Criticism*, 13 (1963), 188–97 (pp. 197, 188).

32 In the first published edition of *Clavics* (London: Enitharmon Press, 2011), there is another end-laden reference to Lowell, at the beginning of the twenty-ninth poem: '*To speak of woe that is in marriage* – Cal | Lowell after the Wife of Bath. Last chance' (p. 39).

240   *Notes*

33 Robert Lowell, 'After Enjoying Six or Seven Essays on Me', *Salmagundi*, 37 (1977), 112–15 (p. 113): 'Looking over my *Selected Poems*, about thirty years of writing, my impression is that the thread that strings it together is my autobiography, it is a small-scale *Prelude*, written in many different styles and with digressions, yet a continuing story – still wayfaring.'

34 Hill, *King Log* (1968), p. 68.

35 These are: 'That Man as a Rational Animal Desires the Knowledge Which Is His Perfection', p. 172; 'Mysticism and Democracy' ('You see the terrain'), p. 183; 'To the Nieuport Scout', p. 195; 'Parentalia' ('The here-and-now finds vigil'), p. 196; the eight parts of 'De Jure Belli ac Pacis', pp. 198–205; the fifth part of 'Cycle', pp. 206–7 (p. 207); 'Parentalia' ('Go your ways'), p. 209; 'Mysticism and Democracy' ('To the Evangelicals'); 'Pisgah', p. 217; the first part of 'Mysticism and Democracy' ('Ill-conceived, ill-ordained'), p. 220 (the second part has thirteen lines); 'Of Constancy and Measure', p. 231; 'Concerning Inheritance', p. 233; and 'Mysticism and Democracy' ('Great gifts foreclosed on'), p. 234.

36 In 'Notebook 38: Canaan', BC MS 20c Hill/2/1/38, p. 190, a draft of 'Parentalia' ('The here-and-now finds vigil') includes the epiphanic marginal note: 'MAKES 14!' See also p. 12 of the same notebook.

37 There are unrhymed fourteen-line poems in five of Hill's collections other than *Canaan*. I include here the versets of *Mercian Hymns* and the free-verse lyrics of *The Triumph of Love*. In the former the fourteen-line poems could not reasonably be called unrhymed sonnets; but the notebooks for *The Triumph of Love* give clear evidence of intention to write unrhymed fourteen-line poems or sections. See 'Notebook 43: The Triumph of Love', BC MS 20c Hill/2/1/43, fols 18^v–19^r, 21^v, 61^v; and 'Notebook 45', fols 32^v, 34^r, 38^v–39^r, 45^v. In *King Log*, excluding 'Funeral Music', the unrhymed fourteen-line poems are: the second part of 'Annunciations', p. 40; 'September Song', p. 44; and 'Cowan Bridge', p. 64. In *Mercian Hymns*, they are: VI, p. 88; X, p. 92; XII, p. 94; and XVI, p. 98. In *The Triumph of Love*, they are: X, pp. 240–41; XVII, p. 243; XXIV, pp. 245–46; LXXXIII, p. 263; LXXXIV, p. 263; LXXXV, pp. 263–64; CII, p. 268; CIII, pp. 268–69; CXV, p. 273; and CXVII, p. 274. In *Without Title*, they are: 'Without Title', p. 484; 'Chromatic Tunes', p. 485; the six parts of 'On the Reality of the Symbol' (pp. 488–90); the three parts of 'Discourse: For Stanley Rosen', pp. 499–500; the fourth part of 'Improvisations for Jimi Hendrix', pp. 502–3 (p. 503); 'Ex Propertio', p. 506; 'On the Sophoclean Moment in English Poetry', p. 508; and the three parts of 'Improvisations for Hart Crane', pp. 512–13. In *A Treatise of Civil Power*, they are: the two parts of 'Holbein', p. 565; 'Masques', p. 567; the four parts of 'To the Lord Protector Cromwell', pp. 571–74; and 'On Looking Through *50 Jahre im Bild: Bundesrepublik Deutschland*', p. 580. I exclude the fourteen-line poems in *Ludo* (14, p. 608; and 25, p. 612) because, although metrically and otherwise they are nowhere near conventional sonnets, they have rhyme schemes.

38 Sherry, *The Uncommon Tongue*, p. 91.

39 Sherry, *The Uncommon Tongue*, p. 91.

Notes

241

40 James notes that the ends of both this fourth sonnet and the seventh sonnet, with its 'carrion birds', owe something to Lowell's (rhymed) sonnet 'Napoleon Crosses the Berezina' (*Lord Weary's Castle*, p. 37), which ends: 'the snow | Blazes its carrion-miles to Purgatory'. See James, *Shades of Authority*, pp. 113–14.

41 Sherry, *The Uncommon Tongue*, p. 96.

42 Frank Kermode, *The Sense of an Ending: Studies in the Theory of Fiction* (New York: Oxford University Press, 1967), p. 25.

43 'Notebook 6', p. 9. The words in italic and scorings out are manuscript additions.

44 Žirmunskij, Рифма, Её история и теория, p. 9.

45 Auden's comment comes to mind: 'On revisions as a matter of principle, I agree with Valery: "A poem is never finished; it is only abandoned"' (W. H. Auden, 'Foreword', *Collected Shorter Poems 1927–1957* (London: Faber and Faber, 1966), p. 16). In this sonnet, the poem may be said to end by abandoning itself.

46 See Smith, *Poetic Closure*, p. 160.

47 Hill uses the phrase 'real cries' again in the concluding eighth part of 'Tenebrae', in *Tenebrae*, p. 140: 'Music survives, [...] Queen of the Air, | and when we would accost her with real cries | silver on silver thrills itself to ice.'

48 Letter to Frank Bidart, 4 September 1976, in *The Letters of Robert Lowell*, ed. by Saskia Hamilton (New York: Farrar, Straus, and Giroux, 2005), p. 656.

49 In the quotation one may detect an echo of Lowell's sonnet 'War', in *Lord Weary's Castle*, p. 39: 'Dead to the world, until their mother, fat | With weeping'.

50 Lowell, 'History', *History*, p. 421.

51 'From a train, we saw cows [...] They fly by like a train window: | flash-in-the-pan moments | of the Great Day, | the *dies illa*'. The Latin is a quote from the Sequence of the Requiem Mass, the *Dies irae* ('Day of wrath'), which considers the final day of creation.

52 Dionysius of Halicarnassus, *On Literary Composition*, in *Critical Essays, Volume II: On Literary Composition. Dinarchus. Letters to Ammaeus and Pompeius*, trans. by Stephen Usher (Cambridge, MA: Harvard University Press, 1985), pp. 208–9.

53 Haffenden, *Viewpoints*, p. 93.

54 'Notebook 13', fol. 5^r. The poem is incomplete here but Hill's marginal numbering of fourteen lines on fol. 9^r demonstrates that he had the sonnet in mind.

55 'Notebook 13', fol. 50^{r-v}. The words '[gone over]' here constitute a guess; I cannot decipher for certain what Hill has actually written.

56 *OED*, 'verset', senses 1, 2; 'versicle', sense 1a.

57 Hill also refers to *The Book of Baruch*'s versets as hymns: 'Each late hymn a form of votive offering to establish an uncertain claim' (*BBGJ* 113, p. 58).

58 Knottenbelt, *Passionate Intelligence*, p. 173.

59 *CP* (1985), pp. 201–2. These notes to *Mercian Hymns* are not reproduced in *Broken Hierarchies*.

242 *Notes*

60 Frederick Brittain, 'Introduction', *The Penguin Book of Latin Verse*, ed. by Frederick Brittain (Harmondsworth: Penguin, 1962), p. lv.

61 Brittain, 'Introduction', p. liv.

62 See Chapter 2, n. 5, above.

63 Roots, as in some sense beginnings, are inextricably tied up with endings elsewhere in Hill's work. The final lines of 'Insert Here' might be helpfully inserted here: 'Let me be, says the dying man, let me fall | upward towards my roots' (*WT*, p. 491).

64 With regard to the consequences of mass immigration into Britain, Powell said, on 20 April 1968, in Birmingham, by then the major city of Offa's and Hill's region: 'Like the Roman, I seem to see "the River Tiber foaming with much blood"' (Enoch Powell, *Reflections: Selected Writings and Speeches of Enoch Powell*, ed. by Rex Collings (London: Bellew, 1992), p. 168). In Virgil's *Aeneid*, the 'Roman' is in fact the Sibyl prophesying: 'bella, horrida bella | et Thybrim multo spumantem sanguine cerno' ('Wars, grim wars I see, and the Tiber foaming with streams of blood'; *Aeneid*, 6.86–87, in Virgil, *Eclogues. Georgics. Aeneid, Books 1–6*, trans. by H. R. Fairclough, rev. by G. P. Goold (Cambridge, MA: Harvard University Press, 1916), pp. 538–39). Hill's allusion to the same passage takes the form of a fragmented sentence that concludes the eighteenth hymn (p. 100): 'To watch the Tiber foaming out much blood'.

65 'Notebook 11', fol. 57^r. The article, by Robert Jackson, is titled 'Enoch Powell: Paradox of politics and poetry', *The Times*, 24 April 1969, p. 11.

66 Hill, 'The Pentecost Castle', §11, *CP* (1985), p. 142.

67 Thomas Day, 'Variant Editions of Geoffrey Hill's "Mercian Hymns"', *PN Review*, 202 (2011), www.pnreview.co.uk/cgi-bin/scribe?item_id=8399.

68 'Notebook 11', fol. 62^r. The two marks above 'FINIS' in the notebook are more elongated than those preceding them.

69 See Hill's notes for the eleventh and thirteenth hymns, *CP* (1985), p. 202.

70 Cf. the possessiveness (and perhaps the obscured autobiography) in both the first epigraph of 'The Pentecost Castle', from Yeats: 'It is terrible to desire and not possess, and terrible to possess and not desire'; and §12 of the same poem: 'each of us dispossessed [...] crying like one possessed' (*T*, pp. 115, 119).

71 'Tom Vaughan an alchemist of the Cross' (*Cl.* 27, p. 817). See also *O* 45: *i. m. R. Williams Parry*, p. 755: 'Yes, we are done; and the great stone threatens'.

72 *CP* (1985), p. 203. 'Notebook 10: Mercian Hymns', BC MS 20c Hill/2/1/10, fol. 2^v. A cutting reads: 'This year's **Bromsgrove Festival** (April 20–May 5) includes several works by Messiaen. What more appropriate way of blazoning this homage to a composer, whose music wrestles with the problems of time, than playing his "Et exspecto resurrectionem mortuorum," a fanfare to raise the dead, three week's [*sic*] earlier?'

73 Knottenbelt, *Passionate Intelligence*, p. 155.

74 'The Hollow Men', §III, *Poems of T. S. Eliot*, p. 82.

75 Donne provides an example of this understanding of the word אדם in Sermon 10, 'Preached to the Lords upon Easter-day, at the Communion, The King being then dangerously sick at New-Market (1619)', *The Oxford Edition of*

Notes 243

the Sermons of John Donne, ed. by Peter McCullough and others (Oxford: Oxford University Press, 2013–), I: *Sermons Preached at the Jacobean Courts, 1615–1619*, ed. by Peter McCullough (2015), p. 127: 'It is not *Adam*, which is another name of man, and signifies nothing but *red earth* [...]'. The Beddoes fragment is cited by his editor in *Poems by the Late Thomas Lovell Beddoes, Author of Death's Jest-book or the Fool's Tragedy, with a Memoir*, ed. by Thomas F. Kelsall (London: W. Pickering, 1851), p. xvi. For the comparison with Beddoes's line I am indebted to a comment by Rob Stanton (listed as '*RDS*'), the second on the webpage in response to an article by David-Antoine Williams, 'Muti-lation at the end of the line', *Poetry & Contingency* blog, https://poetry-contingency.uwaterloo.ca/muti-lation-at-the-end-of-the-line/.

76 The differences in line endings between the original publication in 1971 and the last in 2013 are, to the best of my detection, as follows: the fifth line of hymn III; the sixth and seventh lines of V; the third line of XIII; the ninth and twelfth lines of XIV; the fourth line of XVII; the ninth line of XXI; and the sixth and tenth lines of XXV.

77 Knottenbelt, *Passionate Intelligence*, p. 155.

78 *BH*, p. 81. C. H. Sisson, *The Avoidance of Literature*, ed. by Michael Schmidt (Manchester: Carcanet, 1978), p. 202. Hill notes (*BH*, p. 937): '(It was previously printed privately in Sisson's *Essays* of 1967.)'

79 Knottenbelt, *Passionate Intelligence*, p. 156.

80 'Rose-cheekt *Lawra*, come', the second example from the eighth chapter, on '*Ditties* or *Odes*', in *Observations in the Art of English Poesy*, in *Campion's Works*, ed. by Percival Vivian (Oxford: Oxford University Press, 1909), pp. 50–51.

81 The date is from *BH*, p. 521. In 'Pindarics', §8, *Without Title* (London: Penguin, 2006), p. 42, a poem revised out of the later version of *Pindarics*, Hill claims to have 'cribbed from much | maligned beau Allen Tate pindaric odes'. The ode particularly in question is Tate's 'Ode to the Confederate Dead', the initiator of Hill's poetic imagination (see Chapter 3, n. 19). Of that ode Tate writes: 'It is an ode only in the sense in which Cowley in the seventeenth century misunderstood the real structure of the Pindaric ode. Not only are the meter and rhyme without fixed pattern, but in another feature the poem is even further removed from Pindar than Abraham Cowley was: a purely subjective meditation would not even in Cowley's age have been called an ode' ('Narcissus as Narcissus', *Essays of Four Decades*, p. 602). See Simon Collings, 'Love and Sex in Hill's "Pindarics": Getting Personal', *PN Review*, 230 (2016), www.pnreview.co.uk/cgi-bin/scribe?item_id=9684.

82 *Poems of John Donne*, I, 44–45. See Chapter 1, n. 77.

83 The printer's ornament differs slightly between the initial publication of *Clavics* (London: Enitharmon Press, 2011), in which it is an oblong diamond with a dot in the centre, and the *Clavics* of *Broken Hierarchies* (2013), in which it is a diamond shape made up of four small black diamonds.

Among the reviewers who liken the first section to Herbert's 'The Altar' are Carole Birkan-Berz ('An Emblem of Some Consequence', *Arts of War and Peace*, 1 (2013), https://artswarandpeace.univ-paris-diderot.fr/wp-con tent/uploads/2018/12/rv_4_birkan_hill_clavics_2012.pdf); Jeffrey Hipolito ('Give Me the Key', *The Critical Flame*, http://criticalflame.org/verse/0911_ hippolito.htm); Lachlan Mackinnon ('Discords and Distractions', *The Independent*, 2 June 2011, www.independent.co.uk/arts-entertainment/ books/reviews/clavics-by-geoffrey-hill-2292235.html); and Marcus Waithe ('Dense Settling: Geoffrey Hill's "Broken Hierarchies"', *PN Review*, 219 (2014), www.pnreview.co.uk/cgi-bin/scribe?item_id=9165). Stefan Hawlin corrects these by naming 'The Morning-watch' as the true text adopted and adapted by Hill. See Hawlin, '"Grinding the Textures of Harmony": Heroic Difficulty in Geoffrey Hill's "Clavics"', *English*, 63 (2014), 313–29 (p. 314).

84 Michael Robbins, 'Three Books', *Poetry*, 199 (2011), 171–80 (p. 172).

85 Cf. *BBGJ* 14, p. 7: 'Orthodoxy to make you wince.'

86 *Clavics* (2011), 20, p. 30.

87 Hawlin ('"Grinding the Textures of Harmony"', p. 313, n. 1) erroneously notes that between the editions Hill 'has deleted two poems, added twelve new ones'. Here are the poems as numbered in the first edition of *Clavics* (2011), with, in brackets after each, the corresponding numbered poems from *Clavics* as it appears in *Broken Hierarchies*, along with other information as necessary: 1 (1); 2 (33); 3 (2); 4 (3); 5 (4); 6 (6); 7 (22); 8 (9); 9 (5); 10 (8); 11 (23); 12 (16); 13 (15); 14 (13); 15 (14); 16 (17); 17 (18); 18 (20); 19 (21); 20 (no corresponding poem; but the last five lines of the Vaughan section are used as such in 34 in *BH*); 21 (25); 22 (12); 23 (10); 24 (26); 25 (the Vaughan section, much revised and excluding the last five lines, is used in 34; the Herbert section is used in 11); 26 (28); 27 (27); 28 (29); 29 (no corresponding Vaughan section; the Herbert section is used in 24); 30 (no corresponding poem); 31 (30); 32 (42). The clavics exclusive to *Broken Hierarchies* are: 7; 11 (Vaughan section); 19; 24 (Vaughan section); 31; 32; 34 (Vaughan section, except the last five lines); 35–41.

88 The prochronistic *OED* entry reads: 'CLAVICS: The science or alchemy of keys – *OED*, 2012'. The first epigraph, 'Be very var vith his raklese toyis of Padoa', is from a letter by Robert Logan of Restalrig, a conspirator to abduct James VI of Scotland, an abduction that might have prevented the uniting of the crowns (see, e.g., Alexander Allan Carr, *A History of Coldingham Priory* (Edinburgh: Adam and Charles Black, 1836), p. 203). The second epigraph, '*Ah! taci ingiusto core*' (Ah! be quiet, unjust heart), is the first line of a trio in Mozart's *Don Giovanni*. The drawing is Robert Webb's, after a design by Inigo Jones for Whitehall Palace. The intaglio, marked '*Clausula*.' above and 'The Close.' below, is from the facsimile edition of Comenius's 1659 children's textbook, *Orbis Pictus* (Oxford: Oxford University Press, 1968).

89 See the *Oxford Dictionary of National Biography* entries for the four men (www. oxforddnb.com); see also Hawlin, '"Grinding the Textures of Harmony"', p. 316.

90 Waithe, 'Dense Settling' (para. 18 of 21).

91 'Prayer (I)', *Works of George Herbert*, p. 51.

92 'The Morning-watch', *The Works of Henry Vaughan*, ed. by L. C. Martin, 2nd edn (Oxford: Oxford University Press, 1957), pp. 424–25. The comparison

Notes 245

with Herbert's 'Prayer (I)' is made in *Henry Vaughan: The Complete Poems*, ed. by Alan Rudrum (Harmondsworth: Penguin, 1976), p. 552. Rudrum's notes also quote E. C. Pettet on the poem: 'On paper it may appear rather formal in its patterning of long and short lines' (E. C. Pettet, *Of Paradise and Light: A Study of Vaughan's 'Silex Scintillans'* (Cambridge: Cambridge University Press, 1960), p. 126). As with Hill, one may suggest that the importance of form is more than an appearance.

93 *CCW*, p. 563.

94 '"Instauratio magna" preliminaries', in *The Oxford Francis Bacon*, ed. by Brian Vickers and others (Oxford: Oxford University Press, 1996–), xi: *The Instaurare magna Part II: Novum Organum and Associated Texts*, ed. by Graham Rees and Maria Wakely (2004), p. 2; see pp. 2–47 for Bacon's fully written vision for and plan of the work. Hill refers to the same work earlier: 'We cannot | have some great instauration occurring | by default, can we?' (*TL* CXVII, p. 274).

95 The quoted phrase is from Ephesians 1.10: 'That in the dispensation of the fulnesse of times, he might gather together in one all things in Christ'. In the Libreria Editrice Vaticana's translation of Pope Pius X's encyclical *E supremi*, the phrase is rendered 'to restore all things in Christ' (www.vatican.va/content/pius-x/en/encyclicals/documents/hf_p-x_enc_04101903_e-supremi.html). The phrase was Pius X's motto.

96 Christopher Middleton, in interview with Marius Kociejowski, *Palavers, and A Nocturnal Journal* (Exeter: Shearsman, 2004), p. 88.

97 'Easter-wings', *Works of George Herbert*, p. 43.

98 George Puttenham, *The arte of English poesie* (London: Richard Field, 1589), pp. 76, 78.

99 *OED*, 'skald | scald': 'An ancient Scandinavian poet. Also sometimes in general use, a poet.' The dictionary cites Thomas Percy's *Five Pieces of Runic Poetry from the Icelandic Language*: 'It was the constant study of the northern Scalds to lift their poetic style as much as possible above that of their prose'; and also the 1830 edition of Walter Scott's *Ivanhoe*: 'It will readily occur to the antiquary, that these verses are intended to imitate the antique poetry of the Scalds'. Hill's use of the word connotes suspicion of his own high-minded antiquarianism in using the seventeenth-century forms of *Clavics*.

100 *OED*, 'explode', etymology: 'classical Latin *explōdere*, variant of *explaudere* to drive out by clapping, hiss (a player) off the stage'.

101 To return to a discussion in the first chapter, Hill's question here indicates an answer to one sense of another question, the final line of the seventy-second poem of *Oraclau | Oracles* (p. 764): 'Whose is the spirit moving that dead thing?' The dead thing is the old form: as it happens, Donne's. The spirit, too, may be his; or Hill's.

102 *Poetry of Robert Herrick*, i, 80. For the Lawes setting, consult, e.g., the recording *Songs by Henry & William Lawes* (Hyperion, CDA67589, 2007).

103 Hill observes Marvell gathering time in a more aggressive fashion: 'In October 1666 [Marvell] writes to the Mayor of Hull "really busynesse dos so multiply

246   *Notes*

of late that I can scarce snatch time to write to you". Barely adumbrated in this hasty phrase is that Horatian theme which Marvell, a poet acutely aware of the perils and ecstasies of "snatching time", had found so appealing' (*CCW*, p. 204). Cited in Hawlin, '"Grinding the Textures of Harmony"', p. 327.

104 The Herbert sections that do not have the particular symmetrical rhyme scheme ABCDEEDCBA are: 1–4, pp. 791–94; 6, p. 796; 9, p. 799; 11, p. 801; 16–17, pp. 806–07; 22, p. 812; 28, p. 818; 33, p. 823. This means that thirty of the forty-two Herbert sections have the rhyme scheme above.

105 Joseph Haydn, *The Creation* (London: Novello, Ewer & Co., 1859), pp. ii, 11–12.

106 *Clavics* (2011), 30, p. 40. It is the antepenultimate poem in this edition.

107 *OED*, 'concent, *n.*' ('Now *rare*'), sense 1: 'Harmony of sounds; accord or concord of several voices or parts'. Puttenham's *Arte of English poesie* (p. 53) is cited: 'The harmonicall concents of the artificial Musicke'.

108 Philip Sidney, 'Cleophila', the twelfth of the First Eclogues of *The Countess of Pembroke's Arcadia (The Old Arcadia)*, in *The Poems of Sir Philip Sidney*, ed. by William A. Ringler, Jr (Oxford: Oxford University Press, 1962), pp. 30–31.

109 Gavin Alexander, 'Lyric Poetics?', lecture at Trinity College, Cambridge, 7 March 2017.

110 Demetrius, *On Style*, 140–48, in Aristotle, Longinus, and Demetrius, *Poetics. Longinus: On the Sublime. Demetrius: On Style*, trans. by Stephen Halliwell, W. Hamilton Fyfe, Doreen C. Innes, and W. Rhys Roberts, rev. by Donald A. Russell (Cambridge, MA: Harvard University Press, 1995), pp. 433–39.

111 Middleton, *Palavers*, p. 95.

112 Marius Kociejowski, '"I think you will have the kippers": Memories of Geoffrey Hill', *Stand*, 214 (2017), 45–49 (p. 48). Kociejowski and Middleton are the two dedicatees of *Odi Barbare*.

113 Hill, reading at Emmanuel College, 28 April 2016. See also *OB I*, p. 835: 'Measure loss re-cadencing Sidney's sapphics | Not as words fall but as they rise to meaning'.

114 See also the quasi-sapphic stanza that begins 'Epiphany at Hurcott' (*WT*, p. 497): 'Profoundly silent January shows up | clamant with colour, greening in fine rain, | luminous malachite of twig-thicket and bole | brightest at sundown'.

115 See Hassan, *Annotations*, p. 249.

116 The English translation of the title comes from Horace, *Odes and Epodes*, ed. and trans. by Niall Rudd (Cambridge, MA: Harvard University Press, 2004).

117 *OS XLI*, p. 391: 'This should be called *The Second Book* or *Book | of Stone* maybe, or *Tristia*, or | *You, Mandelstam*'.

118 Kenneth Haynes, the editor of Hill's *Collected Critical Writings*, *Broken Hierarchies*, and *The Book of Baruch by the Gnostic Justin*, uses the word 'adonic' to describe the last line in Hill's sapphic stanza in '"Faith" and "Fable" in the Poetry of Geoffrey Hill', *Christianity and Literature*, 60 (2011), 398–401 (p. 401).

119 The best-known and most important sayings to such effect on Swinburne are T. S. Eliot's. See T. S. Eliot, 'Swinburne as Poet', *The Sacred Wood*

Notes 247

(London: Methuen, 1921), pp. 131–36 (conversely, although in reference to 'honesty' rather than sound, in the subsequent essay, 'Blake', Eliot writes: 'Blake's poetry has the unpleasantness of great poetry' (p. 137)); T. S. Eliot, 'Isolated Superiority', *Dial*, 84 (1928), 4–7. See also the response to Eliot by Veronica Forrest-Thomson, 'Swinburne as Poet: A Reconsideration', written in the 1970s and published from the MS in *The Journal of Pre-Raphaelite Studies*, 15 (2006), 51–71. The introduction of *Swinburne: Selected Verse*, ed. by Alex Wong (Manchester: Fyfield Books, 2015), provides a valuable survey of Swinburne's critical appreciation. There is no entry in the index of Hill's *Collected Critical Writings* for Swinburne; but Hill mentions and cites Eliot's 'Swinburne as Critic' in 'Eros in F. H. Bradley and T. S. Eliot' (*CCW*, p. 559).

120 Algernon Charles Swinburne, 'Sapphics', *Poems and Ballads & Atalanta in Calydon*, ed. by Kenneth Haynes (Harmondsworth: Penguin, 2000), pp. 163–65 (p. 165). Subsequent references are to this edition.

121 Swinburne, 'Sapphics', p. 165.

122 *OED*, 'pennill' ('Plural *penillion*'): 'An improvised Welsh verse sung to a harp accompaniment; a stanza of such verse'.

123 The trope reappears at the end of the twenty-fourth poem (p. 858): 'bringing discharge of measure, | Blasting the home-straight'.

124 Swinburne, 'Sapphics', p. 164.

125 Ratcliffe, 'On Being "a man of the world"', p. 84.

126 Paul Batchelor, 'Geoffrey Hill's measured words', *TLS*, 2 November 2012, 12–13.

127 'The metaphysical | End of desire is always to be real' (*TT* 84: *Preghiera a* ——, p. 928). The word 'real' appears in Hill's writing with peculiar conspicuousness, and seems to be related, at least latterly, to Bradley's use. See n. 47 above.

128 For the epigraphs of 'The Pentecost Castle' (*T*, p. 115), see the fourth section of Chapter 3, 'Impossible rhymes'. The Bradley quotation is from *Essays on Truth and Reality*, p. 10, n. 1.

129 As for Bradley's definition, the question is difficult to answer; in the index of *Essays on Truth and Reality*, the single entry for 'Love' is the note cited above (Index, p. 477).

130 See also 'Orpheus and Eurydice', *U*, p. 33.

131 See Dante, *Divine Comedy*, pp. 23–25 (*Inferno*, Canto 5).

132 The idea of static yearning recalls the Welsh word *hiraeth*, which Rowan Williams calls 'the nearest word in Welsh to *eros*: there is a long or slow movement of "longing"' (Rowan Williams, *The Edge of Words* (London: Bloomsbury, 2014), p. 132). Hill uses the word to title six consecutive poems in *Oraclau | Oracles* (119–24, pp. 780–82). See also *P* 30, p. 552; *O* 13: *near St Beuno's*, p. 745.

133 *The Economist*, 'Poems should be beautiful'.

134 See *OED*, 'will, *v.1*', senses 36, 44b.

135 Middleton, *Palavers*, p. 97.

136 If not for the prefaced 'Argument' of *Hymns to Our Lady of Chartres* (p. 156), which calls the doctrine of the Immaculate Conception of the Blessed Virgin

248   *Notes*

Mary a 'sentimental late intrusion that infantilizes faith', one might have dared to make a comparison between the action of God in the cases of the soul of the Virgin and, here, the light of the sun. ('O dulcis Virgo, you are the stained world's | ransom' (*HOLC* 7, p. 160).)

137 *CCW*, p. 571. The quotation is from Bradley, *Appearance and Reality*, p. 131. Bradley may have Arnold's idea of culture in mind: 'Culture is then properly described not as having its origin in curiosity, but as having its origin in the love of perfection; it is a study of perfection' (Matthew Arnold, *Culture and Anarchy* (Oxford: Oxford University Press, 2009), p. 34).

138 In the first published version of *Odi Barbare* (Thame: Clutag, 2012), the word used here is 'beloved'. Batchelor laments the change as well as numerous others in *Broken Hierarchies*: 'that head-clearing, heart-warming word "beloved" has now been changed to "betimely," muddying the syntax and introducing a fussy note'. Batchelor, 'Weight of the Word'.

139 Hill combines consummation and annulment again, though in a very different context, in *The Book of Baruch*: 'We brought Lübeck to ruin with a mischievous spark, a flick to its old stack of beauties, as if doing so were topmost of civilization's sporting duties; whereas it was a prime experiment in branding a fire-storm with its newly perfected name, as inspiration consummated by the perfect poem. | The imagination suffers annulment; neo-liberal satiety becomes its imaginary coffers' (*BBGJ* 140, p. 75).

140 'East Coker', §IV, *Poems of T. S. Eliot*, p. 190: 'the absolute paternal care | That will not leave us, but prevents us everywhere'.

141 Geoffrey Hill, 'A Reading and Discussion of My Own Writings in the Context of Contemporary British Philosophy and Poetry', Collège de France, Paris, 18 March 2008. Transcribed and cited in Vincent, *Moral Authority*, p. 84.

142 'To the High Court of Parliament' (subtitled 'November 1994'), *C*, p. 171.

143 The word 'dance' and its relatives occur with surprising regularity in Hill's late work. See 'Pavana Dolorosa', §5 of 'Lachrimae', *T*, p. 123; *HOLC* 1, p. 157; 'Cycle', §4, *C*, p. 207; 'Psalms of Assize', §§IV, VII, *C*, pp. 226, 229; *TL* IX, p. 240; CXV, p. 273; CXXXIII, p. 280; *SS* 32, p. 304; 35, p. 306; 52, p. 314; 73, p. 325; 74, p. 325; 95, p. 336; 109, p. 343; 116, p. 346; *OS* VII, p. 357; XVI, p. 366; LXI, p. 411; *SC* title page (in the epigraph from Kafka), p. 419; §2 title ('Courtly Masquing Dances'), p. 431; 2. 42, p. 451; 2. 72, p. 464; 3. 3, p. 472; 3. 14, p. 477; 'Improvisation on 'O Welt ich muss dich lassen'', *WT*, p. 483; 'Improvisations for Jimi Hendrix', §4, *WT*, p. 503; 'Improvisations for Hart Crane', §1, *WT*, p. 512; *P* 31, p. 553; 'The Minor Prophets', *TCP*, p. 559; 'Holbein', §II, *TCP*, p. 565; 'After Reading *Children of Albion* (1969)', §§2, 3, *TCP*, p. 578; 'G. F. Handel, Opus 6', *TCP*, p. 585; *L* 25, p. 612; 51, p. 619; *EV* 14, p. 642; 27, p. 655; 32, p. 660; 40, p. 668; 53, p. 681; *LIV* XX, p. 704; XXXVIII, p. 722; *O* 17: *Ann Griffiths* (III), p. 746; 62: *Ty-tryst* (I), p. 761; 77, p. 766; 135, p. 785; 136: *Welsh apotheosis* (I), p. 786; *Cl.* 3, p. 793; 7, p. 797; 11, p. 801; 25, p. 815; 33, p. 823; 40, p. 830; *OB* V, p. 839; XVIII, p. 852; XXV, p. 859; XXVI, p. 860; XLVIII, p. 882; XLIX, p. 883; *TT* 8, p. 891; 54, p. 915; 55, p. 916; 76: *to Hugh Maxton*, pp. 924–25.

Notes 249

Hill: 'The physical is important to me although – or because – I'm a physically awkward person.' Hill, 'A matter of timing', cited in Ratcliffe, 'On Being "a man of the world"', pp. 70–71.

144 For 'gnomic', see, e.g., *OB* XX, p. 854; LII, p. 886; *BBGJ* 257, p. 138. One of *The Book of Baruch*'s self-characterisations is: 'Vatic one-liners *in memoriam*' (*BBGJ* 242, §2, p. 130).

145 Stephen James adduces some self-reflexive phrases from *Odi Barbare*: 'Into scrap language unpredicted landscape' (*OB* XXXV, p. 869); 'the merest memo' (*OB* XLV, p. 879); 'Proven things not salvageable like collage [...] a token fragment' (*OB* LII, p. 886). See James, 'The Nature of Hill's Later Poetry', p. 59. Agamben, in *The End of the Poem*, cites Walter Benjamin on the end of a poem by Baudelaire: 'it "suddenly interrupts itself, giving one the impression – doubly surprising in a sonnet – of something fragmentary"' (p. 113).

146 Edward Mendelson, 'Editing Auden', *New Statesman*, 17 September 1976, p. 376.

147 See also, e.g., *BBGJ* 2, p. 3; 36, §§6, 7, p. 17; 38, p. 18; 43, p. 20; 56, p. 25; 78, p. 36; 81, p. 38; 83, p. 39; 87, p. 40; 101, §1, p. 48; 103, p. 49; 110, pp. 53–55 (p. 55); 115, p. 59; 117, p. 60; 123, §7, p. 66; 130, p. 70; 133, p. 71; 138, p. 74; 142, p. 76; 150, §1, p. 81; 170, p. 90; 175, p. 93; 178, p. 95; 185, p. 101; 188, p. 103; 190, §3, p. 104; 196, p. 109; 203, p. 112; 207, p. 114; 218, p. 118; 225, p. 121; 230, p. 123; 231, p. 124; 232, p. 125; 234, p. 126; 243, p. 131; 245, p. 132; 246, p. 133; 247, p. 133; 248, p. 134; 249, p. 134; 254, p. 137; 262, p. 141; 263, p. 141; 264, §1, p. 142; 265, p. 142; 266, p. 143; 268, p. 144; 269, p. 144. It is at times a tricky business to distinguish quotations from scare quotes in *The Book of Baruch*, full as it is of words and phrases set in undifferentiated single quotation marks. (It is unclear to me why, in doing this, Hill eschews his usual practice in previous work of using italics to denote quotation; and doubly unclear why there are occasional relapses into this practice, such as in *BBGJ* 155, p. 84.)

Hill, without using the phrase 'scare quotes' (the coinage of Elizabeth Anscombe, mentioned only once by Hill as Wittgenstein's translator in *CCW*, p. 278), cites the *MHRA Style Book* in his essay 'Our Word is Our Bond': 'Avoid the practice of using quotation marks as an oblique excuse for a loose, slang, or imprecise (and possibly inaccurate) word or phrase. Quotation marks should normally be reserved to indicate direct quotation from other writers' (*MHRA Style Book: Notes for Authors and Editors*, ed. by A. S. Maney and R. L. Smallwood (Leeds: MHRA, 1971), p. 16; *CCW*, p. 150). Hill takes lengthy issue with this 'too simplistically exclusive' view, and writes that quotation marks, used as against the *MHRA*'s guidance, are 'a way of bringing pressure to bear and are also a form of "ironic and bitter" intonation acknowledging that pressure is being exerted. They have a satiric function' (*CCW*, pp. 150–51). The title and first sentence of Hill's first collected essay cannot be forgotten in this context: 'The quotation-marks around 'menace' and 'atonement' look a bit like raised eyebrows' ('Poetry as 'Menace' and 'Atonement"', *CCW*, p. 3).

250   *Notes*

148 Agamben, *The End of the Poem*, pp. 112–13. Hill has no 'problem' in defining the unenjambed *Book of Baruch* as a sequence of poems. In 'The End of
the Poem', the essay that gives its title to the English translation of his book,
Agamben defers the question of whether the last verse 'trespasses into prose',
but discusses (in a way that seems relevant to Hill's posthumous book; and
in diction, the translator's, that is redolent of Hill's prose) the example of
Raimbaut d'Aurenga's 'No sai que s'es', in which 'the end of every strophe,
and especially the end of the entire unclassifiable poem, is distinguished by
the unexpected irruption of prose – an irruption that, *in extremis*, marks the
epiphany of a necessary undecidability between prose and poetry' (Agamben,
The End of the Poem, p. 112).

End notes

1 Dante Alighieri, *De vulgari eloquentia*, ed. and trans. by Stephen Botterill
(Cambridge: Cambridge University Press, 1996), II, IX, 2, p. 73. See Agamben,
The End of the Poem, p. 110; Muldoon, *The End of the Poem*, p. 152.
2 Kenneth Haynes, in correspondence with me, writes that 'Hill did not leave
instructions for what he wanted as the [last] poem. It was my decision to conclude
with an unfinished poem (271), rather than, say, terminate the book at 270.'
3 'Notebook 63: A Treatise of Civil Power', BC MS 20c Hill/2/1/63, fols 84ᵛ–85ʳ.
4 Twice, in *The Book of Baruch*, Hill makes reference to funeral sentences: 'The
funeral sentences are here less an act of homage than a *collage* requital of collateral
damage' (*BBGJ* 242, §2, p. 130); 'Take heart, the Funeral Sentences are neither
an act of homage nor a bill for damage' (255, p. 137). The funeral sentences are
seven quotations from Scripture, which the Book of Common Prayer prescribes
for the Burial Service. The capitalisation in the latter of Hill's uses of the term
may more clearly suggest an allusion to William Croft's Burial Service, commonly
known as his *Funeral Sentences* (first published as an appendix to his collection
of anthems *Musica sacra* in 1724), which seems to have been sung at most royal
funerals in Britain since its publication (see Matthias Range, 'William Croft's
Burial Service and Purcell's "Thou Knowest, Lord"', *The Musical Times*, 1906
(2009): 54–68).
5 Matthew 25.13. Cf., e.g., Matthew 24.42–44; Mark 13.33–37; Luke 21.36.
6 Hill, after quoting 'I write | to astonish myself' in a prose piece reflecting on his
work, writes: 'This self-astonishment is achieved when, by some process I can't
fathom, common words are moved, or move themselves, into clusters of meaning
so intense that they seem to stand up from the page, three-dimensional almost'
(Hill, 'A matter of timing'). From the same article: 'I write to create a being of
beautiful energy.'
  The end of writing Hill posits here, 'to astonish myself', is unmistakably
Platonic–Aristotelian, though both philosophers speak of astonishment as a
beginning rather than an end. See Plato, *Theaetetus*, 155d, in *Theaetetus and
Sophist*, ed. and trans. by Christopher Rowe (Cambridge: Cambridge University

Notes 251

Press, 2015), p. 19; Aristotle, *Metaphysics*, 1.982b ('For through astonishment men have begun to philosophize both in our times and at the beginning'), as quoted in Martin Heidegger, *What is Philosophy?*, trans. by Jean T. Wilde and William Kluback (Lanham, MD: Rowman & Littlefield, 1956), p. 81. See also Plotinus: 'For these are the states one should be in regarding something which is beautiful: astonishment, and sweet shock, and longing, and erotic thrill, and pleasurable excitement' (Plotinus, *The Enneads*, ed. by Lloyd P. Gerson, trans. by George Boys-Stones, John M. Dillon, R. A. H. King, Andrew Smith, and James Wilberding (Cambridge: Cambridge University Press, 2017), 1.6.4.16–18, p. 96). There are numerous Scriptural references to astonishment, in Greek θαυμαστός (*thaumastos*), e.g., Revelation 15.1. For more astonishments in Hill, see 'In Ipsley Church Lane 2', *WT*, p. 501; *P* 10, p. 532; 29, p. 551 ('let us not lose | this last astonishment untaxed by grief'); *TT* 46: *i.m. Irma Brandeis*, pp. 911–12; *TT* 87: *on the Marriage of a Virgin* (p. 930); *BBGJ* 229, p. 123 ('It was so provident I could barely speak, miming the astonishment, mining the fabulous lode without diminishment').

7 *TT* 17, p. 895.

8 Henry Cockeram, *The English dictionarie; or, An interpreter of hard English words* (London: 1623, for N. Butter), sig. B7ᵛ.

Bibliography

Works of Geoffrey Hill

Poetry

Broken Hierarchies: Poems 1952–2012, ed. by Kenneth Haynes (Oxford: Oxford University Press, 2013)

Canaan (London: Penguin, 1996)

Clavics (London: Enitharmon Press, 2011)

Collected Poems (Harmondsworth: Penguin, 1985)

'Excerpts from a Work in Progress: III, IV, V', *Iowa Review*, 40 (2010), 191–93

'Excerpts from a Work in Progress: 6, 12, 18, and 34', *Keble College: The Record 2009* (2009), pp. 52–54

For the Unfallen (London: André Deutsch, 1959)

'Four Poems', *Paris Review*, 21 (1959), 98–100

'From "Odi Barbare": VII, VIII, IX', *Christianity and Literature*, 60 (2011), 402–4

'From "Odi Barbare", XXI–XXIII', in *GHC*, pp. 227–29

'From "Odi Barbare"', *Poetry*, 196 (2010), 410–13

'From "Odi Barbare"', *The Baffler*, 19 (2012), 21

'From "Odi Barbare": XVI and XVII', *The New Criterion*, 30.1 (2011), 81–83

'From "The Day Books" IV: ODI BARBARE', *Archipelago*, 6 (2011), 1–5

King Log (London: André Deutsch, 1968)

Mercian Hymns (London: André Deutsch, 1971)

The Mystery of the Charity of Charles Péguy (London: Agenda Editions and André Deutsch, 1983)

New and Collected Poems, 1952–1992 (Boston, MA and New York: Houghton Mifflin, 1994)

'New Poems', *Standpoint*, 24 (2010), pp. 88–91

Odi Barbare (Thame: Clutag Press, 2012)

Oraclau | Oracles (Thame: Clutag Press, 2010)

The Orchards of Syon (Washington, DC: Counterpoint, 2002)

Preghiere (Leeds: Northern House, 1964)

Scenes from Comus (London: Penguin, 2005)

Selected Poems (London: Penguin, 2006)

Selected Poems (New Haven, CT: Yale University Press, 2009)

Somewhere is Such a Kingdom (New York: Houghton Mifflin, 1975)

Speech! Speech! (Washington, DC: Counterpoint, 2000)

Bibliography 253

Tenebrae (London: André Deutsch, 1978)
A Treatise of Civil Power (London: Penguin, 2007)
A Treatise of Civil Power (Thame: Clutag Press, 2005)
The Triumph of Love (London: Penguin, 1998)
Without Title (London: Penguin, 2006)

Lectures, prose, and translation

'Acceptance Speech for the T. S. Eliot Prize', *Image: A Journal of the Arts and Religion*, 28 (2000), 72–77
'Between Politics and Eternity', in *The Poets' Dante: Twentieth-Century Responses*, ed. by Peter S. Hawkins and Rachel Jacoff (New York: Farrar, Straus, and Giroux, 2001), pp. 319–32
'C. H. Sisson', *PN Review*, 39 (1984), www.pnreview.co.uk/cgi-bin/scribe?item_id=6420
'Civil Polity and the Confessing State', *The Warwick Review*, 2 (2008), 7–20
Collected Critical Writings, ed. by Kenneth Haynes (Oxford: Oxford University Press, 2008)
'Confessio Amantis', *Keble College: The Record, 2009* (2009), pp. 45–54
'"The Conscious Mind's Intelligible Structure": A Debate', *Agenda*, 9.4–10.1 (1971–1972), 14–23
'David Wright at Sixty', *PN Review*, 14 (1980), www.pnreview.co.uk/cgi-bin/scribe?item_id=7594
'A deep dynastic wound', Professor of Poetry lecture, University of Oxford, 30 April 2013, http://media.podcasts.ox.ac.uk/engfac/poetry/2013-04-30-engfac-hill.mp3
'The Dream of Reason', *Essays in Criticism*, 14 (1964), 91–101
'The Eloquence of Sober Truth', *TLS*, 11 June 1999, pp. 7–12
The Enemy's Country: Words, Contexture and Other Circumstances of Language (Oxford: Clarendon Press, 1991)
'How ill white hairs become a fool and jester', Professor of Poetry lecture, University of Oxford, 30 November 2010, http://media.podcasts.ox.ac.uk/kebl/general/2010-11-30-hill-poetry-keble.mp3
'I know thee not, old man, fall to thy prayers', Professor of Poetry lecture, University of Oxford, 5 May 2015, http://media.podcasts.ox.ac.uk/engfac/poetry/2015-05-05_engfac_hill.mp3
'"Legal Fiction" and legal fiction', Professor of Poetry lecture, University of Oxford, 5 March 2013, http://media.podcasts.ox.ac.uk/engfac/poetry/2013-03-21-engfac-poetry-hill-2.mp3
The Lords of Limit: Essays on Literature and Ideas (London: André Deutsch, 1984)
'A matter of timing', *Guardian*, 21 September 2002, www.theguardian.com/books/2002/sep/21/featuresreviews.guardianreview28
'Mightier and darker', *TLS*, 23 March 2016, www.the-tls.co.uk/articles/public/mightier-and-darker/
'Orderly Damned, Disorderly Saved', University Sermon preached at Great St Mary's, Cambridge, 16 October 2011, www.yumpu.com/en/document/read/5084440/geoffrey-hill-16-october-2011-great-st-marys-church
'The Poet as Arbiter', *Yorkshire Post*, 3 October 1963, p. 4
Review of William Blake, 'Jerusalem', *The Isis*, 4 March 1953, p. 22

254   *Bibliography*

'Robert Lowell: "Contrasts and Repetitions"', *Essays in Criticism*, 13 (1963), 188–97
Style and Faith (Washington, DC: Counterpoint, 2003)

Secondary works

Adorno, Theodor W., *Prisms*, trans. by Samuel and Shierry Weber (London: Neville Spearman, 1967)
Adorno, Theodor W., 'Punctuation Marks', trans. by Shierry Weber Nicholsen, *The Antioch Review*, 48.3 (1990), 300–5
Agamben, Giorgio, *The End of the Poem: Studies in Poetics*, trans. by Daniel Heller-Roazen (Stanford, CA: Stanford University Press, 1999
Allott, Kenneth, ed., *The Penguin Book of Contemporary Verse: 1918–60* (London: Penguin, 1962)
Andrewes, Lancelot, *XCVI Sermons* (London: Richard Badger, 1632)
Annwn, David, *Inhabited Voices: Myth and History in the Poetry of Geoffrey Hill, Seamus Heaney and George Mackay Brown* (Frome: Bran's Head Books, 1984)
Aquinas, Thomas, *Summa Theologiae*, trans. by Fathers of the English Dominican Province, 2nd edn, 5 vols (London: Burns Oates and Washbourne, 1920)
Aristotle, *The Nicomachean Ethics*, trans. by David Ross (Oxford: Oxford University Press, 2009)
Aristotle, *Physics, Volume I: Books 1–4*, trans. by P. H. Wicksteed and F. M. Cornford (Cambridge, MA: Harvard University Press, 1957)
Aristotle, Longinus, and Demetrius, *Poetics. Longinus: On the Sublime. Demetrius: On Style*, trans. by Stephen Halliwell, W. Hamilton Fyfe, Doreen C. Innes, and W. Rhys Roberts, revised by Donald A. Russell (Cambridge, MA: Harvard University Press, 1995)
Arnold, Matthew, *Culture and Anarchy* (Oxford: Oxford University Press, 2009)
Arnold, Matthew, *Poems* (London: Longman, Brown, Green, and Longmans, 1853)
Ashmole, Elias, ed., *Theatrum Chemicum Britannicum. Containing Severall Poeticall Pieces of our Famous English Philosophers* (London: J. Grismond, 1652)
Attridge, Derek, *Moving Words: Forms of English Poetry* (Oxford: Oxford University Press, 2013)
Auden, W. H., *Collected Shorter Poems 1927–1957* (London: Faber and Faber, 1966)
Augustine, *Enarrationes in Psalmos*, in *Patrologia Latina*, ed. by Jacques-Paul Migne, 221 vols (Paris: Migne, 1841–1855), xxxvii (1861)
Augustine, *Sermones*, in *Patrologia Latina*, ed. by Jacques-Paul Migne, 221 vols (Paris: Migne, 1841–1855), xxxviii (1861)
Austin, J. L., *How to Do Things with Words: The William James Lectures delivered at Harvard University in 1955*, ed. by J. O. Urmson (Oxford: Clarendon Press, 1962)
Baker, Jack, 'The Burden of Authentic Expression in the Later Poetry of Geoffrey Hill', *FORUM: University of Edinburgh Postgraduate Journal of Culture and the Arts*, 12 (2011), www.forumjournal.org/article/view/663/945
Batchelor, Paul, 'Geoffrey Hill's measured words', *TLS*, 2 November 2012, www.the-tls.co.uk/articles/public/geoffrey-hills-measured-words/

Bibliography 255

Batchelor, Paul, 'Weight of the Word, Weight of the World', *Poetry* (July/August 2018), www.poetryfoundation.org/poetrymagazine/articles/147126/weight-of-the-word-weight-of-the-world

Beckett, Samuel, *The Complete Dramatic Works* (London: Faber and Faber, 2006)

Bell, Alexandra, Rebecca Rosen, and Edmund White, 'Strongholds of the Imagination', *The Oxonian Review*, 9.4 (2009), https://web.archive.org/web/20160306200217/http://www.oxonianreview.org/wp/geoffrey-hill

Ben-Merre, David, 'Falling into Silence: Giorgio Agamben at the End of the Poem', *Mosaic: An Interdisciplinary Critical Journal*, 45.1 (2012), 89–104

Berryman, John, *Collected Poems 1937–1971* (New York: Farrar, Straus, and Giroux, 1989)

Birkan-Berz, Carole, 'An Emblem of Some Consequence', *Arts of War and Peace*, 1 (2013), 92–94

Blackmur, R. P., 'An Adjunct to the Muses' Diadem: A Note on E. P.', in *American Critical Essays (Twentieth Century)* (Oxford: Oxford University Press, 1959), pp. 202–10

Blackmur, R. P., 'Irregular Metaphysics', in *Literary Lectures Presented at the Library of Congress* (Washington, DC: Library of Congress, 1973), pp. 136–51

Blackmur, R. P., *Language as Gesture* (New York: Harcourt, Brace, 1952)

Bloom, Harold, ed., *Geoffrey Hill* (New York: Chelsea House, 1986)

Bos, Zachary, 'Note on, reviews of, and a stanza from Hill's Oraclau', *The Wonder Reflex* blog, 27 June 2011, http://thewonderreflex.blogspot.co.uk/2011/06/from-reviews-of-oraclau-and-stanza-72.html

Bradley, F. H., *Appearance and Reality* (Oxford: Oxford University Press, 1930)

Bradley, F. H., *Essays on Truth and Reality* (Oxford: Clarendon Press, 1914)

Bradley, F. H., *Oxford Lectures on Poetry* (London: Macmillan, 1909)

Brittain, Frederick, ed., *The Penguin Book of Latin Verse* (Harmondsworth: Penguin, 1962)

Brown, Clare, and Don Paterson, eds, *Don't Ask Me What I Mean: Poets in their Own Words* (London: Picador, 2003)

Brown, Merle, 'Poetic Omissions in Geoffrey Hill's Most Recent Sequences', *Contemporary Literature*, 20 (1979), 76–95

Burns, Richard, *Keys to Transformation: Ceri Richards & Dylan Thomas* (London: Enitharmon Press, 1981)

Burrow, Colin, 'Rancorous Old Sod', *London Review of Books*, 20 February 2014, pp. 11–13

Butt, John, ed., *The Poems of Alexander Pope* (London: Methuen, 1963)

Buxton, Rachel, 'Transaction and Transcendence: Geoffrey Hill's 'Vision of "Canaan"', *The Cambridge Quarterly*, 34 (2005), 333–63

Cain, Tom and Ruth Connolly, eds, *The Complete Poetry of Robert Herrick*, 2 vols (Oxford: Oxford University Press, 2013)

Calderón de la Barca, Pedro, *La vida es sueño, El alcalde de Zalamea*, ed. by Enrique Rodríguez Cepeda (Madrid: Ediciones Akal, 1999)

Campbell, Jessica, 'Interview: Geoffrey Hill, Oxford Professor of Poetry', *Oxford Student*, 26 May 2011, http://oxfordstudent.com/2011/05/26/interview-geoffrey-hill-oxford-professor-of-poetry/

Carr, Alexander Allan, *A History of Coldingham Priory* (Edinburgh: Adam and Charles Black, 1836)

256 *Bibliography*

Castiglione, Davide, *Difficulty in Poetry: A Stylistic Model* (Cham: Palgrave Macmillan, 2019)

Catechism of the Catholic Church (New York: Doubleday, 2003)

Cave, Terence, *Recognitions: A Study in Poetics* (Oxford: Clarendon Press, 1988)

Chemi, Tatiana, *In the Beginning Was the Pun: Comedy and Humour in Samuel Beckett's Theatre* (Aalborg: Aalborg University Press, 2013)

Chesterton, G. K., 'The Romance of Rhyme', *The Living Age*, 13 March 1920, pp. 656–65

Cicero, *Orator ad M. Brutum*, in *Brutus. Orator*, trans. by G. L. Hendrickson and H. M. Hubbell (Cambridge, MA: Harvard University Press, 1939)

Coburn, Kathleen, and others, eds, *The Collected Works of Samuel Taylor Coleridge*, 16 vols (Princeton, NJ: Princeton University Press, 1969–2001)

Coburn, Kathleen, and others, eds, *The Notebooks of Samuel Taylor Coleridge*, 5 vols (Princeton, NJ: Princeton University Press, 1957–2012)

Cochrane, Harry, 'Quarries of silence: The work and legacy of Geoffrey Hill, who died five years ago', *TLS*, 2 July 2021, p. 20

Coleridge, Samuel Taylor, *Lectures 1808–1819 on Literature*, ed. by R. A. Foakes, 2 vols (London: Routledge & Kegan Paul, 1987)

Collings, Simon, 'Love and Sex in Hill's "Pindarics": Getting Personal', *PN Review*, 230 (2016), www.pnreview.co.uk/cgi-bin/scribe?item_id=9684

Comenius, *Orbis Pictus* (Oxford: Oxford University Press, 1968)

Cook, Eleanor, *Against Coercion: Games Poets Play* (Stanford, CA: Stanford University Press, 1998)

Cook, Eleanor, 'Paronomasia', in *The Princeton Encyclopedia of Poetry and Poetics*, 4th edn, ed. by Roland Greene (Princeton, NJ: Princeton University Press, 2012), pp. 1003–4

Cook, Eleanor, *Poetry, Word-Play, and Word-War in Wallace Stevens* (Princeton, NJ: Princeton University Press, 1988)

Cummings, Brian, *The Literary Culture of the Reformation: Grammar and Grace* (Oxford: Oxford University Press, 2002)

Dante Alighieri, *De vulgari eloquentia*, ed. and trans. by Stephen Botterill (Cambridge: Cambridge University Press, 1996)

Dante Alighieri, *The Divine Comedy: Inferno, Purgatorio, Paradiso*, trans. by Robin Kirkpatrick (London: Penguin, 2012)

Darbishire, Helen, and others, eds, *The Poetical Works of John Milton*, 8 vols (Oxford: Oxford University Press, 1963–2012)

Davie, Donald, 'Fallen Language', *London Review of Books*, 21 June 1984, p. 10

Davies, Hilary, '"The Castaway of Drowned Remorse, the World's Atonement on the Hill"[:] History, Language and Theopoetics: Geoffrey Hill's Dialogue with David Jones in "Mercian Hymns" and "Tenebrae"', *Études anglaises*, 71–72 (2018), 154–67

Davis, Garrick, 'Geoffrey Hill, Prodigal', *First Things*, August 2018, www.firstthings.com/article/2018/08/geoffrey-hill-prodigal

Day, Thomas, 'Savage Indignation and Petty Resentment in Geoffrey Hill's "Canaan", "The Triumph of Love" and "Speech! Speech!"', *Études britanniques contemporaines*, 45 (2013), http://ebc.revues.org/779

Day, Thomas, 'Variant Editions of Geoffrey Hill's "Mercian Hymns"', *PN Review*, 202 (2011), www.pnreview.co.uk/cgi-bin/scribe?item_id=8399

Bibliography

Day, Thomas, 'We All Do', *PN Review*, 210 (2013), www.pnreview.co.uk/cgi-bin/scribe?item_id=8770

De Selincourt, Ernest, and Helen Darbishire, eds, *The Poetical Works of William Wordsworth*, 5 vols (Oxford: Clarendon Press, 1952–1959)

D'Evelyn, Tom, 'Geoffrey Hill and the Metaxy', *VoegelinView* online journal, 9 November 2016, https://voegelinview.com/6070-2/

Dionysius of Halicarnassus, *On Literary Composition*, in *Critical Essays, Volume II: On Literary Composition. Dinarchus. Letters to Ammaeus and Pompeius*, trans. by Stephen Usher (Cambridge, MA: Harvard University Press, 1985)

Dodd, Elizabeth S., *The Lyric Voice in English Theology* (London: Bloomsbury, 2023)

Dodsworth, Martin, 'Geoffrey Hill's Difficulties', in *Strangeness and Power: Essays on the Poetry of Geoffrey Hill*, ed. by Andrew Michael Roberts (Swindon: Shearsman Books, 2020), pp. 174–202

Dooley, David, and others, eds, *The Collected Works of G. K. Chesterton*, 37 vols (San Francisco: Ignatius Press, 1986–2012)

Downing, Ben, 'The Other Harmony of Sentences', *Parnassus*, 23.1 (1998), https://web.archive.org/web/20211209182353/http://parnassusreview.com/archives/377

Drexel, John, 'Geoffrey Hill: The Poet in Winter', *Contemporary Poetry Review*, 7 April 2003, www.cprw.com/geoffrey-hill-the-poet-in-winter

Dryden, John, *The Works of Virgil* (London: Jacob Tonson, 1697)

Duncan, Andrew, 'Geoffrey Hill: Recalcitrant survey 2015', 7 May 2016, *Angel Exhaust* blog, http://angelexhaust.blogspot.co.uk/2016/05/geoffrey-hill-recalcitrantsurvey-2015.html

Eberhart, Richard, *Collected Poems 1930–1976* (London: Chatto and Windus, 1976)

Economist, The, 'Poems should be beautiful', video interview with Geoffrey Hill, 2 December 2011, www.economist.com/prospero/2011/12/02/poems-should-be-beautiful

Eden, Kathy, *Poetic and Legal Fiction in the Aristotelian Tradition* (Princeton, NJ: Princeton University Press, 1986)

Eliot, T. S., *Collected Poems 1909–1962* (London: Faber and Faber, 2002)

Eliot, T. S., 'Isolated Superiority', *Dial*, 84 (1928), 4–7

Eliot, T. S., *On Poetry and Poets* (London: Faber and Faber, 1957)

Eliot, T. S., 'Reflections on Vers Libre', *New Statesman*, 3 March 1917, pp. 518–19

Eliot, T. S., *The Sacred Wood* (London: Methuen, 1921)

Ellmann, Richard, *James Joyce* (Oxford: Oxford University Press, 1959)

Empson, William, *The Complete Poems* (London: Penguin, 2001)

Empson, William, *Seven Types of Ambiguity* (London: Chatto and Windus, 1953)

Empson, William, *Some Versions of Pastoral* (New York: New Directions, 1974)

Erdman, David V., ed., *The Complete Poetry & Prose of William Blake* (New York: Anchor, 1988)

Fafara, Richard, 'Angelism and Culture', in *Understanding Maritain: Philosopher and Friend*, ed. by Deal Wyatt Hudson and Matthew J. Mancini (Macon, GA: Mercer University Press, 1987), pp. 171–80

Feser, Edward, *Scholastic Metaphysics: A Contemporary Introduction* (Heusenstamm: Editiones Scholasticae, 2014)

Ficino, Marsilio, *Opera omnia*, ed. by Paul Kristeller, 2 vols (Turin: Bottega d'Erasmo, 1962)

258   *Bibliography*

Ficino, Marsilio, *Theologia Platonica*, in *Théologie Platonicienne de l'immortalité des ames | Theologia Platonica de immortalitaté animorum*, trans. by Raymond Marcel, 3 vols (Paris: Société d'édition "Les Belles Lettres", 1964–1970)

Finneran, Richard J., ed., *The Collected Poems of W. B. Yeats* (New York: Macmillan, 1996)

Fitzgibbon, Constantine, *The Life of Dylan Thomas* (London: J. M. Dent, 1975)

Forrest-Thomson, Veronica, 'Swinburne as Poet: A Reconsideration', *The Journal of Pre-Raphaelite Studies*, 15 (2006), 51–71

Fowlie, Wallace, *Age of Surrealism* (Bloomington, IN: Indiana University Press, 1972)

Franklin, R. W., ed., *The Poems of Emily Dickinson: Variorum Edition*, 3 vols (Cambridge, MA: The Belknap Press of Harvard University Press, 1998)

Freer, Alexander, '"Love-Runes We Cannot Speak": Sacred and Profane Love in "The Pentecost Castle"', *Literature and Theology*, 26 (2012), 199–213

Gardner, Helen, *The Composition of 'Four Quartets'* (London: Faber and Faber, 1978)

Garrod, H. W., ed., *Keats: Poetical Works* (London: Oxford University Press, 1966)

Gaudern, Mia, *The Etymological Poetry of W. H. Auden, J. H. Prynne, and Paul Muldoon* (Oxford: Oxford University Press, 2020)

Gervais, David, 'Geoffrey Hill: The Poet as Critic', *PN Review*, 162 (2005), www.pnreview.co.uk/cgi-bin/scribe?item_id=2423

Gervais, David, '"A tyme of knots": Geoffrey Hill's Clark Lectures', *The Cambridge Quarterly*, 21 (1992), 389–94

Gibbon, Edward, *The History of the Decline and Fall of the Roman Empire*, 8 vols (London: J. F. Dove, 1821)

Gibson, James, ed., *The Variorum Edition of the Complete Poems of Thomas Hardy* (London: Macmillan, 1979)

Gilman, Ernest B., *The Curious Perspective: Literary and Pictorial Wit in the Seventeenth Century* (New Haven, CT: Yale University Press, 1978)

Grafe, Adrian, 'Geoffrey Hill as Lord of Limit: The Kenosis as a Theological Context of his Poetry and Thought', *Revue LISA*, 7.3 (2009), 50–61

Grandsen, K. W., *John Donne* (London: Longmans, Green, 1954)

Greene, Roland, and others, eds, *The Princeton Encyclopedia of Poetry and Poetics*, 4th edn (Princeton, NJ: Princeton University Press, 2012)

Grierson, Herbert J. C., ed., *The Poems of John Donne*, 2 vols (Oxford: Oxford University Press, 1912)

Haffenden, John, *Viewpoints: Poets in Conversation with John Haffenden* (London: Faber and Faber, 1981)

Hamburger, Michael, 'Circumstances', *PN Review*, 82 (1991), www.pnreview.co.uk/cgi-bin/scribe?item_id=3877

Hamilton, Paul, *Coleridge and German Philosophy: The Poet in the Land of Logic* (London: Continuum, 2007)

Hammond, Paul, ed., *Shakespeare's Sonnets: An Original-Spelling Text* (Oxford: Oxford University Press, 2012)

Hand, Dominic, and Sofía Crespi de Valldaura, '"If I write about destruction it's because I'm terrified of it": An interview with Geoffrey Hill', *The Isis*, 27 April 2015, http://isismagazine.org.uk/2015/04/if-i-write-about-destruction-its-becaus e-im-terrified-of-it-an-interview-with-geoffrey-hill/

Bibliography 259

Harrison, G. B., ed., *Samuel Daniel: A Defence of Ryme; and Thomas Campion: Observations in the Art of English Poesie* (Edinburgh: Edinburgh University Press, 1966)

Hart, Henry, *The Poetry of Geoffrey Hill* (Carbondale, IL: Southern Illinois University Press, 1986)

Hart, Kevin, *Lands of Likeness: For a Poetics of Contemplation* (Chicago: University of Chicago Press, 2023)

Hart, Kevin, 'Longing: Young Geoffrey Hill and the Problem of Religious Poetry', in *Literature and Religious Experience: Beyond Belief and Unbelief*, ed. by Matthew J. Smith and Caleb D. Spencer (London: Bloomsbury, 2022), pp. 55–72

Hart, Kevin, *Poetry and Revelation: For a Phenomenology of Religious Poetry* (London: Bloomsbury, 2017)

Hassan, Ann, *Annotations to Geoffrey Hill's 'Speech! Speech!'* (New York: Glossator Special Editions, 2012)

Haughton, Hugh, '"How fit a title…": Title and Authority in the Work of Geoffrey Hill', in *EW*, pp. 129–48

Hawlin, Stefan, 'The Argument of Geoffrey Hill's "Odi Barbare"', *The Cambridge Quarterly*, 43 (2014), 1–15

Hawlin, Stefan, '"Grinding the Textures of Harmony": Heroic Difficulty in Geoffrey Hill's "Clavics"', *English*, 63 (2014), 313–29

Haydn, Joseph, *The Creation* (London: Novello, Ewer & Co., 1859)

Haynes, Kenneth, 'A Bibliography of the Works of Geoffrey Hill', in *ELW*, pp. 170–216

Haynes, Kenneth, '"Faith" and "Fable" in the Poetry of Geoffrey Hill', *Christianity and Literature*, 60 (2011), 398–401

Haynes, Kenneth and Andrew Kahn, '"Difficult Friend": Geoffrey Hill and Osip Mandelstam', *Essays in Criticism*, 63 (2013), 51–80

Heaney, Seamus, 'An English Mason', in Harold Bloom, ed., *Geoffrey Hill*, pp. 49–53

Hecht, Anthony, *Melodies Unheard: Essays on the Mysteries of Poetry* (Baltimore, MD: Johns Hopkins University Press, 2003)

Heidegger, Martin, *What is Philosophy?*, trans. by Jean T. Wilde and William Kluback (Lanham, MD: Rowman and Littlefield, 1956)

Henisch, Bridget Ann, *The Medieval Calendar Year* (University Park, PA: Pennsylvania State University Press, 1999)

Higgins, Leslie, and Michael F. Suarez, S.J., eds, *The Collected Works of Gerard Manley Hopkins* (Oxford: Oxford University Press, 2006–)

Hipolito, Jeffrey, 'Give Me the Key', *The Critical Flame*, http://criticalflame.org/verse/0911_hippolito.htm

Hirst, Francis W., *The Stock Exchange* (Oxford: Oxford University Press, 1948)

Hobbes, Thomas, *Humane nature* (London: T. Newcomb, 1649)

Hobbes, Thomas, *Leviathan* (London: printed for Andrew Crooke, 1651)

Holland, Jane, 'Wyatt, Geoffrey Hill, and other acts of coitus with the English language', *Raw Light* blog, 28 October 2007, http://rawlightblog.blogspot.co.uk/2007/10/wyatt-geoffrey-hill-and-other-acts-of.html

Hooker, Jeremy, 'Oracular Soundings', *PN Review*, 63 (1988), www.pnreview.co.uk/cgi-bin/scribe?item_id=4963

Hooker, Jeremy, 'Other Land', *Notre Dame Review*, 32 (2011), 248–52

Hopkins, Beau, 'Review', *Stand*, 214 (2017), 84–88

260 *Bibliography*

Horace, *Odes and Epodes*, ed. and trans. by Niall Rudd (Cambridge, MA: Harvard University Press, 2004)

Horne, Philip, 'Bibliography of Works by and about Geoffrey Hill', in *EW*, pp. 237–51

Hurley, Michael D., and Michael O'Neill, *Poetic Form: An Introduction* (Cambridge: Cambridge University Press, 2012)

Hutchinson, Ben, '"Raw with late wisdom": Geoffrey Hill's "A Treatise of Civil Power"', *The Modern Language Review*, 104 (2009), 947–61

Hutchinson, F. E., ed., *The Works of George Herbert* (Oxford: Oxford University Press, 1941)

Ibsen, Henrik, *Brand: A Version for the English Stage*, trans. by Geoffrey Hill (London: Heinemann, 1978)

Ibsen, Henrik, *Brand: A Version for the Stage*, trans. by Geoffrey Hill, 3rd edn (Harmondsworth: Penguin, 1996)

Ibsen, Henrik, *Peer Gynt and Brand*, trans. by Geoffrey Hill (London: Penguin, 2016)

Isaacs, David, 'Self-doubt: Revision and the Late Modernist Crisis of Conscience' (unpublished doctoral thesis, University College London, 2020)

Isaacs, David, '"Unfinished to perfection": Geoffrey Hill, Revision, and the Poetics of Stone', *Textual Practice* 36.7 (2021), https://doi.org/10.1080/09502 36X.2021.1900377

Jackson, Robert, 'Enoch Powell: Paradox of politics and poetry', *The Times*, 24 April 1969, p. 11.

Jaeger, Martha, 'Reflections on the Work of Jung and Rank', *Journal of Psychotherapy as a Religious Process*, 2 (1955), 47–57

James, Stephen, 'The Nature of Hill's Later Poetry', in *Strangeness and Power: Essays on the Poetry of Geoffrey Hill*, ed. by Andrew Michael Roberts (Swindon: Shearsman Books, 2020), pp. 39–63

James, Stephen, *Shades of Authority: The Poetry of Lowell, Hill and Heaney* (Liverpool: Liverpool University Press, 2007)

Jarrell, Randall, 'Fifty Years of American Poetry', *Prairie Schooner*, 37 (1963), 1–27

Jarvis, Simon, 'Prosody as Cognition', *Critical Quarterly*, 40.4 (1998), 3–15

Jarvis, Simon, 'An Undeleter for Criticism', *Diacritics*, 32.1 (2002), 3–18

Jarvis, Simon, 'Why Rhyme Pleases', *Thinking Verse*, 1 (2011), 17–43

Johnson, Daniel, 'Geoffrey Hill and the Poetry of Ideas', *Standpoint*, June 2014, https://web.archive.org/web/20210305032731/https://standpointmag.co.uk/features-june-14-geoffrey-hill-poetry-ideas-daniel-johnson-public-life/

Johnson, Monte Ransome, *Aristotle on Teleology* (Oxford: Oxford University Press, 2005)

Jones, David, *Epoch and Artist* (London: Faber and Faber, 1959)

Jones, Ewan James, *Coleridge and the Philosophy of Poetic Form* (Cambridge: Cambridge University Press, 2014)

Jung, C. G., *Letters*, trans. by R. F. C. Hull, 2 vols (London: Routledge & Kegan Paul, 1972–1976)

Jung, C. G., 'The Psychology of the Child Archetype', in C. G. Jung and C. Kerényi, *Essays on a Science of Mythology* (Princeton, NJ: Princeton University Press, 1969), pp. 70–100

Kant, Immanuel, *Logic*, trans. by Robert S. Hartman and Wolfgang Schwarz (New York: Dover, 1974)

Kelsall, Thomas. F., ed., *Poems by the Late Thomas Lovell Beddoes, Author of Death's Jest-book or the Fool's Tragedy, with a Memoir* (London: W. Pickering, 1851)

Kenner, Hugh, 'Rhyme: An Unfinished Monograph', *Common Knowledge*, 10 (2004), 377–425

Kent, William, 'Doctrine of the Atonement', in *The Catholic Encyclopedia*, www.newadvent.org/cathen/02055a.htm

Kermode, Frank, *The Sense of an Ending: Studies in the Theory of Fiction* (New York: Oxford University Press, 1967)

Kerrigan, John, 'Paul Muldoon's Transits: Muddling through after "Madoc"', *Jacket*, 20 (2002), http://jacketmagazine.com/20/kerr-muld.html

Kilgore-Caradec, Jennifer, 'Reading Geoffrey Hill in 2020: An Introduction', *Études anglaises*, 71.2 (2018), 131–36

King, Henry, 'Fraught Celebration', *PN Review*, 199 (2011), www.pnreview.co.uk/cgi-bin/scribe?item_id=8290

King, Henry, '"Out from under the body politic": Poetry and Government in the Work of C. H. Sisson, 1937–1980' (unpublished doctoral thesis, University of Glasgow, 2013)

Kings, Steven, 'Jung's Hermeneutics of Scripture', *The Journal of Religion*, 77 (1997), 233–51

Knottenbelt, E. M., *Passionate Intelligence: The Poetry of Geoffrey Hill* (Amsterdam and Atlanta, GA: Rodopi, 1990)

Knowlson, James, 'Beckett's "Bits of Pipe"', in *Samuel Beckett: Humanistic Perspectives*, ed. by Morris Beja, S. E. Gontarski, and Pierre Astier (Columbus, OH: Ohio State University Press, 1982), pp. 16–25

Kociejowski, Marius, '"I think you will have the kippers": Memories of Geoffrey Hill', *Stand*, 214 (2017), 45–49

Kwek, Theophilus, 'The Mastery of the Thing', *The Oxonian Review*, ORbits section, https://web.archive.org/web/20160730144923/http://www.oxonianreview.org/wp/the-mastery-of-the-thing/

Kwek, Theophilus, 'Words, Words, Words', *The Oxonian Review*, ORbits section, https://web.archive.org/web/20161012192943/http://www.oxonianreview.org/wp/words-words-words/

Larkin, Philip, *Collected Poems* (London: Faber and Faber, 1988)

Lennard, John, *The Poetry Handbook*, 2nd edn (Oxford: Oxford University Press, 2006)

Leunissen, Mariska, *Explanation and Teleology in Aristotle's Science of Nature* (Cambridge: Cambridge University Press, 2010)

Lezard, Nicholas, 'A growl in his voice, a twinkle in his eye', *The Independent*, 6 February 2005, www.independent.co.uk/arts-entertainment/books/features/a-growl-in-his-voice-a-twinkle-in-his-eye-758572.html

Lock, Charles, 'Corrected Versions and Disputed Titles', review of Geoffrey Hill, *Broken Hierarchies: Poems 1952–2012* (2013), *The Cambridge Quarterly*, 43 (2014), 375–84

Locke, John, *Two Treatises of Government* (London: printed for Awnsham Churchill, 1690)

Logan, William, 'The Absolute Unreasonableness of Geoffrey Hill', in *Conversant Essays: Contemporary Poets on Poetry*, ed. by James McCorkle (Detroit: Wayne State University Press, 1990), pp. 34–47

262   *Bibliography*

Logan, William, *Broken Ground: Poetry and the Demon of History* (New York: Columbia University Press, 2021)

Logan, William, 'Geoffrey Hill, 1932–2016', *The New Criterion*, 35.1 (2016), https://web.archive.org/web/20231212193410/https://newcriterion.com/issues/2016/9/geoffrey-hill-1932a2016

Logan, William, *The Undiscovered Country: Poetry in the Age of Tin* (New York: Columbia University Press, 2005)

Lorca, Federico García, 'Theory and Function of the "Duende"', trans. by J. L. Gilli, in *Toward the Open Field: Poets on the Art of Poetry 1800–1950*, ed. by Melissa Kwasny (Middletown, CT: Wesleyan University Press, 2004), pp. 197–208

Lowell, Robert, 'After Enjoying Six or Seven Essays on Me', *Salmagundi*, 37 (1977), 112–15

Lowell, Robert, *Collected Poems* (London: Faber and Faber, 2003)

Lowell, Robert, *The Dolphin* (London: Faber and Faber, 1973)

Lowell, Robert, *History* (London: Faber and Faber, 1973)

Lowell, Robert, *The Letters of Robert Lowell*, ed. by Saskia Hamilton (New York: Farrar, Straus, and Giroux, 2005)

Luzzi, Joseph, 'The Ends of Poetry: Sense and Sound in Giorgio Agamben and Ugo Foscolo', *Annali d'Italianistica*, 29 (2011), 291–99

Lyon, John, 'Self and Love', *PN Review*, 170 (2006), www.pnreview.co.uk/cgi-bin/scribe?item_id=2782

Lyon, John, and Peter McDonald, eds, *Geoffrey Hill: Essays on His Later Work* (Oxford: Oxford University Press, 2012)

Macaulay, G. C., ed., *The Complete Works of John Gower*, 4 vols (Oxford: Clarendon Press, 1899–1902)

Macfarlane, Robert, 'Gravity and Grace in Geoffrey Hill', *Essays in Criticism*, 58 (2008), 237–56

Mackinnon, Lachlan, 'Discords and Distractions', *The Independent*, 2 June 2011, www.independent.co.uk/arts-entertainment/books/reviews/clavics-by-geoffrey-hill-2292235.html

Maritain, Jacques, *Three Reformers: Luther, Descartes, Rousseau* (New York: Scribner, 1929)

Marlan, Stanton, *The Black Sun: The Alchemy and Art of Darkness* (College Station, TX: Texas A&M University Press, 2005)

Martin, L. C., ed., *The Works of Henry Vaughan*, 2nd edn (Oxford: Oxford University Press, 1957)

Matthews, Steven, 'Geoffrey Hill's Complex Affinities with American Agrarian Poetry', *The Cambridge Quarterly*, 44 (2015), 321–40

McAlpine, Erica, *The Poet's Mistake* (Princeton, NJ: Princeton University Press, 2020)

McCullough, Peter, and others, eds, *The Oxford Edition of the Sermons of John Donne* (Oxford: Oxford University Press, 2013–)

McDonald, Peter, '"But to my Task": Work, Truth, and Metre in Later Hill', in *ELW*, pp. 143–69

McDonald, Peter, *Serious Poetry: Form and Authority from Yeats to Hill* (Oxford: Clarendon Press, 2002)

McGann, Jerome J., 'The Meaning of the Ancient Mariner', *Critical Inquiry*, 8.1 (1961), 35–67

McKenzie, Norman H., ed., *The Poetical Works of Gerard Manley Hopkins* (Oxford: Clarendon Press, 1990)

Bibliography 263

McNeillie, Andrew, 'On Encountering Geoffrey Hill', *Stand*, 214 (2017), 34–38

McNess, Eleanor J., *Eucharistic Poetry* (Lewisburg, PA: Bucknell University Press, 1992)

Mebane, John S., *Renaissance Magic and the Return of the Golden Age* (Lincoln, NE: University of Nebraska Press, 1989)

Merriman, Emily Taylor, 'Raging with the Truth: Condemnation and Concealment in the Poetry of Blake and Hill', *The Journal of Religious Ethics*, 37 (2009), 83–103

Merriman, Emily Taylor, '"Redeemed Swots": Geoffrey Hill's Pedagogically Touched Poetry', *Revue LISA*, 7.3 (2009), 62–73

Meyer, Leonard B., 'The End of the Renaissance? Notes on the Radical Empiricism of the Avant-garde', *The Hudson Review*, 16 (1963), 169–85

Middleton, Christopher, *Palavers, and A Nocturnal Journal* (Exeter: Shearsman, 2004)

Miller, Clarence H., 'Donne's "A Nocturnall upon S. Lucies Day" and the Nocturns of Matins', *Studies in English Literature*, 6.1 (1966), 77–86

Milne, W. S., *An Introduction to Geoffrey Hill* (London: Bellew, 1998)

Mirus, Christopher V., 'The Metaphysical Roots of Aristotle's Teleology', *The Review of Metaphysics*, 57.4 (2004), 699–724

Molan, Michael, 'Milton and Eliot in the Work of Geoffrey Hill', in *GHC*, pp. 81–105

Moore, Henry, 'The Sculptor Speaks', *Listener*, 18 August 1937, pp. 338–40, reproduced in *Henry Moore: Sculptural Process and Public Identity*, Tate Research Publication, 2015, www.tate.org.uk/art/research-publications/henry-moore/hen ry-moore-the-sculptor-speaks-r1176118

Mounic, Anne, 'Le poème, "moulin mystique": Entretien avec Geoffrey Hill', *Temporel*, 28 September 2008, https://web.archive.org/web/20220818015014/ https://www.temporel.fr/Le-poeme-moulin-mystique-Entretien

Muldoon, Paul, *The End of the Poem: Oxford Lectures in Poetry* (London: Faber and Faber, 2006)

Mullen, Benjamin, 'Hill's "A Treatise of Civil Power": Two Editions', *The Pitch Review* blog, 18 January 2010, http://pitchpress.blogspot.co.uk/2010/01/geof frey-hills-treatise-of-civil-power.html

Murphy, Kathryn, 'Geoffrey Hill and Confession', in *ELW*, pp. 127–42

Murphy, Kathryn, 'Hill's Conversions', in *GHC*, pp. 61–80

Murphy, Kathryn, 'In My Opinion, Having Read These Things', *PN Review*, 191 (2010), www.pnreview.co.uk/cgi-bin/scribe?item_id=5981

Newman, John Henry, *Apologia Pro Vita Sua*, ed. by Martin J. Svaglic (Oxford: Clarendon Press, 1967)

Nicholl, Charles, *The Chemical Theatre* (London: Routledge & Kegan Paul, 1980)

Noegel, Scott B., ed., *Puns and Pundits: Word Play in the Hebrew Bible and Ancient Near Eastern Literature* (Bethesda, MD: CDL Press, 2000)

Oras, Ants, 'Milton's Early Rhyme Schemes and the Structure of "Lycidas"', *Modern Philology*, 52 (1954), 12–22

Ovid, *Amores*, in *Heroides. Amores*, trans. by Grant Showerman, rev. by G. P. Goold (Cambridge, MA: Harvard University Press, 1914)

O'Hanlon, Karl, 'Dark with excessive bright', *Blackbox Manifold*, 13 (2014), https://web.archive.org/web/20220704215958/http://www.manifold.group.shef. ac.uk/issue13/KarlO%27Hanlon13.html

264 *Bibliography*

O'Hanlon, Karl, '"A final clarifying": Form, Error, and Alchemy in Geoffrey Hill's "Ludo" and "The Daybooks"', *Études anglaises*, 71.2 (2018), 207–21

O'Hanlon, Karl, '"Noble in his grandiose confusions": Yeats and "Coriolanus" in the poetry of Geoffrey Hill', *English*, 65 (2016), 211–33

O'Hanlon, Karl, 'Ovid in America', *Stand*, 214 (2017), 57–61

O'Hanlon, Karl, '"The Violent and Formal Dancers": John Berryman and Geoffrey Hill', *The Cambridge Quarterly*, 45 (2016), 208–23

O'Leary, Peter, *Thick and Dazzling Darkness: Religious Poetry in a Secular Age* (New York: Columbia University Press, 2017)

Paige, D. D., ed., *The Letters of Ezra Pound 1907–1941* (London: Faber and Faber, 1951)

Parke-Taylor, G. H., *Yahweh: The Divine Name in the Bible* (Waterloo, Ontario: Wilfrid Laurier University Press, 1975)

Paskins, Matthew, 'Hill and Gillian Rose', in *GHC*, pp. 171–85

Pasnau, Robert, 'Thomas Aquinas', in *The Stanford Encyclopedia of Philosophy*, ed. by Edward N. Zalta and Uri Nodelman, https://plato.stanford.edu/archives/spr2023/entries/aquinas/

Pater, Walter, *Studies in the History of the Renaissance* (New York: Oxford University Press, 2010)

Paterson, Don, *The Book of Shadows* (London: Picador, 2004)

Patke, Rajeev S., 'Ambiguity and Ethics: Fiction and Governance in Geoffrey Hill's "Mercian Hymns"', *Connotations*, 20.2–3 (2010–2011), 253–71

Patmore, Coventry, *The Unknown Eros and Other Poems* (London: George Bell and Sons, 1877)

Paulin, Tom, 'The Case for Geoffrey Hill', *London Review of Books*, 4 April 1985, pp. 13–14, www.lrb.co.uk/v07/n06/tom-paulin/the-case-for-geoffrey-hill

Pavese, Cesare, *This Business of Living: Diaries 1935–1950*, trans. by A. E. Murch (London: Quartet Books, 1980)

Péguy, Charles, *Oeuvres en prose complètes*, ed. by Robert Burac, 3 vols (Paris: Gallimard, 1987–1992)

Pennington, Piers, and Matthew Sperling, eds, *Geoffrey Hill and his Contexts* (Bern: Peter Lang, 2011)

Perry, Nathaniel, 'On the Cusp of Devotion: A Squirrel, Doubt and Geoffrey Hill', *The American Poetry Review*, 46.4 (2017), 29–31

Perry, Seamus, *Alfred Tennyson* (Tavistock: Northcote House, 2005)

Perry, Seamus, 'Cute, my arse', review of Geoffrey Hill, *The Book of Baruch by the Gnostic Justin* (2019), *London Review of Books*, 41.17, 12 September 2019, www.lrb.co.uk/the-paper/v41/n17/seamus-perry/cute-my-arse

Pestell, Alex, 'Geoffrey Hill: Poetry, Criticism and Philosophy' (unpublished doctoral thesis, University of Sussex, 2011)

Pestell, Alex, *Geoffrey Hill: The Drama of Reason* (Bern: Peter Lang, 2016)

Pestell, Alex, review of Matthew Sperling, *Visionary Philology: Geoffrey Hill and the Study of Words* (2014), *The Review of English Studies*, New Series, 66 (2015), 597–99

Pestell, Alex, 'Vision, Commerce and Society in Geoffrey Hill's Poetry', *Textual Practice*, 29 (2015), 905–25

Pettet, E. C., *Of Paradise and Light: A Study of Vaughan's 'Silex Scintillans'* (Cambridge: Cambridge University Press, 1960)

Phillips, Brian, 'Review: A Colder Spell to Come', *Poetry*, 188 (2006), 139–47

Bibliography

Phillips, Carl, 'The Art of Poetry LXXX: An Interview with Geoffrey Hill', *Paris Review*, 154 (2000), 270–99

Piette, Adam, 'Review: Geoffrey Hill, Collected Critical Writings', *Blackbox Manifold*, 3, https://web.archive.org/web/20170727133509/http://www.manifold.group.shef.ac.uk:80/issue3/AdamPiette.html

Pinch, Adela, 'Rhyme's End', *Victorian Studies*, 53.3 (2011), 485–94

Plato, *Five Dialogues: Euthypro, Apology, Crito, Meno, Phaedo* (Indianapolis, IN: Hackett, 2002)

Plato, *Symposium*, in *Lysis. Symposium. Gorgias*, trans. by W. R. M. Lamb (Cambridge, MA: Harvard University Press, 1925)

Plato, *Theaetetus and Sophist*, ed. and trans. by Christopher Rowe (Cambridge: Cambridge University Press, 2015)

Plotinus, *The Enneads*, ed. by Lloyd P. Gerson, trans. by George Boys-Stones, John M. Dillon, R. A. H. King, Andrew Smith, and James Wilberding (Cambridge: Cambridge University Press, 2017)

Plutarch, *Moralia*, ed. by H. Cherniss and W. C. Hermbold, 16 vols (Cambridge, MA: Harvard University Press, 1927–2004)

Pollard, Natalie, *Speaking to You: Contemporary Poetry and Public Address* (Oxford: Oxford University Press, 2012)

Poole, Adrian, 'Hill's "Version" of "Brand"', in *EW*, pp. 86–99

Pope, Alexander, *The Correspondence*, ed. by George Sherburn, 5 vols (Oxford: Clarendon Press, 1956)

Pope Pius X, *E supremi*, Libreria Editrice Vaticana, http://w2.vatican.va/content/pius-x/en/encyclicals/documents/hf_p-x_enc_04101903_e-supremi.html

Post, Jonathan F. S., *Henry Vaughan: The Unfolding Vision* (Princeton, NJ: Princeton University Press, 1982)

Potter, Madeline, '"On the Cusp of Devotion": Christian Forms and Difficulties in Geoffrey Hill' (unpublished doctoral thesis, University of York, 2020)

Potts, Robert, 'The praise singer', *Guardian*, 10 August 2002, www.theguardian.com/books/2002/aug/10/featuresreviews.guardianreview15

Pound, Ezra, *Personae: Collected Shorter Poems* (New York: New Directions, 1990)

Powell, Enoch, *Reflections: Selected Writings and Speeches of Enoch Powell*, ed. by Rex Collings (London: Bellew, 1992)

Pritchard, Daniel E., 'Geoffrey Hill: Unparalleled Atonement', *The Critical Flame*, 1 (May–June 2009), http://criticalflame.org/geoffrey-hill-unparalleled-atonement/

Procaccini, Alfonso, 'Pavese: On the Failure of Under-standing', *Italica*, 62 (1985), 214–29

Proclus, *Elements of Theology*, ed. and trans. by E. R. Dodds (Oxford: Clarendon Press, 1963)

Pseudo-Dionysius, *The Celestial Hierarchy*, trans. by the Shrine of Wisdom (Godalming: Shrine of Wisdom, 1949)

Puttenham, George, *The arte of English poesie* (London: Richard Field, 1589)

Quinn, Justin, 'Geoffrey Hill in America', *The Yale Review*, 89.4 (2001), 145–66

Quintilian, *The Orator's Education*, trans. by Donald A. Russell, 5 vols (Cambridge, MA: Harvard University Press, 2001)

Radice, Anthony, 'Making Sense of the Alps', *PN Review*, 145 (2002), www.pnreview.co.uk/cgi-bin/scribe?item_id=1219

266 *Bibliography*

Raff, Jeffrey, *Jung and the Alchemical Imagination* (Berwick, ME: Nicolas-Hays, 2000)

Rahim, Sameer, 'An interview with Geoffrey Hill (1932–2016)', *Prospect*, 20 July 2016, www.prospectmagazine.co.uk/culture/43140/an-interview-with-geoffrey-hill-1932-2016

Raine, Craig, *My Grandmother's Glass Eye* (London: Atlantic Books, 2016)

Raleigh, Walter, ed., *Johnson on Shakespeare* (Oxford: Oxford University Press, 1908)

Range, Matthias, 'William Croft's Burial Service and Purcell's "Thou Knowest, Lord"', *The Musical Times*, 1906 (2009), 54–68

Ratcliffe, Sophie, 'On Being "a man of the world": Geoffrey Hill and Physicality', in *ELW*, pp. 70–88

Read, Herbert, Michael Fordham, and Gerhard Adler, eds, *The Collected Works of C. G. Jung*, trans. by R. F. C. Hull, 20 vols (London: Routledge & Kegan Paul, 1966–1979)

Read, Sophie, 'Puns: Serious Wordplay', in *Renaissance Figures of Speech*, ed. by Sylvia Adamson, Gavin Alexander, and Katrin Ettenhuber (Cambridge: Cambridge University Press, 2011), pp. 81–96

Redfern, Walter, *Puns* (Oxford: Basil Blackwell, 1984)

Reiss, Edward, 'Geoffrey Hill: Poet of Sequences' (unpublished doctoral thesis, University of Leeds, 2021)

Richman, Robert, '"The battle it was born to lose": The Poetry of Geoffrey Hill', *The New Criterion*, 2.8 (1984), 22–34

Ricks, Christopher, *Along Heroic Lines* (Oxford: Oxford University Press, 2021)

Ricks, Christopher, 'Cliché as "Responsible Speech": Geoffrey Hill', *London Magazine*, 8 (1964), 97–98

Ricks, Christopher, *Essays in Appreciation* (Oxford: Oxford University Press, 1996)

Ricks, Christopher, *The Force of Poetry* (Oxford: Clarendon Press, 1984)

Ricks, Christopher, 'Hill's Unrelenting, Unreconciling Mind', in *ELW*, pp. 6–31

Ricks, Christopher, ed., *The Oxford Book of English Verse* (Oxford: Oxford University Press, 1999)

Ricks, Christopher, ed., *The Poems of Tennyson*, 2nd edn, 3 vols (Harlow: Longman, 1987)

Ricks, Christopher, '"Tenebrae" and at-one-ment', in *EW*, pp. 62–85

Ricks, Christopher, *True Friendship* (New Haven, CT: Yale University Press, 2010)

Ricks, Christopher, and Jim McCue, eds, *The Poems of T. S. Eliot*, 2 vols (London: Faber and Faber, 2015)

Ringler, William A., Jr, *The Poems of Sir Philip Sidney* (Oxford: Oxford University Press, 1962)

Robbins, Michael, 'Three Books', *Poetry*, 199 (2011), 171–80

Roberts, Andrew Michael, *Geoffrey Hill* (Tavistock: Northcote House, 2004)

Roberts, Andrew Michael, review of Jeffrey Wainwright, *Acceptable Words: Essays on the Poetry of Geoffrey Hill* (2005), *The Review of English Studies*, New Series, 57 (2006), 854–56

Roberts, Andrew Michael, ed., *Strangeness and Power: Essays on the Poetry of Geoffrey Hill* (Swindon: Shearsman Books, 2020)

Robichaud, Paul, '"Some Wayward Art": David Jones and the Later Work of Geoffrey Hill', in *David Jones: A Christian Modernist?*, ed. by Jamie Callison,

Bibliography

267

Paul S. Fiddes, Anna Johnson, and Erik Tonning (Leiden and Boston, MA: Brill, 2018), pp. 153–66

Robinson, Peter, ed., *Geoffrey Hill: Essays on His Work* (Milton Keynes: Open University Press, 1985)

Rorem, Paul, *Pseudo-Dionysius* (New York and Oxford: Oxford University Press, 1993)

Rose, Gillian, *Love's Work* (London: Chatto and Windus, 1995)

Rowland, Antony, *Holocaust Poetry* (Edinburgh: Edinburgh University Press, 2005)

Rowland, Antony, *Metamodernism and Contemporary British Poetry* (Cambridge: Cambridge University Press, 2021)

Rowland, Antony, 'Reading Holocaust Poetry: Singularity and Geoffrey Hill's "September Song"', *Textual Practice*, 30 (2016), 69–88

Rowland, Antony, 'Re-reading "Impossibility" and "Barbarism": Adorno and Post-Holocaust Poetics', *Critical Survey*, 9 (1997), 57–69

Ruderman, D. B., *The Idea of Infancy in Nineteenth-Century British Poetry: Romanticism, Subjectivity, Form* (New York and London: Routledge, 2016)

Rudrum, Alan, ed., *Henry Vaughan: The Complete Poems* (Harmondsworth: Penguin, 1976)

Russell, Corinna, 'A Defence of Tautology: Repetition in Difference in Wordsworth's Note to "The Thorn"', *Paragraph*, 28 (2005), 104–18

Russell, Jesse, 'Geoffrey Hill, the Holocaust, and the Redemption of British Poetry', *Texas Studies in Literature and Language*, 61.1 (2019), 28–48

Saintsbury, George, *A History of English Prosody*, 3 vols (London: Macmillan, 1906–1910)

Sanesi, Roberto, ed., *The Graphic Works of Ceri Richards* (Milan: Gino Cerastico, 1973)

Saporta, Sol, 'On Meaningful Tautologies', *Anthropological Linguistics*, 28 (1986), 509–11

Saravanamuttu, Dîpti, 'Some Aspects of the Tetragrammaton: On Geoffrey Hill', *Jacket*, 38 (2009), http://jacketmagazine.com/38/hill-by-saravanamuttu.shtml

Schmidt, A. V. C., *Passion and Precision* (Newcastle upon Tyne: Cambridge Scholars Publishing, 2015)

Schmidt, Michael, 'Editorial', *PN Review*, 168 (2006), www.pnreview.co.uk/cgi-bin/scribe?item_id=2655

Schmidt, Michael, review of Christopher Ricks, *True Friendship* (2010), 13 May 2010, *Independent*, www.independent.co.uk/arts-entertainment/books/reviews/true-friendship-by-christopher-ricks-1972540.html

Shaw, Robert B., 'Lowell in the Seventies', *Contemporary Literature*, 23 (1982), 515–27

Sherry, Vincent, *The Uncommon Tongue: The Poetry and Criticism of Geoffrey Hill* (Ann Arbor, MI: University of Michigan Press, 1987)

Sidney, Philip, *An Apologie for Poetrie* (Cambridge: Cambridge University Press, 1891)

Sidney, Philip, *The Defence of Poesie* (London: William Ponsonby, 1595)

Silkin, Jon, 'The Poetry of Geoffrey Hill', *The Iowa Review*, 3.3 (1972), 108–28

Sisson, C. H., *The Avoidance of Literature*, ed. by Michael Schmidt (Manchester: Carcanet, 1978)

Sisson, C. H., 'Beddoes' Best Thing', *London Review of Books*, 20 September 1984, pp. 17–18

268 *Bibliography*

Sisson, C. H., 'Geoffrey Hill's Péguy', *PN Review*, 33 (1983), www.pnreview.co.uk/cgi-bin/scribe?item_id=6643

Smith, Barbara Herrnstein, *Poetic Closure: A Study of How Poems End* (Chicago: University of Chicago Press, 1968)

Sperling, Matthew, 'Greatest living poet', *3:AM Magazine*, www.3ammagazine.com/3am/greatest-living-poet/

Sperling, Matthew, review of John Lyon and Peter McDonald, eds, *Geoffrey Hill: Essays on his Later Work* (2012), *The Review of English Studies*, New Series, 64 (2013), 730–31

Sperling, Matthew, *Visionary Philology: Geoffrey Hill and the Study of Words* (Oxford: Oxford University Press, 2014)

Spinks, Lee, 'Geoffrey Hill and Intrinsic Value', *Essays in Criticism*, 68.3 (2018), 369–89

Sprott, S. Ernest, *Milton's Art of Prosody* (Oxford: Basil Blackwell, 1953)

Stendhal, *Love*, trans. by Gilbert and Suzanne Sale (London: Penguin, 1975)

Stevens, Holly, ed., *Letters of Wallace Stevens* (New York: Knopf, 1966)

Stoppard, Tom, *Plays 5* (London: Faber and Faber, 1999)

Swinburne, Algernon Charles, *Poems and Ballads & Atalanta in Calydon*, ed. by Kenneth Haynes (Harmondsworth: Penguin, 2000)

Tanner, Tony, *Adultery in the Novel* (Baltimore, MD: Johns Hopkins University Press, 1979)

Tate, Allen, *Essays of Four Decades* (London: Oxford University Press, 1970)

Tate, Allen, *The Forlorn Demon* (Chicago: Regnery, 1953)

Thomas, M Wynn, review of Geoffrey Hill, *Oraclau | Oracles* (2010), *Guardian*, 16 October 2010, www.theguardian.com/books/2010/oct/16/oraclau-oracles-geoffrey-hill-review

Thompson, Colin, '"The Resonances of Words": Lope de Vega and Geoffrey Hill', *The Modern Language Review*, 90 (1995), 55–70

Tomlinson, Charles, *The Way of a World* (Oxford: Oxford University Press, 1969)

Travis, Molly Abel, 'Two Formal Elegies', in *Reference Guide to Holocaust Literature*, ed. by Thomas Riggs (Farmington Hills, MI: St James Press, 2002), p. 605

Turing, Alan, Richard Braithwaite, Geoffrey Jefferson, and Max Newman, 'Can Automatic Calculating Machines Be Said to Think?', in *The Essential Turing*, ed. by B. Jack Copeland (Oxford: Clarendon Press, 2004), pp. 487–506

Vaughan, Thomas, *Lumen de lumine, or, A new magicall light discovered and communicated to the world by Eugenius Philalethes* (London: printed for H. Blunden, 1651)

Vickers, Brian, and others, eds, *The Oxford Francis Bacon* (Oxford: Oxford University Press, 1996–)

Vincent, Bridget, 'The Exemplary Poetry of Geoffrey Hill: Authority and Exemplarity in "A Treatise of Civil Power"', *The Modern Language Review*, 110 (2015), 649–68

Vincent, Bridget, *Moral Authority in Seamus Heaney and Geoffrey Hill* (Oxford: Oxford University Press, 2022)

Vincent, Bridget, '"Not an Idle Spectator": Geoffrey Hill as Model Reviewer', *Diogenes*, 60 (2014), 1–11

Virgil, *Eclogues. Georgics. Aeneid, Books 1–6*, trans. by H. R. Fairclough, rev. by G. P. Goold (Cambridge, MA: Harvard University Press, 1916)

Bibliography

Vivian, Percival, ed., *Campion's Works* (Oxford: Oxford University Press, 1909)

Waddell, Helen, *Peter Abelard* (London: Constable, 1939)

Wainwright, Jeffrey, *Acceptable Words: Essays on the Poetry of Geoffrey Hill* (Manchester: Manchester University Press, 2005)

Wainwright, Jeffrey, 'The Impossibility of Death', in *ELW*, pp. 89–111

Waite, A. E., ed. and trans., *The Hermetic and Alchemical Writings of Paracelsus*, 2 vols (London: James Elliott, 1894)

Waithe, Marcus, 'Dense Settling: Geoffrey Hill's "Broken Hierarchies"', *PN Review*, 219 (2014), www.pnreview.co.uk/cgi-bin/scribe?item_id=9165

Waithe, Marcus, 'Empson's Legal Fiction', *Essays in Criticism*, 62 (2012), 279–301

Waithe, Marcus, 'Hill, Ruskin, and Intrinsic Value', in *GHC*, pp. 133–50

Waithe, Marcus, '"Whose Jerusalem"? – Prophecy and the Problem of Destination in Geoffrey Hill's "Canaan" and "Churchill's Funeral"', *English*, 51 (2002), 261–76

Wall, Alan, 'The poet and the dictionary', *The Fortnightly Review*, 13 August 2014, http://fortnightlyreview.co.uk/2014/08/dictionary-poet/

Wall, Alan, 'Questioning the Prose Poem: Thoughts on Geoffrey Hill's "Mercian Hymns"', in *British Prose Poetry: The Poems Without Lines*, ed. by Jane Monson (Cham: Palgrave Macmillan, 2018), pp. 167–76

Ward, Jean, *Christian Poetry in the Post-Christian Day: Geoffrey Hill, R. S. Thomas, Elizabeth Jennings* (Frankfurt a.M.: Peter Lang, 2009)

Wardwell, James, 'Restoring the Broken Themes of Praise: Geoffrey Hill's Ectocentric Christianity', *Stonework*, 2 (2006), http://stonework02.blogspot.co.uk/2006/05/restoring-broken-themes-of-praise.html

Watts, Isaac, *Logick, or, The right use of reason in the enquiry after truth* (London: printed for John Clark and Richard Hett, 1725)

Weil, Simone, *Gravity and Grace*, trans. by Emma Crawford and Mario von der Ruhr (London: Routledge & Kegan Paul, 1952)

Weil, Simone, *The Need for Roots*, trans. by Arthur Wills (Boston, MA: Beacon, 1952)

Wells, Stanley, and others, eds, *The Oxford Shakespeare: The Complete Works: Original-Spelling Edition* (Oxford: Oxford University Press, 1987)

Wesling, Donald, *The Chances of Rhyme* (Berkeley, CA: University of California Press, 1980)

Wilkinson, Judith, 'Geoffrey Hill's "The Pentecost Castle", with Special Reference to Spanish Influences', *English Studies*, 71 (1990), 35–51

Williams, David-Antoine, '"All corruptible things": Geoffrey Hill's Etymological Crux', *Modern Philology*, 112.3 (2015), 522–53

Williams, David-Antoine, 'Broken Hierarchies: Precursor to a Variorum?', *Poetry & Contingency* blog, https://poetry-contingency.uwaterloo.ca/broken-hierarchies-precursor-to-a-variorum/

Williams, David-Antoine, *Defending Poetry* (Oxford: Oxford University Press, 2010)

Williams, David-Antoine, *The Life of Words: Etymology and Modern Poetry* (Oxford: Oxford University Press, 2020)

Williams, David-Antoine, 'Muti-lation at the end of the line', *Poetry & Contingency* blog, https://poetry-contingency.uwaterloo.ca/muti-lation-at-the-end-of-the-line/

Williams, David-Antoine, 'Sorts of Hierarchies', *Poetry & Contingency* blog, https://poetry-contingency.uwaterloo.ca/sorts-of-hierarchies/

Williams, Rowan, *The Edge of Words: God and the Habits of Language* (London: Bloomsbury, 2014)

Williams, Rowan, *Grace and Necessity: Reflections on Art and Love* (London: Continuum, 2005)

Williams, Rowan, 'The Standing of Poetry', in *ELW*, pp. 55–69

Wimsatt, W. K., 'One Relation of Rhyme to Reason', *Modern Language Quarterly*, 5 (1944), 323–38

Wimsatt, W. K., *The Verbal Icon: Studies in the Meaning of Poetry* (Lexington, KY: University of Kentucky Press, 1954)

Wittgenstein, Ludwig, *Philosophical Investigations*, trans. by G. E. M. Anscombe (Oxford: Basil Blackwell, 1963)

Wittgenstein, Ludwig, *Tractatus Logico-Philosophicus*, trans. by C. K. Ogden (London: Kegan Paul, Trench, Trubner & Co., 1922)

Wolfe, Don M., and others, eds, *The Complete Prose Works of John Milton*, 8 vols (New Haven, CT: Yale University Press, 1953–1982)

Wolfe, Gregory, 'Who's Afraid of Geoffrey Hill', *Image: A Journal of the Arts and Religion*, 66 (2010), https://imagejournal.org/article/whos-afraid-geoffrey-hill/

Wong, Alex, ed., *Swinburne: Selected Verse* (Manchester: Fyfield Books, 2015)

Wood, James W., 'The Many Humours of Geoffrey Hill', *Stand*, 214 (2017), 52–55

Wootten, William, *The Alvarez Generation* (Liverpool: Liverpool University Press, 2015)

Wordsworth, William, and Samuel Taylor Coleridge, *Lyrical Ballads: 1798 and 1802* (Oxford: Oxford University Press, 2013)

Wylie, Alex, 'Accountable Survivor', *PN Review*, 179 (2008), www.pnreview.co.uk/cgi-bin/scribe?item_id=3193

Wylie, Alex, 'Eros in Geoffrey Hill's "Scenes from Comus"', *English*, 60 (2011), 198–211

Wylie, Alex, *Geoffrey Hill's Later Work: Radiance of Apprehension* (Manchester: Manchester University Press, 2019)

Wylie, Alex, 'Prophet and Citizen: Fifty Years of Geoffrey Hill's "For the Unfallen"', *PN Review*, 190 (2009), www.pnreview.co.uk/cgi-bin/scribe?item_id=5663

Wylie, Alex, '"This: "Ad Socium"?: Verbal Power in Geoffrey Hill's "The Triumph of Love"', *English*, 63 (2014), 330–46

Yezzi, David, 'Verse in perfect pitch', *The New Criterion*, 7 July 2016, https://web.archive.org/web/20231227010530/https://newcriterion.com/blogs/dispatch/verse-in-perfect-pitch

Young, Charles M., 'Aristotle on Temperance', in *Essays in Ancient Greek Philosophy IV: Aristotle's Ethics*, ed. by John Peter Anton and Anthony Preus (Albany: State University of New York, 1991)

Žirmunskij, V. M., Рифма, Её история и теория [*Rhyme, Its history and theory*] (Petrograd: Academia, 1923)

Index

'accessible' 141

Adam 37, 41, 170–71, 172, 242–43 n.75

Adorno, Theodor 33, 210–11 n.51, 234 n.39

Agamben, Giorgio 16, 196, 198, 206 n.51, 232 n.14, 249 n.145, 250 n.148

alchemy 38, 40–45, 171, 213–14, 242 n.71
  'alchemic-carnal' 40
  Black Sun 41, 43, 44
  in *Clavics* 177
  conjunction 40–42, 213–14 n.72
  limbeck 41–42, 43–44, 214 n.79
  in *Oraclau | Oracles* 43–44

Alexander, Gavin 183

Alighieri, Dante, *see* Dante

ambiguity 18, 25, 32, 143
  'accurate' 27–28
  in 'De Anima' 127–29
  and 'Annunciations' 82
  and deceit 26–27
  Hill on Lowell's 153
  in 'Nachwort' 113
  in *Odi Barbare* 138, 141, 143–44, 190
  in 'The Pentecost Castle' 89, 95
  in *Scenes from Comus* 119
  in 'September Song' 35
  in 'Sobieski's Shield' 124
  in *Al Tempo de' Tremuoti* 101, 102, 144
  in 'Two Formal Elegies' 137–38
  Wainwright on Hill's 208 n.17

in 'Whether Moral Virtue Comes by Habituation' 132–33

anadiplosis 48, 51, 217 nn.14 & 15

anagram 46, 48, 67, 83, 103, 231 n.73

anaphora 111, 183, 184

angels 51, 128–29, 217 n.18, 234–35 n.48

'antiphonal voice of the heckler' (Hill) 78, 84, 85, 176, 238 n.8

antiphony 3, 14, 85, 86, 106, 163, 164, 165

apocalypse 7, 177
  in 'Funeral Music' 155–56
  in *Mercian Hymns* 169–70, 172
  in *Al Tempo de' Tremuoti* 2–3

Aristotle
  anagnorisis 32–33, 210 nn.43 & 44
  astonishment 250–51 n.6
  four causes 8–9, 224 n.87
  meson 53, 218 n.25
  and mimesis 9, 11, 69
  and teleology 9, 204 nn.29 & 30

Arnold, Matthew 33–34, 54, 141–42, 248 n.137

Arrowsmith, William 133

atonement
  in 'De Anima' 128–29
  and 'at-one-ment' 4, 25, 114–15, 146
  Christ's 17, 44, 200
  in *Clavics* 176
  of cultures 165
  in 'Funeral Music' 155
  in *Scenes from Comus* 118
  in *Al Tempo de' Tremuoti* 106–7

272

Index

atonement (*cont.*)
  in 'That Man as a Rational Animal Desires the Knowledge Which Is His Perfection' 123
  in Vaughan's rhyme 87
Auden, W. H. 196, 241 n.45
Augustine 69, 76, 216 n.6
Averroës 154

Bacon, Francis 96, 176–77
balance
  in 'Canticle for Good Friday' 54
  'even' (word) 65, 73
  in *Ludo* 55–58
  in *The Orchards of Syon* 67
  and Ransom 53
  of rhyme 109
  in *Scenes from Comus* 69–71
  in Shakespeare 71–72
  and tautology 59
Batchelor, Paul 188, 228–29 n.52, 248 n.138
Beddoes, Thomas Lovell 150, 172
Bible
  Exodus 34, 137, 225 n.1, 235 n.62
  Judges 76, 224–25 n.92
  Psalms 56, 127, 163, 227 n.32
  Proverbs 132
  Ecclesiastes 67
  Isaiah 3, 63, 201–2 n.7
  Matthew 18, 20, 21, 44, 64, 133, 169–70
  Mark 3, 44
  Luke 44, 126
  John 44, 155, 183, 211 n.59, 221 n.52
  Acts 3
  1 Corinthians 36, 211 n.58
  Ephesians 177, 245 n.95
  Philippians 30
  Colossians 205 n.38
Blackmur, R. P. 44, 72, 77, 105, 215 n.87
Blake, William 62, 74, 98, 150, 205 n.41, 220 n.47, 224 n.84
Blok, Aleksandr 99–100
Bradley, A. C. 96

Bradley, F. H. 51–52
  on 'the End' 189
  on love 189
  on perfection 192–93
  'real' 44, 247 n.127
Bradwardine, Thomas 75, 76
Brittain, Frederick 164
Brunelleschi, Filippo 105
Bunyan, John 23, 30–31, 33

Calderón de la Barca, Pedro 66
Campion, Thomas 79–80, 173, 181–82
Charles I (King of England) 176
Chesterton, G. K. 28, 85, 237 n.82
  on Aristotle's *meson* 53, 218 n.25
  and Christianity 53, 225 n.4
  on rhyme 227 n.33
chiasmus 136, 183
Christ
  His Beatitudes 133
  in 'Canticle for Good Friday' 54
  -child 2, 64
  His Cross 17, 51, 53, 58, 77, 132, 193, 213 n.68, 218 n.24, 221 n.52
  death of 200
  in 'Funeral Music' 154
  'giving up the ghost' 43–44
  His Incarnation 106
  in 'Lachrimae' 37
  in *Mercian Hymns* 170–71
  in 'Ovid in the Third Reich' 98
  in 'The Pentecost Castle' 89
  punning on 'Peter' 20
  His Resurrection 100
  His Second Coming 3, 156, 169–70
  His Transfiguration 18, 24
  as Word 3, 29, 61–62, 64, 73, 76, 129, 177, 201 n.6, 212 n.63, 220–21 n.51
Cicero 122
clavic (form) 174, 175, 177–82
Coleridge, Samuel Taylor 75–76, 212 n.66, 215 n.85
comedy
  in 'Funeral Music' 160
  'the grief of' (Hill) 118–19

in *Odi Barbare* 187
and puns 8, 19, 21, 23
in 'On Reading Blake: *Prophet Against Empire*' 120
in *Scenes from Comus* 40
conduplicatio 59, 183
contingency
in 'De Anima' 128–29
in F. H. Bradley and Hill 189
in Hill's puns 20, 24, 45
of human life 99
in *Ludo* 48
noted by Hill in Vaughan 87
in 'Ovid in the Third Reich' 98
in *Scenes from Comus* 40
in *Al Tempo de' Tremuoti* 105
Cowley, Abraham 173

dance 71, 135, 176, 195, 248–49 n.143
Dante 32, 116, 117, 190–91, 198
Day, Thomas 168
'dead language' 4, 46–47, 49, 52, 165
Demetrius 184
Desnos, Robert 1, 201 n.2
Dickinson, Emily 130–31
Dionysius of Halicarnassus 163
disordinance 49, 52
Dodsworth, Martin 53
Donatello 105
Donne, John
on 'Adam' (word) 242–43 n.75
on language as a 'crooked lymbeck' 214 n.79
'A nocturnall upon S. Lucies day' 42, 149, 173, 214 n.77
in *Oraclau | Oracles* 245 n.101
and poems' endings 114
and style 223–24 n.82

Eberhart, Richard 146–47, 159
Eddington, Arthur Stanley 104
Eliot, T. S.
on Blake 246–47 n.119
on blank verse 151
'Burnt Norton' 95
East Coker 117, 193

on finishing a poem 25, 114–15
Four Quartets 146–47, 188
'Gerontion' 64, 220–21 n.51
'The Hollow Men' 171
on Johnson 150
'Little Gidding' 31–32, 52
'Reflections on Vers Libre' 80–81, 107
on syntax 216 n.5
The Waste Land 164
Empson, William 212 n.66
and ambiguity 26, 36, 143, 237 n.78
'Arachne' 53
Hill and poems of 237 n.77
'Let It Go' 143
Some Versions of Pastoral 220 n.46
epanalepsis 48, 59, 191
equity 108–9
eros 88, 139, 177, 183, 188–89

Fall, *see* original sin
'finesse' (Hill) 148
Fowlie, Wallace 1
fragmentation
in 'Before Senility' 111
in *The Book of Baruch by the Gnostic Justin* 249 n.145
in 'Cycle' 133–35
of Hill's late work 195–96
in *Ludo* 56
in *Mercian Hymns* 171, 172, 195, 166–67, 242 n.64
in 'Nachwort' 113
in *Scenes from Comus* 39, 70, 71, 119
in 'Two Formal Elegies' 137
free will 37–38, 50, 54, 55, 66, 101–2, 105–6

government 61, 105, 109, 123, 166, 172
grace 38, 99
in 'De Anima' 128
in *Brand* 85
in *Clavics* 176
in 'Of Coming into Being and Passing Away' 127

274 *Index*

grace (*cont.*)
  in 'God Little's Mountain' 129
  in *Odi Barbare* 192–93
  in *The Orchards of Syon* 64
  poetry as in or out of 12–13
  the poet's work with 30, 107, 109, 143, 144
  in *Al Tempo de' Tremuoti* 102
  in *The Triumph of Love* 49, 52, 75, 108
  and Weil 88

Hardy, Thomas 104
Haydn, Franz Joseph 181
Haynes, Kenneth 199, 246 n.18, 250 n.2
Hebrew 19–20, 164, 172
Herbert, George 174, 175, 177–78, 221 n.63
Herrick, Robert 120–22
Hill, Geoffrey
  essays:
    'The Absolute Reasonableness of Robert Southwell' 18, 24, 208 n.15
    'Alienated Majesty: Gerard M. Hopkins' 84
    'Caveats Enough in their Own Walks' 45,
    'Of Diligence and Jeopardy' 49
    'Dividing Legacies' 52
    'Dryden's Prize Song' 32
    'Eros in F. H. Bradley and T. S. Eliot' 12–13, 114, 177, 188, 189, 246–47 n.119
    'Gurney's Hobby' 54
    'Language, Suffering, and Silence' 127, 153, 216 n.6
    'Our Word Is Our Bond' 9, 39, 54, 63, 204 n.33, 219 n.30, 249 n.147
    '"Perplexed Persistence": The Exemplary Failure of T. H. Green' 31
    'A Pharisee to Pharisees' 79–80, 86–87

    'Poetry as 'Menace' and 'Atonement'' 21, 24–25, 28, 114–15, 118, 146, 196
    'A Postscript on Modernist Poetics' 37, 78, 189, 192, 222 n.64
    'Redeeming the Time' 78, 81, 114, 176
    'Rhetorics of Value and Intrinsic Value' 107
    'The Tartar's Bow and the Bow of Ulysses' 29
    'Translating Value: Marginal Observations on a Central Question' 19, 30
    'What Devil Has Got into John Ransom?' 53, 94–96
    'Word Value in F. H. Bradley and T. S. Eliot' 188
    '"The World's Proportion": Jonson's Dramatic Poetry in "Sejanus" and "Catiline"' 208 n.20
  lectures 9, 27, 32, 71–72, 139, 149, 153, 206 n.48, 215 n.87, 217 n.20
  poems and collections:
    'De Anima' 127–30
    'Annunciations' 20, 81–82, 83, 212 n.63
    'An Ark on the Flood' 149
    'Before Senility' 110–12
    The Book of Baruch by the Gnostic Justin 12, 61, 62, 63–64, 68, 77, 84, 102, 143, 144, 163–64, 168, 193–97, 199, 206 n.50, 211 n.58, 216 n.10, 220 n.44, 224 n.84, 227 n.29, 229 n.53, 230 n.71, 232 n.10, 248 n.139, 249 nn.147 & 148, 250 n.4
    Canaan 153–54, 193–94
    'Canticle for Good Friday' 54
    Clavics 173–82, 185, 194, 195, 243–44 n.83, 244 nn.87 & 88, 245 n.99
    'Coda' 115–17

Index

275

Collected Poems (1985)
'Of Coming into Being and Passing
  Away' 125–27
'Of Commerce and Society' 135–36
'Cycle' 133–35
The Daybooks 142, 143
'The Dead Bride' 21
'Doctor Faustus' 149
'Epiphany at Hurcott' 246 n.114
Expostulations on the Volcano 1,
  54, 67, 80, 83, 225 n.1
For the Unfallen 82–83, 149, 194,
  239 n.17
'Funeral Music' 90, 149–50,
  153–55, 157–63, 167, 169,
  173, 194, 195, 227 n.25
'Genesis' 149
'G. F. Handel, Opus 6' 122–23
'God's Little Mountain' 129
'Harmonia Sacra' 120–21
Hymns to Our Lady of Chartres
  83, 88, 142–43, 247–48 n.136
'Improvisation on "Warum ist uns
  das Licht gegeben?"' 200
'Improvisations on Jimi Hendrix'
  47
'De Jure Belli ac Pacis' 161
King Log 20–21, 33, 59–60, 82–83,
  96, 153, 227 n.25, 240 n.37
'Lachrimae' 37
Liber Illustrium Virorum 52, 64,
  83–84, 148, 149
Ludo 48, 55–58, 83, 222 n.69,
  231 n.3
'Luxe, Calme et Volupté' 200
'In Memory of Jane Fraser' 96
Mercian Hymns 47, 60, 74, 77,
  84–85, 163–73, 194–95, 240 n.37
'Merlin' 147
*The Mystery of the Charity of
  Charles Péguy* 1, 124, 208 n.23,
  229 n.53
'Nachwort' 112–15
'The Oath' 225 n.97
Odi Barbare 41–44, 138–41,
  142–43, 145, 184–88, 189–93,
  235–36 n.63, 249 n.145

'Offertorium: Suffolk, July 2003'
  228 n.50
Oraclau | Oracles 19, 42–44, 74,
  110, 149, 171, 185, 214 n.77,
  245 n.101, 247 n.132
The Orchards of Syon 27, 30–31,
  55, 58, 60–61, 64–67, 77,
  138, 185, 199–200, 219 n.31,
  221 n.63, 222–23, n.74,
  236 n.64
'Ovid in the Third Reich' 20,
  96–98, 149
'Parentalia ('Go your ways')' 143
'The Pentecost Castle' 60, 66,
  88–96, 167, 193, 242 n.70
Pindarics 19, 28–29, 62, 173,
  243 n.81
'Psalms of Assize' 3
'On Reading Blake: Prophet
  Against Empire' 120
'Requiem for the Plantagenet
  Kings' 58, 147–48, 217 n.15
Scenes from Comus 38–40, 55,
  62, 69–71, 73, 96, 117–20,
  154, 211 n.56, 217 n.14, 222
  n.71
Selected Poems (Penguin) 168,
  172
Selected Poems (Yale) 136
'September Song' 33–36, 137–38,
  210 n.50, 211 n.55, 222 n.73,
  235 n.61
'Sobieski's Shield' 124
'The Songbook of Sebastian
  Arrurruz' 21, 59–60, 163
'Sorrel' 143
Speech! Speech! 20, 22–24, 37, 47,
  57, 60, 127, 142, 185, 218 n.21,
  224 n.87, 236 n.72
'Te Lucis Ante Terminum' 234 n.42
Al Tempo de' Tremuoti 2–3, 36,
  40–41, 60, 68–69, 99–107,
  143–44
Tenebrae 83
'That Man as a Rational Animal
  Desires the Knowledge Which Is
  His Perfection' 123

276   *Index*

Hill, Geoffrey (*cont.*)
  poems and collections: (*cont.*)
    'Three Baroque Meditations' 21,
      47
    A Treatise of Civil Power (2005)
      110–12, 117, 153, 233 n.32
    The Triumph of Love 47, 48–52,
      59, 73–77, 108, 194, 215 n.3,
      216–17 n.12, 222 n.68,
      223 n.81, 240 n.37
    'The Troublesome Reign' 36
    'The Turtle Dove' 36
    'Two Formal Elegies' 136–38
    'Whether Moral Virtue Comes by
      Habituation' 131–33
    'Whether the Virtues are Emotions'
      130–31
    Without Title 189
  translations:
    Brand 85–86
Holy Innocents, the 64, 67
homo incurvatus in se 47–48, 51, 54
Hopkins, Gerard Manley 1, 13, 47,
      114, 192
  'counterpoint' 78
  'inscape' and 'instress' 12, 49, 51
  and silence 61
  'That Nature is a Heraclitean Fire
      and of the Comfort of the
      Resurrection' 223 n.75, 232 n.6
  on Wordsworth 81
Horace 185
humility 128–30, 132
Hurley, Michael D. 148

ideal 105, 114–15, 146–47, 149, 155,
      238 n.4

James, Stephen 149
Jarvis, Simon 80, 226 n.1
Jesus, *see* Christ
Jones, David 11–12, 206 n.48
Jung, Carl 43

Keats, John 137, 150
Kenner, Hugh 80, 81, 107
Kermode, Frank 155–56

Kierkegaard, Søren 146–47
Knottenbelt, E. M. 4–5, 96, 164, 171,
      173
Kociejowski, Marius 184

Larkin, Philip 101
'laus et vituperatio' 133
Lawes, Henry 174
Lawes, William 174, 176, 180
Lowell, Robert
  'Fishnet' 150–53
  History 150, 152, 156–57, 161–62
  'History' 162
  Imitations 150, 153, 239 n.22
  Life Studies 149
  Lord Weary's Castle 149, 160
  'Napoleon Crosses the Berezina'
      241 n.40
  'War' 241 n.49

Macfarlane, Robert 88
marriage 38–40, 55, 70, 96, 154
Mary, the Blessed Virgin 2, 74–75, 99,
      106–7, 247–48 n.36
McDonald, Peter 123
Mendelson, Edward 196
Messiaen, Olivier 171, 243 n.72
metanoia 54–55, 217 n.14, 219 n.29
  in 'Coda' 117
  in *Ludo* 56, 57–58
  in *Odi Barbare* 185
  in *The Orchards of Syon* 55
  in Sappho 184
  in Sidney 183
  in *Speech! Speech!* 57
  in *The Triumph of Love* 48
metaphysics
  in 'De Anima' 128–29
  in *The Book of Baruch by the
      Gnostic Justin* 236 n.64
  in *Clavics* 178, 180
  definitions of 'metaphysical' 223 n.81
  and grammar 74
  Hill on Vaughan's 87
  in 'The Pentecost Castle' 95
  'of poetry' (Hill) 96
  of tautology 76

in *Al Tempo de' Tremuoti* 209 n.37,
    247 n.127
in *The Triumph of Love* 73–74
Meyer, Leonard B. 125
Middleton, Christopher 177, 184, 192
Milton, John
    and Christian paradox 50, 52
    'civil power' 122
    'conjunction' 42
    Eliot, T. S., commenting on 216 n.5
    Lycidas 81
    and rhyme 79, 81, 151
    and *Scenes from Comus* 38, 69–70
    'simple, sensuous, passionate' 44, 85,
        215 n.85
    and standing 55, 219 n.33
Moore, Henry 104
Muldoon, Paul 16, 198,
    206 nn.50 & 51
Murphy, Kathryn 5–6, 47, 54,
    217 n.14
music 27, 78, 79, 80–1, 98, 127, 173
muteness
    in *The Book of Baruch by the
        Gnostic Justin* 61, 63–64
    in 'God's Little Mountain' 129
    of infancy 73, 113
    in *Ludo* 56
    in *In Memoriam* (Tennyson) 62
    in *Pindarics* 61–62
    and 'surds of feeling' (Blackmur)
        77
myth 1, 5, 43, 77, 168, 170, 189–90

Nabokov, Vladimir 181
'necessary closure' (Hill) 148
Niceno-Constantinopolitan Creed 171

O'Neill, Michael 148
obscenity 22, 57, 174
original sin
    its effect on language 31, 47–48, 53,
        177, 199–200
    in Hill's theology 17, 54, 136
    in *The Orchards of Syon* 55
    pun as partial remedy to 30
    in *Al Tempo de' Tremuoti* 69, 106

'terrible aboriginal calamity'
    (Newman) 38
in *The Triumph of Love* 49, 50–51
Ovid 96–98
oxymoron
    of 'civil power' 123
    in 'Cycle' 133
    in 'Fishnet' (Lowell) 152
    in Hill's *Brand* 85–86
    and the 'knack of half-rhyme' 84
    in *Mercian Hymns* 167, 169
    in *The Orchards of Syon* 199
    in 'The Pentecost Castle' 91
    of 'sacrifice' 13
    of this book's title 17
    in *The Triumph of Love* 51
    in Vaughan's rhyme 87

palindrome 47, 48, 53, 57
paradox
    in 'Annunciations' 20
    and composition of poetry 107, 166
    of free will and predestination 37–38,
        50, 66, 102, 105–6
    in 'Funeral Music' 154, 159, 161
    of Hill's metanoia 54
    in Hill's puns 27
    of Hill's rhyme 88, 109
    in 'Improvisation on "Warum ist uns
        das Licht gegeben?"' 200
    'Kierkegaardian' (Hill) 146–47, 152
    in *Mercian Hymns* 166, 167
    in 'Nachwort' 113
    noted by Hill in Ransom 94–95
    noted by Hill in Vaughan 87
    in 'The Pentecost Castle' 90–91
    of rhyming pairs in Hill's *Brand* 85–86
    in 'Stopping by Woods on a Snowy
        Evening' (Frost) 77
    of *verbum infans* 64
parody 52, 60, 175, 177, 200
paronomasia 18, 19
Paterson, Don 134
Paul (Saint) 30, 155
Péguy, Charles 2
Perry, Seamus 62
Peter (Saint) 20

Index

Plato 88
Plutarch 50–51, 217 n.16
Pollard, Natalie 79
polyptoton 48, 49, 50, 183, 186, 223 n.76
Pope, Alexander 79, 83, 106
Pound, Ezra 32, 63, 118–19, 232 n.10, 233 n.26
  'In a Station of the Metro' 113
  'mot juste' 204 n.33
  Ta Hio 109
Powell, Enoch 165–66, 242 n.64
predestination 37–38, 40, 48–50, 66, 100, 102, 105–6
punctuation
  in 'De Anima' 127–30
  in 'Of Coming into Being and Passing Away' 125–27
  in 'Cycle' 133–35
  excess of 136–38
  lack of 124–25
  in *Odi Barbare* 138–45
  revision of 138–42
  in 'Sobieski's Shield' 124
  in 'Two Formal Elegies' 136–38
  in 'Whether Moral Virtue Comes by Habituation' 131–33
  in 'Whether the Virtues are Emotions' 130–31
Puttenham, George 178

Ransom, John Crowe 53, 94–96, 153, 216–17 n.12, 218 n.27
recognition 30–33, 127, 188–89, 209 n.37
Reed, Jeremy 47, 215–16 n.4
restoration 74, 124, 166, 176–77, 179
revision
  of 'Before Senility' 110–12
  of 'Citations II' 112–13
  of *Clavics* 174
  of 'Funeral Music' 158–59
  of *Odi Barbare* 138–41, 236 n.67
  of 'The Pentecost Castle' 91–93
  of *A Treatise of Civil Power* 112
  of *The Triumph of Love* 216–17 n.12
  of 'Two Formal Elegies' 136–38

Richards, Ceri 42–43
Ricks, Christopher 4, 125
  and 'at-one-ment' 232 n.17
  on Donne 114
  on hyphens 93, 222 n.71
  on 'Poetry as 'Menace' and 'Atonement'' 115
  on 'On Reading Blake: Poetry Against Empire' 120
  on *Scenes from Comus* 70
  on 'Two Formal Elegies' 136
  on unrhymed sonnets 150
Robbins, Michael 174
Rowton Heath, battle of 174

sacrifice 13, 17, 54, 56, 86, 136–37, 207 n.56
Saintsbury, George 80
sapphics 138, 142, 182–88, 191–93
Sappho 184, 186
Scholasticism 75–76
'semantic epiphany' (Hill) 146–47, 148, 152, 181, 238 n.4, 250 n.148
sexual love 36–40, 41, 190
Shakespeare, William 42, 141–42, 151, 222 n.69
  King Lear 2
  Measure for Measure 108
  Sonnet 66: 71–72
Sherry, Vincent 136, 154, 155, 156
Sidney, Philip 142, 246 n.113
  Cleophila's (Pyrocles') poem (*Old Arcadia*) 182–84, 191, 192
  The Defence of Poesie 9–11, 36, 44, 148, 204 n.33, 205 n.35
Sisson, C. H. 172, 185
Skelton, John 55
Smith, Barbara Herrnstein 119–20, 148, 233 nn.30 & 33
Smith, James 26
sonnet 84
  'abbreviated' 122, 123
  in Herrick 120–22
  unrhymed 149–63
Sperling, Matthew 4–5, 6, 31, 47, 224 n.87, 234–35 n.48
Stendhal 138–39

Index

Stevens, Wallace 25, 79, 107
Swift, Jonathan 134
Swinburne, Charles Algernon 185–88, 191

Tate, Allen 81, 149, 153, 173, 217 n.18, 243 n.81
tautology
  and evenness 65, 73
  in 'Funeral Music' 161
  and 'God's grammar' 74
  and memory 66–67
  as 'mute desire' 61–64, 77
  and the Name of God 73
  as prayer 73–77
  as redundancy 58–59
  'sublime' (Coleridge) 76
Tennyson, Alfred 62, 220 n.44
Tomlinson, Charles 38, 102
Towton, battle of 153
transfiguration 18, 24–25, 30, 36, 41, 45

Vaughan, Henry 86–87, 174, 175–76
Vaughan, Thomas 41, 174, 214 n.73, 242 n.71
verset 163–66, 168, 169, 170, 172, 193–95

vertical (punctuation mark) 101
Vico, Giambattista 104

Waithe, Marcus 175
Weil, Simone 29, 88
'wilde civility' (Herrick) 122–23
Williams, Rowan 11, 66, 146, 205 nn.41 & 45, 248 n.132
Wimsatt, W. K. 93
Wittgenstein, Ludwig 69, 222 n.68, 223 n.81
  on grammar 74, 223–24 n.82
  'is' (word) 68
  'the logic of the world' 59
  on truth as tautological 66–67
  'unlogical' 74
Wordsworth, William 32, 76, 81, 153

Yeats, W. B. 99
  on finishing a poem 25, 30, 114–15, 143, 147
  in first epigraph of 'The Pentecost Castle' 88, 89–90
  Hill's commentary on 78
  'Swift's Epitaph' 135

Žirmunskij, V. M. 159, 226 n.9

Printed in the USA
CPSIA information can be obtained
at www.ICGtesting.com
JSHW010010280924
70652JS00003B/15